The Supreme Court's
Retreat from
Reconstruction

The Supreme Court's Retreat from Reconstruction

A Distortion of Constitutional Jurisprudence

Frank J. Scaturro

Contributions in Legal Studies, Number 91

GREENWOOD PRESS
Westport, Connecticut • London

Library of Congress Cataloging-in-Publication Data

Scaturro, Frank J.
    The Supreme Court's retreat from Reconstruction : a distortion
of constitutional jurisprudence / Frank J. Scaturro.
        p.   cm. — (Contributions in legal studies, 0147–1074 ; no. 91)
    Includes bibliographical references and index.
    ISBN 0–313–31105–6 (alk. paper)
    1. Civil rights—United States—History—19th century.   2.
Constitutional history—United States.   3. United States—Politics
and government—1865–1900.   4. United States. Constitution.
13th–15th Amendments.   I. Title.   II. Series.
    KF4757   .S29   2000
    342.73'085—dc21   99–15391

British Library Cataloguing in Publication Data is available.

Library of Congress Catalog Card Number: 99–15391
ISBN: 0–313–31105–6
ISSN: 0147–1074

First published in 2000

Greenwood Press, 88 Post Road West, Westport, CT 06881
An imprint of Greenwood Publishing Group, Inc.
www.greenwood.com

Printed in the United States of America

The paper used in this book complies with the
Permanent Paper Standard issued by the National
Information Standards Organization (Z39.48–1984).

10 9 8 7 6 5 4 3 2 1

To the memory of my father,

Salvatore Scaturro

I mean . . . to express an earnest conviction that the court has departed from the familiar rule requiring, in the interpretation of constitutional provisions, that full effect be given to the intent with which they were adopted.

—Justice John M. Harlan,
dissenting in the *Civil Rights Cases*[1]

Far down the ages, when men shall wish to inform themselves as to the real state of liberty, law, religion and civilization in the United States at this juncture in our history, they will overhaul the proceedings of the Supreme Court, and read the decision declaring the Civil Rights Bill unconstitutional and void.

—Frederick Douglass[2]

Contents

Preface

The following study presents both a story and legal analysis, and its hybrid nature calls for some explanation of the author's background and intent. I wrote this account while formally studying law but after an undergraduate (and extracurricular) career in which I wrote primarily as a historian. I considered myself something of a historian (if an amateur one) before I was ever involved in law—my only other published book to date is in the field of history—and my interest in the present study derives from my observations as someone with one foot in each field.

The Civil War–Reconstruction period, which has drawn my particular interest as a student of history, has long struck me as one of the most misunderstood eras in American history. When I entered the realm of constitutional law, it seemed natural that I would become similarly concerned that the constitutional product of that era would also be misunderstood.

There is more overlap between history and law than initially meets the eye, but members of the legal profession, like practitioners in most fields, tend to focus less on seemingly secondary subjects than on their primary field. For many, history lies at most on the periphery of the world of law, so one can expect it to be at least as misunderstood by judges and lawyers as by historians. Because the legal analysis of this study is inseparable from the broader historical framework, and because Reconstruction has been subject to too many divergent interpretations for there to be an "elementary" version common to all students of history, this study devotes more space to history than is typical of primarily legal studies. In fact, the historical dimension of this work presents a thesis of its own: it provides a refutation (if only a partial refutation) of the notion, perhaps most formidably advanced in William Gillette's *Retreat from Reconstruction, 1869–1879*

(1979), that those political leaders who continued to advocate Reconstruction amid public opposition were somehow responsible for its ultimate collapse. In truth, the present account demonstrates that, even apart from the public opposition that alone was probably enough to make Reconstruction unsustainable, the Supreme Court presented a central obstacle to the continuation of a process that, like any other constitutional process, relied for its very existence on the proper interpretation of its constitutional underpinnings. It is unclear how an understanding of the structure of American government could lead historians to conclude that political leaders had a meaningful chance to perpetuate Reconstruction given the Supreme Court of the late nineteenth century. Whether this historical content is seen as the essential backdrop I think it is or simply the product of quirks in my own background and disposition, I wish to emphasize at the outset my awareness of where history ends and law begins. Whatever its value to historians, this study's ultimate analysis and conclusions focus on matters of constitutional law, with historical observations playing a subordinate role. Having said this, I should add a word about the premises of my own legal analysis beyond those that will appear in this study.

I do not adhere to a blanket theory that the Constitution should be subject to either a "strict" or a "loose" construction. Rather, the national blueprint's words deserve a construction that is sensible, given the context in which the people framed it. This statement of theory is not as dogmatic as many might prefer—some may find it too open-ended—but this very imprecision is simply a reality of the nature of language in relation to the principles it is intended to reflect in different contexts. I do not wish at the outset to overstate the imprecision of language, for I do believe that words objectively can be determined to encompass a limited range. The present study, however, concerns a body of law with unusually imprecise text, especially the Fourteenth Amendment.

There is fortunately no need to sacrifice sound constitutional interpretation on the altar of textualism. Judges clearly need to look to more than the dictionary or their own predilections in making their decisions. The United States is a representative democracy. If the Constitution is to be appreciated as the product of such a system, it should be acknowledged at the outset that its principles sprang from a political process—the will of the people, as represented by their elected officials—and not by some oracle or philosopher king from an unreachable stratosphere.

At the same time, although the Constitution dwells in a representative democracy, courts fill the almost paradoxical role of having to apply the Constitution from a realm that is undemocratic and detached from the people. By the fair application of "pure" constitutional principles to all who appear before them, these undemocratic courts, occupied by life-tenured judges at the federal level, can salvage the notion that a representative democracy is still a government of laws and not of men. In order to prevent the undemocratic nature of the realm they occupy from swallowing the representative foundation of the system that supports them, judges must seek a reliable basis of interpretation that respects the circumstances under which the Constitution's own guidelines for ratification were followed.

This is where historical context enters the picture—the question of who *did* bear witness to the establishment of constitutional principles, or more fundamentally, what principles they bore witness to. Put another way, this study adheres to the notion that the Constitution should be interpreted in accordance with its original meaning. Although many originalists cite original intent as their guide, I find *meaning* a more fitting term for proper originalism than *intent* (though the semantic difference is slight enough that the two terms can be used interchangeably to refer to meaning). To the degree that these terms differ, "intent" tends to infer that the hallmark of correct interpretation is the extent to which the consequences of a constitutional provision were contemplated in the minds of its framers. The focus on "meaning" looks at laws for precisely what they are—statements of general principles—just as legislators (at least the better informed ones) understand the product of their work. Making human intent at a given time the supreme guide (assuming this were possible) would compromise the extent to which the system can become one of laws by demanding the limited application of principles ostensibly crafted to be applied consistently.

To reiterate an earlier point, originalism as embraced in this study recognizes where history ends and law begins. It does not promote the use of courts to preserve society as a cross-section of a past historical period, particularly with constitutional amendments that are as revolutionary as the ones discussed. It does, however, attempt to discern certain principles of a past historical period—without any apologies for its extensive use of historical materials beyond the Constitution's own text.

Further defense of originalism is not required here since it will be taken up in the analysis that follows, but before beginning, I should address the increasing hesitation among some scholars in recent years in using legislative history. After all, this study works not only from legislative history, but also from the broader history of the times in which the framers were operating.

I do not see how I could adhere to the above cited principles if I were to do any less. Originalists who shun the use of legislative history and similar materials actually tend to follow a hybrid theory of originalism and textualism that risks collapse under the weight of its own internal contradictions. (In some cases, this group will cite such external sources as the *Federalist Papers* in order to interpret the original Constitution while rejecting corresponding sources to interpret subsequent constitutional amendments, such as the subjects of this study.) The Supreme Court, it shall be seen, demonstrated the problem with such a theory when it sacrificed original meaning to a particularly shrewd use of textual analysis.

On the other end of the spectrum, I recognize activists who shun historical materials (often selectively) in favor of the context of today, working
from the notion that the Constitution evolves over time. The following
study shall address that idea; it should suffice for now to say that by stifling
historical context for the sake of exploring the varied possibilities of the
words of the Constitution, both factions run the risk of demeaning the very
product of representative democracy they seek to interpret.

It follows that components of this work will probably disappoint members of most major current schools of jurisprudential thought. So be it.
Although the present topic is especially ripe for discussion in view of recent
developments in the Supreme Court, this study hopes to distance itself from
the platform of any agenda specific to the time in which it is written. What
matters in the end is that a chapter of constitutional law can be recovered
from the depths of historical misunderstanding and an important part of
America's constitutional heritage finally appreciated on its own terms.

1

Introduction

When the Supreme Court in *United States v. Lopez* (1995)[1] invalidated a
federal statute that made gun possession in a local school zone an offense
on the grounds that it was an overextension of Congress' authority under
the Interstate Commerce Clause,[2] it raised concerns about the constitutional
status of civil rights legislation. Using as its test of constitutionality under
the Commerce Clause "an analysis of whether the regulated activity 'substantially affects' interstate commerce,"[3] the Court based its ruling on the
observation that the "possession of a gun in a local school zone is in no
sense an economic activity that might, through repetition elsewhere, substantially affect any sort of interstate commerce."[4]

Writing for four justices in dissent, Justice Stephen G. Breyer argued that
the Court's line-drawing between commercial and noncommercial activities
was inconsistent with earlier rulings in *Katzenbach v. McClung*[5] and *Daniel
v. Paul*[6] that upheld provisions of the Civil Rights Act of 1964[7] under the
Commerce Clause.[8] Justice Breyer's concerns might become even more pro-
nounced for those who advocate Justice Clarence Thomas' *Lopez* concurrence with the belief that it adheres to the Constitution's original meaning.
Asserting that "our case law has drifted far from the original understanding
of the Commerce Clause,"[9] Thomas contended that as a mere "innovation
of the 20th century,"[10] the " 'substantial effects' test" itself "should be
reexamined."[11]

This suggestion that even the Court's arguably narrow interpretation of
congressional power under the Commerce Clause (at least from the standpoint of the preceding sixty years) was not quite narrow enough[12] seemingly raises an originalist threat not only to *Katzenbach* and *Daniel*, but
also to the Supreme Court precedent that initially validated the Civil Rights

Act of 1964, *Heart of Atlanta Motel v. United States.*[13] Would acceptance of the analysis of the Interstate Commerce Clause set forth either by the Court or by Thomas' concurrence necessitate the overruling of (as the case may be) some or most of the Supreme Court's recognition of the fruits of the Civil Rights Movement in the latter half of the twentieth century?

This question prompts the further question of why the Court during the "Second Reconstruction" felt it must revert to the Interstate Commerce Clause, which dates back to 1787, in the first place rather than to the constitutional provisions produced by the first Reconstruction—the Thirteenth, Fourteenth, and Fifteenth Amendments. The answer can be found in a line of mostly nineteenth-century decisions that, as the nation repudiated Reconstruction, narrowed the federal protection of civil rights that was attempted during the 1860s and 1870s. For those who agree with either the Court in *Lopez* or Thomas' concurrence on originalist grounds, comparing the original meaning of the Reconstruction Amendments with the Court's nineteenth-century pronouncements might be essential to determining the ultimate constitutionality of federal civil rights statutes. For those who advocate the notion of changing the interpretation of the Constitution to fit changing national attitudes, the story of the Supreme Court's role in burying Reconstruction illustrates the disturbing consequences of such a concession.

Although strong opinions for or against the result in *Lopez* make the present topic more intriguing, an examination of the merits of *Lopez* or other Commerce Clause holdings is beyond the scope of this study, as is corresponding consideration of *stare decisis.*[14] Instead, the present focus shall include the Supreme Court's consideration of the Reconstruction Amendments and statutes passed pursuant to them, insofar as they were related to the retreat from Reconstruction, and the resulting distortion of constitutional jurisprudence that lingers even after the Court's more accepting attitude toward civil rights since 1954.

Although there have been twenty-seven amendments to the Constitution, the task of revisiting the original meaning of the Reconstruction Amendments, particularly the Fourteenth, is an especially significant one because no other constitutional change since the original framing in the eighteenth century has had such a profound impact on American law. This task is difficult, however, because unlike the framers of 1787, the framers of 1866 traditionally have not been regarded on their own terms—or in any flattering context for that matter. As W.E.B. Du Bois asserted in his farsighted study of Reconstruction in 1935, "Not a single great leader of the nation during the Civil War and Reconstruction has escaped attack and libel."[15] While the writings of *Federalist Papers* authors James Madison, Alexander Hamilton, and John Jay, as well as the other eminent political philosophers of the framing period, still capture respect and inspire consultation by judges as well as historians, the same cannot be said of the ideas of members of the later generation that created a new legal framework in the aftermath of the Civil War. It is difficult to imagine a Supreme Court justice denying the timelessness of the work of the 1787 framers, but one quoted approvingly from a law review article, "It is very queer to try to protect human rights in the middle of the Twentieth Century by a left-over from the days of General Grant."[16]

For several generations after the end of Reconstruction, histories of the period worked from white supremacist themes that maligned Radical Republicans and celebrated the "Redeemers," as they were called, who were responsible for bringing Reconstruction to an end.[17] The unpopularity of Reconstruction was given a scholarly imprimatur by the school of William A. Dunning, who, like fellow Columbia University professor John W. Burgess, held former slaves and their Republican allies in low esteem and condemned virtually every aspect of Reconstruction.[18] Dunning's final assessment was that

the ultimate root of the trouble in the South had been, not the institution of slavery, but the coexistence in one society of two races so distinct in characteristics as to render coalescence impossible; that slavery had been a *modus vivendi* through which social life was possible; and that, after its disappearance, its place must be taken by some set of conditions which, if more humane and beneficent in accidents, must in essence express the same fact of racial inequality. The progress in the acceptance of this idea in the North has measured the progress in the South of the undoing of reconstruction.[19]

For Burgess, who outdid Dunning in bluntness, it was a "monstrous thing, . . . a great political error, if not a sin," to grant former slaves suffrage, for a "black skin means membership in a race of men which has never of itself succeeded in subjecting passion to reason, has never, therefore, created any civilization of any kind."[20] As a matter of "sound political science the imposition of universal negro suffrage upon the Southern communities . . . was one of the 'blunder-crimes' of the century. There is something natural in the subordination of an inferior race to a superior race, even to the point of the enslavement of the inferior race, but there is nothing natural in the opposite."[21] Dunning's Columbia University colleague appeared more impassioned against those responsible for Reconstruction in the South than he was eager to conduct thorough analysis.[22]

Dunning's students, who displayed more vehemence in their criticism of Reconstruction than their teacher, played an important role in establishing the Dunning School.[23] From them came the assertions that "the part played by the carpet-baggers in the United States senate"—the very group responsible for landmark Reconstruction legislation—"was comparatively slight in respect to legislation of a truly national interest"[24] and that they generally "stood together in support of the worse, rather than the better, matters of legislation."[25] "The real center of interest of every carpet-bagger . . . was the spoils of office" while he had "no understanding of important national questions" and "no deep-seated interest in the welfare of his adopted state."[26] The discriminatory "Black Codes" passed shortly after the Civil War were viewed as "not only . . . reasonable, temperate, and kindly; but, in the main, necessary."[27] Laws to enforce the voting rights of Southern blacks "were in fact out of joint with the times" and "suggest[ed] an autocracy rather than a democracy."[28] It met the Dunning School's approval that such laws "were attacked and emasculated and then relegated to their proper place as curiosities in our political history."[29] That the South after Reconstruction operated with one viable party, "a white man's party, and but one great issue, namely, the maintenance of white supremacy," was motivated by "the simple instinct of self-preservation rather than . . . revenge or hatred," and whatever its negative political effects, "this political solidarity" had once been "so necessary to the preservation of Southern civilization."[30]

The work of Dunning and his students influenced popular histories, textbooks, and fiction for years to come.[31] It attained much popularity through the success of D.W. Griffith's *Birth of a Nation*—a film that, being based on a trilogy that included Thomas Dixon's *The Clansman: An Historical Romance of the Ku Klux Klan* (1905), predictably glorified the Ku Klux Klan—and Claude G. Bowers' national best-seller, *The Tragic Era* (1929).[32]

However much historical revisionism since the twentieth-century Civil Rights Movement has reversed the traditional condemnation of Reconstruction, revisionism has dominated historical thought for far less time than what it replaced. The persistence of a negative attitude toward Reconstruction, even if it seems dead in many circles, continues to present a problem for judges and lawyers for several reasons. First, whether one is a committed originalist or not, the original meaning of the Constitution and the context of history and tradition remain important criteria—even if not the exclusive or predominant ones—for proper constitutional interpretation. Second, the American legal profession is by nature prone to remain a few steps behind the American historical profession in correcting distortions of the past or in comprehending complex historical issues. Reconstruction has been an unusually complicated subject, and the enduring and volatile nature of the debate over what it entailed has left even historians uninformed about many issues that arose during the period.[33]

Third, judges, at least compared to public servants in other realms, are by training conservative and (for many good reasons) disinclined to undo precedent—which is, of course, the product of past times. Even if they could be expected to follow history as well as they follow law, committed originalists interested in rediscovering the original meaning of the Reconstruction Amendments would have to overcome the traditional presumption in favor of precedent—precedent that before 1954 was almost entirely the product of times marked by retreat from, if not outright repudiation of, Reconstruction.

Fourth, lack of awareness of the pervasiveness of the retreat from Reconstruction can lead to the devaluation of original meaning in general. It would be difficult to contend that the Supreme Court was motivated by a rediscovery of nineteenth-century history when it released its opinion in *Brown v. Board of Education*,[34] and it remains to be seen that the failure to utilize the evidence of history was actually a weakness of that decision. It also will be seen that disregard of originalism was one of the very problems that led the Court down the path it took in late–nineteenth-century civil rights jurisprudence. To the extent that the twentieth-century Supreme Court abandoned those nineteenth-century rulings that this study maintains were incorrect as applications of the original meaning of the Reconstruction Amendments, commentators should not feel compelled to treat such results (approvingly or not) as a betrayal of the constitutional mandate the ratifiers issued in 1865, 1868, and 1870.

Finally, because the retreat from Reconstruction occurred such a short time after its birth, those who wish to discern its true meaning have a narrow window of time and space in which they can find information that supports the task of remaining faithful to the Reconstruction Amendments. The vast majority of histories of Reconstruction focus on the years 1865 to 1869 and underemphasize the retreat from Reconstruction during and after the 1870s, leaving those unfamiliar with this history with the greater risk of following seemingly contemporary views on the new amendments as expressions of fidelity to their original meaning while such views truly may express hostility.

In the Court's own debate over the incorporation of the Bill of Rights into the Fourteenth Amendment, Justice Felix Frankfurter expressed more faith in judicial decisions occurring near the time of ratification than in the statements of a proponent of the amendment, "no matter how influential," during the congressional debates over the amendment.[35] Frankfurter's faith in contemporaneous judicial pronouncements may be justifiable as measures of original meaning in most cases, but the Reconstruction Amendments present a different situation, especially because the most contemporaneous interpretations took several years after ratification to come from the Supreme Court. It will be seen that the counterrevolution against Reconstruction followed a similar timetable, so traditional judicial fidelity to precedent is not a phenomenon that would have a chance to work in favor of original meaning. (One can speculate on how different the jurisprudential situation would have been had the Supreme Court had the opportunity to establish precedent on the Fourteenth and Fifteenth Amendments while the national fervor in favor of those amendments was at its peak.)

After a brief review of the history of Reconstruction and the ensuing retreat from it, which is necessary since the original meaning cannot be understood without historical context, this analysis will seek to square the Supreme Court's cases on the Reconstruction Amendments with the original meaning, working primarily with the constructions of legislators in Congress spanning from before ratification to Reconstruction's last legislative feat in 1875.[36] (The term "Reconstruction debates" will be used during this study to refer to congressional debates occurring roughly between 1864, when debates over the Thirteenth Amendment began, and the passage of the Civil Rights Act of 1875.) Information from state legislative debates will be included where possible,[37] as well as statements from the White House and from other participants similarly familiar with the amendments' origins.[38]

2

A Brief Overview of Reconstruction and the Nation's Retreat

Far from being a distinct historical period, Reconstruction was a process that began in conjunction with the last few years of the Civil War—more specifically, with the nation's adjustment to the emancipation of slaves that began largely with the Emancipation Proclamation of 1863, which liberated slaves in the rebelling Confederate states—and the subsequent advance of Union victory.[1] With the end of the war in 1865, there remained a controversy over how to realize the full meaning of Union victory, at the center of which stood more than four million newly freed slaves whose future status remained uncertain. Whatever other issues were involved between 1865 and 1877 (the dates traditionally cited to designate Reconstruction), debates and conflicts over the part former slaves and their descendants would play in the nation's future remained the pivotal questions on which Reconstruction turned.[2]

The first issue of primary concern in this study is the measure that put the final nail in the coffin of American slavery: the Thirteenth Amendment. This amendment, ratified in December 1865,[3] abolished slavery and involuntary servitude throughout the nation and empowered Congress to enforce its provisions in the following language:

Section 1. Neither slavery nor involuntary servitude, except as a punishment for crime whereof the party shall have been duly convicted, shall exist within the United States, or any place subject to their jurisdiction.

Section 2. Congress shall have power to enforce this article by appropriate legislation.[4]

While emancipation had become a clear enough aim of the war, the notion that slavery should be abolished did not preclude debate over the extent to which former slaves would enjoy a change in status. The Thirteenth Amendment was ratified months after the announcement of the lenient Reconstruction policy of Andrew Johnson, who became president after the assassination of Abraham Lincoln. Presidential Reconstruction under Johnson aimed to confer amnesty and pardon on former Confederates who took an oath of allegiance to the Union and support for emancipation, with several exceptions that included high Confederate officials and large property owners who would have to apply individually for presidential pardons.[5] Slaves were not included in the restoration of property rights.[6] This policy assured white Southerners that they would retain the power to define the legal status of former slaves without federal interference;[7] found disapproval among moderate Republicans who respected traditional principles of federalism but desired more civil rights for former slaves;[8] and especially enraged the egalitarian Radical Republicans, who believed that slavery and rights for blacks were the era's most important political issues and that the Civil War authorized a sweeping expansion of national authority to define and protect the rights of all citizens.[9]

The search in the South for a way to pass laws to subordinate blacks followed the end of the war and led to the adoption of the Black Codes, state laws that provided limited property and contract rights while trying to restrict blacks' economic choices apart from plantation labor.[10] The consequent state power to enforce contracts and plantation discipline, to punish those who failed to contract, and to hinder white competition for black laborers reflected a system that seemed intent on restoring to Southern blacks a condition as close as possible to slavery.[11]

By February 1866, both Radicals and moderates, wishing to amend Johnson's policy and to counter the effects of the Black Codes, agreed on two bills addressing the freedmen's plight.[12] The Freedmen's Bureau Act directly financed the bureau of the same name and empowered bureau agents both to assume jurisdiction of cases involving blacks and to punish state officials who denied the civil rights white persons possessed.[13] The Civil Rights Act defined all persons born in the United States, excluding Indians not taxed, as citizens, and it guaranteed to all "citizens, of every race and color" the "same right . . . as is enjoyed by white citizens" to "make and enforce contracts, to sue, be parties, and give evidence, to inherit, purchase, lease, sell, hold, and convey real and personal property," and to enjoy the "full and equal benefit of all laws and proceedings for the security of persons and property."[14] The act also authorized federal officials to prosecute violations in federal courts and included punishment of all persons who denied a citizen civil rights under color of state law.[15] Johnson vetoed both bills,[16] but Congress subsequently overrode both vetoes.[17]

Johnson's vetoes were steps toward a major rupture with congressional

Republicans who were determined to incorporate their understanding of the results of the Civil War into a constitutional amendment; in that form, it would be immune from presidential vetoes and the changing compositions of Congress.[18] On the initiative of Representative Thaddeus Stevens at the start of the Thirty-Ninth Congress, a Joint Committee on Reconstruction (also known as the "Joint Committee of Fifteen") had been established to investigate conditions in the South and report whether any states were entitled to representation.[19] What resulted from its deliberation was the Fourteenth Amendment, which, incorporating the principles of the 1866 Civil Rights Act, included the following provisions (which will be most relevant for purposes of this study):

Section 1. All persons born or naturalized in the United States, and subject to the jurisdiction thereof, are citizens of the United States and of the State wherein they reside. No State shall make or enforce any law which shall abridge the privileges or immunities of citizens of the United States; nor shall any State deprive any person of life, liberty, or property, without due process of law; nor deny to any person within its jurisdiction the equal protection of the laws. . . .

Section 5. The Congress shall have power to enforce, by appropriate legislation, the provisions of this article.[20]

Section two of the amendment essentially recognized former slaves as full persons (rather than three-fifths) for purposes of representation and penalized states that would abridge voting rights of males over twenty-one for reasons other than rebellion or crime by reducing their representation in Congress accordingly.[21] Section three prohibited those who had pledged to support the Constitution and later supported the rebellion from holding office,[22] and Section four repudiated Confederate war debts.[23] Introduced in the House of Representatives in current form on April 30, 1866,[24] the amendment passed the Senate on June 8[25] and the House on June 13[26] and would be ratified on July 9, 1868,[27] but not before Reconstruction entered a new phase.

Public dissatisfaction over presidential Reconstruction had been fueled by racial violence in Memphis in May 1866[28] and particularly by race riots in New Orleans three months later that arose out of a dispute between Radical Republicans and increasingly powerful former Confederates; the latter event resulted in the deaths of thirty-four blacks and three white Radicals, as well as more than 100 people wounded.[29] In the congressional elections of 1866, Republicans won sweeping victories at the polls, outnumbering Democrats and Johnson conservatives in the subsequent Congress by considerably more than was necessary to override a veto.[30] Southern recalcitrance had unintentionally aided the Radical cause, and the controversial issue of black suffrage would return to the congressional agenda, destined to become the most radical component of congressional Reconstruction.[31]

All former Confederate states except Tennessee rejected the Fourteenth Amendment, and Republicans in Congress implemented military Reconstruction over Johnson's vetoes chiefly through three Reconstruction Acts in 1867.[32] The first of these acts divided the other ten Southern states into five military districts, each under the command of an army general.[33] These states would be admitted to representation in Congress only if blacks were permitted to vote under their new state constitutions, if they ratified the Fourteenth Amendment, and if the amendment became part of the Constitution.[34] Congress also required the exclusion of prominent ex-Confederates from public office and retained the right to reject the proposed state constitutions for any reason.[35] Among Congress' efforts to protect its Reconstruction policy was the Tenure of Office Act, which among other things barred the removal of cabinet members without Senate approval during the term of the president who appointed them.[36] Johnson arguably defied this act, which he maintained was unconstitutional, by removing Secretary of War Edwin M. Stanton, and the House voted to impeach him.[37] Johnson escaped conviction in the Senate by one vote.[38]

Although the remainder of Johnson's presidency seemed paralyzed, Reconstruction remained a major issue in the presidential election of 1868. Democrat Horatio Seymour's campaign was dominated in the South by the prospect of undoing Reconstruction[39] while the victorious Republican candidate, General Ulysses S. Grant, fully supported congressional Reconstruction.[40] Starting in January 1869,[41] Congress considered the third Reconstruction measure to become a part of the Constitution, the Fifteenth Amendment, and it was passed by the House on February 25[42] and the Senate on February 26.[43] Grant endorsed the amendment in his First Inaugural Address[44] and played a decisive role in garnering support for the amendment,[45] which at one point seemed headed for defeat.[46] It was ultimately ratified on February 3, 1870, following the president and Congress' firm response to Georgia's removal of black legislators from its state legislature.[47] The Fifteenth Amendment provides the following:

Section 1. The right of citizens of the United States to vote shall not be denied or abridged by the United States or by any State on account of race, color, or previous condition of servitude.

Section 2. The Congress shall have power to enforce this article by appropriate legislation.[48]

A central dilemma facing the federal government throughout Reconstruction was the issue of enforcement. Congress passed five Enforcement Acts between 1870 and 1872 in efforts to protect the newly recognized rights of former slaves and their white Republican allies. The Enforcement Act of May 31, 1870, prohibited the use of force, bribery, threats, intimidation, or other illegal means to obstruct the right to vote based on race, as well as conspiracies to prevent or hinder the enjoyment of rights secured by the Constitution or federal laws.[49] Federal officials were authorized to supervise elections and make arrests, and federal courts had jurisdiction over cases arising under the act.[50] The Enforcement Act of July 14, 1870, which aimed less at the South than at Democratic practices in Northern cities,[51] established that special deputy marshals would police elections in cities of twenty thousand or more with the power to make arrests without warrants.[52] The Enforcement Act of February 28, 1871, further established intensive federal supervision of voting wherever congressional representatives were chosen, required written or printed ballots in congressional elections, and mandated the oversight of election enforcement by various federal election supervisors.[53] Accompanying these measures was the creation of the Department of Justice in 1870, which marked an unprecedented consolidation of the federal government's legal capacity under the attorney general.[54]

The Enforcement Act of April 20, 1871, also dubbed the "Ku Klux Klan Act,"[55] was the most sweeping legislation to counter Southern violence during Reconstruction.[56] It was enacted less than a month after Grant issued a message to Congress announcing a state of lawlessness in the South, the correction of which he deemed "beyond the control of the State authorities" and requiring legislation that "shall effectually secure life, liberty, and property and the enforcement of law in all parts of the United States."[57] The act gave a federal cause of action to any person whose constitutional rights were violated under color of state law; punished conspiracies to hinder constitutional rights through various specified crimes; authorized the president on his own initiative to intervene with federal military force to suppress violence when states could not or would not protect constitutional rights from domestic violence; and permitted the president to suspend the writ of *habeas corpus* and impose martial law when state authorities conspired with armed groups to violate constitutional rights.[58] By its clear terms, this act authorized punishment under federal law for crimes committed by individuals.[59] A final Enforcement Act of June 10, 1872, which was incorporated into an act appropriating funds for sundry civil expenses, expanded federal scrutiny of elections into rural areas without authorizing election supervisors to interfere or make arrests.[60]

The Dunning School was critical of the Enforcement Acts as "belong[ing] logically to a more arbitrary period" and suggestive of "an autocracy rather than a democracy,"[61] but they in fact were a response to violent resistance to the civil and political rights granted by the Reconstruction Amendments. Rampant mob violence by such groups as the Ku Klux Klan, the Knights of the White Camelia, and the White Brotherhood posed the greatest obstacle to the enforcement of federal law.[62] The Klan, the largest and most notorious of these groups, was founded in 1866 as a social club, and in 1867, intent on undoing Reconstruction and restoring white supremacy, it launched a campaign of violence and intimidation against both black and white Republicans that spread to almost every Southern state.[63] The effect of the violence differed from location to location, but particularly in the Deep South, the Klan incapacitated the Republican Party in many areas.[64]

On May 3, 1871, shortly after the passage of the Ku Klux Klan Act, Grant called for "acquiescence in the results of" the Civil War, "now written in our Constitution," and he asserted the federal government's duty to protect "citizens of every race and color" when local communities failed to enforce "equal, just, and impartial laws in every part of our country."[65] This warning was not heeded. On October 17, after being informed that Klan violence in South Carolina was out of control, Grant suspended *habeas corpus* in nine South Carolina counties.[66] This drastic measure was accompanied by a stringent prosecution effort that within one year effectively brought about the death of the Ku Klux Klan and a dramatic decline of violence in the South.[67]

Even after the federal government's efforts, many of which were unprecedented during peacetime, the Southern counterrevolution did not end. Other groups, such as the rifle clubs and Red Shirts of South Carolina, the White Liners of Mississippi, the White Man's Party in Alabama, and the White Leaguers of Louisiana, sought to combine many Klan tactics with social ostracism and economic pressure as more subtle methods of intimidation.[68] They would enjoy more sustained success,[69] in large part because their activity would coincide with a decline in national fervor for Reconstruction.

Besides legal prosecutions, Reconstruction was carried out during the 1870s through the use of federal troops to protect the polls, prevent violence, and support contested state governments, though such measures often were accompanied by reactions against Reconstruction elsewhere. In 1870, for example, Grant sent federal troops to North Carolina in case Governor William W. Holden needed them to suppress violence during the legislative elections that year.[70] Without needing to revert to federal troops, Holden conducted an unpopular military expedition, which included illegal arrests, in two counties he declared to be in a state of insurrection, and while both counties went Republican, Democratic success elsewhere made the election a repudiation of the use of military force.[71]

Four states presented the federal government with the problem of contested elections between 1872 and 1875. The first and most persistently troubled state was Louisiana, where following the 1872 gubernatorial election, the president ordered federal troops to support the government of Republican William P. Kellogg.[72] Supporters of Democratic candidate John McEnery and his legislature did not give up—the rival government even convened separately[73]—and federal troops would suppress the state militia's mutiny against Kellogg and an outbreak of mob violence in New Orleans.[74]

Violence spread to the countryside and often assumed the form of race riots, the worst of which occurred at Colfax after a group of pro-Kellogg blacks, who in accord with a Republican sheriff had taken over a local courthouse in fear of Democratic aggression, were attacked by about two hundred whites of the McEnery faction.[75] About seventy-one blacks and two whites were killed before federal troops restored order, and the bodies of many of the blacks were found mutilated.[76] The statewide civil strife would end in May, but many Northern newspapers blamed the Colfax massacre of Easter Sunday not on Louisiana whites but on Louisiana blacks, Kellogg, and Grant.[77]

Federal intervention occurred again in Alabama in the 1872 state legislative elections when a proposal presented by the White House as a compromise plan effectively secured Republican control of both houses.[78] Grant declined to interfere in Texas following the December 1873 election after the incumbent Republican governor and legislative allies made a rather flimsy claim of election illegality.[79] Arkansas presented a more complicated situation in 1874 when civil war broke out over the gubernatorial election between regular Republican Elisha Baxter and Liberal Republican Joseph Brooks.[80] Baxter represented the political organization of incumbent Governor Powell Clayton, whose power relied on the black vote and the disfranchisement of about 20,000 former Confederates.[81] Brooks initially held control until Grant, after initial neutrality, intervened on Baxter's behalf at Attorney General George H. Williams' urging, based largely on the state legislature's support (the validity of which was questionable).[82] The ensuing situation saw each faction make a dramatic political turn, with Baxter supporting a new constitution that restored suffrage to disfranchised whites and shortened his own term while Brooks, with new support from black Republicans, contended that the constitution was illegal.[83] Grant believed the new constitution to be a dangerous precedent for Reconstruction and changed his earlier opinion on Brooks' legitimacy, but the House of Representatives and Northern opinion blocked further intervention.[84]

The peculiarity of the Arkansas situation, with its gubernatorial contestants largely switching positions in state politics, might have presented a "no-win" situation for the federal government, but the negative public reaction reflected a broader disapproval of Reconstruction that had become manifest by 1874. Two years before, a liberal reform movement in the North had become intimately connected with discontent over Reconstruction, and in 1872, it was embodied in the Liberal Republican Party, which maintained that the federal government should focus less on the "dead," supposedly settled issues of Reconstruction.[85] Grant won a landslide reelection victory that year over a candidate backed by both the Liberal Republicans and the Democrats, but other national issues (like prosperity and foreign policy successes) better explain the 1872 election than any enthusiastic popular mandate for Reconstruction. During Grant's second term,

Reconstruction would meet with increasing hostility from both politicians and the general public. By 1874, the call for a retreat from Reconstruction, accompanied by blatant racism against blacks, was amplified clearly in the North as well as the South.[86] Vice President Henry Wilson believed that Reconstruction faced a "Counter-Revolution."[87]

Nevertheless, even as the nation retreated from Reconstruction, the more ardent supporters of Reconstruction in the federal government, despite the Radicals' waning influence,[88] sought to continue and even advance the effort. Civil rights laws guaranteeing equal access to transportation and public accomodations had been passed in the Deep South as black political influence grew,[89] but such laws (with exceptions) generally were unenforced, segregation being the norm outside the context of governing institutions.[90] (Most blacks tolerated voluntary segregation but insisted that the state remain color-blind, and to the extent that Reconstruction did not produce an entirely integrated society, it starkly contrasted with the state-imposed segregation of future years.[91]) On May 22, 1874, after more than two years of attempts by Senator Charles Sumner (who died on March 10[92]) to pass supplemental civil rights measures[93] and a call in Grant's Second Inaugural Address for the full realization of civil rights inherent in citizenship,[94] the Senate passed a civil rights bill that required equal enjoyment of accomodations in inns, public conveyances, restaurants, theaters, and other places of public amusement, public schools, institutions, land-grant colleges, and cemeteries, as well as banning racial discrimination in jury selection.[95]

Many Republicans had private misgivings about the measure, the controversiality of which was so intense that both parties handled civil rights like "deadly poison"[96] and assumed it never would pass in the House.[97] The Senate version of the bill never reached the House floor,[98] but the debate over civil rights legislation lingered as the elections of 1874 approached. Democrats focused their attack on a particularly controversial provision barring school segregation, finding considerable support across party lines,[99] while many Republicans feared the bill would destroy their party in the South.[100] Despite the desire of some Republicans to bury the bill quietly,[101] its partial passage in May made the "deadly poison" of racial equality—and with it, the rest of Reconstruction—a top issue in the fall elections.[102]

The congressional elections of November 1874 proved catastrophic for the Republicans, who lost eighty-nine seats in the House, bringing the Democrats from occupying less than a third of the House to a majority of sixty seats.[103] (Included among the Republicans who met defeat was Representative Benjamin F. Butler, the floor manager of the civil rights bill.[104]) Similarly, state legislative elections for Senate seats usually filled the seats of Republican incumbents allied with the president with either Democrats or independent Republicans, which both cut the Republican majority in half and destabilized it.[105] State elections represented a similar trend.[106] Disappointment over the depression following the Panic of 1873 might have been the preeminent national concern during the elections, but this preoccupation was supplemented—or perhaps even fueled—by the increasing desire to abandon Reconstruction.[107] General William T. Sherman remarked that Attorney General Williams "may have been right" to believe troops were needed in the South to preserve peace, "but politically he has brought on a catastrophe which will give infinite trouble. The late elections show how common people regard these things."[108]

Nevertheless, days before the Forty-Third Congress ended its session in 1875, it passed the Civil Rights Act, which was substantially similar to the earlier Senate bill but shorn of its provisions regarding schools and cemeteries.[109] The bill marked the final legislative contribution to Reconstruction before the entrance of a Congress that was hostile to civil rights,[110] and in historian Eric Foner's words, the Civil Rights Act stood as "a broad assertion of principle" that "represented an unprecedented exercise of national authority, and breached traditional federalist principles more fully than any previous Reconstruction legislation."[111] Still, while the legislation might have led to many successful attempts at integration, blacks utilized it on a relatively sparse basis,[112] and its unpopularity since the debates over the Senate bill was widespread enough that—typical of the catch-22 situation that faced supporters of strong Reconstruction measures in the mid-1870s—Reconstruction's opponents could use its passage to fuel their cause.[113] The Supreme Court would invalidate the Civil Rights Act of 1875 in the *Civil Rights Cases* (1883).[114]

In his Sixth Annual Message in December 1874, Grant, who then faced the collapse of his Radical congressional support with the start of the next Congress, issued a lament over events in the South that included a significant affirmation of his legal responsibilities:

I regret to say that with preparations for the late election decided indications appeared in some localities in the Southern States of a determination, by acts of violence and intimidation, to deprive citizens of the freedom of the ballot because of their political opinions. Bands of men, masked and armed, made their appearance; White Leagues and other societies were formed; large quantities of arms and ammunition were imported and distributed to these organizations; military drills, with menacing demonstrations, were held, and with all these murders enough were committed to spread terror among those whose political action was to be suppressed, if possible, by these intolerant and criminal proceedings. In some places colored laborers were compelled to vote according to the wishes of their employers, under threats of discharge if they acted otherwise; and there are too many instances in which, when these threats were disregarded, they were remorselessly executed by those who made them. I understand that the fifteenth amendment to the Constitution was made to prevent this and a like state of things, and the [Enforcement] act of May 31, 1870, with amendments, was passed to enforce its provisions, the object of both being to guarantee to all citizens the right to vote and to protect them in the free enjoyment of that right. Enjoined by the Constitution "to take care that the laws be faithfully executed," and convinced by undoubted evidence that violations of said act had been committed and that a widespread and flagrant disregard of it was contemplated, the proper officers were instructed to prosecute the offenders, and troops were stationed at convenient points to aid these officers, if necessary, in the performance of their official duties. Complaints are made of this interference by Federal authority; but if said amendment and act do not provide for such interference under the circumstances as above stated, then they are without meaning, force, or effect, and the whole scheme of colored enfranchisement is worse than mockery and little better than a crime.[115]

Acknowledging that this interference "with the affairs of a State" was "repugnant to public opinion," the president conveyed his desire to avoid such actions and asserted their legitimacy when he took them:

The theory . . . that there is to be no further interference on the part of the General Government to protect citizens within a State where the State authorities fail to give protection . . . is a great mistake. While I remain Executive all the laws of Congress and the provisions of the Constitution . . . will be enforced with rigor, but with regret that they should have added one jot or tittle to Executive duties or powers. . . . Treat the negro as a citizen and a voter, as he is and must remain. . . . Then we shall have no complaint of sectional interference.[116]

Despite the nation's attitude, Grant intervened in Mississippi in December 1874 to crush a bloody campaign of racial intimidation in the vicinity of Vicksburg with federal troops; these troops replaced a fraudulently installed Democratic sheriff with a Republican.[117] He also continued to support the Kellogg government in Louisiana in what would become the most controversial occurrence of federal intervention in the South. After crushing a *coup d'etat* in New Orleans by pro-McEnery forces in September 1874,[118] the president, anticipating problems in the wake of Democratic intimidation and fraud in the November state legislative elections,[119] authorized General Philip H. Sheridan to investigate the matter and assume command if necessary.[120] Crisis came in January 1875, when anti-Kellogg forces illegally entered the lower chamber and tried to gain control by seating five Democrats. Sheridan ejected the five Democrats from the statehouse, and the nation was swept with anger toward Washington.[121] That Reconstruction had become a major political liability was manifest by the public reaction.

Congressman James A. Garfield wrote in his diary when he learned of Sheridan's actions, "This is on the whole the darkest day for the Republican Party and its hopes I have ever seen since the war," and even Vice President Wilson, who in his legislative career had established an impeccable record in support of Reconstruction, told Garfield that Grant was "the mill-stone around the neck of our party that would sink it out of sight."[122] A Senate compromise decided that Louisiana's lower house would be Democratic while preserving Republican control in the state senate and perhaps saving the Kellogg regime.[123]

In 1876, the Supreme Court supplemented the public reaction against Reconstruction with its decisions in *United States v. Reese*[124] and *United States v. Cruikshank*,[125] which directly undermined federal efforts to protect blacks during Reconstruction. As remains to be discussed in fuller detail, *Reese* struck down provisions of the first Enforcement Act in 1870[126] while *Cruikshank* applied to the same act an interpretation of the Fourteenth and Fifteenth Amendments narrow enough to overturn the only three convictions the federal government had secured out of the Colfax massacre.[127] By crippling federal enforcement, these decisions helped usher in the end of Reconstruction,[128] and they were met by public approval.[129] With both Congress and the Supreme Court having abandoned Reconstruction, it remained only for the president to complete the federal government's retreat. Grant remained dedicated to Reconstruction until the end of his term, but the election of 1876 would determine his successor. The Republican presidential campaign in 1876 distanced itself from Reconstruction, and the Republican candidate, Governor Rutherford B. Hayes of Ohio, seemed eager for conciliation toward the South.[130]

The incident in Louisiana in 1875, despite its unpopularity, would not mark the last instance of federal intervention in the South. Although Grant, showing hesitation about sending troops unless it was necessary,[131] failed to send sufficient troops to Mississippi to prevent a campaign of intimidation against blacks from giving the Democrats sweeping victories on election day in 1875,[132] this result was attributable to various miscommunications rather than a conscious policy of abandonment.[133] The following year, Grant suppressed open intimidation by South Carolina rifle clubs, and he employed the military to keep the elections in both South Carolina and Louisiana untainted by fraud.[134] Election disputes followed in both states in which the president fully supported Republican Governor Daniel H. Chamberlain, who polled the largest Republican majority in South Carolina history,[135] while only tentatively supporting Republican Stephen B. Packard in Louisiana until his victory as governor was confirmed.[136]

These disputes, however, were eclipsed temporarily by the larger electoral crisis over who had been elected president—an issue that could be resolved only by deciding which candidate received the electoral votes of the three remaining Republican states in the South (South Carolina, Louisiana, and Florida), as well as a disputed elector in Oregon.[137] The Electoral Commission created to settle the election gave all disputed electoral votes to Hayes,[138] and the bargaining process among politicians that helped secure the settlement of the electoral crisis was said to center around a deal to restore "home rule" to the South.[139] It is impossible to determine the precise terms of the Compromise of 1877,[140] as it became known, but a policy of nonintervention in the South during the next presidential administration was made likely by political factors independent of any election controversy, including the posture of the Republican Party at that point and the nomination of Hayes.[141]

The new president was publicly inaugurated on March 5, 1877, and in April, Hayes withdrew the last remaining troops in the South from their posts in South Carolina and Louisiana, allowing both Republican regimes to succumb to Democratic "home rule" as the Solid South was born.[142] During his presidency, Hayes would make no substantial effort in the South to utilize any enforcement legislation that remained intact.[143] However much his Reconstruction policy resembled that of Andrew Johnson, he faced no significant political opposition toward his course amid a national attitude that welcomed the end of Reconstruction.[144]

Over the years following 1877, the South witnessed the erosion of political rights for blacks, a process that took place abruptly in the Deep South and more gradually in the border and Upper South.[145] In the New South that emerged, former slaves and their descendants found themselves in a system that was oppressive on economic, political, and social fronts, and a new standard of race relations would take root that would be embedded in Southern segregation laws during the 1890s.[146]

Such was the framework within which the Supreme Court operated in the late nineteenth century.

3

The Supreme Court's Retreat from Reconstruction

A. PRELUDE TO RETREAT

It is noteworthy that the Court's initial decisions during the 1860s, when national fervor for Reconstruction still ran high, consistently deferred to congressional plans for the South, usually by finding no jurisdiction. In *Mississippi v. Johnson* (1867),[1] the Court avoided an action to enjoin President Johnson from enforcing the Reconstruction Acts of March 2 and 23, 1867, by holding that the Court lacked jurisdiction over the president's executive and political duties.[2] The following year, the Court dismissed a similar suit against Secretary of War Stanton on the grounds that it presented a political question beyond the Court's subject-matter jurisdiction.[3] In *Ex Parte McCardle* (1869),[4] the Court avoided yet another challenge to the Reconstruction Acts by upholding Congress' repeal of the provision of the Habeas Corpus Act allowing appeals to the Supreme Court.[5] *Texas v. White*,[6] decided the same year as *McCardle*, would be celebrated for holding secession to be constitutionally impossible and the Union to be indestructible.[7] The case's central issue is beyond the scope of this study, but the decision did include the Court's refusal to question the constitutionality of the Reconstruction Acts and "the paramount authority of Congress."[8]

It is also worthy of mention that the Civil Rights Act of 1866 was held to be constitutional in two separate cases between 1866 and 1867 in which Supreme Court justices sat on circuit. In *United States v. Rhodes*,[9] after interpreting the authorization for "appropriate" legislation in Section 2 of the Thirteenth Amendment in light of the Court's landmark opinion in *McCulloch v. Maryland*[10] and similar supporting authorities, Justice Noah Swayne described the provision as involving "a legislative, and not a judicial question" unless "the authority given has been clearly exceeded."[11] He had "no doubt of the constitutionality of the act in all its provisions. It gives only certain civil rights."[12] Chief Justice Salmon P. Chase reached the same result on the act's constitutionality under Section 2 in *In re Turner*.[13]

B. THE COURT'S DECISIONS DURING THE 1870s

1. *Blyew v. United States*

During the 1870s, cases regarding the Reconstruction Amendments and accompanying statutes tended to reach different results in the Supreme Court from those of the previous decade, though it was not until *Blyew v. United States* (1872)[1] that the Court would test a Reconstruction law on its merits.[2] *Blyew* arose from the murder of a blind and elderly black woman by two white men in Kentucky.[3] The incident was witnessed by two blacks who were denied the right to testify in Kentucky courts solely on account of their race, prompting the case's removal to federal district court under the Civil Rights Act of 1866. This statute gave the district court jurisdiction over causes "affecting persons who are denied, or cannot enforce in the courts or judicial tribunals of the State, or locality, where they may be, any of the rights secured to them by the first section of the act."[4]

The Court held that federal courts lacked jurisdiction on the grounds that witnesses in a criminal prosecution were "not persons affected by the cause."[5] Otherwise, Justice William Strong wrote for the Court, if all those who might be called as witnesses were intended to be included as persons affected, any case between whites could be heard by a federal court at the suggestion that a black citizen was or might be an important witness.[6] Additionally, the murder victim could not be a person affected because she was dead.[7]

Justice Joseph P. Bradley, who dissented along with Swayne, argued that the Civil Rights Act was intended to carry out the Thirteenth Amendment "and to place persons of African descent on an equality of rights and privileges with other citizens of the United States."[8] According to Bradley, Section 1 of the act, which defined national citizenship and its accompanying rights,[9] was intended to abolish all state laws that discriminated against blacks (including examples of the Black Codes that Bradley cited).[10] "To deprive a whole class of the community of" the right to furnish aid in bringing an offender to justice, wrote Bradley, "is to brand them with a badge of slavery; is to expose them to wanton insults and fiendish assaults; is to leave their lives, their families, and their property unprotected by law."[11] The dissent further called the Court's denial that prosecutions intended to redress the killing of helpless people were " 'causes affecting the persons' . . . a view of the law too narrow, too technical, and too forgetful of the liberal objects it had in view."[12]

Deeming it obvious that the law covered a black victim who "is merely wounded or maimed, but is still capable of making complaint" and "has the doors of justice shut in his face" on racial grounds, Bradley found no decisive difference in a case in which the victim was dead.[13] Given his view that prosecutions for crimes against blacks are causes that "most seriously affect them" under the Civil Rights Act, Bradley had "no doubt" of Congress' power under Section 2 of the Thirteenth Amendment.[14] He explained this power in the following terms:

Slavery, when it existed, extended its influence in every direction, depressing and disfranchising the slave and his race in every possible way. Hence, in order to give full effect to the National will in abolishing slavery, it was necessary in some way to counteract these various disabilities and the effects flowing from them. Merely striking off the fetters of the slave, without removing the incidents and consequences of slavery, would hardly have been a boon to the colored race. Hence, also, the amendment abolishing slavery was supplemented by a clause giving Congress power to enforce it by appropriate legislation. No law was necessary to abolish slavery; the amendment did that. The power to enforce the amendment by appropriate legislation must be a power to do away with the incidents and consequences of slavery, and to instate the freedmen in the full enjoyment of that civil liberty and equality which the abolition of slavery meant.[15]

It is significant, in view of his later opinions, that Bradley initially recognized the self-executing nature of Section 1 of the Thirteenth Amendment while he recognized Section 2 as a supplement for Congress to exercise a broader sweep of power beyond the strict command of the preceding section.

While congressional debates contemporaneous with the debates over the Thirteenth Amendment and Civil Rights Act do not address the specific statutory question the Court faced, Bradley's general view of Section 2 of the Thirteenth Amendment was well supported in Congress. Bradley was clearly correct that the Civil Rights Act was meant to target the Black Codes,[16] and laws limiting former slaves' capacities as witnesses in court were common examples of such laws.[17] Senator Lyman Trumbull spoke affirmatively of Section 2 as "put[ting] it beyond cavil and dispute" that Congress could secure the rights accompanying freedom.[18] Early in 1866, he flatly denied the idea that the amendment had

merely taken from the master the power to control the slave and left him at the mercy of the State to be deprived of his civil rights. . . . Such was not the intention of Congress, which proposed the constitutional amendment, nor is such the fair meaning of the amendment itself. With the destruction of slavery necessarily follows the destruction of the incidents to slavery. When slavery was abolished, slave codes in its support were abolished also.

Those laws that prevented the colored man going from home, that did not allow him to buy or to sell, or to make contracts; that did not allow him to own property;

that did not allow him to enforce rights; that did not allow him to be educated, were all badges of servitude made in the interest of slavery and as a part of slavery. They never would have been thought of or enacted anywhere but for slavery, and when slavery falls they fall also. . . . With the abolition of slavery should go all the badges of servitude which have been enacted for its maintenance and support.[19]

Senator Oliver P. Morton, though not a member of Congress when the Thirteenth Amendment and Civil Rights Act were passed, seemed to contradict the Court's future holding when in 1871 he asserted that Kentucky's law denying blacks the right to testify in court in any case to which a white person is a party "nullifies" the 1866 act.[20]

Blyew may be seen as the start of the Court's retreat from Reconstruction,[21] but it represented a relatively small step because the issue involved was a narrow one of statutory construction and the Court did not narrow its interpretation of any amendment or invalidate a civil rights statute. More sweeping decisions still awaited the Court.

2. The Privileges and Immunities Clause and the *Slaughter-House Cases*

a. Background: Justice Bradley, *Live-Stock Dealers' & Butchers' Ass'n* and *Hall*

The *Slaughter-House Cases*[1] would provide the Court its first major opportunity to interpret the Fourteenth Amendment[2] five years after its ratification, by which time the general public already was on the verge of its condemnation of Reconstruction. The chronology of the Court's first opportunity invites a glance at Justice Bradley's earlier interpretation of the amendment in 1870, when *Live-Stock Dealers' & Butchers' Ass'n v. Crescent City Live-Stock Landing & Slaughter-House Co.*[3] came to him as a circuit justice.

The case involved a suit for an injunction seeking to restrain the defendants, the Crescent City Company and the local police board, from suspending proceedings to suppress the business of the complainants in slaughtering animals and selling meat under a Louisiana law giving the Crescent City Company the exclusive right to conduct such business in and near New Orleans.[4] Although Bradley determined that the Civil Rights Act of 1866 did not apply, he found the Fourteenth Amendment to be "much broader in its terms."[5] Comparing the Privileges and Immunities Clause of Section 1 of the Fourteenth Amendment to the Privileges and Immunities Clause of Article IV Section 2,[6] Bradley found that the earlier provision, which prohibited discrimination "against the citizens of other states," embraced much less than the later one, which "demands that the privileges and immunities of all citizens shall be absolutely unabridged, unimpaired."[7]

The "essential privileges which belong to a citizen of the United States" might "be difficult to enumerate or define," Bradley conceded, but they included the ability "to adopt and follow such lawful industrial pursuit—not injurious to the community—as he may see fit" subject to constitutional regulations.[8] Distinguishing this privilege of "ordinary pursuits and employments" from "the exclusive right to use a franchise" and similar public rights involving a public charge, as well as licenses "open to all proper applicants," Bradley found the scheme to confer "a monopoly of a very odious character."[9] Although he found a fundamental privilege to be violated, Bradley ultimately did not issue the injunction only because the court lacked statutory authorization, thus requiring the complainants to pursue relief through the state courts until, if necessary, it reached the Supreme Court on appeal from the state's highest court.[10]

It is worthy of additional mention that between the circuit case and the ascendance of the *Slaughter-House Cases* to the Supreme Court, Bradley was primarily responsible for the opinion issued in *United States v. Hall* (1871),[11] the first significant judicial reaction to Fourteenth Amendment enforcement legislation,[12] even though the watershed decision was handed down by Judge (later Justice) William B. Woods. Repeating an advisory opinion Bradley had sent him almost verbatim,[13] Woods overruled a demurrer to an indictment under the first Enforcement Act and issued an opinion for his circuit that recognized the freedom of speech and other rights enumerated in the first eight amendments of the Bill of Rights as constitutionally protected privileges and immunities.[14] According to *Hall*, Congress had the power under the Fourteenth Amendment to protect these privileges and immunities by appropriate legislation against "unfriendly or insufficient state legislation," and as the denial of equal protection of the laws "includes inaction as well as action, . . . denying the equal protection of the laws includes the omission to protect, as well as the omission to pass laws for protection."[15] This rationale, formulated while Reconstruction still ran strong, raises issues that will remain of key importance in subsequent discussion of later Supreme Court cases.

b. The Court's Opinion in the *Slaughter-House Cases*

The *Slaughter-House Cases*, which brought the Louisiana law involved in Bradley's circuit case to the Supreme Court,[16] were decided by a five-to-four margin in 1873. Justice Samuel F. Miller, whose views on Reconstruction were originally sympathetic[17] but later grew increasingly hostile toward Radical politics,[18] wrote the Court's opinion. The case itself did not deal with the rights of former slaves, but it raised such fundamental issues of Fourteenth Amendment interpretation that it would lay the groundwork for later civil rights cases.

Nevertheless, the Court attempted to place the entire case within a category apart from what it viewed as the "one pervading purpose" behind the recent amendments—"the freedom of the slave race, the security and firm establishment of that freedom, and the protection of the newly-made freeman and citizen from the oppressions of those who had formerly exercised unlimited dominion over him."[19] The Fourteenth Amendment's "main purpose was to establish the citizenship of the negro,"[20] and the Court even admitted doubt that the Equal Protection Clause would ever apply (absent "a strong case") to categories other than racial discrimination.[21]

Miller emphasized the difference between state citizenship and citizenship of the United States and asserted that the Privileges and Immunities Clause addressed only the privileges and immunities of citizens of the United States.[22] Making reference to the Constitution's original Privileges and Immunities Clause, the Court quoted from the 1823 circuit opinion of Justice Bushrod Washington in *Corfield v. Coryell*:

[W]hat are the privileges and immunities of citizens of the several States? We feel no hesitation in confining these expressions to those privileges and immunities which are *fundamental*; which belong of right to the citizens of all free governments, and which have at all times been enjoyed by citizens of the several States which compose this Union, from the time of their becoming free, independent, and sovereign. What these fundamental principles are, it would be more tedious than difficult to enumerate. They may all, however, be comprehended under the following general heads: protection by the government, with the right to acquire and possess property of every kind, and to pursue and obtain happiness and safety, subject, nevertheless, to such restraints as the government may prescribe for the general good of the whole.[23]

The start of this excerpt actually misquotes Washington by inserting the word "of" between "citizens" and "the several States," where the word "in" appeared in the 1823 opinion.[24] This quotation also includes several minor alterations and omission of "the enjoyment of life and liberty" in its list of privileges and immunities.[25]

The earlier clause, Miller wrote, aimed solely to dictate to the states that those rights they granted their citizens, whatever they were, must be given to citizens of other states in their jurisdiction.[26] With the exception of "very few express limitations" the Constitution imposed on the states—for example, "the prohibition against ex post facto laws, bills of attainder, and laws impairing the obligation of contracts"—and "a few other restrictions, the entire domain of the privileges and immunities of citizens of the States" rested within state, not federal, constitutional and legislative power.[27]

Considering the far-reaching consequences of subjecting such a large domain of previously acknowledged state powers to federal control under the recent amendments, the Court found it "irresistible" absent clearer language to conclude that the Fourteenth Amendment had no such sweeping impact.[28] The recent amendments, it asserted, lacked "any purpose to destroy the main features of the general system."[29] Thus under the Court's interpretation, the claimed right was not covered by the Fourteenth Amendment's Privileges and Immunities Clause.[30]

c. The *Slaughter-House* Dissents

The 1873 decision evoked three dissents, the first of which, written by Justice Stephen J. Field, was joined by Chief Justice Chase and Justices Swayne and Bradley. Except for the provisions of the law requiring the landing and slaughtering of animals below New Orleans and requiring the inspection of animals before they were slaughtered, Field described the act in "all other particulars" as "a mere grant to a corporation created by it of special and exclusive privileges by which the health of the city is in no way promoted."[31] Since the situation presented "the naked case, unaccompanied by any public considerations," of the deprivation of the "right to pursue a lawful and necessary calling" that was taken from every citizen and given to a single corporation in a large area for twenty-five years,[32] Field viewed the only question involved as "whether the recent amendments to the Federal Constitution protect the citizens of the United States against the deprivation of their common rights by State legislation."[33] The dissent answered this question in the affirmative, according to what it viewed as the intention of the framers and the ratifying states.[34]

Field followed with some discussion of the Thirteenth Amendment and the Civil Rights Act as aiming to secure practical freedom,[35] but he found it unnecessary to rest his argument with the earlier constitutional provision because he felt the Fourteenth Amendment covered the case.[36] Before that amendment, he explained, there had been a difference of opinion over whether there existed any citizenship independent of that of the state,[37] but Section 1 "changes this whole subject" by recognizing "in express terms, if it does not create, citizens of the United States" such that a "citizen of a State is now only a citizen of the United States residing in that State. The fundamental rights, privileges, and immunities which belong to him as a free man and a free citizen, now belong to him as a citizen of the United States, and are not dependent upon his citizenship of any State."[38] This explanation differed from the majority's emphasis on the distinction between state and national citizenship.

To define the "privileges and immunities which are secured against abridgment by State legislation,"[39] the dissent looked to the Civil Rights Act of 1866, objections to which it admitted the Fourteenth Amendment was adopted to obviate,[40] and to the famous passage in *Corfield*, which it quoted more accurately than the majority.[41] "The privileges and immunities designated," Field asserted, "are those *which of right belong to the citizens of all free governments*,"[42] and under Article IV Section 2 they could be enjoyed equally between citizens of the several states while in the same state.[43] Under the Fourteenth Amendment, the dissent concluded, the same equality of privileges and immunities secured by Article IV between citizens of different states is secured between citizens of the United States, and what Article IV does for the protection of citizens of one state against the creation of monopolies in favor of citizens of other states, the Fourteenth Amendment does for the protection of every U.S. citizen against the creation of any monopoly.[44]

After elaborating on the definition of monopoly and the pedigree of the privilege against monopolies,[45] Field concluded that "[t]his equality of right, with exemption from all disparaging and partial enactments, in the lawful pursuits of life, throughout the whole country, is the distinguishing privilege of citizens of the United States" and protected by the Fourteenth Amendment.[46]

Bradley's dissent added that the Fourteenth Amendment settles that national citizenship is "primary" while state citizenship is "secondary and derivative,"[47] and "the right of any citizen to follow whatever lawful employment he chooses to adopt (submitting himself to all lawful regulations)" is protected against invasion by the states.[48] Citizens of every free government, contended Bradley, have rights of life, liberty, and property that can be taken away only by due process of law or modified "by lawful regulations necessary or proper for the mutual good of all," and the "right to choose one's calling" and the calling itself are liberty and property interests, respectively, that could not be "arbitrarily assailed."[49] "[T]o say that these rights and immunities attach only to State citizenship, and not to citizenship of the United States" seemed to Bradley "to evince a very narrow and insufficient estimate of constitutional history and the rights of men, not to say the rights of the American people."[50] Bradley noticed Miller's misquotation of *Corfield* and found it significant that Justice Washington had spoken of "citizens *in* a State"—that is, "citizens as such"— and not "citizens *of* a State."[51]

Bradley acknowledged that the Constitution before the recent amendments specified only a few personal privileges and immunities of citizens: prohibitions against bills of attainder, ex post facto laws, laws impairing the obligation of contracts, and others.[52] Others were enumerated even though they were expressly secured only against the federal government,

such as the right of *habeas corpus*, the right of trial by jury, of free exercise of religious worship, the right of free speech and a free press, the right peaceably to assemble for the discussion of public measures, the right to be secure against unreasonable searches and seizures, and above all, and including almost all the rest, the right of *not being deprived of life, liberty, or property, without due process of law*.[53]

By declaring these rights to be "among the privileges and immunities of citizens of the United States"—or more strongly stated, "of all persons, whether citizens or not"[54]—Bradley indicated his support for the incorporation doctrine, an issue that would play a more central role in later cases. For Bradley, fundamental privileges and immunities were no less real or inviolable even if the Constitution were silent regarding them.[55]

A third dissent by Swayne added little to the substantive debate but called the recent amendments "a new departure" and "an important epoch" in constitutional history.[56] Before the Civil War, Swayne remarked, "ample protection was given against oppression by the Union, but little was given against wrong and oppression by the States. That want was intended to be supplied by [the Fourteenth] amendment."[57] This dissent read like an endorsement of the amendment itself, calling the national government "glaringly defective" in its previous lack of authority "to secure to every one within its jurisdiction the rights and privileges enumerated, which, according to the plainest considerations of reason and justice and the fundamental principles of the social compact, all are entitled to enjoy."[58]

It might be added as an afterword that all of the remaining dissenters of the *Slaughter-House* Court would join the unanimous opinion in *Bartemeyer v. Iowa*, a case argued at the same time but decided in 1874.[59] Here the Court rejected the argument that a state law predating the Fourteenth Amendment regulating traffic in intoxicating liquors violated the Privileges and Immunities Clause, holding that "the right to sell intoxicating liquors . . . is not one of the rights growing out of citizenship of the United States."[60] In joining this opinion, Swayne, Field, and Bradley indicated the limits of their dissents by acknowledging the validity of the legitimate exercise of the police power of the states.[61]

d. The *Slaughter-House Cases* in View of Congressional Understandings

The congressional debates that occurred during Reconstruction cast much light on the debate that occurred on the Court in the *Slaughter-House Cases*. They do not address the question of a privilege against monopoly, which was not a particularly important issue during Reconstruction, but they do suggest answers to other questions that came to provide a significant foundation for the judicial retreat from Reconstruction.

Although the vast majority of debates over Reconstruction measures occurred in a racial context, scattered statements indicate that the Fourteenth Amendment's terms, which do not mention race, were not understood to be confined to blacks or to racial categories in general. The role of the 1866 Civil Rights Act is important in any evaluation of the Fourteenth Amendment because it largely served as its precursor, yet Miller, unlike the dissent, failed entirely to consider this important bill in his opinion for the Court.[62] Senator Trumbull, the author of the Civil Rights Act, asserted during debates over the bill that it "applies to white men as well as black men."[63] When Senator Richard Yates soon afterwards expressed the view that he favored the rights of all people, not only blacks,[64] he was expressing a shared interest of Radical Republicans in breaking down all irrelevant discrimination, not only that which was driven by race.[65] Senator Edgar Cowan, a conservative Republican who supported President Johnson and would vote against the Fourteenth Amendment,[66] complained that the civil rights bill could be construed to "confer upon married women, upon minors, upon idiots, upon lunatics, and upon everybody native born in all the States, the right to make and enforce contracts."[67]

This statement might have appeared a visibly shallow attempt to raise alarm, but it was unaccompanied by any statement refuting the dissent in the *Slaughter-House Cases*. It is also noteworthy that an 1867 bill to abolish peonage in New Mexico reveals the application of the Thirteenth Amendment, the terms of which are no more indicative of a racial aim than those of the Fourteenth, to whites as well as blacks.[68]

In a dialogue between Congressmen John A. Bingham, the principal author of Section 1 of the Fourteenth Amendment, and Robert S. Hale, the latter representative construed the intent behind the proposed amendment to extend practically only to blacks in former Confederate states, but Bingham replied that it applied to all white loyalists and "to other States also that have in their constitutions and laws to-day provisions in direct violation of every principle of our Constitution."[69] Similar sentiments could be found on the state level during the ratification debates.[70]

During later debates over the Fifteenth Amendment, Representative George S. Boutwell asserted that the Privileges and Immunities Clause "is for all or it is for nobody" and that it applied to all who are citizens of the United States, whether they were born in Africa, Denmark, or Ireland, and whether they were black or white.[71] Senator William M. Stewart's 1870 bill to extend equal protection to aliens, which would be added to the first Enforcement Act, also indicates congressional intent that extended beyond race.[72] The accompanying debates included a statement by Bingham that under the Fourteenth Amendment, immigrants were "entitled to the equal protection of the laws" by both the state and the federal Constitution.[73] Democratic Senator Eugene Casserly asserted that the Fourteenth Amendment conferred "on all persons equal protection before the law" in order to contrast it with the more limited classes covered by the Fifteenth Amendment.[74] Reacting to the *Slaughter-House Cases*, Senator Frederick T. Frelinghuysen asserted in 1874 that all three Reconstruction Amendments "apply equally to all races."[75] Senators Timothy O. Howe[76] and Boutwell[77] made similar statements about the Fourteenth Amendment's application beyond blacks during the debates over what became the Civil Rights Act of 1875.

Although Congress did not specify all of the potential categories of discrimination the Fourteenth Amendment addressed, the Court's apparent skepticism toward claims made by non-blacks for nonracial reasons reflects a narrower construction of the amendment than the essentially unrefuted views of legislators throughout Reconstruction.

The notion that the privileges and immunities mentioned in the Fourteenth Amendment gave the federal government no new powers over the states or operated in a context that followed the Court's distinction between state and national citizenship finds support predominantly among opponents of Reconstruction. Like Justice Miller, the Democratic theory worked from its understanding of the original Privileges and Immunities Clause (in which most courts had concurred) as protecting only travelers from one state in another state from sectional discrimination without protecting citizens against their own state's laws.[78] This theory was accepted by some Republican supporters of the Fourteenth Amendment as well,[79] but without impacting their understanding of the new constitutional measure.

The debates over the 1871 Ku Klux Klan Act and the subsequent Civil Rights Act gave several Democratic legislators the opportunity to express views of the Fourteenth Amendment Privileges and Immunities Clause that seem to support the Court's conclusion, if not all of its premises. Senator Thomas F. Bayard, Sr., asserted that the Fourteenth Amendment "gave to citizens of the United States no privileges or immunities, no rights that they had not before its adoption."[80] Its only effect, he felt, was to enlarge the class of people who could be considered citizens and to prevent state discrimination "against native-born or naturalized citizens."[81] Senator George Vickers spoke of the later Privileges and Immunities Clause in relatively narrow terms as a reenactment of the earlier one,[82] and like the Court, he drew a sharp distinction between privileges of state and national citizenship, contending that the Fourteenth Amendment addressed only the latter.[83] Representatives William S. Herndon[84] and William E. Finck (who had voted against the Fourteenth Amendment),[85] as well as Senators Allen G. Thurman[86] and Thomas Bayard,[87] supported a similar emphasis on dual citizenship. Thurman acknowledged that citizens of the United States possessed rights, privileges, and immunities, but he believed that they were all enumerated in the Constitution.[88]

Among Republicans, Trumbull asserted during the 1871 Ku Klux Klan Act debates that the Fourteenth Amendment had "not extended the rights and privileges of citizenship one iota," and displaying skepticism toward the notion of undefined national privileges, he maintained that the "Constitution says no such thing as that a State shall not abridge the privileges of any citizen."[89] His views seemed at that point to conform to those of the Court, though a recurring problem throughout this study in interpreting Trumbull's postratification views is that he moved toward Liberal Republicans and ultimately the Democrats during the 1870s (the Democrats nominated him for governor in 1880), a shift that corresponded to his growing opposition to Reconstruction.[90]

During the accompanying House debates in April 1871, Congressman Charles W. Willard asserted that a citizen under Article IV Section 2 had been entitled only to "an equality of privileges and immunities with the citizens of the State in which he may happen to be" and that the Fourteenth Amendment did not add to these privileges and immunities.[91] Congressman John Ambler Smith, a relatively conservative Republican from Virginia who served for one term, expressed in 1875 that the Fourteenth Amendment neither added to a citizen's fundamental rights nor covered state privileges and immunities.[92] A fourth Republican, Senator Matthew H. Carpenter, similarly expressed support for the Court's dual citizenship interpretation in 1875,[93] but this position was taken amid a stark about-face from his earlier Radical stands following his defeat for re-election.[94] His earlier views had included a direct contradiction of Trumbull's above cited 1871 views.[95]

That the Privileges and Immunities Clause did not add to previously existing privileges and immunities also was asserted by Democrats Roger Q. Mills[96] and William B. Read[97] in the House, though without more this proposition does not contradict the *Slaughter-House* dissent. The predominant Republican theory behind the original Privileges and Immunities Clause gave rise to a different conception of preexisting rights. As early as 1864, Henry Wilson referred to the 1787 clause in terms that included the First Amendment as a privilege of every American citizen with which no state could "interfere without breach of the bond which holds the Union together"—and which the slave states had violated.[98] A number of other Republicans made similar charges about Southern violations of freedom of speech and Article IV Section 2.[99]

The Republican theory of the Constitution motivating the Fourteenth Amendment Privileges and Immunities Clause was most thoroughly explained early in 1866 by Bingham himself:

[I]n view of the fact that many of the States—I might say, in some sense, all the States of the Union—have flagrantly violated the absolute guarantees of the Constitution of the United States to all its citizens, it is time that we take security for the future, so that like occurrences may not again arise to distract our people and finally to dismember the Republic.

When you come to weigh these words, "equal and exact justice to all men," go read, if you please, the words of the Constitution itself: "The citizens of each State (being *ipso facto* citizens of the United States) shall be entitled to all the privileges and immunities of citizens (supplying the ellipsis "of the United States") in the several States." This guarantee is of the privileges and immunities of citizens of the United States in, not of, the several States. This guarantee of your Constitution applies to every citizen of every State of the Union; there is not a guarantee more sacred, and none more vital in that great instrument. . . .

I propose . . . that hereafter there shall not be any disregard of that essential guarantee of your Constitution in any State of the Union. And how? By simply adding an amendment to the Constitution to operate on all the States of this Union alike, giving to Congress the power to pass all laws necessary and proper to secure to all persons—which includes every citizen of every State—their equal personal rights; and if the tribunals of South Carolina will not respect the rights of the citizens of Massachusetts under the Constitution of their common country, I desire to see the Federal judiciary clothed with the power to take cognizance of the question, and assert those rights by solemn judgment, inflicting upon the offenders such penalties as will compel a decent respect for this guarantee to all the citizens of every State.[100]

Bingham's conception of privileges and immunities, putting aside his interpretation of Article IV, bears close resemblance to the dissents in the *Slaughter-House Cases*, even down to his concern (similar to Bradley's) over "citizens of the United States in, not of, the several States." It is not the extent to which Bingham and his colleagues misconstrued the original Privileges and Immunities Clause that is at issue, but rather what understanding motivated the later Privileges and Immunities Clause that faced the Court in the *Slaughter-House Cases*.

Trumbull in 1866 expressed widely felt frustration over the failure to enforce what many Republicans conceived to be privileges and immunities,[101] a concern that was closely related to calls for federal action, whether statutorily or constitutionally based, to enforce "natural" or "inherent" rights of life, liberty, and property.[102] Congress would turn to legislation before amending the Constitution itself.

Miller's failure to consider two pieces of legislation in 1866 helps explain why his opinion misses the additional evidence both bills provide of the dominant idea that citizens did (or should) possess fundamental rights as national citizens. Both § 1 of the civil rights bill and § 7 of the Freedmen's Bureau bill contained identical lists of civil rights and immunities later intended to be incorporated into the Privileges and Immunities Clause—rights to contract; to buy, sell, and own property; to sue, be parties, and give evidence; and to have the full and equal benefit of laws for the security of persons and property.[103] "These I understand to be civil rights," declared Trumbull, "fundamental rights belonging to every man as a free man, and which under the Constitution as it now exists we have a right to protect every man in."[104] Senator John B. Henderson, who believed with other Republicans that these measures aimed to enforce the original Privileges and Immunities Clause, described the bills as "imperative" to preserve the results of the Civil War.[105] That the bills imposed uniform civil rights on all people was one of the most basic observations one could make,[106] but though someone who did not read beyond the Court's opinion might have viewed such measures as unfathomable.

In the view of House Judiciary Chairman James F. Wilson, citizens possessed of "the great fundamental rights embraced in the bill of rights" were

"entitled to a remedy," and the civil rights bill was justifiable under Article
IV Section 2 and corresponding implied congressional powers, recognized
in *Prigg v. Pennsylvania*,[107] to enforce the Bill of Rights against the
states.[108] For like-minded Republicans,[109] the Fourteenth Amendment
would merely provide a new means of enforcement.[110] To the extent that
Bingham and his Republican allies differed, it was primarily in the belief
that Congress lacked an appropriate enforcement mechanism and that one
would have to be supplied by the Fourteenth Amendment. There was no
basic difference in the conception of Article IV Section 2 as conferring
substantive rights that included fundamental guarantees in the Bill of
Rights,[111] and thus no difference in the resulting understanding of the Fourteenth Amendment—regardless of who had been more correct earlier.

During the debates over Bingham's early proposal for the Fourteenth
Amendment, Congressman Frederick E. Woodbridge described the measure's purpose as empowering Congress to pass "those laws which will give
to a citizen of the United States the natural rights which necessarily pertain
to citizenship" and "those privileges and immunities which are guarantied
to him under the Constitution of the United States."[112] The amendment in
its final version was given a broad interpretation by Senator Andrew J.
Rogers, a Democratic opponent of the amendment who tried to alarm his
colleagues by defining "all the rights we have under the laws of the country" as "privileges and immunities."[113] The Privileges and Immunities
Clause would "prevent any State from refusing to allow anything to anybody embraced under this term of privileges and immunities," including
the rights to vote, marry, contract, be a juror, or be a judge or president.[114]

Those who dismissed Rogers as an alarmist had less reason to ignore
Bingham's reiteration of his view that the amendment supplied Congress'
inability to act to "protect by national law the privileges and immunities
of all the citizens of the Republic and the inborn rights of every person"
against state infringement.[115] Bingham mentioned the Eighth Amendment
prohibition of cruel and unusual punishment and the right to protection in
life, liberty, and property as part of these privileges.[116] In the Senate, Luke
P. Poland repeated the widespread Republican belief that the Fourteenth
Amendment would remedy the fact that states had been allowed to disregard the original Privileges and Immunities Clause.[117]

Senator Jacob M. Howard, another amendment supporter, acknowledged
a similar goal to secure "enforcement" of privileges and immunities whenever
citizens "go within the limits of the several States of the Union."[118] Privileges and immunities, he admitted, were not precisely defined, but the Constitution contained the original Privileges and Immunities Clause "for some
good purpose" with "some results beneficial to the citizens of the several
States" in view, "or it would not be found there."[119] Both Article IV Section
2 as described by Justice Washington and the first eight amendments were
covered by the Fourteenth Amendment, Howard asserted, and under Sec-

tion 5 of the new proposed amendment, Congress could finally exercise power to "compel" the states "at all times to respect these great fundamental guarantees."[120]

However clear Howard's definition was, the Fourteenth Amendment drew criticism by its opponents for the uncertain terms of the Privileges and Immunities Clause,[121] which according to Howard included "a great number of particulars,"[122] but Bingham had few apparent reservations about this.[123] So, it would seem, did the House, which passed the Fourteenth Amendment following a speech by Thaddeus Stevens that praised Section 1 for settling legal uncertainty and declaring the "great privilege" of citizenship "to belong to every person born or naturalized in the United States."[124]

Several interpretations of the Privileges and Immunities Clause followed congressional passage. During the debates over the Fifteenth Amendment, Boutwell described the clause in terms that rejected the Court's later attempt to separate state from national privileges:

One of the immunities . . . and privileges of a citizen of the United States is that he shall be a citizen of the State where he resides, and the inhibition applies as well to the deprivation of rights derived directly from the States as to those rights derived directly from the United States Government. It is a comprehensive inhibition upon the States. They cannot deprive a citizen of the United States of any privilege and immunity which he may enjoy as a citizen of the United States; they cannot deprive him of any privilege and immunity which he may enjoy, or which any other citizen may enjoy as a citizen of the State in which he resides.[125]

In an 1872 debate, Senator John Sherman, who like Boutwell voted for the Fourteenth Amendment, similarly rejected such distinctions and asserted that privileges and immunities included all rights conferred by the common law.[126]

The Ku Klux Klan Act of 1871 was intended to cover all rights, privileges, and immunities inherent in national citizenship.[127] Representative Samuel Shellabarger and Senator George F. Edmunds, both of whom had voted for the Fourteenth Amendment, used the occasion to assert both the fundamentality of the privileges and immunities of citizenship and Congress' corresponding enforcement power.[128] An 1871 House Judiciary Committee report rejecting a request for women's suffrage reiterated that the Privileges and Immunities Clause did not add national privileges and immunities to those embraced by Article IV Section 2, but did aim to limit the states.[129] Senators Morton[130] and Lot M. Morrill[131] contended as well the next year that privileges and immunities were preexisting, a nondispositive proposition that Frelinghuysen, a Radical who recognized the courts' construction of Article IV Section 2, had denied during the Ku Klux Klan Act debates.[132]

Frelinghuysen asserted that the Fourteenth Amendment did not merely establish " 'equality' between whites and blacks," but also for the first time "asserts United States citizenship and defines some of its privileges and immunities" which the federal government could enforce.[133] The senator proceeded to cite Justice Bradley's opinion in *Live-Stock Dealers' & Butchers' Ass'n* approvingly, indicating further his differences with the *Slaughter-House* majority, and added that since the Fourteenth Amendment came into being, "citizenship of the United States is primary, underived, and independent of State citizenship."[134] Edmunds also recognized the amendment's new principle that "every person born in the United States shall first and always be a citizen of the nation, and second, and as a consequence, be a citizen of the State in which he resides."[135]

During the debates over the Civil Rights Act of 1875, Frelinghuysen repeated his earlier views and applied them to the nondiscrimination policy in the bill: "as no State under the old Constitution could discriminate in law against a citizen of another State as to fundamental rights to any greater degree than it did against a citizen of its own State, of the same class, so now no State must discriminate against a citizen of the United States merely on account of his race."[136] Morton added that "the privileges and immunities of citizens of the State . . . are treated as being identical with the privileges of citizens of the United States under the fourteenth article."[137] Boutwell, now a senator, expressed views concurring with both Morton and Frelinghuysen on the nondiscrimination principle.[138] For him, the Fourteenth Amendment secured "citizens of the United States their rights as citizens of the several States; and the first right is the right of equality before the law."[139] Edmunds closed the debates over the Civil Rights Act with a strong assertion of the Fourteenth Amendment's protection against discrimination in "common rights."[140]

It should be added, given the temptation to dismiss the importance of a decision by a single Supreme Court justice,[141] that *Corfield* was widely recognized by the Reconstruction Congress and cited to define privileges and immunities in contexts both supporting and contradicting the majority of the Court in 1873—but usually the latter.[142] As citations of judicial cases in Congress went, it is noteworthy that through the debates over the Civil Rights Act of 1875, the *Slaughter-House Cases* were expressly cited with approval or disapproval that was largely correlated to the level of support for Reconstruction. The Court's opinion was cited with approval by Democrats James B. Beck,[143] Alexander H. Stephens (the former Confederate Vice President),[144] Herndon,[145] John D. Atkins,[146] Milton I. Southard,[147] Thomas M. Norwood,[148] Thurman,[149] Read,[150] Finck,[151] and Republican John Ambler Smith.[152] Senator Carpenter argued from the Court's opinion against the constitutionality of the 1875 civil rights bill,[153] but he did not necessarily do so on the merits: although it might be said to be "incorrect," he contended, it "still . . . must be admitted that the" Court's decision "exist[s], and that" it "prescribe[s] for the judicial department of the Government a rule which must be applied to this bill."[154]

Several Republicans cited the Court's opinion with disapproval, including Frelinghuysen (who also endorsed Bradley's circuit opinion),[155] Boutwell,[156] Howe,[157] and Edmunds (who found the Court's opinion "radically" different from "the intent of the Framers and the construction of the language used by them").[158] Congressman George F. Hoar additionally cited *Live-Stock Dealers' & Butchers' Ass'n* approvingly.[159]

In the end, support for the dissents' interpretations of the Privileges and Immunities Clause, without looking specifically at the right against monopolies, is abundant from statements made during the framing and early history of the Fourteenth Amendment. Among the four Republican legislators cited above who made floor statements that supported the majority, only Trumbull had voted for the Fourteenth Amendment,[160] and given his postratification political career, it is difficult to attach decisive weight to statements he made in 1871. Otherwise, congressional debates infer a strong correlation between Democratic opposition to Reconstruction and the Court's interpretation while pro-Reconstruction Republicans overwhelmingly contradicted the opinion. Not only is it clear that the Privileges and Immunities Clause was understood by its supporters as conferring substantive rights against state infringement beyond the Democratic (judicially recognized) construction of the original Constitution, but congressional statements go as far as to support Bradley's suggestion of the incorporation doctrine, an issue that remains to be dealt with in a subsequent section.[161]

That the Court wrongly interpreted the Privileges and Immunities Clause in 1873 has been accepted by most scholars,[162] but there are exceptions such as Judge Robert H. Bork who find it to be "quite properly" that the clause has "remained a dead letter."[163] Perhaps the most remarkable observation for originalists, in view of the fact that the 1873 decision remains good law, is that Justice William H. Moody's opinion for the Court in *Twining v. New Jersey* (1908) admitted thirty-five years later that the *Slaughter-House Cases* "[u]ndoubtedly . . . gave much less effect to the Fourteenth Amendment than some of the public men active in framing it intended."[164] The framers viewed the Privileges and Immunities Clause as the Fourteenth Amendment's central provision, devoting far less attention to the Equal Protection Clause, and the first major distortion of constitutional jurisprudence during the Court's retreat from Reconstruction arose out of the narrowing of the former clause to the point that the Equal Protection Clause would be given the sole role of absorbing much of the Privileges and Immunities Clause's intended protection.[165]

e. *Bradwell*: Application of the *Slaughter-House* Principle

In a decision upholding the denial of a woman's admission to the state bar because of her sex, *Bradwell v. Illinois* (1873) extended the *Slaughter-House* rationale to hold that the right to admission to practice in a state's courts is not one of the "privileges and immunities belonging to citizens of the United States."[166] Senator Carpenter argued for the plaintiff "that the fourteenth amendment opens to every citizen of the United States, male or female, black or white, married or single, the honorable professions as well as the servile employments of life; and that no citizen can be excluded from any one of them."[167] The Court, however, felt otherwise. Working from the *Slaughter-House Cases*, Justice Miller's majority opinion emphasized the distinction between citizenship of a state and of the United States: "it would seem that, as to the courts of a State, it would relate to citizenship of the State, and as to Federal courts, it would relate to citizenship of the United States."[168]

By determining the area at issue not to be covered by the Privileges and Immunities Clause at all, the Court avoided the need for an analysis of the legitimacy of the discrimination involved, but none of the four *Slaughter-House* dissenters joined Miller's opinion. Instead, Justices Swayne and Field joined a concurrence by Bradley that, while not denying that fundamental privileges and immunities of citizenship merited protection in the context at issue, held that women enjoyed no fundamental privilege or immunity to practice law.[169] Chief Justice Chase, who had about three weeks to live when the decision was announced, dissented without opinion.[170] The merits of the concurrence's conclusions on sex discrimination will not be explored because that particular issue did not deal with Reconstruction, but the Court's recognition of an entire state sphere as beyond the scope of the Privileges and Immunities Clause is significant to note as a reaffirmation of a holding that later would come to impact former slaves.

3. *Railroad Co. v. Brown:* The Court and Segregation in 1874

One of the curiously neglected Supreme Court cases dealing with racial discrimination in the nineteenth century is the high court's first post–Civil War segregation case, *Railroad Co. v. Brown* (1874).[1] At issue in this case was an 1863 statute prohibiting the exclusion of any person on account of color from the cars of the Washington and Alexandria Railroad Company, which Congress authorized to extend its road into Washington, D.C.[2] The railroad had employed a policy of separate but equal cars, and when Kate Brown, a black woman employed by the Senate, tried to enter a particular car reserved "for white ladies, and gentlemen accompanying them," an employee of the railroad company ordered her to go to another car.[3] Nevertheless, she entered the car for white women, and the employee "put her out with force, and, as she alleged, some insult."[4]

In a unanimous decision, the Court rejected the separate but equal arrangement of the railroad company as "an ingenious attempt to evade a compliance with the obvious meaning of the requirement" of the law.[5] It acknowledged that a literal construction of the statute might produce a different result, but the Court looked to the broader context that gave rise to the law, including the accompanying discussion in Congress about "the discrimination in the use of the cars on account of color, where slavery obtained, which was the subject of discussion at the time, and not the fact that the colored race could not ride in the cars at all."[6] This ruling should be kept in mind when turning to the Court's subsequent holding on segregation thirty-two years later.

The Court's conclusions in 1874 were well supported. During the Senate debates ten years earlier over streetcar discrimination in the nation's capital, Sumner, arguing for a resolution securing blacks the "equal enjoyment of all railroad privileges in the District of Columbia,"[7] charged that whenever the railroad company "exclude[s] a colored person from any one of their cars they do it in violation of law."[8] He saw freedom from segregation as a part of "the full enjoyment of all the privileges of the railway in this District."[9] "[A]ny other conclusion," he asserted, "authorizes a corporation to establish a *caste*, offensive to religion and humanity, injurious to a whole race now dwelling among us, and bringing shame upon our country."[10]

The opposition did not construe Sumner's amendment differently. Senator Thomas A. Hendricks, who consistently opposed civil rights measures during the 1860s, observed,

I understand the position to be taken in the Senate of the United States . . . that the negro is now the peer of the white man; that he shall take his seat in the same cars; that there shall not be any police arrangement or regulation to exclude him from the cars of the white man, although there is a sufficient accommodation provided for him separately, but that he shall be forced into social equality with the white man.[11]

Hendricks concluded that "the purpose of the majority" was "to place" blacks "on terms of social, political, and legal equality with the white race."[12] Henry Wilson later would announce in a speech against segregation that he did "not desire to go against prejudices" but felt that the government should "protect rights, if we do it over prejudices and over interests, until every man in this country is fully protected in all the rights that belong to beings made in the image of God."[13] Sumner's amendment passed the Senate by a close vote,[14] as did another Sumner amendment three months later providing that "there shall be no exclusion of any person from any car on account of color."[15]

The incident involving Kate Brown became a matter of congressional concern in 1868. A report that year by the Senate Committee on the District of Columbia reviewed the situation and, citing the 1863 law governing the railroad, observed that it "appears that Congress has already provided that said company shall not make any discrimination against passengers on account of race or color."[16] Sumner viewed the matter, including the multiple injuries that Brown received, as "dastardly,"[17] and other senators shared his outrage. John Conness wanted to "put an end to this system of cowardly treatment that is dealt to unoffending persons when they are in public conveyances" and added, "let black and white be protected alike; I am for their equal protection"[18]—an interesting use of this Fourteenth Amendment term in the segregation context. Charles D. Drake decried the fact that "negroes are to be tolerated in the cars of that road while they are in a servile capacity; but the octaroon, between whom and the white woman by whose side she sits it were difficult to discover the difference, if she goes as a free woman, not charged in a servile capacity for any one, is to be rudely thrust from the cars while southern blackguards sit there with impunity!"[19] Morton denounced the incident as "an outrage growing out of the prejudice against color."[20] James W. Nye cited the 1863 law chartering the railroad and not only seemed to agree with the Court's later decision, but also contended that the railroad company by its actions had forfeited its charter.[21] Waitman T. Willey saw the incident as "prejudice against the colored race" taking "active form" and resulting in "outrages upon the rights and privileges and immunities of that race."[22]

Congress did not often deal with segregation during the 1860s, but existing evidence supports the Court not only on principle, but also on the very case that would face the nation's highest tribunal. While the statute at issue existed apart from, and in fact preceded, the Fourteenth Amendment, it sheds significant light on the framers' conception of equality in the segregation context that is scarce during the Fourteenth Amendment debates themselves. It will be of additional interest in subsequent discussion of constitutional issues that, with the exception of Drake and Morton, the 1868 statements cited above all came from senators who had voted for the Fourteenth Amendment,[23] and Morton probably merits status as a framer as well because he served as the governor of Indiana during ratification and took considerable interest in the amendment.[24]

4. *Minor v. Hapersett* and Suffrage under the Fourteenth Amendment

In *Minor v. Hapersett* (1875),[1] the Court, in the spirit of the *Slaughter-House Cases*, held that the Fourteenth "amendment did not add to the privileges and immunities of a citizen. It simply furnished an additional guaranty for the protection of such as he already had."[2] (Shellabarger in later years would expressly refute this holding as a violation of many of the framers' intentions.[3]) Finding suffrage not to be among the privileges and immunities of citizenship, the Court rejected a claim that the Constitution protected women against sex discrimination in the exercise of suffrage[4] and cited the express terms of Section 2 of the Fourteenth Amendment to support this holding.[5]

Although its premises might not always have conformed to the framers' intentions for reasons already discussed, the Court's ultimate holding did not mark another retreat from Reconstruction since evidence strongly refutes the notion that the Fourteenth Amendment was intended to cover suffrage. Statements from both supporters and opponents of Reconstruction overwhelmingly support the notion that suffrage was not a privilege of citizenship and not covered by the Fourteenth Amendment.[6] One can find statements after Congress passed the Fourteenth Amendment contending otherwise,[7] but of the legislators who both fit this category and had voted for the amendment, only one, Edmunds, had not contradicted his earlier statements during the debates, and his interpretation was too widely opposed for one to consider it a reasonable reflection of the original understanding.[8] Where the context of voting was concerned, the Court in *Minor* did not stray from the framers' understanding in view of both the debates and the text of Section 2.[9] Whatever the fate of women's suffrage, it was still supposed that the right to vote of former slaves would be protected by the Fifteenth Amendment.

5. The Fifteenth Amendment and *United States v. Reese*

a. *United States v. Given*

In 1873, Justice Strong handed down a decision as circuit justice upholding an indictment under § 2 of the first Enforcement Act of 1870 in *United States v. Given*,[1] the language of which would remain important in view of other Supreme Court cases. Besides affirming Congress' exercise of power under the Fifteenth Amendment, Strong maintained that the "thirteenth, fourteenth, and fifteenth amendments of the constitution have confessedly extended civil and political rights, and, I think, they have enlarged the powers of congress"[2]—a statement that causes one to wonder why Strong joined opinions suggesting the contrary about the extension of privileges and immunities. The justice proceeded to describe the fundamental purposes of the amendments in terms that encompassed the rights of private persons:

The primary object of the thirteenth, and of the first sections of the fourteenth and fifteenth [amendments] was to secure to persons certain rights which they had not previously possessed. Thus the thirteenth amendment made the right of personal liberty a constitutional right. The fourteenth assured the right of citizenship to all persons born or naturalized in the United States, and subject to the jurisdiction thereof. And the fifteenth defined partially that which constitutes citizenship and which belongs to citizenship as such. It recognizes, as a right of citizenship, exemption from disability on account of race, color, or previous condition of servitude, in the determination of a right to vote. It practically declares that citizenship, irrespective of color or race, confers a right to vote on equal terms or conditions with those that are required for voters of another race or color. It places white and colored persons on equal footing as respects the elective franchise. . . . It is true the amendment is in form a prohibition upon the United States, and upon the states, but it is not the less on that account an assertion of a constitutional right belonging to citizens as such. Surely it cannot be maintained that it conferred no rights upon persons. There are very many instances to be found in the constitution as it was before the recent amendments, in which rights of persons have been recognized and secured without any express grant.[3]

If the Constitution once gave a slave owner the right to reclaim a fugitive slave[4] through congressional penal legislation against individuals, Strong reasoned, "much more are the rights secured, recognized, and guaranteed by the thirteenth, fourteenth, and fifteenth amendments objects of legitimate protection by the law-making power of the federal government."[5] Those amendments "manifestly intended to secure the right guaranteed by them against any infringement from any quarter."[6] Section 2 of the Fifteenth Amendment "[m]anifestly . . . was adopted for a purpose" and must "confer some effective power."[7] Without even feeling the need to narrow his holdings to the case's context of a tax collector charged with racial discrimination in a jurisdiction in which paid taxes were a prerequisite of the right to vote,[8] Strong called it

an exploded heresy that the national government cannot reach all individuals in the states. It cannot invade the state domain. It cannot take cognizance of offences against state sovereignty. But when state laws have imposed duties upon persons, whether officers or not, the performance or non-performance of which affects rights under the federal government . . . , I have no doubt that congress may make the non-performance of those duties an offence against the United States, and may punish it accordingly. This is not invading the state domain. . . . Undoubtedly, an act, or an omission to act, may be an offence both against the state law and the laws of the United States. Any other doctrine would place the national government entirely within the power of the states, and would leave constitutional rights guarded only by the protection which each state might choose to extend to them. The fault of this objection to this indictment is, it fails to apprehend that the fifteenth amendment secured rights to every citizen, and that it gave congress power to protect them.[9]

Thus Strong's theory of the Reconstruction Amendments in 1873 did not rely on a distinction between state and private actors or between state actions and omissions. The lack of such distinctions seems effortless enough that Strong does not appear even to have been particularly aware of the probability of strong challenges to his premises.[10] It also did not concern him that the exercise of federal power might overlap with state functions since the federal government's power was premised on affirmative rights existing directly between the federal government and individual citizens. Strong's early impressions, like those of Bradley, should be kept in mind when turning to the line of cases that would challenge them one by one.

b. The Court's opinion in *Reese*

United States v. Reese[11] was the first Supreme Court decision to interpret the Fifteenth Amendment,[12] and it was the first of two 1876 cases that dealt a substantial blow to congressional efforts during Reconstruction. At issue was whether an indictment under §§ 3 and 4 of the first Enforcement Act was valid against two inspectors of a municipal election in Kentucky for refusing to receive and count the vote of a black citizen on grounds of race, color, or previous condition of servitude.[13] "The Fifteenth Amendment does not confer the right of suffrage upon any one," wrote Chief Justice Morrison R. Waite for the Court, but "prevents the States, or the United States, . . . from giving preference, in this particular, to one citizen of the United States over another on account of race, color, or previous condition of servitude."[14] Appropriate legislation under Section 2, therefore, should address wrongful refusal based on these three categories but cannot "impose penalties for every wrongful refusal to receive the vote of a qualified elector at State elections."[15]

Section 3 of the Enforcement Act was conceded not to expressly limit the offense of an inspector of elections to the three categories addressed in the amendment, but it was argued that the provision was so limited when considered together with preceding sections.[16] The Court rejected this argument, explaining that as the Fifteenth Amendment substantially changed earlier practice of leaving the regulation of elections entirely to states, neither a citizen nor an inspector should be placed in a situation in which an honest error in construing a penal statute may put him in danger of prosecution.[17] "Every man should be able to know with certainty when he is committing a crime."[18] As for Section 4, the Court ruled that it did not even contain words of limitation or reference "manifesting any intention to confine its provisions to the terms of the Fifteenth Amendment."[19] Rather, it aimed to punish "all persons, who, by force, bribery, &c., hinder, delay, &c., any person from qualifying or voting" without confining its language to the amendment's three categories.[20]

Reasoning that the Court could not reject the part of the challenged provisions that was unconstitutional and retain the remainder, Waite maintained that introducing words of limitation into a penal statute "would be to make a new law, not to enforce an old one," so he concluded that Congress had "not as yet provided by 'appropriate legislation' for the punishment of the offence charged in the indictment."[21]

c. Justice Hunt's Dissent

The Court's judgment was eight to one, with Justice Nathan Clifford finding the indictment invalid on different grounds[22] and Justice Ward Hunt alone in dissent. Hunt observed that "the intention of Congress on this subject is too plain to be discussed."[23] Section 1 contained "a general announcement that" the right to vote was "not to be embarrassed by the fact of race, color, or previous condition."[24] Section 2 required "that equal opportunity shall be given to the races in providing every prerequisite for voting" and provided civil damages and criminal penalties for any officer violating it.[25] When a collector refused to let a citizen pay a capitation tax (the prerequisite to voting in that locality) on racial grounds, Hunt contended after describing the fourth count of the indictment, a case arose under the provision of § 3 covering "the person so offering and failing as aforesaid"—the person who had made the offer that was rejected on racial grounds—and who was entitled to vote "as if he had, in fact, performed such act."[26] Section 4 similarly addressed any person who illegally hindered or prevented any citizen from voting in any election "as aforesaid."[27] "By the words 'as aforesaid,' the provisions respecting race and color of the first and second sections of the statute are incorporated into and made a part of the third and fourth sections,"[28] Hunt contended, and "[u]nless so construed," the words "are wholly and absolutely without meaning."[29]

Unlike Waite, Hunt in his opinion made specific reference to research of Senate debates at the time the bill was passed and observed that the bill was viewed by its drafters in accordance with his views.[30] The requirement of particularity in indictments or penal statutes, in his opinion, was carried by the Court to such an "extravagant extent" that it allowed "good sense" to be "sacrificed to technical nicety" in some cases.[31] Precedent established that the object of statutory construction was "to ascertain the legislative intent" and not allow the words to "be narrowed to the exclusion of what the legislature intended to embrace."[32] "Especially should this liberal rule of construction prevail," Hunt added, "where, though in form the statute is penal, it is in fact to protect freedom."[33] Both § 3 and § 4 provided for the punishment of election inspectors who refused votes on racially discriminatory grounds and therefore were sufficient.[34]

Turning to the constitutionality of the law, Hunt pointed out that the protected person must be a citizen of the United States with a right to vote, and he thought it would be "both illiberal and illogical to say that this protection was intended to be limited to" elections for federal officials.[35] Acknowledging prior state power to refuse the ballot "to any class of persons" subject to reduced congressional representation under Section 2 of the Fourteenth Amendment, Hunt asserted that the Fifteenth Amendment was passed to protect the rights of freedmen more effectively.[36] It embraced "the right to vote in its broadest terms," covering local or state elections as well as federal elections.[37] From this conclusion, Hunt proceeded to hold that the inspectors' refusal was a refusal by Kentucky since the "State" in the Fifteenth Amendment "can act only through its agents" and the inspectors exercised state power.[38]

Like Strong in *Given*, Hunt rejected the contention that Congress could not enact penal laws and that its enforcement power was limited to correcting incorrect state court decisions as bringing "to an impotent conclusion the vigorous amendments on the subject of slavery."[39] In view of the inferior effectiveness of alternatives, he found the 1870 penal legislation to be "not only the appropriate, but the most effectual, means of enforcing the amendment."[40] Hunt turned to congressional power recognized in cases like *Prigg* under the Fugitive Slave Clause[41] and concluded that in the 1842 case, even despite the lack of an express congressional enforcement authority, the same principle applied that should apply in the case of the Fifteenth Amendment: Absent "all positive provision to the contrary, . . . the national government is bound through its own departments, legislative, judicial, or executive, to carry into effect all the rights and duties imposed upon it by the Constitution."[42]

d. *Reese* in View of Political Understandings

The Court's assumption (unchallenged by Hunt) that the Fifteenth Amendment prevents only discrimination based on the three enumerated categories while leaving the power to regulate suffrage as a general matter with the states is well supported by congressional statements.[43] Some legislators added expressions of regret that the amendment (or similar proposals) did not confer a clearer grant of affirmative authority to the federal government to regulate suffrage or officeholding more broadly and uniformly.[44]

When one looks within the bounds of the three categories protected by the Fifteenth Amendment against discrimination, however, the intended affirmative character of the amendment is apparent. Senator Stewart saw the amendment as "a declaration to make all men, without regard to race or color, equal before the law."[45] Senator Roscoe Conkling saw it as a "proposition to divest" the states "of the power of discriminating invidiously against persons of a certain race in respect of their right to vote."[46] Representative James Dixon, a conservative Republican who did not vote for either the Fourteenth or the Fifteenth Amendment,[47] called the amendment a change of "radical character, which proposes to take from the States their power over suffrage and invest that power in the National Government."[48] Bingham explained the amendment with reference to other negative constitutional limitations in affirmative terms clearly consistent with Hunt:

There are other negative provisions in the Constitution of the United States; for example, the express negative provision that "no State shall pass any law impairing the obligation of contracts." By virtue of your judiciary act, as it has been in force from the foundation of the Government to this day, that limitation upon the power of the States is uniform, and whenever or where ever any State has undertaken by legislative enactment or by constitutional provision, if you please . . . to impair the obligation of contracts, that wrong has, by the operation of your law, been righted; so that the provision of the Constitution has operated uniformly. Whenever Congress has the power under the Constitution to enforce the limitations of that instrument, even upon States, the exercise of the power will be as uniform as the exercise of any affirmative power can possibly be. It must be so; it cannot be otherwise.[49]

Upon ratification, President Grant celebrated the "measure which makes at once 4,000,000 people voters who were heretofore declared by the highest tribunal in the land not citizens of the United States, nor eligible to become so" as possessing "grander importance than any other one act of the kind from the foundation of our free Government to the present day."[50]

Such statements recognize no distinction between state and national citizenship—or the right to vote in state versus national elections, consistent with Hunt's dissent. Howard expressly found the proposed amendment to apply "as clearly by its terms to the citizen of Vermont, and his right to vote . . . is as clearly subject to the language of this clause as is the right of any person residing in a Territory or in the District of Columbia."[51] Grant expressly endorsed Strong's conclusion in *Given* that the protection of the Fifteenth Amendment and Enforcement Acts "extends to State as well as other elections."[52]

The Enforcement Act debates themselves included a number of statements that tracked judicial debates. The provisions at issue in *Reese* originated in the Senate,[53] where Thurman, inconsistent with *Given* and Hunt's dissent, denied congressional power to "regulate the duty of officers created by State authority,"[54] an argument to which supporters of the bill seemed oblivious. Stewart, for his part, presented a summary of the bill consistent with Hunt's. "In the first place," he began, "it makes it the duty of all officers charged with doing any act which is a prerequisite to voting to furnish to all men, without distinction of color, an equal opportunity of performing it."[55] Immediately following was an interpretation of §§ 3 and 4:

In the next place, if a person is otherwise qualified to vote, and attempts to qualify himself by registering, or paying taxes, performing the acts required, and he fails by reason of being unlawfully prevented, then he shall go to the polls with his vote. The next section provides that if any person—this goes outside of the officers— intimidate him while he is attempting to qualify himself by performing the prerequisites, or by any other unlawful means attempt to prevent him from performing that prerequisite, or if any person shall prevent him unlawfully from voting by threats or by any other mode of obstruction, then that person shall be guilty of an offense.[56]

The latter part of this statement, as in Hunt's understanding, lacks any meaning without the previously stated ban on racial discrimination.

Whether interpretations of power under Section 2 of the Fifteenth Amendment were affirmative or negative consistently correlated to the speaker's support of or opposition to Reconstruction. Carpenter found this section to confer "ample and full" power to furnish a remedy for those who suffer injury,[57] and Edmunds concurred, adding the need to fix a floor for damages in anticipation of unfriendly juries.[58] Democrat John P. Stockton, who was not in the Senate when the Fifteenth Amendment was passed, thought that "the fifteenth amendment will enforce itself" and preferred no enforcement bill.[59] Sherman found it "manifest" from Section 2 "that the framers of the fifteenth amendment contemplated that some law should be passed by Congress to enforce it, and that without it it would not have the full force and sanction of law."[60]

Turning to the bill itself, however, Sherman said that he found sections 2 and 3 "too vague and indefinite to found an indictment upon," though he focused his initial criticism on section 2's phrase, "if any such person or officer shall refuse or knowingly omit to give full effect to this section," not on the "as aforesaid" phrases in Sections 3 and 4.[61] Carpenter responded to Sherman that it was necessary "to provide for every contingency in every State" to "frame a section of such generality of description as will include all the cases."[62] The discussion that followed covered a hypothetical similar to the situation in *Reese*:

[CARPENTER:] [S]uppose a particular instance; here is a man entitled on paying a tax to have his name registered and to vote in a certain State. He goes and offers to pay the tax, and the officer will not receive it. When you come to draw the indictment, of course you must draw it specifying the time, place, and circumstances constituting the offense; but you cannot embody an indictment in your act. You must have the act punish the offense generally, and then the indictment must specify the circumstances coming within the provisions of the act. An indictment in that case should charge that at a certain time and place John Smith refused to permit John Jones to pay the tax which wo[u]ld have authorized him to vote; and that would be a proper indictment, and would be clearly within the language of this section.

Mr. SHERMAN. I should like to see a lawyer attempt to frame an indictment where the gist of the offense was that a man failed to give full effect to a section of a particular statute. I think it would be impossible to do it. I think it would be open to general and special demurrer; and therefore I think, instead of "to give full effect to this section," the words "to perform such duty required by such law or regulation" should be inserted. Then you have it distinctly. . . .

Sherman subsequently turned to the provision of Section 3 involved in *Reese*:

[A]n offer to do an act shall be held and considered to be as the act itself—
    And the person so offering, and failing as aforesaid to have otherwise qualified, shall be entitled to vote in the same manner and to the same extent as if he had in fact performed such act.

This provision will, in my judgment, repeal or impair every registry law in the United States of America. . . . Suppose a thousand men should go up to the polls and say, "We tried to be registered and could not be because the officer would not allow us to be," or something of that kind. The man is not bound to take an oath; he is not bound to furnish proof; he is not bound to prove by affidavit that he was denied the right to register. . . . [T]he refusal to a colored man of the right to be registered, shall be held as equivalent to his registering; and that applies to white men as well as to others. . . . [U]nder the operation of the first clause of this third section any body of men who will go up and say, not testify, not prove by affidavit, but simply declare that they have been refused the right to be registered, will have the right to vote, and all your registry laws are overruled. That is not the purpose, certainly, of any committee.[63]

Sherman's primary difficulty—the potential breakdown of all registry laws, "the evasion of the law which . . . could be committed by classes of men in the large cities"[64]—appears different from the Court's primary difficulty, and it would remain to be seen whether the senator shared the Court's particular objection.

Morton's question to the Senate, "whether it is in the power of Congress to make provision for punishing violations of the right of suffrage except those violations go to the question of color, race, or previous condition of servitude,"[65] more directly introduced the Court's concern. Edmunds replied that no one would claim such a power, and Morton continued, "It seems to me that the Senate bill is broader than the [Fifteenth] amendment" before expressing his preference for the bill that originated in the House.[66]

Senator William T. Hamilton asserted that as a negative constitutional provision, the Fifteenth Amendment, which he called "this wicked amendment," was strictly self-executing.[67] With this premise, he predictably concluded that §§ 3 and 4 were too broad for reasons similar to the Court's and found the House bill to be a better draft.[68] Senator Carl Schurz, although he would staunchly oppose Reconstruction and become a Liberal Republican leader,[69] argued that the bill did enforce the Fifteenth Amendment while depriving the states of none of their legitimate power.[70]

Howard felt it would be better to approve the House bill since it brought fewer objections[71] and because he feared the possibility that "a very 'strict construction' court of justice" might

refuse to apply the remedies which are proper in the case to punish individuals for interrupting, preventing, delaying, or hindering the colored man from the peaceful and free exercise of his right of suffrage; which was the great object we had in view in proposing this amendment to the people of the United States.

Against such a construction of the amendment I take this occasion to protest. It is not in harmony with the views of the advocates and friends of the amendment, and if carried out by courts the clause itself will be stripped in a large degree of that remedial and protective justice which was in the minds of its authors when it was under discussion in these Chambers.[72]

Later during the same day of debate, Sherman made another statement in response to Senator Thurman that more directly than his prior comments addressed the issue the Court faced:

[T]hat Congress has a right by appropriate legislation to prevent any State from discriminating against a voter on account of his race, color, or previous condition of servitude. . . . is all, I believe, that is claimed by any one on this side of the Chamber as to the authority conferred by the fifteenth amendment. I have looked over the proposition submitted by the Judiciary Committee of the Senate and the proposition sent to us by the House of Representatives, and I can see no provision in them but what is intended simply to prevent a discrimination on account of race, color, or previous condition of servitude. I think the fourth section of the Senate amendment is badly worded, although even in that section the word "aforesaid," referring to the previous section, shows clearly enough that the intention of its framers was to confine the operation of that section to offenses against the fifteenth amendment; that is, an attempt to discriminate between voters on account of race, color, or previous condition of servitude.[73]

Sherman's interpretation thus fits squarely with that of Hunt, and while he and Howard clearly preferred the House draft, their statements indicate it was for reasons other than that they would agree with the Court's 1876 holdings.

Joseph S. Fowler, a Tennessee Republican who voted against the Fifteenth Amendment,[74] found the bill's constitutionality "doubtful" for targeting state officers who failed to execute state laws, but not on originalist grounds.[75] He asserted that while Section 1 conferred power that was "wholly passive," Section 2

may go further and give the power to enforce the right by legislative action. . . . It is a question of doubt whether any more power is conferred by the auxiliary than by the primary. It is certainly true of all the other primary and auxiliary powers in the Constitution, and has been so held by the ablest commentators on the Constitution. That it was intended by Congress to confer the power is doubtless true; but that it does, is another and a different question.[76]

Fowler's conception of the framers' intent was no different from that of fellow Republicans who supported Reconstruction legislation, but the Tennessee senator displayed less hesitation to disregard congressional intent. His comments prompted a response by Morton:

[W]hat is the spirit and the true intent of the fifteenth amendment, as we all remember it when it passed in this Chamber, as will be shown by the Congressional Globe, by all the discussions, as it is understood by the country? What is the true intent and spirit of that amendment? It is that the colored man, so far as voting is concerned, shall be placed upon the same level and footing with the white man, and that Congress shall have the power to secure to him that right. Is not that the spirit and the intent of that amendment as we all remember it when it passed this Chamber, that the colored man shall be placed on the same footing in regard to voting with the white man, and that Congress shall have the power to secure him in the enjoyment of that right?

Now, the ground these Democratic Senators take is, that any law passed by Congress abridging the right of the colored man to vote is simply unconstitutional and void; that any law or constitution adopted by a State to abridge the right of the colored man to vote is simply unconstitutional and void; and there it stops. If it stops there, what is the use of the second section of the article, which declares that Congress shall have the power by appropriate legislation to enforce it? That second section is intended to give to Congress the power of conferring upon the colored man the full enjoyment of his right. We so understood it when we passed it. The debates will show that that was the understanding.

If the construction adopted by the Senator from Tennessee and others is correct the second section is a nullity; the whole effect of the fifteenth amendment is that any State law prohibiting colored suffrage is void; and there it stops. That is their argument. If it stops there, the second section is nugatory and unnecessary. We know that the second section was put there for the purpose of enabling Congress itself to carry out the provision. It was not to be left to State legislation. If there is any doubt about the understanding with which that was passed we can refer to the debates in the Globe, for it is but little over a year ago since it was done. We know that it was put there for the purpose of enabling Congress to take every step that might be necessary to secure the colored man in the enjoyment of these rights.

Now, sir, we take both of these sections together, we construe them in harmony with each other, and they give to us all the power that is claimed by this bill.[77]

Morton's discussion of the framers' (very recent) intent is difficult to refute, and his assertion of congressional power under Section 2 at the end of this passage contradicts his earlier expressed belief that the Senate bill seemed broader than the Fifteenth Amendment. Perhaps his earlier statement truly aimed to convey preference for the House bill. At any rate, his later statement plus his ultimate vote in favor of the Enforcement Act[78] point more strongly to Morton's belief in the bill's constitutionality.

The House debates over the provisions originating in the Senate proceeded along partisan grounds. Congressman Michael C. Kerr asserted that §§ 2, 3, and 4 extended to election matters not covered by the Fifteenth Amendment,[79] and fellow Democrats Beck[80] and Clarkson N. Potter[81] expressed similar sentiments on the bill's unconstitutionality. Republicans like Noah Davis[82] and Washington Townsend,[83] however, presented broader views of Section 2 of the Fifteenth Amendment and conveyed distrust of the states when left to their own devices.

Questions regarding the framers' perceptions of the constitutionality of the Senate version of §§ 3 and 4 are most decisively answered by the legislation's passage in both houses.[84] Statements about the act after its passage reflected the positions of the speakers on Reconstruction. Democrat Francis

P. Blair, Jr., took occasion during later debates over a supplementary enforcement act to describe the 1870 act as an unconstitutional attempt to cover fraud in voting regardless of the race involved, an argument consistent with that of the Court.[85] Praise for the bill as a measure addressing the categories of discrimination covered by the Fifteenth Amendment (consistent with Hunt's dissent), however, came from Radical Republicans Bingham[86] and Morton[87] as well as the moderate Garfield.[88]

On the surface, even without analysis of the content of contemporary congressional debates, the task of defending the Court's holding in *Reese* on originalist grounds may appear an almost absurdly simple task because the provisions that were struck down were based on a constitutional amendment that had just been ratified under a virtually identical Congress. (Courts generally are not expected to charge the framers of an amendment with misunderstanding their own understanding.) Nevertheless, it might be argued that the Court based its ruling on longstanding principles of statutory construction independent of a particular understanding of the Fifteenth Amendment. Implicitly accepting this conclusion are those commentators who emphasize poor drafting by legislators as a factor in the collapse of Reconstruction.[89] In the end, however, this criticism places disproportionate blame on the wrong branch of the federal government. While one can plausibly suggest, working with the benefit of 20–20 hindsight, that the Reconstruction Congress could have tried to give the Court less room for invalidating the Enforcement Act by passing an alternative to the Senate bill, it is difficult to conclude that Congress was the decisive culprit in the fate of the 1870 law. Not only was Hunt's opinion better supported by both the Senate debates and judicial precedent, but the Court's method of construction was in fact the *first* of its kind on the question of overbroad statutes.[90]

The fate of *Reese* in the twentieth century remains to be discussed, but it is noteworthy that the Court in 1987 would recognize as a longstanding rule of interpretation that a party waging a "facial challenge to a legislative Act . . . must establish that no set of circumstances exists under which the Act would be valid."[91] Not only did the Enforcement Act, even by the *Reese* Court's interpretation, cover at least some circumstances that the Fifteenth Amendment addressed, but the case at bar also involved one such instance of racial discrimination, even though the Court decided to invalidate §§ 3 and 4 on their face. Although *Reese* set an unusual standard that for many years would be applied to federal civil rights laws,[92] its pedigree is questionable enough to suggest that the fate of the Enforcement Act rests not with an oversight by Congress as much as with a judicially created anomaly that conveniently conformed to the national attitude toward Reconstruction.

6. *United States v. Cruikshank*

a. The Court's Opinion in *Cruikshank*

On the same day *Reese* was decided, the Supreme Court handed down its opinion in *United States v. Cruikshank*.[1] This case, which as mentioned earlier arose from the Colfax massacre, involved an indictment under § 6 of the first Enforcement Act, which provided:

That if two or more persons shall band or conspire together, or go in disguise upon the public highway, or upon the premises of another, with intent to violate any provision of this act, or to injure, oppress, threaten, or intimidate any citizen with intent to prevent or hinder his free exercise and enjoyment of any right or privilege granted or secured to him by the Constitution or laws of the United States, or because of his having exercised the same, such persons shall be held guilty of felony, and, on conviction thereof, shall be fined or imprisoned, or both, at the discretion of the court,—the fine not to exceed five thousand dollars, and the imprisonment not to exceed ten years,—and shall, moreover, be thereafter ineligible to, and disabled from holding, any office or place of honor, profit, or trust created by the Constitution or laws of the United States.[2]

Of the sixteen counts of the indictment, the first eight charged the defendants with "banding" and the second eight with "conspiring" together to "injure, oppress, threaten, and intimidate" black citizens "with the intent thereby to hinder and prevent them in their free exercise and enjoyment of rights and privileges 'granted and secured' to them 'in common with all other good citizens of the United States by the constitution and laws of the United States.' "[3]

Reasoning that a protected right must be "granted or secured by the Constitution or laws of the United States" in order to bring the case under the statute,[4] Chief Justice Waite, writing for the Court, proceeded to reiterate the *Slaughter-House Cases*' ruling that emphasized the difference between the rights of state and national citizenship and corresponding obligations to the two governments (state and federal) in which a citizen resides.[5] Waite emphasized the separation of powers between the two levels of government and pointed out that the federal government was limited to those powers contained in the Constitution, other powers being "reserved to the States or the people."[6]

The Court then rejected the first and ninth counts stating the intent to hinder and prevent the exercise of the "lawful right and privilege to peaceably assemble together" with other U.S. citizens "for a peaceful and lawful purpose" on the grounds that it "was not . . . a right granted to the people by the Constitution."[7] Waite's opinion viewed the First Amendment prohibition on Congress from abridging the right "to assemble, and to petition the Government for a redress of grievances"[8] as limiting only the federal government, not the states.[9] Still, the Court found the right of peaceable assembly "for the purpose of petitioning Congress for a redress of grievances, or for any thing else connected with the powers or the duties of the national government," to be "an attribute of national citizenship" within federal sovereignty that was covered by the statute. The case at bar, however, did not involve such a situation.[10]

The Court made a similar holding on the second and tenth counts identifying "bearing arms for a lawful purpose" as a protected right, employing its understanding that the Second Amendment restricted only federal power.[11] The Court found counts three and eleven charging intent to deprive the named citizens' "respective several lives and liberty of person without due process of law" to be "even more objectionable" on the ground that "[t]his is nothing else than alleging a conspiracy to falsely imprison or murder citizens of the United States," no more a federal duty than punishment of false imprisonment or murder.[12] The Due Process Clause, Waite asserted, "adds nothing to the rights of one citizen as against another. It simply furnishes an additional guaranty against any encroachment by the States upon the fundamental rights which belong to every citizen as a member of society."[13]

Counts four and twelve alleged intent to prevent and hinder the named black citizens in "the free exercise and enjoyment of their several right and privilege to the full and equal benefit of all laws and proceedings . . . for the security of their respective persons and property" in Louisiana and the United States that were enjoyed at that particular time and place by white citizens.[14] The Court rejected these counts for lacking an "allegation that this was done because of the race or color of the persons conspired against," which reduced it ("[w]hen stripped of its verbiage") to "nothing more than that the defendants conspired to prevent certain citizens of the United States . . . from enjoying the equal Protection of the laws of the State and of the United States."[15] Turning to the Equal Protection Clause, the Court asserted that the provision "does not . . . add any thing to the rights which one citizen has under the Constitution against another" and that the federal government is limited only to preventing the states from denying the equality of rights, a duty that originated and remains with the states.[16] The Court also maintained that the 1866 Civil Rights Act was not implicated since the counts did not allege "that the wrong contemplated against the rights of these citizens was on account of their race or color."[17]

The Court next struck down counts six and fourteen, which alleged an intent to hinder and prevent black citizens from exercising their "right and privilege to vote at any election to be thereafter by law had and held by the people in and of . . . Louisiana, or by the people of and in the parish of Grant," finding no support in either the Fourteenth or Fifteenth Amendment.[18] The Court applied *Minor*'s holding under the Fourteenth Amendment that the United States has not conferred the right to vote on anyone, and it enunciated its belief that the counts reflected a lack of racial intent under the Fifteenth Amendment: "We may suspect that race was the cause of the hostility; but it is not so averred. . . . Every thing essential must be charged positively, and not inferentially. The defect here is not in form, but in substance."[19]

Counts seven and fifteen alleged the intent "to put the parties named in great fear of bodily harm, and to injure and oppress them, because . . . they had voted 'at an election before that time had and held according to law by the people of' " Louisiana on November 4, 1872.[20] Finding "nothing to show that the elections voted at were any other than State elections, or that the conspiracy was formed on account of the race of the parties against whom the conspirators were to act,"[21] the Court dismissed the counts as "really of nothing more than a conspiracy to commit a breach of the peace within a State"—"mere police duty in the States" that did not belong to the federal government in such a case.[22]

The Court concluded that all of the above counts did not contain criminal charges that were indictable under federal law, having failed to "show that it was the intent of the defendants, by their conspiracy, to hinder or prevent the enjoyment of any right granted or secured by the Constitution."[23] Four counts still remained to be considered. Two of them (five and thirteen) charged the intent "to hinder and prevent the parties in their respective free exercise and enjoyment of the rights, privileges, immunities, and protection granted and secured to them respectively as citizens of the United States, and as citizens of . . . Louisiana," on account of the named parties' race and color.[24] Both these and the other two counts (eight and sixteen) charged the intent to hinder and prevent the parties "in their several and respective free exercise and enjoyment of every, each, all, and singular the several rights and privileges granted and secured to them by the constitution and laws of the United States."[25]

In these counts the Court found "no specification of any particular right," the language being "broad enough to cover all," and it concluded that by failing to be sufficiently specific, they lacked "the certainty and precision required by the established rules of criminal pleading."[26] The only convictions the federal government had attained from the Colfax massacre were thus reversed in a unanimous judgment, with Justice Clifford concurring separately in the judgment.[27]

b. Analysis of *Cruikshank* and the Incorporation Debate

b.1. *The Court and Congressional Understandings*

The Court's opinion in *Cruikshank* was based on both the premises of the *Slaughter-House Cases* and a specificity requirement paralleling that of *Reese* in some ways. Even putting aside the national notoriety of the Colfax massacre and the fact that the elections of November 4, 1872, included both congressional and presidential elections,[28] the Court's opinion in *Cruikshank* is problematic both in its narrow requirements on allegations of racial discrimination and in its general holdings on the Privileges and Immunities Clause.

The allegations made it clear that the victims who were being deprived of various rights, privileges, and immunities were citizens "of African descent and persons of color,"[29] but the Court still found them fatally defective. Conceding that the only constitutional right to vote applied to nondiscrimination based on the Fifteenth Amendment's stated categories, was the Court correct that allegations of infringement of the right to vote of citizens who were described in terms of their race and color was decisively different from those that would have added a phrase to the effect of "on account of their race and color?"[30] Did the absence of those words materially alter those counts to the point that they did not provide clear notice?

The Court's inability to detect allegations of racial discrimination becomes even less convincing when one focuses on the fourth and twelfth counts, which centered on "the full and equal benefit of all laws and proceedings . . . for the security of their respective persons and property . . . enjoyed" at that time and place "by white persons."[31] These counts are, if anything, more clear for identifying the victims' race in addressing racial discrimination than the judicially accepted 1866 Civil Rights Act's provision that citizens shall have the same right "to full and equal benefit of all laws and proceedings for the security of person and property, as is enjoyed by white citizens."[32] As for those counts that did expressly include the words "by reason of and for and on account of" the victims' "race and color,"[33] the Court would strike them on vagueness grounds.

The Court's insistence on clear allegations of racial discrimination presents problems apart from its requirements for clarity, because its interpretation of the Privileges and Immunities Clause builds on departures from the original understanding in the *Slaughter-House Cases*. Three such departures were the language expressing skepticism about applying the Fourteenth Amendment to situations other than racial discrimination; the emphasis on the distinction between national and state citizenship (and corresponding privileges and immunities); and a conception of privileges and immunities narrow enough to preclude the application of the Bill of Rights to the states. The first two already have been explored in view of congressional debates, and they suggest that Waite was unwarranted in being preoccupied with racial discrimination (outside of the voting context) in the first place, as well as with the distinction of peaceably assembling to petition state instead of federal authorities.[34] The third deviation, the yet unexplored debate over the incorporation doctrine, merits its own focus as a matter of substantial judicial attention.

Before turning to that subject, however, it should be mentioned that the validity of the Court's attitude toward the federal protection of life and personal liberty against conspiracy remains an open question that might best be reserved for discussion of its later review of § 2 of the Ku Klux Klan Act. Section 2 was a provision, recognized as having the same constitutional basis as § 6 (congressional power to enforce the privileges and immunities of citizenship), which aimed to define crimes with greater particularity than the 1870 statute, including express mention of murder.[35]

Insofar as congressional efforts to address individual crimes against the person, which one might say culminated in the 1871 act, extended to murder, any blanket dismissal by the Court of "the power of the United States to punish for a conspiracy to falsely imprison or murder within a State"[36] seems unwarranted. This is not to say, however, that § 6's language concerning "any right or privilege" under the Constitution or federal law intended to allow indictments for such crimes under the sheer language of the Due Process Clause. The provision covered many personal crimes where it prohibited conspiracies "to injure, oppress, threaten, or intimidate any citizen," but it added the condition of "intent to prevent or hinder" the enjoyment or exercise of federal rights or privileges.[37]

The third and eleventh counts charging intent to deprive the victims of their lives and personal liberty without due process might have been correctly invalidated with less sweeping language than Waite used, for the Court simply could have looked to the unique language and understanding of the Due Process Clause and the life, liberty, and property it protects. This issue therefore may be placed in a different category from those personal rights not dependent upon due process. While the deprivation of life and personal liberty by private actors may be covered by federal law in terms of injury, oppression, or threats that aim to infringe on one or more rights or privileges, as in the prosecution's seventh and fifteenth counts, the Due Process Clause alone does not render it appropriate to punish private conspiracies against life, liberty, and property per se. The harm instead must target some other right found in the Constitution. Otherwise, the statute would seem to mandate punishment for deprivations of personal liberty (that is, injury, oppression, threats, and so forth) with no underlying aim other than the deprivation of a person's liberty—a result that would make the statute's language confusing and redundant. The Due Process Clause of the Fourteenth Amendment certainly retains meaning, but it will be shown that it is in a different category from other constitutional provisions in the context of punishment of private conspiracies. Precisely where life, liberty, and property interests under the Due Process Clause should fit into the congressional enforcement of privileges or immunities will remain for discussion of the Court's consideration of the Ku Klux Klan Act.

In 1873, the year the nationwide response to the Colfax massacre foretold the popular demand for an end to Reconstruction, the *Slaughter-House* Court was sharply divided five to four on the first decision to interpret the

Fourteenth Amendment. In 1876, after that popular demand had become manifest, the Colfax massacre indictments met their final defeat in a unanimous decision joined by the three remaining *Slaughter-House* dissenters. Several months after *Reese* and *Cruikshank* were handed down, Morton asserted on the Senate floor, "The fourteenth and fifteenth amendments which we supposed broad, ample, and specific, have, I fear, been very much impaired by construction, and one of them in some respects almost destroyed by construction."[38] *Cruikshank* stands as a repudiation of the framers' intent,[39] as Shellabarger seems to have acknowledged in later years:

[W]hen the great opinion appeared . . . in Cruikshank's case, also holding [like *Minor*] that the "Fourteenth Amendment adds nothing to the rights of one citizen against another," and that when the framers of the Fourteenth Amendment inserted therein the provisions creating national citizenship, prohibiting the abridgment of the privileges thereof, and prohibiting the States from depriving any person of life, liberty, or property, or of the equal protection of the laws, and giving to Congress power to enforce these provisions, such framers did not mean to add anything to the rights of one citizen against another; meant not to add anything to the rights of American citizens save the right to be dealt with as equals; that these framers did not design to enable Congress to legislate *affirmatively* and *directly* for the protection of civil rights, but only to use corrective and restraining legislation as against the States; then many of the framers of these Amendments received *information* regarding their intentions which was *new*.[40]

This comment applies as well to *Cruikshank*'s ruling on the application of the First and Second Amendments to the states, which would best be addressed in a broader discussion of the incorporation debate.

b.2. The Incorporation Doctrine

i. Supreme Court trends. In his letter to Judge Woods in 1871, Justice Bradley expressed his belief that the fundamental privileges and immunities mentioned in Section 1 of the Fourteenth Amendment embraced "those which in the Constitution are expressly secured to the people, either as against the action of the Federal Government, or the State Government."[41] Bradley's belief in the application of rights mentioned in the Bill of Rights to the states through the Privileges and Immunities Clause was evident in his dissent in the *Slaughter-House Cases*. In *Cruikshank*, despite his circuit opinion in that case,[42] he joined a Supreme Court decision that rejected incorporation, and so his (and the Court's) position would remain for the rest of his career.

Another case handed down during the same term as *Cruikshank, Walker v. Sauvinet*, rejected a black man's claim that a Louisiana law was void to the extent that it deprived him of a trial by jury after a licensed keeper of a coffee house refused him refreshments "on the ground that he was a man of color."[43] The Seventh Amendment, the Court held with Justices Field and Clifford dissenting, applied only to federal courts while state courts remain free to regulate their own courts "in their own way," so a "trial by jury in suits at common law pending in the State courts is not . . . a privilege or immunity of national citizenship" binding upon the states under the Fourteenth Amendment.[44]

The Court would follow with several additional rejections of the incorporation doctrine, though some claims the Court faced came through the Due Process Clause rather than the Privileges and Immunities Clause. In *Hurtado v. California* (1884),[45] the Court rejected, over Justice John M. Harlan's dissent,[46] a claim that the Due Process Clause of the Fourteenth Amendment requires an indictment by a grand jury in a prosecution by the state for murder.[47] In *O'Neil v. Vermont* (1892),[48] the Court declined to consider a claim based on the Eighth Amendment prohibition of cruel and unusual punishment in a case applying to a sentence under a state liquor law, and dissents by Field and Harlan (the latter opinion being joined by Justice David J. Brewer) embraced the incorporation doctrine under the Privileges and Immunities Clause.[49]

In *Maxwell v. Dow* (1900),[50] the Court refused to invalidate both a prosecution that occurred under an information rather than by a grand jury[51] and a criminal trial by eight instead of twelve jurors.[52] Besides declining to read a grand jury requirement into the Fourteenth Amendment, the Court's holding, working from precedents including the *Slaughter-House Cases, Bradwell, Minor,* and *Cruikshank,* went on to reject the notion that the first eight amendments were incorporated by the Fourteenth Amendment.[53] The Court also dismissed a Senate speech cited in argument that asserted that the first eight amendments were privileges and immunities under the Fourteenth Amendment:

[T]he question whether the proposed amendment itself expresses the meaning which those who spoke in its favor may have assumed that it did, is one to be determined by the language actually therein used and not by the speeches made regarding it.

What individual Senators or Representatives may have urged in debate, in regard to the meaning to be given to a proposed constitutional amendment, or bill or resolution, does not furnish a firm ground for its proper construction, nor is it important as explanatory of the grounds upon which the members voted in adopting it.[54]

Indeed, the Court displayed little enthusiasm for Reconstruction-era congressional interpretations throughout its nineteenth-century Fourteenth Amendment jurisprudence, and although it might have found all of the language clear, Harlan, dissenting with an ardent embrace of the Republican theory during Reconstruction, asserted that the Court's interpretation "is opposed to the plain words of the Constitution, and defeats the manifest object of the Fourteenth Amendment."[55]

The Court's rejection of the incorporation doctrine would not quite be universal at the end of the nineteenth century. In *Chicago, Burlington & Quincy R.R. v. Chicago* (1897), the Court applied to the states the Fifth Amendment guarantee that private property would not be taken for public use without just compensation—a ruling that was based on the Due Process Clause, not the Privileges and Immunities Clause.[56] In *Gitlow v. New York* (1925), the First Amendment guarantees of freedom of speech and of the press were similarly construed.[57] No broad acceptance of the incorporation doctrine occurred during the first half of the twentieth century, but in *Palko v. Connecticut* (1937),[58] the Court acknowledged the incorporation of some immunities "implicit in the concept of ordered liberty" under the Due Process Clause[59] while rejecting the notion that the first eight amendments were included.[60]

Perhaps the most visible debate over incorporation on the Court during the twentieth century occurred in *Adamson v. California* (1947)[61] between Justice Frankfurter concurring[62] and Justice Hugo L. Black in dissent.[63] Frankfurter defended the Court's rejection of incorporation on grounds of longstanding judicial doctrine, apparently accepting no more than the narrow "ordered liberty" exception, and he contended that of the forty-three justices who interpreted the Fourteenth Amendment over the preceding seventy years, only one "eccentric exception" (Harlan) believed that the amendment incorporated the first eight amendments.[64] While he did have roughly contemporaneous Supreme Court opinions on his side, Frankfurter seems to have overlooked the apparent advocacy of incorporation by Bradley, Field, and Brewer, even if their views were not constant throughout their careers. Four justices dissented from the *Adamson* Court's refusal to incorporate the right against compelled self-incrimination, and Black appended to his opinion evidence to support his full acceptance of the incorporation doctrine in "reliance upon the original purpose of the Fourteenth Amendment."[65]

Over the years that followed, the Court would undermine its previous rejections of the incorporation doctrine in a series of cases that one by one would apply many provisions of the Bill of Rights to the states.[66] Between 1961 and 1968 alone, the Court would read into the Fourteenth Amendment the Fourth Amendment protection against unreasonable searches and seizures;[67] the Eighth Amendment protection against cruel and unusual punishment;[68] the Fifth Amendment right to be free of compelled self-incrimination;[69] and Sixth Amendment rights to counsel in all criminal cases,[70] to confront opposing witnesses,[71] to a speedy trial,[72] to the compulsory subpoena of favorable witnesses,[73] and to trial by jury in criminal cases.[74] Still, the Court has neither embraced the complete incorporation of the first eight amendments into the Fourteenth Amendment nor utilized the Privileges and Immunities Clause for the selective incorporation that has taken place. The Second Amendment right to bear arms, the Third

Amendment freedom from compulsion to quarter soldiers in one's home, the Fifth Amendment grand jury requirement, the Seventh Amendment right to a jury trial in many civil cases, and the Eighth Amendment ban on excessive fines and bail have never been incorporated.[75]

ii. Congressional understandings. Statements from the 1866 debates and from congressional sessions that soon followed do not reflect the level of opposition to incorporation that existed on the nineteenth-century Court. In his long defense of his original proposal for the Fourteenth Amendment, Bingham asserted that the measure would empower Congress "to enforce the bill of rights as it stands in the Constitution today" as privileges of American citizenship.[76] He made the common Republican appeal for a federal enforcement power that was lacking in order to enforce national privileges and immunities,[77] including a desire to overrule *Barron v. Baltimore*,[78] which had held that the Fifth Amendment applies only to the federal government.[79] Bingham's desire to enforce the Bill of Rights was a central aspiration of Republicans, and James F. Wilson argued for the civil rights bill on that ground.[80] As matters stood, Bingham felt compelled to oppose the civil rights bill due to the lack of federal power to enforce the Bill of Rights.[81] Believing "that the enforcement of the bill of rights is the want of the Republic," he urged the adoption of his proposed amendment.[82]

Congressman Hale attacked Bingham's proposal in statements that Charles Fairman has construed as a refutation of the incorporation doctrine,[83] but such an interpretation is unsupported. A careful reading indicates that Hale's long attack was based on apprehension over the extension of congressional power to matters traditionally left to state or municipal laws, not over the states being bound by the Bill of Rights because he already thought they were so bound.[84] He saw the first ten amendments as negative provisions "defining and limiting the power of Federal and State legislation,"[85] and in reference to Bingham, "If he claims that those provisions of the constitution or the laws of Oregon are inconsistent with the bill of rights contained in the Constitution of the United States, then I answer that his remedy is perfect and ample, and the courts may be appealed to to vindicate the rights of the citizens, both under civil and criminal procedure."[86] When pressed by Bingham, Hale admitted that he did "not know of a case where it has ever been decided that the United States Constitution is sufficient for the protection of the liberties of the citizen,"[87] and he apparently was unfamiliar with *Barron*.[88] The New York congressman worked from a vague "impression that there is that sort of protection thrown over us in some way" by the Bill of Rights—an impression that "may be entirely mistaken"—but he "prefer[red] to go on with" his "own speech" rather than pursue what he viewed merely as "a very interesting side issue."[89]

Other statements about fundamental rights, privileges, and immunities that included some or all of the Bill of Rights can be found both during the 1866 debates over the civil rights bill and the Fourteenth Amendment and afterward. Shellabarger admitted during debates over the bill that it was "impossible to settle or define what are all the indispensable rights of American citizenship," but it was "perfectly well settled" that two of them were "the right of petition and the right of protection in such property as it is lawful for that particular citizen to own."[90] Representative Roswell Hart asserted that "it is the duty of the United States to guaranty that" the states enjoy "all privileges and immunities of other citizens," the free exercise of religion, the right to bear arms, the right against unreasonable searches and seizures, and the command of the Due Process Clause.[91]

During debates over the final version of the Fourteenth Amendment, Bingham cited state violations of the prohibition against cruel and unusual punishment as an infringement on national privileges and immunities.[92] In the Senate, Howard, in a speech aiming to present the views of the Joint Committee of Fifteen in Chairman William P. Fessenden's absence, defined privileges and immunities to include

the personal rights guarantied and secured by the first eight amendments of the Constitution; such as the freedom of speech and of the press; the right of the people peaceably to assemble and petition the Government for a redress of grievances, a right appertaining to each and all the people; the right to keep and bear arms; the right to be exempted from the quartering of soldiers in a house without the consent of the owner; the right to be exempt from unreasonable searches and seizures, and from any search or seizure except by virtue of a warrant issued upon a formal oath or affidavit; the right of an accused person to be informed of the nature of the accusation against him, and his right to be tried by an impartial jury of the vicinage; and also the right to be secure against excessive bail and against cruel and unusual punishments.[93]

Not only was this a clear statement of the meaning of privileges and immunities, but it went entirely unquestioned by members of both the majority and minority party.[94]

After the ratification of the Fourteenth Amendment, one can find additional statements acknowledging its incorporation of one or more rights enumerated in the first eight amendments. Bingham[95] and Fowler[96] asserted in broad terms that the Constitution protected the right to a jury trial in criminal cases. Representative William Lawrence maintained that the Due Process Clause covered both a common-law jury trial requirement and the condemnation of private property for public use.[97] Senator Frelinghuysen found the prohibition against taking private property without just compensation to be covered by the Privileges and Immunities Clause.[98] An 1871 House Judiciary Committee report written by Bingham asserted that the Privileges and Immunities Clause was adopted to "remedy" the "defect" inherent in judicial holdings "that the first eight articles of amendment of the Constitution were not limitations on the power of the States."[99] A House report of the Committee on Reconstruction that same year asserted the need of a statutory provision "intended to enforce the well-known constitutional provision guaranteeing the right in the citizen to 'keep and bear arms.' "[100]

During the debates over the Ku Klux Klan Act, Representative Horace Maynard stated that § 2 of the bill covered "all privileges and immunities secured by the Constitution," including "any of the personal rights which the Constitution guaranties to the citizen—freedom of speech, of the press; in religion, in house, papers, and effects; from arrest without warrant, from being twice put in jeopardy for the same offense; indeed, every personal right enumerated in the Constitution."[101] Bingham delivered a long speech on the Privileges and Immunities Clause in which he asserted that "privileges and immunities of citizens of the United States . . . are chiefly defined in the first eight amendments to the Constitution of the United States."[102] He proceeded to cite the eight amendments verbatim and added, "These eight articles I have shown never were limitations upon the power of the States, until made so by the fourteenth amendment."[103] Congressman Henry L. Dawes, who like Bingham had voted for the Fourteenth Amendment,[104] similarly asserted that the first eight amendments were included among citizens' privileges and immunities.[105]

During the debates over the civil rights bill in 1872, a dialogue occurred between Senators Sherman and Carpenter, the latter not being a framer of the Fourteenth Amendment, in which Sherman was challenged on his assertion, "The Constitution of the United States declares that every man shall have an impartial trial by jury."[106] Carpenter contended that the constitutional right Sherman cited applied only to federal courts, so "how does it authorize us to legislate for the State courts?"[107] "To answer that question," Sherman replied, "I would go back again to the fourteenth amendment; and I say that the right of trial by jury is one of the privileges and immunities of every American citizen."[108] (Besides embracing incorporation, this statement disregards the Court's later method of line-drawing between state and national privileges and immunities.) Whatever the case was "before the adoption of the recent amendments," Sherman asserted, "here is this last voice of the public will, which we are bound to obey, which declares that every man shall have the protection of this immunity and privilege."[109] The dialogue was a rare occurrence, for it marked an apparent assertion of the incorporation doctrine that was followed by a seeming denial. Carpenter's line of questioning was perhaps too indirect to make a clear contention about the doctrine itself, though Morton assented later that day to the proposition that the Constitution did not guarantee the right to trial by jury.[110]

Refutations of the incorporation doctrine are scarce even among Democrats. Representative Beck called "the amendments to the Constitution . . . all limitations on the General Government and not applicable to the States" in 1869,[111] but in 1874, while arguing that the civil rights bill overextended its constitutional limits, he read the Bill of Rights as the privileges and immunities protected against state abridgment by the Fourteenth Amendment; far from a controversial theory, the incorporation doctrine almost appeared an acceptable *minimum* for the interpretation of the Fourteenth Amendment.[112] Senator Stockton denied congressional power to legislate in order to enforce the Bill of Rights against the states, but even he acknowledged that the Fourteenth Amendment "prohibits the States from doing what the Congress was always prohibited from doing."[113] Senator Norwood spoke in unflattering terms about the Fourteenth Amendment, but he did acknowledge that

the instant the fourteenth amendment became a part of the Constitution, every State was that moment disabled from making or enforcing any law which would deprive any citizen of a State of the benefits enjoyed by citizens of the United States under the first eight amendments to the Federal Constitution. And as the first eight amendments were a prohibition on the General Government as to the privileges and immunities of the citizens of the States named in those amendments, so the fourteenth amendment was and is a prohibition on the States, forbidding them to abridge the same privileges and immunities.[114]

In spite of the available evidence, several scholars have concluded that the Fourteenth Amendment was not understood to incorporate the first eight amendments against the states. Fairman saw "the record of history" as standing "overwhelmingly against" Justice Black in *Adamson*,[115] but his analysis was based almost entirely on omissions of the incorporation doctrine during the Fourteenth Amendment debates.[116] His thesis would merit more weight if in fact the incorporation of the Bill of Rights were virtually unknown at the time, but there were lawyers who were neither Republicans nor congressmen in 1866 who were aware of the framers' acceptance of the doctrine.[117]

As for Bingham and others who did mention the enforcement of the Bill of Rights, Fairman essentially concluded that by omitting to discuss it on several occasions, the congressman and any like-minded framers themselves were confused.[118] Viewed as a whole, however, Bingham's views are quite coherent. They consisted of his conception of Article IV Section 2 as conferring substantive national rights to all citizens; the inclusion of the Bill of Rights as national privileges and immunities; the notion that the original Privileges and Immunities Clause applied the Bill of Rights against the states, but that Congress could not enforce it; and that the Fourteenth Amendment supplies such enforcement power.[119] Richard L. Aynes has effectively shown that Bingham's views reflected "a clear constitutional theory," that Fairman misread his statements and ignored much context, and that his views were shared by many judges, lawyers, and politicians.[120]

Perhaps the most common argument against the incorporation doctrine on originalist grounds is that most supporters did not mention the application of the Bill of Rights to the states, while floor statements do show that the Fourteenth Amendment was intended to incorporate the same principles as the Civil Rights Act.[121] It is unreasonable to insist, however, that the framers use the term "Bill of Rights" because they generally conceived of privileges and immunities in even broader terms and because they often named particular rights among the first eight amendments without citing the entire Bill of Rights.[122] Some scholars dismiss certain statements of rights as too broad and references to particular rights as too narrow, thus missing the essential understanding.[123] Republican thought through the congressional campaign of 1866 actually reflected a consensus that the rights of American citizens would be protected by the Fourteenth Amendment, and most believed that the states already were bound by the Bill of Rights.[124] Furthermore, the Civil Rights Act was seen as an extension of Bill of Rights protection to blacks, and whatever their view of this legislation, not one Republican in the Thirty-Ninth Congress stated an understanding or wish that the first eight amendments would not apply to the states.[125] (*Barron v. Baltimore*'s appearance in Republican floor statements were invariably accompanied by an appeal for its reversal.[126])

In view of this background, Justice Black's own response to his chief critic, speaking as a former senator, carries much weight: "Professor Fairman's 'history' relies very heavily on what was *not* said in the state legislatures that passed on the Fourteenth Amendment" while "my legislative experience has convinced me that it is far wiser to rely on what *was* said."[127] Although little of the 1866 debates dealt with the imposition of the Bill of Rights on the states, the several statements of framers supporting the incorporation doctrine, in part or in its entirety, were never contradicted.[128] In the end, the framers' understanding of the Fourteenth Amendment is best realized not by a selective incorporation theory, but by the incorporation of the first eight amendments of the Constitution through the Privileges and Immunities Clause.[129] *Cruikshank* and later cases rejecting incorporation proceeded on an entirely different understanding, and even after the changes of the 1960s, the incorporation that has occurred has been selective, resting on the Due Process Clause, while the Privileges and Immunities Clause remains neglected.

7. *Hall v. Decuir:* Segregation and the Interstate Commerce Clause

Commentary on the Supreme Court's Reconstruction cases through the 1870s should not omit mention of *Hall v. Decuir* (1878).[1] This case (as the Court treated it) involved a Louisiana Reconstruction act requiring that those engaged in interstate commerce give all persons traveling on their public conveyances in the state "equal rights and privileges in all parts of the conveyance, without distinction or discrimination on account of race or color."[2] Since "exclusive power has been conferred upon Congress in respect to the regulation of commerce among the several States"[3] and congressional inaction allowed the owner of the segregated steamboat at issue to adopt "reasonable rules and regulations for the disposition of passengers," the Court ruled that the state could not require "those engaged in the transportation of passengers among the States to carry colored passengers in Louisiana in the same cabin with whites."[4]

The Court's judgment was unanimous, though Miller, Strong, and Hunt had expressed approval of the law in conference.[5] Clifford concurred separately in the judgment with a defense of segregated cabins and dining saloons "for the plain reason that the laws of Congress contain nothing to prohibit such an arrangement."[6] His reasoning included perhaps the first explicit post–Fourteenth Amendment approval of the "separate but equal" doctrine on the high court: "Substantial equality of right is the law of the State and of the United States; but equality does not mean identity, as in the nature of things identity in the accommodation afforded to passengers, whether colored or white, is impossible, unless our commercial marine shall undergo an entire change."[7] The Court's opinion did not shape Fourteenth Amendment jurisprudence, but it might have appeared to indicate a willingness to leave segregation in the states' hands where other constitutional problems did not exist. Between 1881 and 1891, nine Southern states passed Jim Crow laws segregating transportation.[8]

C. THE JURY DISCRIMINATION CASES: EXCEPTION TO THE RETREAT

1. The Court and Jury Discrimination, 1880–1883

Although they followed the end of Reconstruction, most of the Court's jury discrimination cases during the 1880s stand as an exception to its nineteenth-century trend of departing from the framers' intent.[1] In *Strauder v. West Virginia* (1880),[2] a black murder defendant had removed his case to federal court in the face of a West Virginia law excluding blacks from jury service.[3] Pointing out with renewed originalist fervor the need to construe the Fourteenth Amendment "liberally, to carry out the purposes of its framers,"[4] Justice Strong asserted for the Court that the Fourteenth Amendment declared "that the law in the States shall be the same for the black as for the white."[5] The amendment intended "to strike down all possible legal discriminations against those who belong to" the newly emancipated race.[6] Since it protected "life and liberty against race or color prejudice," Strong explained, it could not "be maintained that compelling a colored man to submit to a trial for his life by a jury drawn from a panel from which the State has expressly excluded every man of his race, because of color alone," was not denied equal protection.[7] Although the Fourteenth Amendment's language was "prohibitory . . . every prohibition implies the existence of rights and immunities" that included "an immunity from inequality of legal protection, either for life, liberty, or property."[8]

Citing *Prigg*, Strong pointed out that Congress did not even need an "express delegation of power" to be able to protect a right or immunity.[9] The Court had no difficulty upholding under Section 5 of the Fourteenth Amendment the case's removal under § 641 of the Revised Statutes, which authorized defendants to remove proceedings when they could not enforce rights granted by civil rights laws in state court.[10] The act, in Strong's view, incorporated into "statute what had been substantially ordained by the" Fourteenth Amendment.[11]

In *Virginia v. Rives*,[12] a companion case to *Strauder*, the Court once again faced a black murder defendant attempting to remove his case to federal court.[13] Blacks were eligible for jury service under Virginia law,[14] however, and the argument presented to the Court alleged strong racial prejudice in the community precluding an impartial trial, as well as the consistent failure in the county to allow blacks to serve as jurors in cases in which their race was interested.[15] The grand jury that found the indictment were all white, and the defendant's request to have one-third or some portion of the venire composed of members of his race was denied.[16] Section 1 of the Fourteenth Amendment, Strong maintained, referred "to State action exclusively, and not to any action of private individuals."[17] Section 641 did not apply to all cases in which a defendant might be denied equal protection of the laws since it authorized removal only before trial, not after it commenced, and thus did not embrace a case in which a state court engaged in a discriminatory application of a state law after a trial's commencement.[18] Strong found the statute to reach "primarily, if not exclusively," state constitutional and legislative discrimination, the absence of which left only the apprehension of a denial of rights in court that could not be manifested until trial commenced.[19]

The Court thus decided the case as an interpretation of the removal statute rather than as a constitutional matter; because § 641 did not reach the case, Strong maintained, it would be left to the revisory power of higher state courts, and ultimately to review by the Supreme Court.[20] If a "subordinate officer of a State" violated state law by the deprivation of a right granted by the state, the Court adopted a presumption that "the court will redress the wrong" or that its "error will be corrected in a superior court."[21] Finally, because a "mixed jury in a particular case is not essential to the equal protection of the laws," the Court did not find the denial of the motion to modify the racial composition of the venire to violate the Fourteenth Amendment.[22]

Still another companion case, *Ex Parte Virginia*,[23] dealt with a county court judge who was arrested under § 4 of the Civil Rights Act of 1875 for excluding certain blacks from juries because of their race.[24] Strong, writing again for the Court, described a primary purpose of the Thirteenth and Fourteenth Amendments as raising "the colored race from that condition of inferiority and servitude in which most of them had previously stood, into perfect equality of civil rights with all other persons within the jurisdiction of the States."[25] Following *Strauder,* the Court pointed out both the "equal right to an impartial jury trial, and such an immunity from unfriendly discrimination" as the Fourteenth Amendment guarantees that Congress can enforce under Section 5.[26] The Court consequently rejected the argument defending the state's right to control the selection of jurors as an attempt to disregard the Constitution's limitations on state power.[27] Strong also rejected the state's contention that the judge, performing his official duty, was immune from prosecution: Jury selection, he asserted, was not necessarily a judicial act, and his actions additionally were unauthorized by the state law under which he was operating.[28] Justices Field and Clifford dissented in both this case and *Strauder.*[29]

All three jury discrimination cases were reaffirmed in *Neal v. Delaware* (1881), another removal case under § 641 in the jury discrimination context.[30] There the Court did not find a justification for removal because it determined that the state law at issue did not exclude blacks from jury duty. The Delaware statute, passed in 1848, confined jury service to those who could vote, and the state constitution of 1831 granted voting rights only to "free white male citizens" who met certain qualifications.[31] Although the state itself did not change this language, Justice Harlan, writing for the Court, found that the Fifteenth Amendment had "[b]eyond question" invalidated the racially discriminatory provision, so jury discrimination in Delaware resulted from neither its constitution nor its laws, thus putting the case beyond the reach of § 641 under the rationale of *Rives.*[32]

The *Neal* Court did find a denial of equal protection where a state court refused to consider a black defendant's allegations that members of his race had been purposely excluded from both the grand jury that indicted him and the petit jury that tried him.[33] The showing "that no colored citizen had ever been summoned as a juror in the courts of the State" despite a black population of more than 20,000 in 1870 and more than 26,000 in 1880 in a population under 150,000 "presented a *prima facie* case of denial" of constitutional protection, asserted Harlan, and the state court's determination that blacks were unqualified for jury service was "a violent presumption."[34] Chief Justice Waite and Justice Field dissented from this equal protection holding.[35]

Justice Harlan reiterated the Court's holdings on the constitutional prohibition against jury discrimination in his majority opinion in *Bush v. Kentucky* (1883)[36] and applied them to Kentucky jury commissioners insofar as they restricted selections of grand jurors to whites under Kentucky law.[37]

The principle of *Neal* did not determine the same outcome in this case, Harlan explained, because the state defeated the presumption that its discriminatory laws were invalidated by the Fourteenth Amendment when it twice enacted statutes excluding blacks from juries *after* ratification.[38] Of the two indictments of the defendant in the case, the Court found the removal of the first to federal court under § 641 to be legitimate, but the second indictment was not deemed removable because it followed a state court ruling that the discriminatory jury statute was unconstitutional.[39] Waite, Field, and Horace Gray dissented.[40]

Under the jury discrimination cases, the Equal Protection Clause, unlike the Privileges and Immunities Clause in preceding cases, was interpreted to confer broad substantive rights that extended to matters of state jury selection. Where the claims of black defendants failed, it was generally due to a construction of a particular statute on a procedural question—removal— that Congress arguably had not addressed when drafting § 641, not to a narrow construction of potential congressional power under the Constitution. Discrimination always remained redressable on appeal to higher state courts and ultimately the Supreme Court even where a criminal proceeding could not be removed to federal court. Otherwise, the Court consistently found jury discrimination to be addressed by the Equal Protection Clause. The request for a portion of the jury to be black in *Rives* was defeated, but it was presented as a claim of constitutional entitlement to black jurors rather than as a claim of discrimination. The defendant might have met with more ultimate success if his motion before the trial judge simply had alleged a prima facie case of jury discrimination in the county in terms similar to those in *Neal* rather than a claim that more closely resembled an overreaching claim of entitlement.

2. Contemporary Legislative Views on Jury Discrimination and the Constitution

Jury discrimination was not specifically addressed during the Fourteenth Amendment debates, but the subject did appear subsequently in Congress, at which point the sides taken strongly corresponded to support for or opposition to the amendment. In the House, Halbert E. Paine called the exclusion of blacks from juries in Virginia "a gross violation of the fourteenth amendment," basing his argument on the Privileges and Immunities Clause.[1] Henry Wilson proposed an ill-fated amendment in the Senate that included a provision binding Virginia against racial discrimination in jury selection,[2] but Bingham in the House believed that "if to sit upon juries be a right of the citizen secured by the Constitution. . . . it is sacred and safe under the Constitution and is imperiled by such legislation" setting a condition upon Virginia's readmission.[3]

Morton found it "essential to the protection of the rights and immunities of people of all races that they shall not be excluded from the jury-box because of race,"[4] and he also argued that such jury discrimination was proscribed by the Equal Protection Clause.[5] If one could not be excluded from being a witness on account of color, a matter that the 1866 Civil Rights Act specifically addressed, Morton reasoned that one could not consistently be excluded from jury service either.[6] Sumner also saw the right to sit on a jury as protected by the Equal Protection Clause and found it indistinguishable from the right to testify.[7] Working from his view of the constitutional right to an impartial trial, Sherman found the right to sit on a jury to be a privilege and immunity of citizenship.[8] Edmunds found the same right protected by the Equal Protection Clause and the "privilege and immunity of a citizen . . . to stand on an equality irrespective of color."[9] During the Senate debates over § 4 of the Civil Rights Act of 1875, which prohibited racial discrimination in jury selection, Frelinghuysen spoke of such discrimination as a violation of the Equal Protection Clause[10] while George Boutwell made similar assertions under both this and the Privileges and Immunities Clause.[11]

All of these legislators except Morton, who otherwise qualifies as a framer, were members of Congress who had voted for the Fourteenth Amendment in 1866,[12] and their views usually were supplemented by support for accompanying congressional power to protect against jury discrimination. Two state legislative committees on federal relations also maintained that the Fourteenth Amendment would entitle blacks to jury duty during the state ratification debates.[13] The position of supporters of the amendment relied variably on both the Privileges and Immunities Clause and the Equal Protection Clause—usually the latter—although the Court would draw only from the latter provision for its conclusions.

On the other side of the constitutional debate over jury discrimination, one finds several Democrats and one exceptional Republican. During the Virginia readmission debate, Representative Frederick Stone, a Maryland Democrat, asserted the right of the states to regulate their own jury systems.[14] Over the course of the several Civil Rights Act debates during the 1870s, Thurman denied that the right to sit on a jury was a privilege of national citizenship or that the Equal Protection Clause covered it; otherwise, all citizens would be equally entitled to sit on juries, including those who did not speak English.[15] Senator John W. Stevenson of Kentucky considered former slaves unqualified for jury duty and denied federal power to ban jury discrimination, adding that white juries in his state were fair to blacks.[16] Representative Henry D. McHenry asserted the exclusive right of states to determine the qualifications of jurors in their own courts,[17] and Senator John B. Gordon, the former Confederate general, found the sought congressional "supervision over juries of State courts" to be "extraordinary."[18] Senator Augustus S. Merrimon felt similarly and refuted both the constitutionality of § 4 of the Civil Rights Act and the equal protection argument on grounds that "equal protection of the laws" required merely the impartial administration of justice, regardless of the color of the jurors.[19] Thomas Bayard contended that it followed from *Bradwell*, which decided against a "right to practice law as a profession before State courts," that the Fourteenth Amendment would not protect "the supposed right to sit on juries."[20]

The one Republican supporter of Reconstruction who played a prominent role in denying the applicability of the Fourteenth Amendment to jury selection was Senator Carpenter. He believed that Congress could not ban jury discrimination in state courts because it was powerless to regulate official positions in the state under any constitutional amendment.[21] Because the Fourteenth Amendment did not extend to political privileges, Carpenter reasoned, the federal government could not control qualifications for a juror any more than those for a judge. If it were otherwise—if Congress had the power to pass a jury discrimination provision—he would vote for it "in a moment."[22] The senator rejected the comparison between the right to testify and the right to serve as a juror, finding the latter not to be a fundamental privilege inherent in citizenship.[23] Like Bayard, Carpenter came to see *Bradwell*, the case in which he had argued unsuccessfully, as supporting his argument.[24] A proposed amendment by Carpenter to strike out the jury discrimination provision in Sumner's civil rights bill in 1872 was decisively defeated.[25] In the end, Carpenter, a nonframer whose arguments were repeatedly countered by those who were more directly involved in the ratification of the Fourteenth Amendment, stands as a Republican anomaly on the jury issue.

The issue of jury discrimination is a singular instance in which the nineteenth-century Supreme Court adopted the interpretation of Republican supporters of Reconstruction rather than that of opposing Democrats. It did not utilize the Privileges and Immunities Clause, which it might have done under the Republican theory of equality of rights were it not for recent precedent, but it did reach the same results under the Equal Protection Clause. Still, one of the jury cases, *Rives*, contained dictum about the Fourteenth Amendment's "reference to state action exclusively, and not to any action of private individuals," which would come to play a role in the Court's subsequent cases.

D. THE FOURTEENTH AMENDMENT STATE ACTION DOCTRINE: *UNITED STATES V. HARRIS*, THE *CIVIL RIGHTS CASES*, AND *BALDWIN V. FRANKS*

1. *United States v. Harris*

In 1883, William Woods, now a Supreme Court justice, issued an opinion for the Court in *United States v. Harris*[1] that contrasted to his opinion twelve years earlier as a circuit judge in *United States v. Hall.* At issue was an indictment of the defendant Harris and nineteen others under § 5519 of the Revised Statutes for conspiracy to deprive four people, who were under arrest and in custody of a deputy sheriff, of the equal protection of the laws by lynching them.[2] Section 5519, which was originally part of § 2 of the Ku Klux Klan Act,[3] set criminal penalties for people who

conspire or go in disguise upon the highway or on the premises of another for the purpose of depriving, either directly or indirectly, any person or class of persons of the equal protection of the laws or of equal privileges or immunities under the laws, or for the purpose of preventing or hindering the constituted authorities of any State or Territory from giving or securing to all persons within such State or Territory the equal protection of the laws.[4]

Searching for constitutional authorization for this provision, Woods dismissed the Fifteenth Amendment on the grounds that it did not confer suffrage on anyone and that the statute did not mention the right protected by that amendment.[5] Sections one and five of the Fourteenth Amendment fared no better. Citing dictum from *Cruikshank* about the amendment's simple guarantee against state encroachment of fundamental rights[6] and the dictum in *Rives* about state action, Woods interpreted both Section 1 and Section 5 as confined to redressing state action:

When the State has been guilty of no violation of its provisions; when it has not made or enforced any law abridging the privileges or immunities of citizens of the United States; when no one of its departments has deprived any person of life, liberty, or property without due process of law, or denied to any person within its jurisdiction the equal protection of the laws; when, on the contrary, the laws of the State, as enacted by its legislative, and construed by its judicial, and administered by its executive departments, recognize and protect the rights of all persons, the amendment imposes no duty and confers no power upon Congress.[7]

Since § 5519 "is directed exclusively against the action of private persons, without reference to the laws of the State or their administration by her officers," the Court held it was not authorized by the Fourteenth Amendment.[8]

Woods found the Thirteenth Amendment to be an insufficient basis for the act as well. Applying the method of statutory construction it used in *Reese*, the Court concluded that since the statute "covers any conspiracy between two free white men against another free white man to deprive him of any right accorded him by the laws of the State or of the United States," its provisions "are broader than the Thirteenth Amendment would justify."[9] Additionally, Woods reasoned, if the Thirteenth Amendment authorized § 5519, the amendment would give Congress "power to punish every crime by which the right of any person to life, property, or reputation

is invaded," thus "invest[ing] Congress with power over the whole cata-
logue of crimes."[10] The Court rejected Article IV Section 2 as a basis for
the act as well, holding that it was "directed against state action" and
aimed to prevent discrimination between citizens of each state and of other
states.[11] Harlan dissented from the Court's judgment on jurisdictional
grounds.[12]

Of all the issues the Court reviewed, its interpretation of the Fourteenth
Amendment would prove the most important because that provision was
intended to be the broadest grant of protection for civil rights. Although
Woods worked from precedent in his opinion for the Court, *Harris* was
truly the first Supreme Court case to determine its result from a "state
action" requirement under the Fourteenth Amendment. Still, a more thorough articulation of the "state action" requirement, along with a lengthy
dissent refuting the Court's analysis, awaited a landmark case that would
be handed down later in 1883.

2. The *Civil Rights Cases*

a. Justice Bradley and the Court's Opinion

While advising then-Judge Woods on the disposition of *Hall* in 1871,
Justice Bradley had written of the Fourteenth Amendment as an active guarantee against the failure of the states to take appropriate action to insure
equal protection. Whatever state action concept he then embraced included
inaction as well as action—"the omission to protect as well as the omission
to pass laws for protection."[1] His views of the amendment embraced the
application of appropriate legislation to individuals: "Since it would be
unseemly for Congress to interfere directly with state enactments, and as it
cannot compel the activity of state officials, the only appropriate legislation
it can make is that which will operate directly on offenders and offenses
to protect the rights the Amendment secures."[2] Bradley was aware that the
recent amendment entailed the entry of the federal government into an area
traditionally reserved for the states, but "it must be remembered that it is
for the purpose of protecting federal rights: and these must be protected
whether it interferes with the domestic laws or domestic administration of
laws."[3]

At a later time, Bradley wrote on the file containing drafts of his letters
to Woods, "The views expressed in the foregoing letters were much modified by subsequent reflection, so far as relates to the power of Congress
for enforcing social equality between the races."[4] This change of view
would be reflected in Bradley's opinion for the Court in the *Civil Rights
Cases* (1883).[5] Facing the Court were several cases arising under the prohibitions of §§ 1 and 2 of the Civil Rights Act of 1875 against racial
discrimination in inns, theaters, and railroads.[6]

Beginning his exploration of whether congressional power existed to pass the statute, Bradley observed that "[o]f course, no one will contend that the power to pass it was contained in the Constitution before the adoption of the last three amendments,"[7] a statement that would be of considerable relevance in the next century. Section 1 of the Fourteenth Amendment, he continued, was meant to address "State action of a particular character," not "[i]ndividual invasion of individual rights."[8] "It nullifies and makes void all State legislation, and State action of every kind, which" violates the provisions of Section 1.[9]

It does not invest Congress with power to legislate upon subjects which are within the domain of State legislation; but to provide modes of relief against State legislation, or State action, of the kind referred to. It does not authorize Congress to create a code of municipal law for the regulation of private rights.[10]

In Bradley's opinion, Congress would be making municipal law and superseding state legislatures if it were to legislate on the areas covered by the Due Process and Equal Protection Clauses:

It is absurd to affirm that, because the rights of life, liberty, and property (which include all civil rights that men have), are by the amendment sought to be protected against invasion on the part of the State without due process of law, Congress may therefore provide due process of law for their vindication in every case; and that, because the denial by a State to any persons, of the equal protection of the laws, is prohibited by the amendment, therefore Congress may establish laws for their equal protection.[11]

Put another way, Congress could adopt "corrective" but "not general legislation" such as the 1875 provisions, which operated on all states regardless of the protection they provided their citizens; otherwise, Bradley found it "difficult to see where it is to stop. . . . [W]hy should not Congress proceed at once to prescribe due process of law for the protection of" life, liberty, and property "in every possible case, as well as to prescribe equal privileges in inns, public conveyances, and theatres?"[12] To reach such a conclusion would be to make the "unsound" assumption that where states are prohibited from acting "in a particular way on a particular subject" and Congress has enforcement power, "this gives Congress power to legislate generally upon that subject" rather than simply remedying state action.[13] The Court's analysis did not extend to those areas where Congress had "direct and plenary powers of legislation over the whole subject," but it found the Fourteenth Amendment to be corrective. The 1875 act, on the other hand, was deemed "primary and direct" in its effect, taking "immediate and absolute possession of the subject of the right of admission to inns, public conveyances, and places of amusement" while superseding state law on that subject.[14]

Turning to Section 2 of the Thirteenth Amendment, the Court conceded that Congress "has a right to enact all necessary and proper laws for the obliteration and prevention of slavery with all its badges and incidents," but found "the denial to any person of admission to the accommodations and privileges of an inn, a public conveyance, or a theatre" to fall beyond this category.[15] The Black Codes under slavery excluding blacks from inns and public conveyances were means of preventing slaves from escaping, Bradley acknowledged, but they were not "part of the servitude itself."[16] The Civil Rights Act of 1866 aimed at "those fundamental rights which are the essence of civil freedom," but the Court found the subject matter of the 1875 law to extend beyond this realm into the adjustment of "what may be called the social rights of men and races in the community."[17] The refusal of access to an inn, a public conveyance, or a place of public amusement "has nothing to do with slavery or involuntary servitude," and maintaining otherwise "would be running the slavery argument into the ground."[18]

After a commentary on the need for there to be "some stage in the progress of" the former slave's "elevation when he takes the rank of a mere citizen, and ceases to be the special favorite of the laws," the Court, having found no authorization under the Thirteenth or Fourteenth Amendment, struck down §§ 1 and 2 of the Civil Rights Act.[19]

b. Justice Harlan's Dissent

Justice Harlan stood alone in dissent, though former Justices Swayne and Strong indicated their agreement with him from their retirement.[20] Charging that Bradley's opinion sacrificed "the substance and spirit of the recent amendments . . . by a subtle and ingenious verbal criticism," Harlan accused the Court of departing from the original intent with which the amendments were adopted.[21] Like previous judicial opinions upholding congressional civil rights statutes, his dissent cited *Prigg* to argue for congressional power to enforce constitutional provisions conferring rights without having to leave this function to the states.[22] According to the *Prigg* doctrine, repeated in *Strauder*, Harlan maintained that congressional power under the Thirteenth Amendment "to secure the enjoyment of such civil rights as were fundamental in freedom" would have been conferred by Section 1 alone, but such authority was intended to be made clear by Section 2.[23] The majority having conceded the power to eliminate the incidents of slavery in a "direct and primary" form, "operating upon the acts of individuals, whether sanctioned by State legislation or not," Harlan found it "impossible" to question the constitutionality of the Civil Rights Act of 1866 and found that the Thirteenth Amendment allowed the protection of blacks from racial discrimination.[24]

The dissenting justice proceeded to explore the legal rights of blacks with respect to public conveyances, inns, and places of public amusement. Citing numerous precedents addressing public conveyances, he concluded that "a railroad corporation is a governmental agency, created primarily for public purposes," and "[i]f the corporation neglect or refuse to discharge its duties to the public, it may be coerced to do so by appropriate proceedings in the name or in behalf of the State."[25] Harlan thus found the right "to use an improved public highway, upon the terms accorded to freemen of other races" to be among rights fundamental enough "to be deemed the essence of civil freedom."[26] "The Thirteenth Amendment alone obliterated the race line, so far as all rights fundamental in a state of freedom are concerned," Harlan concluded.[27] He applied to inns the same conclusions he applied to railroads, characterizing the innkeeper as exercising "a quasi public employment" and thus being barred from discriminating based on race.[28]

Places of public amusement, Harlan continued, were "established and maintained under direct license of the law," under authority that came from the public of which blacks were a part.[29] The Court's opinion in *Munn v. Illinois* (1877)[30] had upheld state-imposed maximum charges for grain storage in certain warehouses in Illinois, even though it was private property at issue, holding that "[p]roperty does become clothed with a public interest when used in a manner to make it of public consequence, and affect the community at large."[31] Harlan quoted this ruling and held that the same observation applied to places of public amusement.[32] He also found the notion that Congress had "entered the domain of State control and supervision" to be unconvincing since it simply had declared that there should be no racial discrimination in public conveyances, inns, and places of public amusement; it had not prescribed their general conditions.[33] Having called such discrimination a "badge of servitude," Harlan found the Thirteenth Amendment to apply before even considering the Fourteenth Amendment.[34]

He proceeded to discuss the Black Codes passed between the Thirteenth Amendment's adoption and the Fourteenth Amendment's proposal as a means of keeping blacks in a condition of practical servitude. He pointed out that the latter amendment was proposed to "meet this new peril to the black race, that the purposes of the nation might not be doubted or defeated" and congressional power could be further enlarged.[35] Recalling the purposes of the recent amendments expressed in the *Slaughter-House Cases* to protect blacks,[36] Harlan found that the Fourteenth Amendment, according to its language and his earlier analysis, necessarily implied congressional power to pass legislation "to protect a right derived from the national Constitution" and not merely to place negative prohibitions upon state action.[37]

Emphasizing the affirmative character of the language of Section 1 of the Fourteenth Amendment, Harlan asserted that citizens were placed "within the direct operation of" the Privileges and Immunities Clause and that citizenship may be protected not merely by the judiciary, "but by congressional legislation of a primary direct character."[38] When the Fourteenth Amendment was passed, blacks became entitled to the fundamental privileges and immunities of citizenship and could claim within a state's jurisdiction all privileges and immunities granted to whites; otherwise, states could pass "discriminating class legislation" withholding from a particular race privileges and immunities recognized as fundamental.[39] Harlan articulated the principle of equality inherent in citizenship as follows:

Citizenship in this country necessarily imports at least equality of civil rights among citizens of every race in the same State. It is fundamental in American citizenship that, in respect of such rights, there shall be no discrimination by the State, or its officers, or by individuals or corporations exercising public functions or authority, against any citizen because of his race or previous condition of servitude.[40]

Working from the holdings of *Reese* and *Cruikshank* that freedom from discrimination in voting on account of race, color, or previous condition of servitude was granted by the federal government, Harlan asserted that "exemption from race discrimination, in respect of civil rights, against those to whom State citizenship was granted by the nation," was no less "a new constitutional right" for blacks, "derived from and secured by the national Constitution."[41]

Why, therefore, should the federal government be prohibited from enforcing the right by "legislation of a primary direct character," considering the Court's longstanding doctrine, articulated in *Prigg* and later in both *Reese* and *Strauder*, that Congress could protect any right proceeding from the Constitution absent a positive delegation of power to the state legislatures?[42] Harlan quoted the rule of construction articulated by Chief Justice John Marshall in *McCulloch v. Maryland*:

The sound construction of the Constitution must allow to the national legislature that discretion, with respect to the means by which the powers it confers are to be carried into execution, which will enable that body to perform the high duties assigned to it in the manner most beneficial to the people. Let the end be legitimate, let it be within the scope of the Constitution, and all means which are appropriate, which are plainly adapted to that end, which are not prohibited, but consistent with the letter and spirit of the Constitution, are constitutional.[43]

By confining Fourteenth Amendment power to the correction of state action, Harlan charged, the Court reversed "the policy which the general government has pursued from its very organization," and its view was "plainly repugnant" to Section 5's grant of power to enforce all provisions of the amendment, including the grant of citizenship in Section 1.[44] Ironically, accepting the Court's analysis would lead to the "anomalous result" that while Congress could pass, as it did in the case of the fugitive slave laws, "the most stringent laws . . . in vindication of slavery and the right of the master, it may not now, by legislation of a like primary and direct character, guard, protect, and secure the freedom established, and the most essential right of the citizenship granted, by the constitutional amendments."[45]

The equal enjoyment of civil rights was understood to be threatened by "the hostile action of corporations and individuals" as well as "unfriendly State legislation," and given the goal of protection and the inherent right of citizenship to be free of racial discrimination, it was clear to Harlan that the Civil Rights Act was appropriate legislation.[46] As for state legislation violating the Privileges and Immunities Clause, it could not be enforced in the first place since the judiciary could invalidate it.[47]

Harlan further disagreed that his interpretation would allow Congress to pass a municipal code "covering every matter affecting the life, liberty, and property of the citizens of the several States." "The personal rights and immunities recognized in the prohibitive clauses of the amendment were, prior to its adoption, under the protection, primarily, of the States," he asserted, "while rights, created by or derived from the United States, have always been . . . primarily, under the protection of the general government."[48] The right of freedom from racial discrimination he placed in the latter category.[49] States still retained the same power to define their own citizens' civil rights as before, except that they were subject to congressional legislation securing privileges and immunities derived from the recent amendments—a category including this new constitutional right against discrimination.[50] If congressional legislation could not reach the discriminatory actions of "individuals and corporations, exercising public functions," Harlan asserted that "we shall enter upon an era of constitutional law, when the rights of freedom and American citizenship cannot receive from the nation that efficient protection which heretofore was unhesitatingly accorded to slavery and the rights of the master."[51]

Even if he were to concede the state action doctrine, Harlan maintained that the Court still would be wrong, for the cases at bar dealt with "agents or instrumentalities of the State" just as *Ex Parte Virginia* did—railroad corporations, innkeepers, and managers of places of public amusement falling into this category "[i]n every material sense applicable to the practical enforcement of the Fourteenth Amendment."[52] Additionally, while he agreed "that government has nothing to do with social, as distinguished from technically legal, rights of individuals," Harlan felt that the Civil Rights Act addressed the latter category of rights; government had nothing to do with bringing "its people into social intercourse against their wishes."[53] Finally, he suggested that the act might be upheld under the Interstate Commerce Clause in the case involving railroad discrimination, where such a claim was presented to the Court, even though the 1875 law failed to cite this provision as its constitutional authorization.[54]

In his closing passages, Harlan found the majority's statement about blacks being "the special favorite of the laws" to be "scarcely just," and he condemned the "class tyranny" confronting every step of the national effort to secure the rights of "freemen and citizens" to black people.[55] He finished with an appeal based on original intent and the need to avoid placing policy judgments above the recent amendments:

If the constitutional amendments be enforced, according to the intent with which, as I conceive, they were adopted, there cannot be, in this republic, any class of human beings in practical subjection to another class, with power in the latter to dole out to the former just such privileges as they may choose to grant. The supreme law of the land has decreed that no authority shall be exercised in this country upon the basis of discrimination, in respect of civil rights, against freemen and citizens because of their race, color, or previous condition of servitude. To that decree—for the due enforcement of which, by appropriate legislation, Congress has been invested with express power—every one must bow, whatever may have been, or whatever now are, his individual views as to the wisdom or policy, either of the recent changes in the fundamental law, or of the legislation which has been enacted to give them effect.[56]

3. The State Action Doctrine and Section 5 of the Fourteenth Amendment: The Constitutional Basis for § 2 of the Ku Klux Klan Act of 1871 and §§ 1 and 2 of the Civil Rights Act of 1875

The doctrine of the *Civil Rights Cases*, which might be viewed as a fuller explanation of the result of *Harris*, invites a reexamination of the original understanding of the several issues involved in those cases from the standpoint of the framers of the Reconstruction amendments, particularly the Fourteenth, and their contemporaries in the Reconstruction Congresses. As shall be seen, these issues received special attention in the debates over both § 2 of the Ku Klux Klan Act of 1871 and §§ 1 and 2 of the Civil Rights Act of 1875. Each debate shall be reconsidered separately, along with the constitutional question presented by federal legislation against various individual crimes in § 2 of the 1871 act. (Of the two statutes the Court faced in 1883, the Ku Klux Klan Act posed a greater challenge to the limits of Section 5 of the Fourteenth Amendment.) First, the general debates shall be reviewed apart from consideration of the specific sections involved in *Harris* and the *Civil Rights Cases* for their illumination of issues facing the Court in 1883.

a. Preliminary Views on the Doctrine of the *Civil Rights Cases*

a.1. The Thirteenth Amendment and the Civil Rights Act of 1866

During debates over civil rights legislation in 1866, legislators were divided over the scope of the congressional power authorized by the first of the two amendments on which §§ 1 and 2 of the 1875 Civil Rights Act would be defended—the Thirteenth. Democratic Senators Hendricks[1] and Willard Saulsbury[2] and Representatives Samuel S. Marshall,[3] Rogers,[4] and Anthony Thornton[5] spoke of the amendment as extending only to the abolition of slavery, not to congressional power to confer equal privileges or civil rights to former slaves. As these legislators pointed out, it followed from this premise that the Thirteenth Amendment provided insufficient justification for the Civil Rights Act of 1866. Cowan, who had voted for the amendment[6] but opposed virtually all Reconstruction measures, similarly asserted that it went no further than to break the bond between master and slave.[7]

It also might be cited as support for the Court's position on the Thirteenth Amendment that some Republicans who defended the Civil Rights Act, including James F. Wilson, looked to other provisions, such as the Privileges and Immunities Clause, for the bill's constitutional authorization.[8] Columbus Delano, like Bingham,[9] disagreed, articulating in a lengthy speech his belief that the federal government lacked power to pass the bill.[10] George R. Latham similarly found the Thirteenth Amendment insufficient, though he felt the interpretation of the amendment ultimately was a task for the judiciary.[11] Not enough congressmen held this view to prevent the Civil Rights Act from being passed, however, or to override President Johnson's veto.[12]

For all the skepticism one finds in Congress about the scope of the Thirteenth Amendment, there is ample support for the notion that Section 2 affirmatively can secure the rights associated with freedom. During the debates over the Thirteenth Amendment, Representative Ebon C. Ingersoll asserted that the provision "will secure to the oppressed slave his natural and God-given rights," which he viewed as being "as sacred in the sight of Heaven as those of any other race." He included in this category the right to "live in a state of freedom . . . to till the soil, to earn his bread by the sweat of his brow, and enjoy the rewards of his own labor," and to have "the endearments and enjoyment of family ties."[13]

The subject of natural rights or of privileges and immunities generally did not come up during the rest of the debates, but they did arise afterward. Senator Sherman spoke of the power to enforce privileges and immunities under Section 2 and to redress racial discrimination—the only question being where racial distinctions were being made throughout the states that Congress should address.[14] Henry Wilson advocated the "policy of emancipation" that "carries with it equality of civil rights and immunities."[15] Under Section 2, Trumbull expressed "no doubt that . . . we may destroy all these discriminations in civil rights against the black man; and if we cannot, our constitutional amendment amounts to nothing."[16] The amendment, in the senator's view, gave Congress the "right to pass any law which, in our judgment, is deemed appropriate, and which will . . . secure freedom to all people in the United States," and such legislation would punish "those who undertake to deny" the former slaves "their freedom."[17] Shellabarger asserted his general wish that the judiciary "would begin to look at the Constitution in the light of the Declaration of Independence, which said . . . that 'all men are created equal.' "[18]

Under such a view of Section 2, the 1866 Civil Rights Act was clearly constitutional, and arguments to this effect were made on the floor by Representatives Burton C. Cook[19] and Martin R. Thayer[20] and Senators Wilson,[21] Stewart,[22] and Yates.[23] Wilson and Stewart also asserted that it was the understanding of the framers that the amendment empowered Congress to pass laws conferring rights of freedom on former slaves.[24] For Cook, Section 2 had no meaning if it did not mean "first, that Congress shall have power to secure the rights of freemen to those men who had been slaves" and "secondly, that Congress should be the judge of what is necessary for the purpose of securing to them those rights."[25] Dreading the prospect of the Supreme Court declaring the civil rights bill unconstitutional, Henderson compared such a scenario to the *Dred Scott* decision: "the present period would be no better for the rights of the negro than that when the Supreme Court once before supposed he had no rights which the white man was bound to respect."[26] The question then would arise "whether four million people can be peacefully held nominally free, but actually slave."[27] Such statements offer more support to Justice Harlan's premises than to the Court's, even if they seem to fall short of addressing the specific issue in the *Civil Rights Cases*.

a.2. The Fourteenth Amendment

Henderson's scenario would not play out with respect to the Civil Rights Act of 1866, which as seen was held to be constitutional under the Thirteenth Amendment by three justices on circuit.[28] Justice Harlan's assertion that its constitutionality was unquestionable was not challenged by the Court, but the very fact that the Civil Rights Act of 1875 met a different fate under both Section 2 of the Thirteenth Amendment and Section 5 of the Fourteenth Amendment than the earlier act had with only Section 2 enacted is curious. It appears even more curious when one realizes that the Fourteenth Amendment was deemed a stronger basis for civil rights legislation—that it was passed in part precisely to dispel doubts about the strength of the Thirteenth Amendment. This seems to have been recognized by both supporters and opponents of Reconstruction.

During the 1866 Civil Rights Act debates, Willard Saulsbury contrasted the status of slavery, to which he found the Thirteenth Amendment confined, with the bill's aims, and he suggested that an amendment including the bill's terms would have granted the sought constitutional authorization that he found lacking.[29] Delano, a supporter of Reconstruction who doubted the constitutionality of the 1866 bill, believed that "the fundamental law should be amended so as to enable Congress to protect and secure the rights of all her citizens in any and in every State where unjust, unequal, and discriminating legislation calls for the increase of the powers of the General Government."[30]

During the Fourteenth Amendment debates, Congressman Finck made it a point to assert that if it was necessary to adopt Section 1, the Civil Rights Act was unconstitutional when it was passed.[31] Senator James R. Doolittle charged the Joint Committee of Fifteen with proposing the amendment because they feared that the Civil Rights Act "was without validity unless a constitutional amendment should be brought forward to enforce it."[32] Representative Henry J. Raymond supported the principle of the bill but felt that it lacked constitutional warrant, adding that many members who voted for the bill "also doubted the power of Congress to pass it, because they voted for the amendment by which that power was to be conferred."[33] His point does not seem to have acknowledged those who, like Representative Thomas D. Eliot, both voted for the bill "under a conviction that we have ample power to enact into law the provisions of that bill" and advocated the adoption of the Fourteenth Amendment in order to "settle the doubt which some gentlemen entertain upon that question."[34] Raymond also omitted the other plausible motive to adopt an amendment: security against the fear of changing congressional majorities repealing the Civil Rights Act.[35]

That the Fourteenth Amendment was considered at least as strong a basis for civil rights legislation as the Thirteenth Amendment also was reflected in the reenactment of the 1866 bill in the first Enforcement Act in 1870.[36] Other civil rights laws during the 1870s were debated with a focus on the authorizing scope of the Fourteenth Amendment, not the Thirteenth, the later amendment apparently being understood as the broader grant of power.[37] The most radical such law, the Ku Klux Klan Act, was entitled "An Act to enforce the Provisions of the Fourteenth Amendment to the Constitution of the United States, and for other Purposes."[38] While there was much basis for Justice Harlan's position on the Thirteenth Amendment in the original understanding, the lone dissenter actually could have afforded to lose that argument because the Fourteenth Amendment was understood to be the stronger basis for civil rights legislation.

In contrast to the internal Republican division displayed by legislators over the Thirteenth Amendment, the division over the Fourteenth Amendment and the 1866 Civil Rights Act that the amendment was intended to incorporate[39] strongly reflected the debate that occurred on the Court—except that the majority and minority were reversed. During debates over the 1866 bill, members of the Democratic minority made charges similar to Bradley's that Congress was attempting to interfere unduly with state police power. Senator Reverdy Johnson had a problem with the notion of repealing many of the laws creating inequalities between the races because he felt they were "passed under the police power, which has always been conceded as a power belonging to the States."[40] Willard Saulsbury more adamantly expressed that the "bill positively deprives the State of its police power of government."[41] Michael Kerr found "the regulation of the ordinary civil relations of the negro to the society in which he lives, by the enactment of laws of a local and merely municipal character to control his contracts, and bestow upon him civil privileges having no necessary connection with his personal freedom" to be both unconstitutional and "revolutionary of the most valuable principles of our Government."[42] Rogers made a similar denunciation of Congress' interference with a state's "internal police, statutes, and domestic regulations" and its tendency to centralize government against the intent of the founders.[43] Senator Garrett Davis found the bill unconstitutional, its principle undeniably authorizing "all that would be required to force upon the States their entire civil and criminal bodies of law."[44]

On the Republican side, legislators during debates over the Civil Rights Act expressed broad hopes of securing civil equality and abolishing discrimination without expressing any such reservations about the invasion of police power. In defense of the bill he authored, Trumbull described "any statute which is not equal to all" as a "badge of servitude" prohibited by the Constitution.[45] (Six years later, he would emphasize that the bill was "confined exclusively to civil rights and nothing else, no political and no social rights," and expressed views agreeing with the Court's opinion.[46]) Praising an order by General Grant protecting blacks in the South from prosecution for offenses for which whites were not punished equally, Henry Wilson insisted that "Southern legislators and people must learn . . . that the civil rights of the freedmen must be and shall be respected; that these freedmen are as free as their late masters; that they shall live under the same laws, be tried for their violation in the same manner, and if found guilty punished in the same manner and degree."[47]

Representative Samuel W. Moulton viewed the object of the civil rights bill as "the amelioration of the condition of the colored people" and the end of "discrimination between whites and blacks."[48] He expressly refuted the argument that the bill infringed on states' "local laws and usages" because it only proposed the elimination of discrimination and the enforcement of "unjust and unequal local civil laws" against blacks.[49] James F. Wilson pointed out that the bill addressed only "civil rights or immunities," which he defined as including the "natural rights of man" and "equality in the exemptions of the law" without indicating where he would stand on railroad, inn, or theater discrimination.[50] Wilson's language was more contained than that of Democratic Representative William E. Niblack, who later expressed "no doubt" that Congress intended to nullify "all State constitutions and State laws making any discrimination against negroes, mulattoes, Indians who pay taxes, Chinamen, or Gypsies, on account of their color or race."[51]

The issues raised during the Civil Rights Act debates returned during the Fourteenth Amendment debates and afterward. During discussion of Bingham's original proposal of the amendment, Democratic Congressmen Rogers[52] and John A. Nicholson[53] protested the intrusion into state sovereignty of the congressional enforcement of rights, privileges, and immunities on the grounds that it defied the design of the federal system from its inception. On the Republican side, Representative Hiram Price openly acknowledged the process of "laying anew . . . the foundations of this Government" and sought a constitutional guarantee to "protect all citizens."[54] To secure in the Constitution "the equal protection of . . . personal rights" was precisely Bingham's aim.[55]

The final version of the Fourteenth Amendment was met by many statements acknowledging its aim of securing the equality of rights among citizens. The content of the amendment was described not as negative prohibitions, but as national rights in affirmative terms that seem to have foretold Harlan's dissent. Raymond stated that he would vote "cheerfully" for the amendment out of his desire to secure "an equality of rights to all citizens of the United States" through "the exercise of powers conferred upon Congress by the Constitution."[56] For Howard, the amendment's effect of "establish[ing] equality before the law" was essential to republican government.[57] Howe referred to laws denying certain rights to hold land, collect wages, sue, and testify and added that these were "not the only particulars in which unequal laws can be imposed"[58]—suggesting that the amendment extended to unequal laws in every particular without the sort of line-drawing in which the Court engaged in 1883.

Shortly after passage, Representative Joseph H. Defrees spoke of the amendment in terms of what the federal government had secured directly to all citizens:

Section one indisputably fixes the character of those who are entitled to be regarded as citizens of the United States or citizens of the several States, and secures to all life, liberty, and property, and places all persons upon an equality, regardless of their condition or color, so far as equal protection of the law is concerned.[59]

The ratification debates in the states included numerous additional statements about the amendment's effect of securing civil rights or equality before the law.[60]

Opposing such a view of the affirmative nature of the Fourteenth Amendment and the rights conferred by Section 1 were several comments suggesting that the entire provision, including Section 5, was merely corrective of violations by the state—a theory that resembled the Court's state action doctrine. There is support, even from Republican advocates of Reconstruction, for the notion that the Civil Rights Act of 1866 was only corrective,[61] but since this statute was an analogue of Section 1 rather than the amendment in its entirety, it is unhelpful for analysis of the key provision involved in the state action debate—Section 5. Among such Republicans, only Delano, advocating a constitutional amendment authorizing the 1866 civil rights bill he otherwise believed to be unconstitutional in a speech during the debates over the legislation, expressed the view that such an amendment should be more contained than Bingham's original proposal—one that "would not allow" Congress "to go in the first instance to secure" guaranteed "rights, but allow it to go only when the States refuse to apply and give such security under the fundamental law of the nation."[62] Delano would vote for the Fourteenth Amendment in its final form,[63] but the ultimate understanding of the precise difference between Bingham's original and final proposals will remain a question for further discussion of § 2 of the Ku Klux Klan Act.

Looking from the Fourteenth Amendment debates on, it is not until after the amendment's passage that one finds evidence of support for an interpretation embracing a state action requirement. Starting in 1870, however, several legislators, almost exclusively Democrats, did promote the Court's later doctrine. Senator Hamilton, who it will be recalled considered the Fifteenth Amendment a "wicked amendment,"[64] asserted that the "prohibitions to the State" in Section 1 of the Fourteenth Amendment do "not thereby confer upon Congress power over the subject-matter of such denial; and if this general proposition be sound, then" the first Enforcement Act "is all wrong; not only wrong, but monstrous in its wrong."[65] Casserly believed the Fourteenth Amendment dealt "with the act of a State; with the constitution or law of a State; and if you will, for the sake of the argument, with an officer of the State acting under color of a State law or constitution."[66] Congress lacked "even a color of authority to go any further and deal with private individuals" who violated the amendment "out of their own heads."[67] Casserly argued that the very wording of the Fourteenth Amendment, in contrast to the language in the preceding amendment that might be construed to cover individuals, supported his point. Directly addressing his fellow senators, he added, "when you were framing these three amendments, the thirteenth, fourteenth, and fifteenth, and intended to act upon the individual wrongdoer without regard to the State or his relation to the State, you knew how to express that intention."[68] This argument appears to be an implicit acceptance of textualism (at least one conception of the text) over intent.

Various versions of the state action doctrine reappeared the following year. One exceptional case among the Republican framers, Representative John F. Farnsworth, maintained that the Fourteenth Amendment invalidated only state laws (not even state administration of the laws), but his statement came five years after the amendment's passage in a remarkable about-face.[69] Basing his position on the adoption of the final version of the amendment over Bingham's first proposal, the Illinois congressman read his version of the state action doctrine from the events of five years earlier. He reviewed several statements from 1866 that actually fell far short of his proposition because they comprised at most general fears of centralization that, as remains to be explored in greater detail,[70] are best explained as positions other than advocacy of the state action doctrine.[71] His argument both constituted an unsupported interpretation of the 1866 debates—an interpretation that Shellabarger, Garfield, and Bingham denied, the last maintaining that the amendment's final form incorporated his earlier version—and relied on a remarkable admission that the Reconstruction laws for which he previously had voted were unconstitutional.[72] Included in Farnsworth's statements was a deceptive quotation of a statement from Bingham in 1866: "Every word of the proposed amendment is to-day in the Constitution of our country, save the words conferring the express grant of power upon the Congress of the United States."[73] Bingham had made this statement when only his original proposal stood before Congress and the final version, including Section 5, was not even an issue, and it does nothing to support Farnsworth's position. It should be added that most of the legislators Farnsworth cited were still in Congress at the time—Bingham, William D. Kelley, Hale, Stewart, and Poland—and all five of them would vote for the Ku Klux Klan Act, the greatest statutory defiance of the state action doctrine.[74]

This is not to suggest that Democrats opposed to Reconstruction did not make statements similar to Farnsworth's. In the Senate, Frank Blair adopted an interpretation of the debates similar to the Illinois representative's on no more evidence, and he maintained that the Fourteenth Amendment applied only to state legislation.[75] Blair[76] and Representative Edward I. Golladay[77] asserted flatly that Section 5 does not apply to Section 1. Representative William S. Holman similarly believed that a "State can only act through her legislative department" and that it would take "some affirmative act of law" for a violation of the amendment to come about.[78] For Representative Edward Y. Rice, it was "sophistry" to seek "to maintain that a denial of power to the States is equivalent to an affirmative grant of power to the Congress or the Government of the United States."[79] Another House Democrat, John B. Storm, found the guarantees of Section 1 of the Fourteenth Amendment (but not the Fugitive Slave Clause) to be "wholly negative in their character" and enforceable only through courts "rather than by absorbing the local jurisdiction of the States through penal statutes and police regulations operating within their limits."[80] Stockton, citing the title of the act, asserted that it was "much more for other purposes than to enforce the fourteenth amendment" because the bill was "not in any sense appropriate legislation" under Section 5.[81] Garrett Davis believed that Congress was empowered only to nullify state laws that discriminated against blacks or to confer jurisdiction to federal courts in such cases.[82] Liberal Republican James G. Blair, whose faction shared the Democratic theory of Reconstruction, believed that the Fourteenth Amendment applied to states in their "corporate and legislative capacity . . . and not against the individuals, as such, of the States."[83] Davis was the only one of these legislators who had been in Congress when the Fourteenth Amendment was passed.[84]

The debates contained far more affirmative characterizations of the rights protected by the Fourteenth Amendment and refutations of the notion that the provision was strictly corrective—statements that extend before congressional passage and ratification—than views supporting the state action doctrine. Working from a historical context that makes it clear that the central problem facing Congress during Reconstruction was private action, this trend should be no mystery. Indeed, Republicans reflected an ongoing concern with state *inaction* to correct private wrongs in addition to state action as narrowly defined by the Court in 1883.[85]

As early as the Civil Rights Act debates in 1866, Senator Henry S. Lane maintained, "We should not legislate at all if we believed the State courts could or would honestly carry out the provisions of the constitutional amendment; but because we believe they will not do that, we give the Federal officers jurisdiction."[86] Congressman Lawrence maintained that "there are two ways in which a State may undertake to deprive citizens of these absolute, inherent, and inalienable rights: either by prohibitory laws, or by a failure to protect any one of them."[87] Upon presenting his first proposal for the Fourteenth Amendment, Bingham asserted that while the "immortal bill of rights embodied in the Constitution[] rested for its execution and enforcement hitherto upon the fidelity of the States," an amendment was needed to give "the whole people the care in future of the unity of the Government which constitutes us one people" amid the "utter disregard of these injunctions of your Constitution" by officials in the former Confederate states.[88]

Such concerns persisted through the debates following ratification. During the debates over the readmission of Virginia, when various attempts were being made to bind that state to respect several civil rights through legislation, Stewart pointed out that the Fourteenth Amendment best provided for civil rights; if it were necessary to pass a law addressing any of the issues presented in that particular debate, "it can be done for all the States under the power conferred by the fourteenth amendment to the Constitution."[89] This statement repudiates the notion that Congress should be constrained by such reservations as the Court expressed in the *Civil Rights Cases* about "general" legislation that binds the nation without depending on whether the states covered were in violation of the amendment.[90]

Congressional approval of the first Enforcement Act, which was passed under the Fourteenth as well as the Fifteenth Amendment,[91] provides additional refutation of the state action doctrine because the measure clearly extended beyond state action. Senator John Pool, the author of § 6 among other provisions of the act,[92] though not in Congress when the Fourteenth Amendment was passed,[93] offered an explanation of state omission that would be flatly inconsistent with the Court's:

> The civil rights bill [of 1866] was to be enforced by making it criminal for any officer, under color of any State law, "to subject, or cause to be subjected, any citizen to the deprivation of any of the rights secured and protected" by the act. If an officer of any State were indicted for subjecting a citizen to the deprivation of any of those rights he was not to be indicted as an officer; it was as an individual. And so, under [Section 1 of] the fourteenth amendment . . . the word "deny" is used . . . in contradistinction to the first clause, which says, "No State shall make or enforce any law" which shall do so and so. That would be a positive act which would contravene the right of a citizen; but to say that it shall not deny to any person the equal protection of the law it seems to me opens up a different branch of the subject. It shall not deny by acts of omission, by a failure to prevent its own citizens from depriving by force any of their fellow-citizens any of these rights. . . .
>
> [T]he liberty of a citizen of the United States, the prerogatives, the rights, and the immunities of American citizenship, should not be and cannot be safely left to the mere caprice of States either in the passage of laws or in the withholding of that protection which any emergency may require. If a State by omission neglects to give to every citizen within its borders a free, fair, and full exercise and enjoyment of his rights it is the duty of the United States Government to go into the State, and by its strong arm to see that he does have the full and free enjoyment of those rights.[94]

Pool clearly believed that "individuals may prevent the enjoyment of . . . rights which are conferred upon the citizen by the fourteenth amendment,"[95] and those who voted for his provisions apparently agreed. The following year, he reiterated his belief in the amendment's coverage of state omissions to protect citizens and in the federal government's power to respond to such situations by acting directly to protect its citizens.[96]

During the Ku Klux Klan Act debates, Bingham issued a lengthy rebuttal to Farnsworth rejecting the state action doctrine. Since its framing, he asserted, the Constitution had allowed the federal government to punish individuals—a power that had been practiced since 1789—and Section 5 of the Fourteenth Amendment applied to all other sections, including Section 1.[97] That Congress could legislate "for the better protection of the people in the rights thereby guarantied to them against States and combinations of individuals" he had "no doubt, for the reason that it is a closed question, absolutely closed."[98] Under the three recent amendments, he found congressional power "to protect the rights of citizens against States, and individuals in States, never before granted."[99] These rights included those found in the first eight amendments, and quoting Daniel Webster, Bingham emphasized individual responsibility to maintain the Constitution rather than relying on "the plighted faith of the States as States."[100] Furthermore, the congressman maintained, Congress could pass a "preventive" law rather than reverting to "remedial and punitive" measures to enforce the amendment: "Why not in advance provide against the denial of rights by States, whether the denial be acts of omission or commission, as well as against the unlawful acts of combinations and conspiracies against the rights of the people?"[101] He defended the Ku Klux Klan Act under this rationale.[102]

Assertions would follow from more junior legislators that the Fourteenth Amendment was "a positive and substantive declaration and bestowal of constitutional right"[103] and that it conferred "a new right . . . to the protection of the laws."[104] Regarding the prohibitory language of the amendment, Edmunds asserted, "Although the word ['denial'] is negative in form, it is affirmative in its nature and character. It grants an absolute right."[105] He also found it "absurd" to consider the amendment as addressing state legislators to the exclusion of state executive and judicial departments.[106]

The Ku Klux Klan Act defied the state action doctrine not only in § 2, which remains to be considered separately, but also in § 3, which authorized the president to suppress "insurrection, domestic violence, unlawful combinations, or conspiracies" to deprive people of certain rights, privileges, and immunities in any state, regardless of whether state authorities "shall either be unable to protect, or shall, from any cause, fail in or refuse protection of the people in such rights."[107] Shellabarger, who reported the bill in the House from the Judiciary Committee,[108] justified § 3 with a recognition of federal power to respond to an omission by a state under the Fourteenth Amendment:

> The laws must be, first, equal, in not abridging rights; and second, the States shall equally protect, under equal laws, all persons in them. . . . [W]henever a State denies that protection Congress may by law enforce protection. . . . To say in such a case as that that Congress cannot protect until it is invited to protect by the State which is doing the mischief, which is making the denial, is to attribute absurdity to the provision. . . . [W]hen an Executive of a State or a Legislature of a State finds a state of violence which deprives the people of their rights, and when this State and Executive refuse to call on the United States for help, then they have denied the equal protection of the laws.[109]

Utilizing definitions of the word "deny" he had drawn from dictionaries, Representative Aaron F. Perry, who agreed on § 3's constitutionality, maintained that the Fourteenth Amendment's "command is that no State shall fail to afford or withhold the equal protection of the laws."[110] Defining the

"State" primarily as "the people" with a citation from *Texas v. White*, he proceeded to interpret the amendment to mean

that the people of a State, with more or less definite political and governmental relations, shall neither abridge nor permit to be abridged those rights, deny nor fail to afford the equal protection of the laws to any persons. On any construction these privileges and immunities are given by the Constitution and placed under the guardian care of Congress.[111]

Representative Lionel A. Sheldon felt similarly about § 3's constitutionality and thought that the contrary theory "must be impalpable logic . . . to those whose lives[,] liberties, and property are all at the mercy of organized bands of marauders who can safely defy the power or command the inactivity of the State authorities."[112] Garfield also believed that § 3 would be constitutional insofar as it "punishes persons who under color of any State law shall deny or refuse to others the equal protection of the laws," though he would not find the provision to be authorized if it attempted "to punish a mere violation of a State law."[113]

Other statements inconsistent with the state action doctrine followed in other Ku Klux Klan Act debates. Representative John Beatty found that the "State, from lack of power or inclination, practically denied the equal protection of the law to" various people who had been victims of violence due to their political opinions.[114] Expressing outrage over crimes committed by the Ku Klux Klan, Congressman Clinton L. Cobb charged that "the people who have paralyzed the arm of the State authority" were alone responsible for compelling "the application of national power."[115] "How can it be an interference with the rights of the States," asked Benjamin Butler, "for the laws of the United States to afford that protection to its citizens which the State fails or neglects to do for itself?"[116] Representative John Coburn, who found just as much a denial of equal protection in the systematic failure of justice in a state as in a positive statute, actually found punishing individuals to be preferable to "the more thorough method of superseding State authority," but he added that "Congress has both remedies, and can use both or either as the emergency may require."[117] He also expressed greater faith in federal courts for their independence and lack of susceptibility to local prejudice.[118]

Another congressman, Jeremiah M. Wilson, asserted that the term "State" should be broadly interpreted in the Fourteenth Amendment to extend to all departments, including a "refusal to legislate equally for the protection of all . . . or a failure to do so, through inability."[119] While addressing disorder in the South in 1871, Senator Frelinghuysen asserted the following interpretation of Section 1:

A State denies protection as effectually by not executing as by not making laws. The amendment says a State is not to abridge the privileges and immunities by making or enforcing any laws, and it is denying protection by failing to make or by failing to enforce proper laws.[120]

Daniel D. Pratt cited the same definitions of "deny" in the Senate that Perry had articulated in the House and claimed "that when . . . equal protection is withheld, when it is not afforded, it is denied, and the occasion at once arises for legislation by Congress to carry this covenant into effect."[121] Pratt did not believe Congress could punish juries that refused to convict or state officials who refused to do their duty, but he felt that "Congress may enact a law of general application everywhere, exactly adapted to the existing evils in the South and which shall stop this flow of blood. There cannot be a wrong without the power to provide a remedy."[122]

Flatly contradicting the Court, Edmunds asserted that

over all the rights and over all the duties and over all the guarantees that the Constitution of the United States enumerates, the power of the United States, by legislation, by punishment, by any of the methods which legislation may resort to, to enforce constitutional duties and obligations may and must act directly upon the citizen; and that it is entirely immaterial whether the State may or can do the same thing for the same act or not; and, therefore, that it is no objection to the constitutional exercise of power by Congress that the States themselves in the case of these disorders in the South may, if they will, punish the same things according to their own laws.[123]

The Vermont senator offered additional criticism of the doctrine that he thought was eroding the Fourteenth Amendment:

[N]ow being adopted as the greatest security settled through the course of centuries as a protecting, as an affirmative right in the citizen—those interests of liberty and property and life to which he is entitled—now for the first time it is attempted to be frittered away by the statement that it is a mere negative declaration, a kind of admonitory prohibition to a State, and that Congress is to invade the rights of the States and the liberties of the people when, these rights being denied, when criminals go unpunished by the score, by the hundred, and by the thousand, when justice sits silent in her temple in the States, or is driven from it altogether, it interposes in their behalf.[124]

President Grant shared the outrage over rampant violence that was being "justified or denied by those who could have prevented it" and asserted in 1874 that the "theory . . . that there is to be no further interference on the part of the General Government to protect citizens within a State where the State authorities fail to give protection" was "a great mistake."[125]

Besides repudiating the state action doctrine, the Reconstruction debates are replete with corresponding assertions of the scope of Section 5 that contradict the Court. Howard reviewed Section 5 more than any other member of Congress during the debates over the Fourteenth Amendment, and he asserted, "Here is a direct affirmative delegation of power to Congress to carry out all the principles of all these guarantees, a power not found in the Constitution."[126] He believed that "section one is a restriction upon the States, and does not, of itself, confer any power upon Congress. The power which Congress has, under this amendment, is derived, not from that section, but from the fifth section, which gives it authority to pass laws which are appropriate to the attainment of the great object of the amendment."[127] For Howard, the section was "indispensable" for the amendment to be carried out.[128]

This interpretation was not challenged, and it appears even more convincing in view of the understanding of the Thirteenth Amendment's analogous Section 2 reflected in the Civil Rights Act.[129] Even those doubting the extent of the Thirteenth Amendment's scope were addressed during the debates when Poland, pointing out Congress' "desire and intention to uproot and destroy all" discriminatory state laws "in the passage of . . . the civil rights bill," acknowledged doubts over the reach of such congressional power among

persons entitled to high consideration. It certainly seems desirable that no doubt should be left existing as to the power of Congress to enforce principles lying at the very foundation of all republican government if they be denied or violated by the States, and I cannot doubt but that every Senator will rejoice in aiding to remove all doubt upon this power of Congress.[130]

Democrats in the minority did not address Section 5 during the 1866 debates, with the exception of Hendricks. The Indiana senator asserted that Section 5

provides that Congress shall have power to enforce, by appropriate legislation, the provisions of the article. When these words were used in the amendment abolishing slavery they were thought to be harmless, but during this session there has been claimed for them such force and scope of meaning as that Congress might invade the jurisdiction of the States, rob them of their reserved rights, and crown the Federal Government with absolute and despotic power. As construed this provision is most dangerous. Without it the Constitution possesses the vitality and vigor for its own enforcement through the appropriate departments.[131]

Hendricks' alarm over the provision actually supports Howard's interpretation.

Ratification debates in the states reflected similarly broad interpretations. That broad congressional enactments could follow the amendment seemed obvious,[132] and several state leaders or legislative committees even believed that the amendment would grant Congress the authority to define its own scope of power, including the definition of privileges and immunities.[133]

Such statements were accompanied by interpretations of the dangerous potential of authorizing congressional intervention in the states to protect citizens.[134] Maryland's Joint Committee on Federal Relations reported that all provisions of the Fourteenth Amendment "must be read in the light of the fifth section, and of the interpretation already given by Congress to the same language in the Thirteenth Amendment."[135] Several newspapers at the time viewed the amendment as authorizing Congress to pass a wide scope of laws that would limit the states' power to legislate.[136]

Over the years following ratification, congressional interpretation underwent little change. Sumner asserted that "Congress has plenary power to enforce" citizens' "immunities and privileges."[137] Pool, in his speech during the debates over the Enforcement Acts, asserted the following on Section 5:

It is only when a State omits to carry into effect the provisions of the civil rights act, and to secure the citizens in their rights, that the provisions of the fifth section of the fourteenth amendment would be called into operation. . . .

There is no legislation that could reach a State to prevent its passing a law. It can only reach the individual citizens of the State in the enforcement of law. You have, therefore, in any appropriate legislation, to act on the citizen, not on the State. If you pass an act by which you make it an indictable offense for an officer to execute any law of a State by which he trespasses upon any of these rights of the citizen it operates upon him as a citizen, and not as an officer. Why can you not just as well extend it to any other citizen of the country? . . .

. . . That the United States Government has the right to go into the States and enforce the fourteenth and the fifteenth amendments is, in my judgment, perfectly clear, by appropriate legislation that shall bear upon individuals. I cannot see that it would be possible for appropriate legislation to be resorted to except as applicable to individuals who violate or attempt to violate these provisions. Certainly we cannot legislate here against States.[138]

The following year, Shellabarger offered further support for Harlan's dissent in a speech defending the Ku Klux Klan Act:

[S]hall it be endured now that those decisions which were invoked and sustained in favor of bondage shall be stricken down when first called upon and invoked in behalf of human rights and American citizenship? No, Mr. Speaker, no; I appeal to them as fixing the interpretation of the Constitution in this regard and as authorizing affirmative legislation in protection of the rights of citizenship under Federal law.

Shellabarger rejected arguments

that there is no legislation executing those other provisions of the Constitution denying powers to the States, as, for example, those providing that no State shall make any law impairing the obligation of contracts or make treaties, and all those similar prohibitions. The fact that there has been no legislation upon those subjects . . . is simply because there has been no need of any. The decision of the Supreme Court of the United States, striking down the State laws which attempted to invade those provisions of the Constitution, ended the State legislation. But that would not do where personal rights were invaded by the States. Hence Congress has never hesitated to provide the necessary affirmative legislation to enforce the personal rights which the Constitution guaranties, as between persons in the State and the State itself. There is the distinction. In my mind our legislative and judicial history renders our position wholly impregnable. So long as your Constitution continues to guaranty the rights of American citizenship, so long you can "by law," to adopt the language of the fifth section of the fourteenth amendment, enforce these rights of American citizenship.[139]

This interpretation follows from the predominant Republican view of the Fourteenth Amendment as an affirmative conferral of substantive personal rights—clearly a broader view of the amendment than is allowed by the state action requirement.

The 1871 debates included other similar or broader statements. Carpenter contrasted the Fourteenth Amendment with such provisions as the prohibition on impairing the obligation of contracts that he maintained were left to the judiciary to enforce; the amendment revolutionized government by clothing Congress "with the affirmative power and jurisdiction to correct the evil."[140] Representative William L. Stoughton found Section 5's authority to be "subject to no restrictions or limitations. It is for Congress in its discretion to determine what legislation is appropriate, and its decision is binding upon every other department of the Government."[141] Morton found the Equal Protection Clause to cover a state's failure to secure equal protection and seemed to suggest that the Court's future doctrine amounted to a virtual nullification of Section 5:

Whether that failure [to secure equal protection] is willful or the result of inability can make no difference, and is a question into which it is not important that Congress should enter. . . . [The Equal Protection Clause] is in its nature an affirmative provision, and not simply a negative on the power of the States. Will it be pretended that the meaning would be changed if it read, "every person in the United States shall be entitled to the equal protection of the laws?" It means to confer upon every person the right to such protection, and therefore gives to Congress the power to secure the enjoyment of that right. . . .

The Government can act only upon individuals. . . . If the effect of the amendment is simply that the United States shall exert a negative upon a State, it amounts to but very little, and in fact would result only in a lawsuit, and would, in effect, nullify the concluding section of the amendment, which gives to Congress the power to enforce the amendment by appropriate legislation.[142]

Congressman Dawes, during a speech affirming the power to secure privileges and immunities (including the Bill of Rights), similarly questioned whether the Constitution "was so empty" that it embodied "merely . . . abstract principles without carrying with it by its own force the power by legislation" or "other proper means" to secure the rights, privileges, and immunities of citizenship.[143]

Representative Jeremiah M. Wilson found the three recent amendments to "confer full and complete authority to pass" the Ku Klux Klan Act, and he described the argument that the Fourteenth Amendment is "a mere limitation upon the powers of the State" that "cannot be enforced by congressional legislation" as "a plausible argument, but utterly unsound."[144] In his opinion, Congress had the power under Section 5 to pass such a bill to enforce the rights, privileges, and immunities of citizens.[145] "Nobody pretends that" Section 1 "is a grant of 'affirmative power;' " explained Wilson, "but I do contend that it is an affirmative declaration of a right in every person within the jurisdiction of the laws of a State, the right of equal protection. The grant of power is in the fifth section."[146] This section made Congress "the exclusive judge of" both "the necessity for the application of remedies" and "what the remedies shall be."[147] The congressman ultimately reached the following three conclusions:

1. The provisions "no State shall deny" and "Congress shall have power to enforce" mean that equal protection shall be provided for all persons.
2. That a failure to enact the proper laws for that purpose, or a failure to enforce them, is a denial of equal protection.
3. That when there is such a denial Congress may enact laws to secure equal protection.[148]

Two senators outraged by the rampant violence in the South, Frelinghuysen[149] and Pratt,[150] maintained that the Fourteenth Amendment's conferral of citizenship granted Congress power to enforce the rights, privileges, and immunities of all citizens directly, and both acknowledged that a state could violate the amendment by failing to make or execute laws. Frelinghuysen pointed out that the states still held authority over municipal matters while the federal government controlled national matters, but he accepted that the scope of congressional power would mean the "General Government and the States have concurrent jurisdiction in many municipal matters."[151] Senator Arthur I. Boreman emphasized the amendment's application to all citizens and interpreted Section 5 in view of James Madison's assertion in the *Federalist Papers*, "A right implies a remedy."[152] In the House, Ulysses Mercur recognized the capacity of "wicked combinations and conspiracies" of individuals to prevent states from securing equal protection, from which it followed that Section 5 authorized the congressional intervention that was necessary to secure equal protection.[153]

It should be added that floor statements of the Republican theory of the

Reconstruction amendments utilized two of the key pre-Reconstruction precedents Justice Harlan cited in support of his position. *McCulloch* was cited in a similar manner by James F. Wilson[154] and Lawrence[155] in support of the 1866 civil rights bill, and by Sumner,[156] Lawrence again,[157] and Hale[158] during debates anticipating the 1875 act. *Prigg* and the fugitive slave laws were used to support the scope of congressional power as well by James F. Wilson in the Thirteenth Amendment context[159] and by Shellabarger,[160] Representative David P. Lowe,[161] Boreman,[162] and Lawrence[163] in the Fourteenth Amendment context.

b. The Constitutional Debate over § 2 of the Ku Klux Klan Act

b.1. Bingham's Original Proposal and the Question of Federal Protection of Life, Liberty, and Property

The general interpretations of the Fourteenth Amendment cited above, though they might reveal some variations in theory among legislators (mostly a matter of emphasis), reflect an impressive degree of consensus on the constitutional issues that ultimately faced the Court. Issues surrounding the congressional power directly to protect life, liberty, and property interests mentioned in the Due Process Clause and the constitutional basis for § 2 of the Ku Klux Klan Act met with more divided opinion among supporters of Reconstruction. The complexity of these issues, which include questions about the scope of congressional power that might never be fully answerable by direct inferences from the debates alone, merits special focus.

The Reconstruction debates would raise questions extending back to the failure of Bingham's original proposal for the Fourteenth Amendment: "The Congress shall have power to make all laws which shall be necessary and proper to secure to the citizens of each State all privileges and immunities of citizens in the several States, and to all persons in the several States equal protection in the rights of life, liberty, and property."[164] Representative Ignatius Donnelly praised this proposal as a means to enforce "all the guarantees of the Constitution," including "its sacred pledges of life, liberty, and property."[165] Bingham himself deemed congressional power to enforce rights of life, liberty, and property an obvious necessity:

[W]hat an anomaly is presented today to the world! We have the power to vindicate the personal liberty and all the personal rights of the citizen on the remotest sea, under the frowning batteries of the remotest tyranny on this earth, while we have not the power in time of peace to enforce the citizens' rights to life, liberty, and property within the limits of South Carolina after her State government shall be recognized and her constitutional relations restored.[166]

Bingham affirmed the broad power of his amendment in a dialogue with Hale:

Mr. HALE. I desire . . . to ask [Bingham] . . . whether in his opinion this proposed amendment to the Constitution does not confer upon Congress a general
power of legislation for the purpose of securing to all persons in the several States
protection of life, liberty, and property, subject only to the qualification that that
protection shall be equal.

Mr. BINGHAM. I believe it does in regard to life and liberty and property as I
have heretofore stated it; the right to real estate being dependent on the State law
except when granted by the United States.

Mr. HALE. Excuse me. If I understand the gentleman, he now answers that it
does confer a general power to legislate on the subject in regard to life and liberty,
but not in regard to real estate. I desire to know if he means to imply that it extends
to personal real estate.

Mr. BINGHAM. Undoubtedly it is true. . . . [U]nder the Constitution the personal property of a citizen follows its owner, and is entitled to be protected in the
State into which he goes.

Mr. HALE. The gentleman misapprehends my point, or else I misapprehend his
answer. My question was whether this provision, if adopted, confers upon Congress
general powers of legislation in regard to the protection of life, liberty, and personal
property.

Mr. BINGHAM. It certainly does this: it confers upon Congress power to see to
it that the protection given by the laws of the States shall be equal in respect to life
and liberty and property to all persons.[167]

This dialogue ultimately fails to establish a clear position on whether Congress would possess plenary power over life, liberty, and property under
Bingham's proposal apart from passing legislation to equalize the protection of those subjects in the states.

James F. Wilson, in a speech defending the constitutionality of the 1866
Civil Rights Act, advocated the protection of a citizen's "right of life, liberty, and property," asserting Congress' power "to provide the necessary
protective remedies" when the state deprived a citizen of these rights without due process.[168] This statement, however, did not take a clear stand on
the scope of congressional power over life, liberty, and property interests,
being primarily concerned with existing congressional power to enforce the
Bill of Rights.

In a general attack on both the civil rights bill and the early Bingham
proposal, Rogers made broad assertions on the need to preserve state sovereignty and attacked the proposed amendment for attempting "to take
away the rights of the States with regard to the life, liberty, and property
of the people."[169] Hale, who unlike Rogers ultimately would vote for the
Fourteenth Amendment,[170] feared that the Bingham proposal would allow
Congress to override "all State legislation, in its codes of civil and criminal
jurisprudence and procedure, affecting the individual citizen"[171] and that it
was "a grant of power in general terms—a grant of the right to legislate

for the protection of life, liberty, and property, simply qualified with the condition that it shall be equal legislation."[172]

Other future supporters of the Fourteenth Amendment seemed to think, like Hale, that Bingham's proposal went too far, though their precise reasons were not always clear. Representative Thomas T. Davis was concerned that "[a]n amendment which gives in terms to Congress the power to make all laws to secure to every citizen in the several States equal protection to life, liberty, and property, is a grant for original legislation by Congress."[173] Congress, he felt, would be the judge of the scope of such equal protection and pass universal legislation that "may circumscribe it and limit it, if only it make it equal," thus encroaching upon state functions.[174] Roscoe Conkling, a representative at the time, indicated his opposition to the measure as a member of the Committee of Fifteen without providing reasons for his position, but he expressed his intention to move to postpone its consideration and hinted that he believed the amendment went too far.[175]

Representative Giles W. Hotchkiss articulated his views a bit more clearly. As he understood it, Bingham's intention was "to provide that no State shall discriminate between its citizens and give one class of citizens greater rights than it confers upon another," an object in which he fully concurred, but he added that he would vote to postpone consideration of the amendment because he did "not regard it as permanently securing those rights."[176] He understood "the amendment as now proposed by its terms to authorize Congress to establish uniform laws throughout the United States upon the subject named, the protection of life, liberty, and property," and he was "unwilling that Congress shall have any such power. . . . Should the power of this Government . . . pass into the hands of the rebels, I do not want rebel laws to govern and be uniform throughout this Union."[177] He further explained the rationale behind his dissatisfaction and proposed an alternate way of drafting the amendment:

The first part of this amendment . . . is precisely like the present Constitution; it confers no additional powers. It is the latter clause wherein Congress is given the power to establish these uniform laws throughout the United States. Now, if [Bingham's] object is, as I have no doubt it is, to provide against a discrimination to the injury or exclusion of any class of citizens in any State from the privileges which other classes enjoy, the right should be incorporated into the Constitution. It should be a constitutional right that cannot be wrested from any class of citizens, or from the citizens of any State by mere legislation. But this amendment proposes to leave it to the caprice of Congress; and your legislation upon this subject would depend upon the political majority of Congress, and not upon two thirds of Congress and three fourths of the States.

Now, I desire that the very privileges for which the gentleman is contending shall be secured to the citizens; but I want them secured by a constitutional amendment that legislation cannot override. Then if the gentleman wishes to go further, and provide by laws of Congress for the enforcement of these rights, I will go with him.

But now, when we have the power in this government, the power in this Congress, and the power in the States to make the Constitution what we desire it to be, I want to secure those rights against accidents, against the accidental majority of Congress. . . . Place these guarantees in the Constitution in such a way that they cannot be stripped from us by any accident, and I will go with the gentleman. . . . I think . . . [Bingham] is not sufficiently radical in his views upon this subject. I think he is a conservative. [Laughter.] . . .

His amendment is not as strong as the Constitution now is. The Constitution now gives equal rights to a certain extent to all citizens. This amendment provides that Congress may pass laws to enforce these rights. Why not provide by an amendment to the Constitution that no State shall discriminate against any class of its citizens; and let that amendment stand as a part of the organic law of the land, subject only to be defeated by another constitutional amendment. We may pass laws here to-day, and the next Congress may wipe them out. Where is your guarantee then?[178]

The House voted to postpone the measure soon after Hotchkiss spoke,[179] and Bingham's original proposal never would be reconsidered.

A corresponding discussion of the proposal did not take place in the Senate, but Stewart, though advocating the enforcement of the Privileges and Immunities Clause, did take one occasion to express reservations about the prospect of Congress "legislat[ing] fully upon all subjects affecting life, liberty, and property, and in this way secur[ing] uniformity and equal protection to all persons in the several States."[180] Besides entailing Congress equalizing the protection of life, liberty, and property in states with "very dissimilar" laws, Stewart feared that "there would not be much left for the State Legislatures" because "the great body of the laws of the several States as in fact of any government relate to the protection of life, liberty, and property."[181] It would be difficult to equalize laws in Massachusetts and South Carolina, Stewart pointed out, and the senator concluded that "the grammatical, legal, and necessary construction of this proposed amendment can hardly have been intended by its framers."[182]

Legal scholar Alfred Avins describes Hotchkiss' proposal as urging a "limitation on state power, *rather than* a grant of power to Congress [emphasis added]" and suggests that the redraft that followed would form the basis of the state action doctrine.[183] This seriously misstates the congressman's views, for Hotchkiss' argument was based largely on the belief that Bingham's proposal was *insufficient* to secure rights, particularly because it was subject to changing congressional majorities. The proposed redraft thus would secure privileges to citizens regardless of possible future congressional hostility, and Hotchkiss' statement, contrary to the impression one gets from Avins, expressly endorsed the idea of Congress going farther to pass enforcement legislation. (The New York congressman also advocated a more effective conferral of substantive privileges to citizens.) Hotchkiss' objection, insofar as he felt the amendment went too far, seems to have been limited to the prospect of plenary congressional authority over matters concerning life, liberty, and property. He neither advocated the state action doctrine as a general interpretation nor suggested that the amendment should be strictly self-executing.

Repudiating Farnsworth's previously cited version of the 1866 debates, Bingham asserted in 1871 that the difference between his initial and final proposals was that the adopted amendment was stronger: "It is, as it now stands in the Constitution, more comprehensive than as it was first proposed and reported in February, 1866. It embraces all and more than did the" earlier proposal.[184] The change of wording, he explained, occurred after he reflected, as he had not done before, on Chief Justice Marshall's holding in *Barron*: "Had the framers of these [first eight] amendments intended them to be limitations on the powers of the State governments they would have imitated the framers of the original Constitution, and have expressed that intention."[185] Bingham continued that Section 1 of the amendment was drafted accordingly as a means of applying the amendments to the states.[186]

In the end, even putting aside Bingham's later explanation, one can ask two questions: (1) Do the debates surrounding the postponed Bingham proposal and its subsequent redraft vindicate the state action doctrine? and (2) Do the debates and redraft support a broad interpretation of the final form of the Fourteenth Amendment with regard to congressional power to enforce its Due Process Clause, or does the Bingham proposal's failure indicate a congressional consensus that Congress in fact should have narrower authority over life, liberty, and property interests?

The postponement of Bingham's proposal, given language that might have seemed at once too strong and too weak, could have occurred (depending on the individual legislator) out of concern that the proposal went either too far or not far enough. The debates, however, are largely ambiguous on that issue—at least before looking to later recollections. Nevertheless, one must answer the first question in the negative, especially in view of the failure of the debates to embrace the state action doctrine and the ample statements rejecting that doctrine at other points. (As has been shown, available evidence demonstrates the implausibility of Farnsworth's attempt to rewrite the history of the 1866 debates five years later.) Some legislators' broad generalizations that the first proposal went too far is hardly a basis for the state action doctrine, even given the change in language, since there was a perfectly plausible alternate explanation for such reservations that specifically was articulated: the possibility of blanket, plenary congressional authority over issues of life, liberty, and property (as long as such power would be applied equally). This observation partially answers the second question—but only partially. Among statements from supporters of the Fourteenth Amendment after as well as before the Bingham proposal, one encounters a division of views on the subject of life, liberty, and property and a debate that would not come to fruition until Congress debated the Ku Klux Klan Act.

Before 1871, the issue was addressed on a sporadic and often ambiguous basis. During the 1866 debates over the civil rights bill, Delano expressed reservations over the possibility that congressional authority would "swallow up all or nearly all of the rights of the States with respect to the property, the liberties, and the lives of its citizens" and "enable Congress to exercise almost any power over a State."[187] During the Fourteenth Amendment debates, the effect of the Due Process Clause was rarely mentioned, but Garrett Davis quoted the provision and recorded his objection to it "because in relation to her own citizens it belongs to each State exclusively, as being of her own reserved sovereignty and rights, to regulate that matter."[188] Coming from a Democrat, this statement appears at first glance to be a remarkable concession on the scope of the enforcement of the Due Process Clause, though in view of reservations expressed in other contexts by Republicans, it does not quite have the same effect as Hendricks' lone Democratic statement on the scope of Section 5. (As in the case of Section 5 generally, Democrats after ratification would no longer embrace the same interpretation of the amendment as they did when they were attempting to articulate its danger for purposes of defeating it.) On the other hand, Henderson expressed a view shortly before the Senate vote on the amendment that seems to have reflected that of several other Republicans already discussed when he referred to "life, liberty, and property" as "absolute or inalienable rights" that "ought never to be taken away without due process of law."[189]

Defrees asserted soon after the House vote that Section 1 of the Fourteenth Amendment "indisputably . . . secures to all life, liberty, and property."[190] A few weeks later, Representative Jehu Baker called the Due Process Clause "clearly right and necessary to liberty" and expressed his view that while the Constitution already had declared (in the Fifth Amendment) that no person generally would be deprived of life, liberty, or property without due process, the later clause particularly provided a "wholesome and needed check" on the state.[191] This statement reflects a lack of awareness of *Barron*, and given his context and assumptions, it is unclear whether and to what extent Baker would have limited congressional power to legislate on life, liberty, and property.

State ratification debates included several statements recognizing the Fourteenth Amendment as protecting the right to life, liberty, and property, though some focused on securing these rights for blacks.[192] Several opponents spoke apprehensively of the prospect of federal power that they maintained could extend to all matters involving life, liberty, and property of citizens.[193] Governor David Walker of Florida warned that Section 1 and Section 5 "taken together give Congress the power to legislate in all cases touching the citizenship, life, liberty or property of every individual in the Union, of whatever race or color, and leave no further use for the State governments."[194] Maryland's Joint Committee on Federal Relations reported, "The proposition to vest in Congress the power of supervision, interference and control over State legislation affecting the lives, liberty and property of its citizens and persons subject to its jurisdiction, is virtually to enable Congress to abolish the State governments."[195] Pennsylvania Representative John S. Mann, a supporter of the amendment, expressed his view of the amendment's broad scope from a starkly different perspective: "What is the worth of a government that willfully neglects to protect all its citizens in their rights of life, liberty and property?"[196]

During debates over the Fifteenth Amendment in 1869, Congressman George F. Miller maintained that Section 1 of the preceding amendment "was intended to protect life, liberty, and property, and especially that class of colored people who had been in slavery."[197] The following year, Fowler asserted that "[i]f an attempt is made to deprive any citizen of his life, liberty, or property without due process of law the Government may enter the State and protect him."[198] During the debates over the first Enforcement Act, Casserly maintained that it was

extremely plain that the criminal or illegal acts of a private person in a State, in depriving another of his life by murder, or of his liberty by false imprisonment, or of his property by stealing it, all "without due process of law," could never give to Congress the right to interfere. Otherwise Congress might take to itself, under pretense of enforcing the fourteenth amendment, the entire criminal and civil jurisdiction in the States of offenses and trespasses against life, liberty, and property by private persons acting without any color of State authority.[199]

A report of the House Committee on Reconstruction on the "protection of loyal and peaceable citizens in the South" issued in February 1871 discussed violence in the South and maintained that deprivations of life, liberty, and property by individuals amid state omissions to prevent and punish them were sufficient for congressional action:

The fourteenth amendment . . . has vested in the Congress . . . the power, by proper legislation, to prevent any State from depriving any citizen of the United States of the enjoyment of life, liberty, and property. But it is said that this deprivation of life, liberty, and property, of which complaint is made, . . . is not done by the State but by citizens of the State. But surely, if the fact is as your committee believe and assert it to be, that the State is powerless to prevent such murders and felonies as your committee have described . . . and if, added to that, comes the inability of the State to punish the crimes after they are committed, then the State has, by its neglect or want of power, deprived the citizens of the United States of protection in the enjoyment of life, liberty, and property as fully and completely as if it had passed a legislative act to the same effect.[200]

b.2. Debates over the Validity of § 2 of the Ku Klux Klan Act

In a speech in Ohio shortly after the ratification of the Fourteenth Amendment, Garfield, who would play an important role in debates over § 2, told a Democrat in the audience, "If you persist in forming Ku-Klux Klans in the South to murder Union men, white or black, we propose to use the bayonet. . . . We propose to see the rights, liberties, and lives of Union men, white and black, protected. This has been the object of congressional reconstruction from the beginning to the end."[201] This concern would reach the height of its national attention following Grant's message to Congress on March 23, 1871, reporting that a "condition of affairs now exists" in some states "rendering life and property insecure" and that "the power to correct these evils is beyond the control of the State authorities."[202] The president recommended "such legislation as in the judgment of Congress shall effectually secure life, liberty, and property and the enforcement of law in all parts of the United States,"[203] and Congress formed a special joint committee in response that drafted the Ku Klux Klan Act.[204]

Evidence and corresponding denunciations of rampant crime in the South occupied much congressional attention, and the desire in Congress to arm the president with power to suppress such violence was manifest.[205] The intention of protecting life, liberty, and property in the South was clear from early in the debates, though not always without qualification. Initially, Benjamin Butler had proposed in the House a lengthy bill intended (in his words) "to protect loyal and peaceable citizens in the South in the full enjoyment of their rights, persons, liberty, and property,"[206] but Garfield was interested in discussing what deficiency in § 6 of the first Enforcement Act Congress was interested in remedying, adding his enthusiasm to aid the passage of "anything that is in the line of constitutional legislation to protect life and property in the South."[207] Senator Adelbert Ames distinguished the "single murder at the North with or without political significance" that "may not need national interference" with the need for the federal government to prevent former Confederates from using all their "power to deprive by violence and fraud citizens of every right" while states were failing to give requisite protection.[208] Senator Frederick A. Sawyer articulated the necessity of finding or creating by statute the authority to protect citizens from such violence in order to avoid anarchy,[209] but Thurman asserted that the constitutional question presented was whether Congress could "punish ordinary murder, ordinary assault and battery, ordinary crimes, such as punishable by the State law," which he felt it could not.[210]

A Senate resolution submitted by Sherman sought legislation correcting organized violence by the (mostly) former Confederates who were "overthrowing the safety of person and property, and the rights which are the primary basis of civil government, and which are guarantied by the Constitution."[211] In the House, Shellabarger reported a shorter committee bill in lieu of Butler's following Grant's message,[212] the second section of which began by describing punishable crimes as follows:

That if two or more persons shall, within the limits of any State, band or conspire together to do any act in violation of the rights, privileges, or immunities of another person, which, being committed within a place under the sole and exclusive jurisdiction of the United States, would, under any law of the United States then in force, constitute the crime of either murder, manslaughter, mayhem, robbery, assault and battery, perjury, subornation of perjury, criminal obstruction of legal process or resistance of officers in discharge of official duty, arson, or larceny; and if one or more of the parties to said conspiracy shall do any act to effect the object thereof, all the parties to or engaged in said conspiracy, whether principals or ac[c]essories, shall be deemed guilty of a felony. . . . [213]

Shellabarger pointed out, as Justice Hunt would in his *Reese* dissent, the rule of interpretation "liberally and beneficently" construing constitutional and statutory provisions "in aid of the preservation of human liberty and human rights."[214] Section 2, he added, aimed to supply the alleged deficiency of § 6 of the first Enforcement Act, which some asserted was too vague in defining particular acts constituting crimes and which also might be construed to apply only to voting since the act generally purported to enforce the Fifteenth Amendment.[215] The Ohio congressman asserted that § 2 "rests upon exactly the same legal ground" as § 6, the only difference being the "greater exactness" with which the later provision defined the offenses.[216] Both sections, he maintained, may be based on the following legal principle:

when the United States inserted into its Constitution that which was not in it before, that the people of this country, born or naturalized therein, are citizens of the United States and of the States also in which they reside, and that Congress shall have power to enforce by appropriate legislation the requirement that their privileges and immunities as citizens should not be abridged, it was done for a purpose, and that purpose was that the United States thereby were authorized to directly protect and defend throughout the United States those privileges and immunities which are in their nature "fundamental" . . . and which inhere and belong of right to the citizenship of all free Governments.[217]

He went on to articulate the application of Section 5 to all provisions of Section 1 of the Fourteenth Amendment, understood in accordance with the dominant Republican theory, including his earlier cited analogies to the fugitive slave laws.[218]

On the Democratic side, Kerr refuted Shellabarger's interpretation of the Fourteenth Amendment, using some premises that were consistent with the Court's post-1873 doctrine. After rejecting the notion that any new congressional power proceeded from the amendment's "merely declaratory" grant of citizenship, he stated that the recent amendment's Privileges and Immunities Clause, unlike that of Article IV Section 2, protected only the privileges of national citizenship while the Due Process Clause was only procedural.[219] The Privileges and Immunities Clause, Kerr argued, "needs no legislation to enforce it" while the Due Process Clause "give[s] no power to Congress or to the United States to supersede State laws."[220] He considered the Equal Protection Clause to be merely declaratory of preexisting law, adding that it "manifestly involves no grant of power."[221] Thus § 2 was "pregnant in every line with vice, usurpation, and danger," looking "to the complete subversion of the power of the States to enforce their criminal laws, adopt and execute their own policy, or protect their own citizens and society."[222]

On the same day Shellabarger and Kerr's statements were articulated, Stoughton made a protracted description of unpunished violence in the South[223] and asserted, "It is a fundamental principle of law that while the citizen owes allegiance to the Government he has a right to expect and demand protection for life, person, and property."[224] He added, however, that it was unnecessary "to rest upon this inherent and undeniable right to protect our own citizens" because the Equal Protection Clause both authorized and compelled congressional action:

When thousands of murders and outrages have been committed in the southern States and not a single offender brought to justice, when the State courts are notoriously powerless to protect life, person, and property, and when violence and lawlessness are universally prevalent, the denial of the equal protection of the laws is too clear to admit of question or controversy. Full force and effect is therefore given to section five. . . . The authority thus conferred is subject to no restrictions or limitations. It is for Congress in its discretion to determine what legislation is appropriate, and its decision is binding upon every other department of the Government. The inquiry, if any arises, is not what Congress may do, but what it may not do.[225]

By this point in the debates, two basic justifications had been articulated for the constitutionality of § 2—one apparently based on a conception of the federal government's power to protect life, liberty, and property directly, the other looking instead for an equal protection rationale limited to the state's discriminatory execution of such protections.

While Democrats and Republican opponents of Reconstruction generally would reject both theories, the views of most Republicans varied in emphasis. Representative George F. Hoar embraced an equal protection argument, emphasizing how a state government that was republican in form could be unrepublican under the Constitution when conspiracy rendered life and property insecure in the administration of laws.[226] He recognized that there could be occasional imperfections in the administration of justice in some states (for example, Vermont, Massachusetts, and Wisconsin), but he distinguished "the incidental evils which attend upon republican government," with which Congress could not interfere, from cases (which it was Congress' duty to discern) where "these evils have attained such a degree as amounts to the destruction, to the overthrow, to the denial to large classes of the people of the blessings of republican government altogether."[227] For Hoar, such statewide, systematic injustice amounted to a denial of equal protection by omission.[228]

Representative Austin Blair criticized the "constitutional hair-splitting" that he perceived while citizens were being denied their rights, privileges, and immunities under Section 1 of the Fourteenth Amendment and asserted the nation's duty to protect them where the states would not.[229] Garfield later asked for the definition of the "rights, privileges, and immunities" protected in § 2 against conspiracy, to which Maynard answered "any of the personal rights which the Constitution guaranties to the citizen," naming as examples rights contained in the First, Fourth, and Fifteenth Amendments, as well as the Double Jeopardy Clause.[230] It would apply to any conspiracy to expel all Northerners or "carpet-baggers" from the community or to prevent blacks from voting.[231] Benjamin Butler asserted his sense of the necessity of congressional action by inverting his proposition: "Is it one of the rights of a State not to protect its citizens in the enjoyment of life, liberty, and property, and thereby deny him the equal protection of the laws, so that, when the General Government attempts to do for the protection of the citizen what the State has failed to do, is it to be held an interference with the rights of the State?"[232]

Several first-term House members defended the bill's constitutionality on terms similar to those of their more senior colleagues. Perry reminded the House of the conditions giving rise to the bill and listed among them violations of the Privileges and Immunities Clause, the Due Process Clause, and the Fifteenth Amendment.[233] James Monroe illustrated the Constitution as a means rather than an end and argued that the pending legislation entailed the extension of older principles to new circumstances.[234] Lowe asserted the need to insure the rights and privileges of citizens through the bill, whether or not deprivations came directly from state laws, and he found power under Sections 1 and 5 together "to secure to citizens the actual enjoyment of the rights and privileges guarantied."[235] Horace B. Smith found congressional power to punish assault and battery, murder, and conspiracy unquestionable where it was "necessary to guaranty to the poor voters of the South their constitutional rights."[236]

In the Senate, Morton viewed the bill as clearly punishing organizations that denied citizens equal protection and security in their lives and property, and he added that the "protection of the people in their lives, liberty, and property is the highest duty of a government."[237] Morton deemed it necessary for the federal government to assume control because "these crimes are the result of confederated action, the result of a common and widespread purpose," intended "not . . . simply for the gratification of individual malice, revenge or aggrandizement, but for the accomplishment of a general design extending not only throughout a State, but throughout many States."[238]

House Democrats for the most part articulated some version of Kerr's argument about the act's unconstitutional intrusion into the states. Washington C. Whitthorne did not see how two people combining to punish a suspected trespasser by assault and battery would not be covered by § 2 and maintained that a liberal interpretation of congressional power over life, liberty, and property would subordinate all state functions to Congress.[239] Stevenson Archer and James R. McCormick felt the bill usurped state criminal authority, and they asserted that the judiciary alone was capable of doing what was necessary to enforce the Fourteenth Amendment.[240] Storm[241] and Edward Rice[242] concluded that § 2 was unconstitutional as well, working from the premise that both Sections 1 and 5 of the Fourteenth Amendment added no new power. As for the Due Process Clause, Storm believed it referred to the " 'process of law' of the States, not the 'process of law' of the United States," and thus did not authorize the legislation.[243] McHenry maintained that a state already confers equal protection where it provides criminal penalties and that Congress could not punish individuals for wrongs of the state when a state already has conferred equal protection.[244] James H. Slater found § 2 to extend to an ordinary conspiracy to commit larceny and suggested the difficulty in finding a limit to congressional authority to protect life, liberty, and property; the act, he concluded, aimed to "assume jurisdiction over the domestic concerns of the several States."[245] Samuel S. Cox, who in his memoirs years later would call the Fourteenth Amendment "a monument to the satanic malice of the radical party,"[246] criticized the bill as an "arbitrary enactment[]" that unconstitutionally attempted to enlarge federal jurisdiction over crimes in the states while not having any relationship to state action.[247]

James G. Blair, the Liberal Republican freshman, found § 2's suggested justification to be a dangerous assertion of federal power contrary to his own advocacy of the state action doctrine.[248] In the Senate, Frank Blair viewed the bill as an attempt to punish those who violated state laws and questioned the validity of Congress' premise that it could act on its own determination that the state's administration of laws was unequal.[249]

Although most differences among regular Republicans consisted of which constitutional justifications for § 2 they chose to emphasize, there occasionally were those who expressly rejected certain justifications—if not all of them. Farnsworth, who it has been seen voted for the Fourteenth Amendment in 1866 and switched from his earlier views supporting Reconstruction legislation, essentially endorsed the state action theory.[250] The

Illinois Republican argued that the fact that § 2 addressed conspiracies gave it no greater constitutionality than if it were to address ordinary crimes by individuals—such as larceny, which was a deprivation of property—but Shellabarger disagreed, pointing out that the section addressed conspiracies to defeat fundamental rights of citizenship articulated in either constitutional or statutory law.[251] It already has been shown that Farnsworth's premises interpreting the Fourteenth Amendment after his about-face are difficult to accept as the theory of the framers, and it is unclear why his conclusions on § 2 should be any more convincing.

Two second-term Republican congressmen from Illinois, Jesse H. Moore and John B. Hawley, found constitutional problems with § 2, though only Moore ultimately would decline to vote for the bill.[252] Moore reiterated Democratic arguments on both § 2's unconstitutional intrusion into state powers to prescribe criminal codes and the Fourteenth Amendment's failure to grant new rights and powers.[253] Hawley's understanding of the committee interpretation presented no constitutional problems for him, but he believed many interpreted the bill "to mean that the criminal laws of the United States as applicable to those places where the United States has exclusive jurisdiction, so far as the crime of murder and the other crimes therein mentioned are concerned, are extended over all the United States," which he could not accept as constitutionally authorized.[254] Shellabarger attempted to clarify such misunderstandings as concerned Moore:

The whole design and scope of the second section of this bill was to do this: to provide for the punishment of any combination or conspiracy to deprive a citizen of the United States of such rights and immunities as he has by virtue of the laws of the United States and of the Constitution thereof. The mentioning of these particular acts is simply resorted to as a convenient method of confining the wrongs to the class of cases which would be in fact and in law an infraction of the rights of national citizens. They are limitations, and are not meant to intimate that the crime of murder or manslaughter or anything of that kind can be punished under this bill, if the crime be merely that. It is merely a method of nomenclature, of description.[255]

Hawley approved of § 2 provided that it was given this construction and not applied to ordinary crime; added to his approval of § 3,[256] Hawley's understanding was a far cry from the state action doctrine, and his only problem with § 2 was an interpretation that in Congress tended to be adopted only by its opponents.

Garfield's lengthy speech on the Fourteenth Amendment and his justification for § 2 would be a key to understanding the theory of moderate supporters of the Ku Klux Klan Act. The Ohio congressman, who had become more skeptical about Reconstruction in 1871, had privately expressed his legal reservations about pushing legislative efforts beyond constitutional bounds.[257] He began his speech by praising the value of decentralized government and employing citations from the 1866 debates to support the notion "that the power to protect the life and property of private citizens within the States, was left by the Constitution exclusively to the State governments."[258] He acknowledged that the three recent amendments "to some extent enlarged the functions of Congress" but reviewed the history of the original Bingham proposal, including the Hale-Bingham dialogue and statements from Conkling and Hotchkiss, to show, over Bingham's objection, that its failure arose from opposition to allowing the federal government to protect life, liberty, and property directly.[259] Thus he concluded that the final version of the amendment could not incorporate the understanding of control over life, liberty, and property contained in the original Bingham proposal.[260] It already has been shown that there is evidence, beyond what Garfield cited, to support his conclusion (though the congressman's citations of the debates over the final version of the Fourteenth Amendment included unhelpfully vague expressions of disappointment that the amendment did not go far enough).[261]

Looking at each clause in Section 1 of the Fourteenth Amendment, the congressman proceeded to develop an interpretation that would justify § 2 of the statute only under the Equal Protection Clause. The grant of citizenship in Section 1, he maintained, was not a grant of power to Congress to protect "all the fundamental rights of persons and property within the States."[262] Similarly, he believed that Shellabarger and Hoar had construed the Privileges and Immunities Clause too broadly, leaving the "irresistible" conclusion that Congress had "original jurisdiction over all questions affecting the rights of the person and property of all private citizens within a State."[263] The Due Process Clause, Garfield added, was copied from the Fifth Amendment, except that it comprised a limitation on states.[264] It was the Equal Protection Clause that the future president considered "the chief and most valuable addition" to Section 1—"a broad and comprehensive limitation on the power of the State governments, and, without doubt, Congress is empowered to enforce this limitation by any appropriate legislation."[265] Under this clause, state laws "may be unwise, injudicious, even unjust; but they must be equal in their provisions, . . . covering all and resting upon all with equal weight."[266]

Turning to the enforcement of the amendment, Garfield spoke approvingly of the previous Enforcement Acts as providing ample protection of voting rights, and he added that "it is undoubtedly within the power of Congress to provide by law for the punishment of all persons, official or private, who shall invade" constitutional rights.[267] Appreciating the problem then facing the South and Grant's request, Garfield proposed a theory on which Congress could act in § 2 of the bill without unwarranted intrusion upon state power by operating under the Equal Protection Clause. The congressman described the "systematic maladministration" or "neglect or refusal to enforce" laws that were "just and equal on their face" as a denial of equal protection that Congress could remedy.[268] This acknowledgment of the sufficiency of state omission to trigger congressional action is clearly inconsistent with the state action doctrine, though Garfield's speech ultimately advocated what appeared a substantially modified version of the doctrine. He suggested that § 2 be amended to apply to such a denial and thus remove the objections of many legislators, adding his interest in recording his own interpretation of the recent amendments to counter others that he found unwarranted.[269]

Shellabarger challenged Garfield on his understanding that the future president was suggesting that the provisions of Section 1 were mere negations of state power and that Congress lacked power to enforce the privileges and immunities of citizenship directly, but Garfield responded that he did not embrace these assumptions.[270] Rather, he believed that "with the fifteenth amendment superadded, Congress is armed with more than a mere negative power, and had the right to pass the enforcement law of May last."[271] Whatever constitutional problems Garfield found with § 2, he evidently was satisfied with its subsequent replacement because he ultimately would vote for it.[272] In the end, Garfield's speech is difficult to accept insofar as it denies the affirmative nature of constitutional protections under the Fourteenth Amendment and corresponding congressional power under the Equal Protection Clause, but it presents a formidable interpretation of the Due Process Clause and original congressional reservations about direct legislative power over life, liberty, and property per se.

The day after Garfield's speech, Shellabarger proposed several revisions to the bill, including the ultimately adopted language of § 2 that the Court would face in *Harris*.[273] He described the object of the amended § 2 in terms of redressing crimes motivated by an attack on the equality of rights—

to confine the authority of this law to the prevention of deprivations which shall attack the equality of rights of American citizens; that any violation of the right, the *animus* and effect of which is to strike down the citizen, to the end that he may not enjoy equality of rights as contrasted with his and other citizens' rights.[274]

Cook, who had voted for the Fourteenth Amendment five years earlier, expressed approval for the provision.[275] He maintained that Congress generally could not punish an ordinary individual crime such as assault and battery—except in emergency situations where state authorities were overwhelmed by combinations preventing them from enforcing such laws—but the legislation at issue was based on the proposition "that wherever the Constitution of the United States secures a right to a citizen Congress may enforce and protect that right."[276] As an "absolute test" of this proposition, Cook added, "Congress may legislate to protect any right the denial of which by a State court would give the citizen affected thereby a right to appeal to the Supreme Court of the United States for redress."[277] Affirmative rights belonging to national citizenship that could be protected by federal legislation, the Illinois congressman felt, existed regardless of whether constitutional clauses were worded in affirmative or negative terms.[278] The bill was based on the right "to have the equal protection of the laws" through the executive, legislative, and judicial branches of the states, as well as protection from "every combination of men by force and intimidation or threat" who hinder state authorities in all branches from granting equal protection.[279]

Two speeches by second-term Republicans toward the end of the House debates shed additional light on § 2. Willard pointed out the federal government's lack of power to punish "offenses against life and property, as such"—which had made him doubtful about the earlier § 2's constitutionality because it practically abolished state criminal jurisdiction over the named crimes—but he approved of the current version because it assumed, under what he viewed as the committee's interpretation, "that the Constitution secured, and was only intended to secure, equality of rights and immunities, and that we could only punish by United States laws a denial of that equality."[280] As for the Due Process Clause, he found that it "added nothing to the rights belonging to citizenship," and "whatever may have been added to the character of citizenship by" its words was "not at all involved in the bill before the House."[281]

In another speech, Horatio C. Burchard explained that he had found the earlier version of § 2 to be unconstitutional. Because Section 5 of the Fourteenth Amendment gave Congress no more power than already existed in the original Constitution's Necessary and Proper Clause, and because Section 1 of the amendment granted no new privileges and immunities of citizenship not already in Article IV Section 2, he reasoned that Congress could have no more power over ordinary felonies than before.[282] (This conclusion, he added, did not change under the incorporation theory because such issues were not involved in evaluating § 2's constitutionality.[283]) Burchard viewed the amendment as a limitation on state legislation and execution and pointed out that § 2 "makes no reference to State laws or the action or non-action of State authority[. I]t relates to the crimes and conspiracies of private individuals."[284] Still, while he found no basis for the legislation in the Due Process Clause, he maintained that the Equal Protection Clause could be violated by all state officials as well as by "secret combinations of men . . . allowed by the Executive to band together to deprive one class of citizens of their legal rights without a proper effort to discover, detect, and punish the violations of law and order."[285]

Burchard argued that Section 1 of the amendment originally "was not understood or intended" to "confer upon Congress the power to enforce its provisions upon private individuals by general affirmative legislation."[286]

Just as the amendment allowed Congress to punish state officials who made or executed unconstitutional laws or neglected their constitutional duties, however, it also allowed such power to punish "willful and wrongful attempts of individuals to prevent such officers performing such duties."[287] The basis for § 2 being the Equal Protection Clause to the exclusion of the other clauses of Section 1 of the amendment, he asserted his understanding that the "gravamen of the offense is the unlawful attempt to prevent a State through its officers enforcing in behalf of a citizen of the United States his constitutional right to equality of protection."[288]

Burchard's articulation of the most conservative constitutional basis advanced for authorizing § 2 was substantially adopted in a statement by a representative who had been in the Senate in 1866. Poland, who expressed general agreement with Farnsworth's above-cited constitutional views, asserted that Congress generally could not punish ordinary crimes against person and property under the Fourteenth Amendment, but that it could punish a state's denial of equal protection or an individual's interference with the state officials' duty under the Equal Protection Clause.[289] He disagreed with an earlier concern Farnsworth had raised about the possibility of double punishment by pointing out that concurrent penal laws by the federal and state governments had been adopted in several contexts for many years.[290]

The amended House bill passed by a party-line vote that remarkably included Farnsworth, the one Republican framer whose floor statements during the 1871 debates appeared to endorse the Court's state action doctrine, voting for passage.[291] The Illinois congressman's views generally supporting the Court's 1883 holdings, stated *before* § 2 was amended, might have been subject to the same qualification as articulated in the substantially modified version of the state action doctrine of legislators like Burchard—significantly, a version that dictated a different verdict on § 2's constitutionality from that reached by *Harris*.

In debates over the Senate bill that followed, Edmunds, who was in charge of the bill, interpreted § 2 not to reach

what might be called a private conspiracy growing out of a neighborhood feud of one man or set of men against another to prevent one getting an indictment in the State courts against men for burning down his barn; but, if in a case like this, it should appear that this conspiracy was formed against this man because he was a Democrat, . . . or because he was a Catholic, or because he was a Methodist, or because he was a Vermonter, . . . then this section could reach it.[292]

The senator added that the act punished only conspiracy and that it did not punish acts pursuant to conspiracies, which he would have preferred to be included.[293] Edmunds spoke of life, liberty, and property affirmatively as interests to which citizens were entitled and rejected interpretations of Section 1 of the Fourteenth Amendment as a merely prohibitory section.[294]

Like several moderate Republicans in the House, Trumbull stated his belief that Congress lacked authority over "the general rights of person and property" (i.e., ordinary private crimes), though he expressed no objection to enacting a law that would protect a person from "inequality of legislation" in laws depriving life, liberty, or property without due process.[295] Thus Congress, in his view, could not punish conspiracies to "obstruct the due course of justice in a State," but only conspiracies "to deny the equal protection of the laws"—a position similar to the more conservative theories supporting the House bill. The senator's criticism of the bill for "undertaking to punish persons for violating State laws, without reference to any violation of the Constitution or laws of the United States" resembled attacks on the early version of the House bill.[296] Unlike the regular Republicans who made such criticisms, however, Trumbull, as might be expected from his emerging disillusionment with Reconstruction, would not vote for the act.[297] For the Illinois senator's benefit, Edmunds cited the part of § 2 expressly punishing conspiracies to obstruct state officials in giving everyone the equal protection of their laws, but Trumbull suggested that the section was accompanied by other clauses that conferred additional power on Congress.[298]

With an understanding of the Fourteenth Amendment as being confined to state action, Senate Democrats condemned § 2 for overreaching the Constitution. Thomas Bayard protested the "consolidation of power" implicit in Congress' attempt to punish crimes between citizens of the same state as an invasion of the state's police power.[299] Thurman conceded the constitutionality of § 2 insofar as it punished treason or deterred federal officers from performing their duties, but he added that Congress lacked power to punish people for obstructing state officials or otherwise removing impediments created by private individuals because that would constitute merely crimes against the state.[300] He further asserted that the provision punishing conspiracy to deprive citizens of equal privileges or immunities or equal protection was too vague for a criminal statute.[301] Vickers found no justification for the bill absent state legislation depriving people of life, liberty, and property, and he charged that it was "unjust and factious" to interpret "the conduct of a few disguised men who commit wrong and avoid detection" to be a violation by the state.[302] The bill passed in the Senate by a party-line vote; those voting against it included Trumbull and Schurz, who would be prominent figures in the emerging Liberal Republican movement.[303]

In the end, the several theories of the Fourteenth Amendment expressed on the floor regarding congressional power over individual crime and on the different versions of § 2 do not support the Court's version of the state action doctrine—unless one decides to embrace the theory endorsed almost exclusively by Democrats (joined in the 1870s by Liberal Republicans) who earlier had opposed the amendment out of fear of its expansion of congressional power in the first place.[304] The rights protected by the Fourteenth Amendment were characterized in affirmative terms by Republican supporters from the outset, and the embrace in 1871 by a handful of Republicans, such as Burchard and Poland, of the idea that private individuals could be punished only when they hindered state officials appears to be something of a retreat from the more affirmative assertions of preceding years. Even if this notion, which comprised the most conservative position of supporters of § 2, were accepted, the Court's judgment in *Harris* on corresponding counts in its indictments could not be justified—except on the flawed mode of statutory construction adopted in *Reese*. Burchard's view is difficult to accept as the original understanding not simply because it follows negative assumptions about the nature of Fourteenth Amendment rights, but also because the very terms of § 2 went farther.

Indeed, all members of Congress who had voted for the amendment in 1866 and were still serving voted for the Ku Klux Klan Act by the time the final vote was cast on April 19, 1871, except for Trumbull, who was well on the way to his own retreat from Reconstruction, and three others, all of whom ultimately were recorded as absent or not voting for the bill.[305] Before concluding that even these four legislators had embraced the Court's doctrine from the outset, it should be added that all but one of them—Representative Oakes Ames—had voted for the first Enforcement Act the preceding year, § 6 of which, besides being inconsistent with the state action doctrine, is difficult to distinguish in constitutionality from § 2 of the Ku Klux Klan Act.[306]

Perhaps in the attempt to simplify the 1871 debates in terms of degrees of support for the state action requirement among framers, Avins erroneously identifies the positions of Garfield, Bingham, and Cook with that of Poland, which he appears to embrace himself.[307] A more careful look at their statements indicates a conception of a direct relationship between the federal government and individual citizens under the Fourteenth Amendment and a corresponding willingness to have Congress punish certain private crimes, though this willingness was sometimes qualified by whether a state had omitted to perform its duty. Avins' unduly narrow conception of congressional power under the original understanding of the Fourteenth Amendment seems to arise from confusion over the nature of divisions concerning the *scope* of private action that could be addressed.[308]

To lump together all statements during the Reconstruction debates expressing reservations over congressional punishment of crimes committed by individuals is to meld life, liberty, and property into the same category as equal protection, which misunderstands the distinctions existing within such reservations. Statements dating back to the original Bingham proposal for the Fourteenth Amendment reflect concern even among Radicals that

Congress should not be allowed to legislate on matters relating to the protection of life, liberty, and property per se, which in practical terms would mean congressional authority to address all matters of legislation. These and other statements opposing the notion that Congress should address ordinary crimes had little to do with concern over federal punishment of individuals as opposed to states or state officials, but are better understood as reservations about the scope of criminal punishment reaching all matters of life, liberty, and property. It was not generally seen to follow from the Due Process Clause, read in conjunction with Section 5, that Congress possessed plenary power over all issues of life, liberty, and property, but Republicans, including moderates such as Garfield, did approve of the notion of congressional power to protect equality under the law as a basis for the 1871 statute. One could find many general expressions of hope by Republicans on both the federal and state levels since 1866 that Congress protect life, liberty, and property, but ultimately, it was not plenary power over such matters, but the ability to enact equality of protection that Republicans as a group came to embrace. The Equal Protection Clause thus was not intended to be confined to the state action doctrine, but can one consistently reach a different conclusion about the Due Process Clause?

This is an additional question for those interested in formulating a coherent originalist interpretation of the Fourteenth Amendment, because there is little basis either textually or from the debates not to apply Section 5 to all clauses of Section 1. How, one may ask (as Justice Bradley essentially did), could one reach any conclusion other than the Court's without granting Congress power over all matters of life, liberty, and property? In response—and Harlan's dissent might not have offered a direct, convincing reply to the Court on this point—it should be noted that the Due Process Clause does not address all deprivations, but only those that occur without due process. When Storm stated that the Due Process Clause referred to the " 'process of law' of the States,"[309] he raised an important point. The clause, it would seem, focuses on due process instead of the enumerated matters that are subject to such process since they are understood as a general matter to be defined by the states in the first instance. The clause received relatively little attention from Congress during Reconstruction except as an application of its Fifth Amendment counterpart to the states, and there is no less reason to view it primarily as a procedural clause. Process being by definition a matter of state action, one might read the clause inherently as addressing state functions—not because of the phrase "nor shall any State," but because of the term "due process of law." Thus, given the words of § 6 of the first Enforcement Act of 1870 involved in *Cruikshank*,[310] language merely mentioning rights, privileges, and immunities of citizenship will not legitimate punishment based on a count alleging deprivations of life or personal liberty alone.

Analysis of the Fourteenth Amendment in view of the congressional debates, however, does suggest possible consequences of applying Section 5 to the Due Process Clause. First, it can be suggested that Congress might justify intervening in the states to protect life, liberty, and property where the state's process breaks down and does not vindicate such interests, even though the state may define those interests in the first instance. Under this possible interpretation, in practical terms—and in the situation Congress faced during Reconstruction—there was a lack of due process, or process had broken down, with respect to protecting the life, liberty, and property (as defined by state laws) of a certain class of citizens. Congressional action in such a situation, as one might say generally of Reconstruction, is difficult to distinguish from the equal protection-based aims explicitly sought by moderates as well as Radicals except insofar as it might depend more specifically on a state's failure or private parties' hindrance of state authorities, so it was not necessary for legislators to articulate as clearly or as often their intentions for the Due Process Clause and Section 5.

One also could suggest that Congress was authorized to intervene beyond redressing procedural deficiencies only to the extent that the Due Process Clause includes a substantive component of fundamental rights that legislators perceived to be violated during Reconstruction. The question of whether and to what extent the Due Process Clause protects substantive rights "implicit in the concept of ordered liberty"[311] is a particularly complex issue, and it is not clear that this (narrow) category would be any broader than the fundamental privileges and immunities of citizenship. Still, several statements during the debates might be construed as desires to punish rampant violence that systematically violated the minimum security of life, liberty, and property demanded by the Due Process Clause—or, if one prefers, by the fundamental guarantees in the Privileges and Immunities Clause. It would be difficult to maintain that Congress believed it had power as a general matter to secure a minimal level of security of life, liberty, and property because that would entail some degree of power to legislate on murder, assault, robbery, and other such crimes by themselves, but combined with a general requirement of the unavailability of due process, such congressional power might be more plausible. Under this interpretation, if the states failed in their obligation to protect such minimal guarantees, whether the systematic failure or sheer lack of due process applied to a class of citizens or to an entire state—whether it was actually legalized or virtually legalized by the failure to execute a law—Congress could intervene and provide such protection itself.

Ultimately, Congress did not clearly choose to adopt either interpretation in 1871. The above suggestions of possible interpretations of Sections 1 and 5, though not repeating explicit arguments from the floor, merely attempt to reconcile the varied and sometimes amorphous views of the supporters of Reconstruction with a constitutional provision that, like any other, deserves coherent interpretation. However, there ultimately did not exist a consensus among Republicans in 1871 that congressional legislation generally should encompass issues of life, liberty, or property raised by the violence Congress primarily wished to address in the South. This does not mean that Section 5 does not apply to the Due Process Clause. Instead, it seems that Reconstruction did not ultimately require a resolution of the allowable scope of Section 5 power with respect to this provision, perhaps because equal protection proved both sufficient and easier for strict constructionists to quantify than the components of the Due Process Clause. Indeed, the statements during the debates reacting to violence in the South collectively seem to blur intentions to protect life, liberty, and property; to secure equality in life, liberty, and property; and to achieve equal protection of the law.[312] (It often is not even clear to what extent assertions about equality in life, liberty, and property were based on the Privileges and Immunities Clause, the Due Process Clause, or the Equal Protection Clause.) Only the last of these concepts was explored thoroughly and affirmed almost across the board by Republicans.

This study, confining itself to analysis of the pedigree of certain Supreme Court holdings, cannot purport to resolve all issues of originalist interpretation behind Sections 1 and 5. It can aim for greater clarity, even though it leaves certain ambiguities beyond the issues that faced the Court. One can discern general guidelines from the original understanding that demonstrate that Section 5 could be applied consistently to all provisions of Section 1 without necessitating either the state action doctrine or plenary congressional power over life, liberty, and property interests. Perhaps the Court did not need to deal with remaining ambiguities for the precise reason that they were ambiguities—because Congress lacked the need to clarify them in the first place. The laws the Court faced in *Harris* and the *Civil Rights Cases* originated not so much out of concern that a particular right, privilege, or immunity was being denied all the occupants of certain states, but more out of concern that a certain class of citizens was not covered or protected equally by laws already in existence. The contemporary concern therefore was more with congressional power to enforce equality under the law under Section 5—which alone was sufficient to have decided *Harris* differently—and that issue would arise again during the debates over Reconstruction's last civil rights law.

c. Debates over §§ 1 and 2 of the Civil Rights Act of 1875 and its Precursors

c.1. The Forty-Second Congress

Sumner regularly had introduced ill-fated bills banning discrimination in public accommodations and transportation, as well as in schools and juries, but it was not until December 1871 that such a bill would be debated on the floor; it was offered as an amendment in an effort by several Senate

Radicals to attach it to an amnesty bill removing Fourteenth Amendment disqualifications from most former Confederates.[313] From this first debate on, legislators dealt with many of the same issues as the Court would in the *Civil Rights Cases*, including the meaning of civil rights in the segregation context and the proposed amendment's effects on state power.

In a debate with Sumner, Republican Joshua Hill, a former Know-Nothing congressman who had been in the Senate for less than a year, did not find segregation in the facilities addressed by the amendment to be "offensive" or a denial of civil rights, and he considered it a matter of municipal regulation subject to state law.[314] On the Democratic side, Thurman, also in dialogue with Sumner, denied in strong terms the constitutional basis for the proposal's attempt to treat every innkeeper, theater manager, and railroad conductor as the state.[315] To this Sumner replied that a hotel, theater, and railroad corporation each was "a legal institution" that "already, to a certain extent," was "within the domain of law. . . . Whoever seeks the benefit of the law, as the owners and lessees of theaters do, as the common carriers do, as hotel-keepers do, must show equality."[316]

Sumner later articulated more fully the distinctions he drew between realms that were and were not subject to desegregation, explaining that each person's

house is his "castle," and this very designation, borrowed from the common law, shows his absolute independence within its walls; nor is there any difference, whether it be palace or hovel; but when he leaves his "castle" and goes abroad, this independence is at an end. He walks the streets; but he is subject to the prevailing law of Equality; nor can he appropriate the sidewalk to his own exclusive use, driving into the gutter all whose skin is less white than his own. . . . Equality in all institutions created or regulated by law, is as little a question of society.[317]

The Massachusetts senator asserted that his amendment was merely a supplement of the 1866 Civil Rights Act and that its constitutionality was as unquestionable.[318] He then articulated point by point how public inns, conveyances, theaters, and other places of public amusement were public institutions subject to regulation under the common law and obligated to serve their applicants equally.[319] Sumner's defense of his amendment clearly foretold Harlan's dissent.

Hill disagreed with Sumner's analysis, contending that "a man's house" does not "cease to be his castle whenever he chooses to convert it into a house of entertainment, and to take a license from the proper authority as a hotel-keeper or a boarding-house keeper."[320] He thus asserted that "the hotel-keeper is entitled to all the discrimination in regard to his guests that other men have in admitting them into their houses."[321] Vickers considered Sumner's proposal to be a forfeiture of state and federally granted charters and found it too "palpably unconstitutional" for extended comment to be necessary.[322] He later would express at greater length his belief that the bill infringed upon reserved state powers over its subject matter.[323] Thurman criticized the amendment for its application to states that had not deprived any of their citizens of their privileges and immunities, adding that the provision addressed only privileges and immunities and did not fall under the Equal Protection Clause. The Fourteenth Amendment, he asserted, did not authorize interference until the state passed or enforced an unconstitutional law.[324] In a later debate with Sumner, Thurman took issue with the Republican senator's analysis of the common law, including his belief that Congress possessed power over matters regulated by state law.[325]

Morton, in yet another dialogue involving Thurman, defended "the right of a man to the equal enjoyment of the privileges of traveling" as "a citizen of the United States" and the federal government's right to protect that privilege.[326] He also countered the belief of "a Democrat brought up in the old State-rights school of Virginia," for whom the Fourteenth and Fifteenth Amendments were "very difficult . . . to comprehend," that "the State must first deny before the Government can enforce" since that would allow only judicial invalidation, not legislation.[327] The Fourteenth and Fifteenth Amendments, he asserted, expressly left the remedy for their violation to Congress, which must act "by affirmative legislation."[328]

Thurman admitted that he did not find the Civil Rights Act of 1866 constitutional, a premise Justice Bradley (at least in earlier years) did not share, and he spoke of the Fourteenth Amendment as merely prohibitory of state action[329] and reached conclusions resembling the Court's:

What is [Morton's] argument? It is that privileges, immunities, life, liberty, property, and the protection of the laws in the United States are all taken in charge, and are under the guarantee of the Constitution of the United States, and that thus taken in charge and under its guarantee and protection, Congress has a right to legislate upon any subject whatsoever, according to its own discretion, that relates to the privileges, the immunities, the life, the property, or the liberty of a citizen of the United States; that it is wholly indifferent and immaterial whether a State has legislated upon that subject or not; that it is wholly immaterial what are the laws of a State, that the acts of Congress passed in pursuance of the Constitution are the paramount law of the land, and that Congress may, therefore, enter upon this subject as *res integra*, as a new thing, and may in its own discretion, without any reference to State legislation, State judicial decision, State custom, or State practice, make just such a code of laws as it sees fit to make. If this is the case, then all local self-government is wiped out in this land; for there is not one subject of legislation, . . . not even a tax bill, that may not be referred to the category of the privileges, the immunities, the liberty, the life, the property, or the protection of the citizen. If this interpretation of the Constitution be true, then the Federal Government has swallowed up every State government as completely as the prophet Jonah was swallowed by the whale.[330]

Garrett Davis denied that Congress could integrate hotels or theatrical companies on the basis of a state-granted charter, adding that the privileges and immunities of citizens of the United States did not cover such private associations.[331]

Frelinghuysen conceded that a law generally regulating the subjects of the bill absent an express grant of power in the Constitution would be invalid, but he added that it was constitutional to leave all such regulation to the states, as Sumner's proposal did, "excepting that it provides that every citizen shall be treated as a citizen, be he white or colored."[332] The New Jersey senator suggested, as did Senator John Scott, that the bill could be perfected, but Edmunds and Conkling replied that they supported the measure in principle, preferring to defer discussion about ironing out details.[333]

In a rare display of disapproval by a Radical, Lot M. Morrill, who had voted for the Thirteenth and Fourteenth Amendments, criticized Sumner's proposal as unconstitutional in a long speech on the recent amendments.[334] He contended that the adoption of the Citizenship Clause in Section 1 of the Fourteenth Amendment had not changed anything, but simply declared what the law already was.[335] The Thirteenth Amendment was "a mere negation" that "affirms nothing" besides freedom—and that only "by implication"—and Morrill did not interpret it as reaching Sumner's proposal to legislate on church accommodations.[336] Sumner replied that the bill made no pretension to legislate on accommodations, but only to abolish "an original pretension of slavery" and have Congress abolish racial discrimination.[337] Morrill, who was not persuaded, moved on to the Privileges and Immunities, Due Process, and Equal Protection Clauses and asserted that "in no proper sense can the fourteenth amendment be regarded as a substantive grant of power. It is in terms, in essence and effect, a prohibition to the States."[338] Although he did not object to congressional power to desegregate "common carriers" on "national highways," the senator described the privileges and immunities of citizenship in terms similar to those of the 1866 Civil Rights Act and added that they differed from Sumner's claimed rights to the same accommodations, which touched "rights of a strictly domiciliary character, and so not in our province."[339] The proposal thus invaded the "personal, social, religious, domiciliary rights of the people of the States."[340]

Sumner later responded to Morrill by asserting the Thirteenth Amendment's abolition of slavery "in length and breadth and then in every detail" and Congress' corresponding power, adding that the Fourteenth Amendment surely would remove any doubt left by its predecessor as to his proposal's constitutionality.[341] Morrill flatly rejected the Thirteenth Amendment argument and, responding to what he viewed as one of Sumner's misunderstandings, maintained that the Civil Rights Act of 1866 was authorized by the original Privileges and Immunities Clause, not the Thirteenth Amendment.[342] Morrill's statement might be seen as a response to Justice Harlan's point about the 1866 act, but his assumptions were highly problematical from the standpoint of the act's legislative history—even before contrasting his views with the actual meaning of the original Privileges and Immunities Clause.

Morrill's suggestion that the Senate Judiciary Committee had reported against Sumner's bill because it was unconstitutional provoked a reply from Edmunds, who explained that the committee's actions were based "chiefly on the ground that the [1866] civil rights bill was adequate to accomplish the protection which the citizen was entitled to, and that this was unnecessary legislation. We never reported against the bill upon the ground that its chief and leading features were unconstitutional."[343] Carpenter, another committee member, indicated agreement with the bill's "principle" and "substance" and confined most of his expressed reservations to the provisions banning discrimination in churches under the First Amendment and in juries (as already discussed)—not to the public accommodations and transportation at issue in the *Civil Rights Cases*.[344] He added, however, that the right to use benevolent institutions like cemeteries should depend on their support at public expense rather than on their incorporation, and he expressed his hope for a future amendment that would address common carriers supported at public expense or endowed by public use and inns or places of amusement for which a license from any legal authority was required.[345] Dismissing the notion that the recent amendments were adopted merely as negations on the states, Carpenter articulated the necessity of "positive enactments" by Congress to secure the amendments' principles.[346] Unlike Morrill, Carpenter construed the original Privileges and Immunities Clause according to the old Democratic theory, but he added that the Fourteenth Amendment's analogous clause extended beyond this to protect all citizens in the exercise of the privileges and immunities of national citizenship, which could be enforced by Congress.[347] Sherman supported Sumner's bill and embraced all rights under the common law as the privileges and immunities of citizenship.[348]

Republican Senator Orris S. Ferry, who was not in Congress during the Fourteenth Amendment debates, argued that the amendment did not allow Congress to legislate directly on the full scope of subjects in Section 1, and he criticized Sumner, Morton, and Carpenter for promoting the subversion of the former structure of government.[349] Under their logic, he argued, the federal government would possess "complete legislative authority over every interest affecting the life, liberty, and property of every citizen of the United States" while "absolutely nothing" would be left to state legislatures.[350] Carpenter interjected that where state laws fail to apply equal punishment to blacks and whites for murder, Congress could punish murder offenses directly, but Ferry disagreed.[351]

Democrat James K. Kelly saw the situation as Ferry did and argued that if Congress could intervene to protect blacks from racial discrimination, it could legislate on behalf of all whites as well, thus taking full control of "all offenses, wherever they may arise and whoever may be injured."[352] Soon before the vote on the Sumner amendment, Stevenson and Republican Thomas W. Tipton also remarked that the legislation was unconstitutional for intruding on the state domain.[353]

The Sumner amendment passed on February 9, 1872, thanks to the tie-breaking vote of Vice President Schuyler Colfax, who had voted for the Fourteenth Amendment in 1866 as Speaker of the House.[354] Excluding Colfax, twelve of the fourteen present legislators in the Senate who had voted for the Fourteenth Amendment voted for Sumner's amendment, the exceptions being Trumbull and Morrill.[355] The Democrats and Liberal Republicans who opposed Sumner's rider proceeded to vote against the amended amnesty bill, dropping the votes in support below the required two-thirds.[356]

A recurring theme over the course of the debates was the characterization of the right at issue in Sumner's proposal as a social rather than a civil right, a characterization on which Justice Bradley would rely in his opinion for the Court. This distinction arose often in debate but is easy to misinterpret, because different legislators defined the term "social rights" differently. One could find broad support among both the original supporters and opponents of the Fourteenth Amendment for the proposition that the amendment was intended to address civil and not social rights, but the consequences of this proposition depend decisively on the definitions employed.

Sumner himself, perhaps the preeminent spokesman for egalitarian causes in Congress, acknowledged a realm of social questions that the law did not attempt to address, including one's selection of associates, but he drew the line at "anything created or regulated by law," which "must be opened equally to all without distinction of color."[357] He soon afterward spoke disparagingly of criticisms that relied on a definition of social equality, acknowledging the term's ambiguity: "This is no question of society; no question of social life; no question of social equality, if anybody knows what this means. . . . Each person . . . is always free to choose who shall be his friend, his associate, his guest."[358] Working from his earlier cited distinctions between one's home and a public highway, the senator pointed out that "nobody pretends that Equality in the highway, whether on pavement or sidewalk, is a question of society."[359]

Democratic Senator Eli Saulsbury differed with Sumner, finding his measure to be "one not only of social equality, but of social equality enforced by pains and penalties."[360] Norwood attacked Sumner's "exceedingly abhorrent" amendment on similar grounds.[361] "What [Sumner's] bill aims to accomplish—disguise it as you may—is social equality in the inn," added Thurman.[362] Republicans embracing the amendment shared no such characterization about intruding into the social realm. Henry Wilson doubted that "the distinctions between the races" would be forgotten in the future but maintained that "[w]hatever differences of opinion there may be in regard to" one race's superiority, "one thing is clear, that there should be no distinction recognized by the laws of the land."[363]

The issue of social equality surfaced in the House during debate over a bill never acted on, which was similar to Sumner's but phrased to exclude the Chinese.[364] Charges that the bill imposed social equality came from Liberal Republican James G. Blair,[365] Conservative James C. Harper,[366] and Democrats McHenry[367] and Andrew King.[368] Blair also criticized the bill for unconstitutionally intruding into state affairs.[369] McHenry argued that innkeepers and other private businessmen had the liberty to discriminate in their businesses and that the bill gave blacks a special advantage over whites.[370]

When the Senate again considered the amnesty bill on May 8, Trumbull argued that Sumner's bill named social rights, not civil rights, and he defined the latter as natural rights such as those enumerated in the Civil Rights Act of 1866.[371] Several Republican senators took issue with Trumbull over the course of his speech, including Sherman, who asserted that the legislation aimed to enforce the 1866 act and included rights that were as much civil rights as those named in the earlier act.[372] Boreman, despite reservations about other provisions of the bill, indicated that he had no constitutional scruples about the issues raised by what turned out to be the precursors of §§ 1 and 2 of the 1875 bill.[373] Republican James L. Alcorn of Mississippi asked why the bill must extend into his state, where blacks could travel in first-class cars without being insulted, and Sumner replied, "We must legislate generally; there must be one law for every part of the country, the law of equal rights."[374] On the Democratic side, Thomas Bayard attacked the bill as an intrusion into the police power of the state,[375] and Stockton maintained that it interfered with the people's social rights.[376] Following a rather complex series of votes, the Sumner provision was retained on the amnesty bill, again by Colfax's vote.[377]

Later that same day, Conkling, with the support of Edmunds and Morton, proposed that the bill be confined to institutions supported by taxes, and Sumner agreed—with the qualification that publicly authorized institutions still would be covered whether or not they were tax-supported.[378] So amended, the civil rights amendment once again was attached to the amnesty bill after a couple of votes, and the latter again failed to pass the Senate.[379] Both sides were deadlocked.[380]

Debates over attempts to attach the civil rights amendment or a variety of other amendments to the amnesty bill ensued.[381] Trumbull asserted that the civil rights bill was misnamed because it was truly a bill for social rights, and Sumner responded with extended quotes from Frederick Douglass refuting the distinction the Illinois senator was making about social equality.[382] Casserly found the amendment "grossly and wantonly unconstitutional in many of its leading provisions."[383] Thurman proposed an amendment to strike the provision addressing places of public amusement and entertainment, but it was rejected.[384] A separate civil rights bill proposed by Carpenter lacking school or jury provisions and resembling the provisions the Court faced in the *Civil Rights Cases* passed the Senate during a night session in Sumner's absence, and over the adamant objection of the Massachusetts senator, the amnesty bill subsequently was passed without Sumner's amendment.[385] In the House, Carpenter's bill would receive the vote of a majority without reaching two-thirds on more than one occasion, and it ultimately disappeared into seeming oblivion.[386]

c.2. The Forty-Third Congress

In his Second Inaugural Address in 1873, Grant reopened the issue of civil rights legislation by urging its passage in the following terms:

The effects of the late civil strife have been to free the slave and make him a citizen. Yet he is not possessed of the civil rights which citizenship should carry with it. This is wrong, and should be corrected. To this correction I stand committed, so far as Executive influence can avail.

Social equality is not a subject to be legislated upon, nor shall I ask that anything be done to advance the social status of the colored man, except to give him a fair chance to develop what there is good in him, give him access to the schools, and when he travels let him feel assured that his conduct will regulate the treatment and fare he will receive.[387]

In his Fifth Annual Message in December 1873, the president repeated his request for "a law to better secure the civil rights which freedom should secure, but has not effectually secured, to the enfranchised slave."[388]

That same month, debates began in the House on civil rights legislation, which had been introduced in both houses at the start of the first session of the Forty-Third Congress in the form of bills to desegregate schools, common carriers, inns, theaters, cemeteries, and places of public amusement, besides banning jury discrimination.[389] Benjamin Butler, who introduced the House bill that in modified form would be passed in 1875,[390] described the legislation as a mere reaffirmation of the rights conferred by the common law and as a means of securing the privileges and immunities of citizenship.[391] He believed that state legislatures or courts often fell short of passing or carrying out laws to enforce civil rights and added an observation about a practical difficulty in state enforcement that would be alleviated by federal legislation:

when a railroad-car is in full speed, twenty miles an hour, passing from one State to another, and a negro is taken neck and heels and thrown out of the car, it may be difficult to tell whether that was done on one side or the other of the State line.

In one State there may be a law enforcing his rights, and in the other State there may be no such law.[392]

Butler's argument both provided a Fourteenth Amendment argument for the legislation and lent support to the notion that Congress could desegregate railroads under the Interstate Commerce Clause.

Robert B. Elliott, a black Republican from South Carolina, argued that even though the matters addressed in the bill were state and not national privileges under the doctrine of the *Slaughter-House Cases*, the same issues were subject to congressional power to address discrimination under the Equal Protection Clause.[393] Lawrence also found the law supported by the Equal Protection Clause. Like Butler, he maintained that the legislation secured only preexisting rights against racial discrimination.[394] He added that, as demonstrated by the Enforcement Acts of 1870–71, it denied equal protection when state judges failed to enforce existing law—here, the common law relating to public accommodations.[395] The word "protection" in the Equal Protection Clause, he asserted, referred to "every benefit to be derived from laws," so use of a common carrier, though not a protection of preexisting rights, was a legally conferred benefit to which all persons had a right that a state could not omit to protect.[396] Reviewing the original debates over the Fourteenth Amendment that he had witnessed, Lawrence concluded, "The debates show that these distinct assertions of the powers to be conferred on Congress by the fourteenth amendment were not controverted. No one ventured to deny them."[397] William H. H. Stowell added that hotels and railroads were legal institutions established or chartered by law and subject to state regulations and that the bill sought to ordain that such "legal institutions shall be for the benefit of all alike."[398] Richard H. Cain, a black South Carolina Republican, saw the legislation's aim as only "equal laws, equal legislation, and equal rights throughout the length and breadth of this land."[399]

House Democrats echoed arguments made in other contexts about the unconstitutionality of the legislation. Beck found no authority for the legislation in the Constitution and cited the *Slaughter-House Cases* to support his position.[400] Mills construed the privileges and immunities of citizenship to be those enumerated in the Constitution, such as those in the Bill of Rights, and argued that the rights contained in the bill were not in this category because Congress could abolish them at will.[401] Milton J. Durham saw no more right to intrude upon state sovereignty in matters of theater or hotel discrimination than to regulate similarly people's private homes.[402] John M. Bright[403] and Robert Hamilton[404] asserted that the Fourteenth Amendment applied to the states rather than individuals and that the bill did not extend to privileges and immunities that Congress could address. A similar assertion of the state action doctrine came from John D. Atkins, who added that the bill operated on the states regardless of whether they had discriminated.[405] Other Democrats asserting that the bill unconstitutionally invaded state functions included William S. Herndon,[406] Aylett H. Buckner,[407] and Milton I. Southard.[408]

Several Democrats also promoted the notion that separate but equal facilities were allowed (if not a matter of state right) under the Fourteenth Amendment. Buckner argued that the construction of the Equal Protection Clause articulated by the bill's promoters would invalidate all separation by sex in the named facilities and condemned the "interference with the rights of private property and the rules and regulations of society."[409] Atkins agreed that segregation with the enjoyment of equal advantages by both races was not inconsistent with equal protection.[410]

In the Senate, Sumner's last civil rights bill was reported in January 1874.[411] The Massachusetts senator died on March 11 while the legislation was in the Senate Judiciary Committee, and he urged the bill's passage as his last request.[412] When the bill was debated on the floor, Frelinghuysen defended it in a long speech that included characterizations similar to Sumner's:

Inns, places of amusement, and public conveyances are established and maintained by private enterprise and capital, but bear that intimate relation to the public, appealing to and depending upon its patronage for support, that the law has for many centuries measurably regulated them, leaving at the same time a wide discretion as to their administration in their proprietors. This body of law and this discretion are not disturbed by this bill, except when the one or the other discriminates on account of race, color, or previous servitude.[413]

The senator listed three grants of power from the Constitution: (1) "the thirteenth, fourteenth, and fifteenth amendments, considered together and in connection with the contemporaneous history"; (2) the Privileges and Immunities Clause of the Fourteenth Amendment; and (3) the Equal Protection Clause.[414] Citing the *Slaughter-House Cases*, he asserted that the recent amendments were intended "to wipe out every consequence of [slavery]; to prevent State legislation of every kind that discriminated on account of race, color, &c., and make the race formerly in servitude equal in all respects to other citizens."[415]

Frelinghuysen conceded that visiting inns or theaters did not constitute privileges or immunities of national citizenship, but it was, he asserted, such a privilege not to experience racial discrimination in these areas.[416] The Equal Protection Clause, he felt, prohibited all racial discrimination, not just where it reached "gross injustice and hardship" (the Court's term): "Any discrimination is injustice and hardship," and the clause prohibited "all discrimination" and favored "perfect [e]quality before the law."[417] Because Congress could not force the hand of state legislatures and could "only deal with the offenders who violate the privileges and immunities of citizens of the United States," the New Jersey senator defended the penalties the proposal imposed and similarly defended accompanying civil remedies.[418] Pratt added that the bill guaranteed common-law rights, but with a more adequate remedy than strictly judicial alternatives.[419]

Norwood maintained that the Fourteenth Amendment was similar to Article I Section 10's limitations on the states, which federal courts were intended to enforce, and "until a State shall attempt to abridge" a citizen's "rights, Congress has no power to act."[420] Thurman made a similar comparison to the original Constitution and found the Thirteenth as well as the Fourteenth Amendment to be inapplicable to individuals.[421] Morton asked him how Congress could enforce the prohibitions if they applied only to states in their corporate capacity, and Thurman, before reiterating his criticism of the bill for intervening in the absence of discriminatory laws, replied that Congress could only confer jurisdiction on federal courts.[422]

Morton justified punishing individuals on the grounds that it was impossible for Congress to "operate upon the States as such," and only Congress could be the judge of appropriate legislation.[423] The Indiana senator's views on the Equal Protection Clause were similar to Lawrence's, construing "protection" to extend to all benefits and to "forbid[] all discriminations of every character against any class of persons, being citizens of the United States."[424] Racial discrimination in places of public amusement or transportation would not be allowed since the state licensed and regulated them.[425] Morton also asserted that the framers of the Fourteenth Amendment "understood that a law passed by a State in contravention of it would be void," but he added that they intended to supplement the "roundabout and costly remedy" of pursuing the courts with penal legislation:

Rights are protected by penal enactments, by punishing the violator of them. A State makes a law. Under cover of that law one man violates the rights of another. To simply have the law declared void is no vindication of the right. That is no punishment of the criminal. We desire to protect the right by punishing the wrongdoer; and all we say is that no law made by a State in violation of this amendment shall protect the criminal from punishment. And that is the only efficient and successful enjoyment of these amendments that the people can have. That was precisely what was intended at the time the fourteenth amendment was adopted, and the discussion will show it. . . . [I]n my judgment the very highest franchise that belongs to any citizen of the United States as such is the right to go into any State and there to have the equal enjoyment of every public institution, whether it be the court, whether it be the school, or whether it be the public conveyance, or whether it be any other public institution, for pleasure, business, or enjoyment, created or regulated by law.[426]

Stockton suggested that Sumner's construction held "equal" to mean "the same" and criticized the provision on accommodations and conveyances for its intrusion into state affairs.[427] Howe emphasized that the bill merely banned racial discrimination—that it "lays not an ounce of weight upon any man of any color, but it lifts burdens from some"—and expressed alarm at Thurman's theory that the Fourteenth Amendment, for which he had voted, addressed only states and not individuals.[428] He proceeded to articulate his own view of the amendment:

I think that clause of the Constitution says . . . that every one of both the classes mentioned are citizens both of the United States and of the State in which they reside, and that no State shall impair their privileges or deny them the equal protection of the laws, and it charges the Congress of the United States to see that condition is realized by every one of these citizens. It means all that or it means nothing.[429]

Later that day, Alcorn made a speech that marked a change in position from his earlier opposition to the bill, describing theaters and public hotels as licensed institutions with public obligations and asserting the need for Congress to go forward regardless of the *Slaughter-House Cases*.[430] "Congress is called upon to legislate," the Mississippi senator concluded, "and when it comes to legislate it must legislate . . . in conformity with the Constitution—equality before the law."[431]

The Democrats then attacked the bill in an all-night filibuster.[432] Senator Henry Cooper contended that Congress lacked power to pass the act and that the contrary construction of the Fourteenth Amendment would entail congressional power to legislate against murder since a citizen's life was "the dearest of all the inalienable rights of a citizen."[433] Merrimon[434] and William Hamilton[435] found the bill an unconstitutional interference with the state's police power to regulate business and defended separate facilities for each race. During an argument between Edmunds and first-term California Republican Aaron A. Sargent over the latter's tolerance of school segregation, the Vermont senator spoke in absolute terms about congressional duty to redress discrimination based on origin or color without compromising.[436] Sargent suggested, however, that the Fourteenth Amendment did not ban racial segregation, just as it did not ban segregation by sex.[437] The civil rights bill passed the Senate by a vote of twenty-nine to sixteen.[438]

Debate on the House bill occurred on a sporadic basis for the remainder of the first session. Democrat William B. Read asserted that Congress lacked power to pass the civil rights bill,[439] and Republican Roderick R. Butler of Tennessee expressed his contentment with segregation.[440] James T. Rapier, a black representative from Alabama, described desegregation as a matter of securing rights and declared, "I am degraded as long as I am denied the public privileges common to other men."[441] Another Republican, Chester B. Darrall, promoted desegregation and predicted that public approval for it would come within five years.[442]

After their major election defeat in the fall, the "lame-duck" Republican

Congress convened for its second session in 1875.[443] In the House, John Roy Lynch, a black Mississippi representative, asserted congressional power under Sections 1 and 5 of the Fourteenth Amendment to abolish racial distinctions.[444] A debate followed soon afterward between Finck and Hale, both of whom were in the House in 1866, over the constitutionality of the measure. Finck asserted that the Fourteenth Amendment only prohibited certain forms of state action without authorizing such a congressional instrusion into local affairs, and when Hale pressed him to explain the significance of Section 5, the Democratic congressman responded "that this fifth section of the amendment confers no power upon Congress which it did not already possess."[445] Democrat Eppa Hunton articulated the same position as Finck.[446] Both he and John Ambler Smith, the conservative Virginia Republican, cited the *Slaughter-House Cases* to defend the position that the bill constituted an unwarranted invasion of state sovereignty.[447] Conservative Thomas Whitehead reached the same position from "a common-sense stand-point," expressly finding no need even to refer to the 1873 decision.[448]

Hale, whose relatively conservative position among Fourteenth Amendment supporters in 1866 has been seen, made an important concession about the original understanding of the recent amendment as expanding congressional power contrary to Finck's argument (though he seems to have forgotten that the *Congressional Globe* recorded his vote in favor of the amendment in 1866[449]):

I well remember . . . that it was my fortune, standing alone in my party, to oppose the fourteenth amendment by my vote and by my voice, upon the ground . . . that it *did* change the constitutional powers of legislation of Congress, that it changed the theory of our Government, and introduced a range of legislation by Congress utterly lacking in the old Constitution or in any previous amendments to it except the thirteenth. I voted against the fourteenth amendment on that ground alone, fully conceding the propriety of the provisions of the article, except the last section, claiming that that section was to a certain extent a revolution of our form of government in giving Congress a control of matters which had hitherto been confined exclusively to State control. In the position I then took I certainly understood in the Thirty-ninth Congress that my friend from Ohio [Finck], whose opinion on legal and constitutional questions I value highly, fully concurred. I understood that the entire body of his political associates on the other side of the House in that Congress concurred with me.[450]

Apply the Court's holding in *McCulloch* to the Fourteenth Amendment, Hale urged his colleagues,

and I ask any lawyer on this floor to tell me where he finds authority to say that under those provisions Congress is limited to legislation to correct the action of States, to provide a tribunal which may review such action, and to provide for some measure of criticism or correction of such action, and not for legislation in the first instance to remedy the great evil against which the amendment proposes to guard.[451]

Hale both asserted the constitutionality of the legislation and asserted, without revealing his own vote on the particular pending measure, that it was the duty of Congress to pass appropriate legislation to enforce the Fourteenth Amendment.[452] Democrat Lucius Q. C. Lamar, the future Supreme Court justice, pressed Hale to cite state laws that violated the Fourteenth Amendment, and Ellis H. Roberts interjected that it could not be denied "that in certain States of the Union there are no laws guaranteeing those rights to the several classes of our citizens," indicating that this omission was sufficient cause for congressional legislation.[453]

The bill, which had been amended to omit the clause desegregating schools, ultimately passed the House by a vote of 162 to 99, with twenty-eight recorded as not voting.[454] Twelve legislators in the House who had voted for the Fourteenth Amendment in Congress (one as a senator) remained, and they all voted for the Civil Rights Act along with two others who were recorded as "not voting" in 1866.[455] One representative who voted against the 1875 bill, Democrat James W. Nesmith, was in the Senate in 1866, but he had been absent for the vote on the Fourteenth Amendment.[456] None of the five representatives still in the House who had voted against the amendment in 1866 voted for the bill.[457]

The bill still awaited passage in the Senate and was debated at length on February 26, 1875. Like Alcorn in the House, George Boutwell in the Senate asserted the constitutionality of the civil rights bill and urged the need to go forward regardless of the *Slaughter-House Cases*.[458] Both he[459] and Morton[460] reiterated the latter's earlier articulated belief that the Equal Protection Clause refers to equal benefits and that the Fourteenth Amendment consequently requires complete equality before the law. "The State may make the law as it seems proper"; the Indiana senator asserted, "but whatever shall be the character of that law it must apply equally to all races upon the same precise conditions."[461] Thurman remarked that the Fourteenth Amendment did not apply to race more than other categories—ignorance of the English language, for instance—and that it covered individuals as much as it covered classes.[462] Thomas F. Bayard similarly commented that race deserved no special scrutiny and suggested that the Fourteenth Amendment additionally applied only to states, not to what he regarded as an invasion of state power for the purpose of securing "the enjoyment of each individual's supposed rights."[463] Supreme Court precedent, he added, demonstrated that "the right of a man to go into an inn or into a rail-car or a theater or concert-room . . . belongs to him as a citizen *of a State* and not as a citizen of the United States."[464]

Carpenter's earlier cited about-face was articulated the next day, February 27, though as previously explained, his position might have arisen more from deference to Supreme Court precedent than to his views on the amendment.[465] The Wisconsin senator drew distinctions between state and national privileges as Bayard had.[466] He added that the provision address-ing public conveyances "might be sustained as a regulation of commerce if confined to that commerce over which Congress possesses the power of regulation—commerce with foreign nations, among the several States, or with the Indian tribes"—but it was not accordingly confined in its wording because it applied to all transportation within the states.[467]

In the time remaining before the final Senate vote, John A. Logan asserted the necessity of the Civil Rights Act under Section 5 of the Fourteenth Amendment in view of state constitutions that (like Connecticut's) included the word "white."[468] William Hamilton called the arguments of proponents of the bill "confused, uncertain, unfixed" for their varying citation of the Privileges and Immunities Clause and Equal Protection Clause as the basis of the bill.[469] Edmunds had the last word, and he described the Constitution as

a bill of rights for the people of all the States, and no State has a right to say you invade her rights when under this Constitution and according to it you have pro-tected a right of her citizens against class prejudice, against caste prejudice, against sectarian prejudice, against the ten thousand things which in special communities may from time to time arise to disturb the peace and good order of the commu-nity.[470]

The senator denounced segregation and affirmed "common rights" that included "the right to go peaceably in the public streets, the right to enjoy the same privileges and immunities, without qualification and distinction upon arbitrary reasons, that exist in favor of all others."[471] The bill, he concluded, protected such rights, which could not be invaded on racial or religious grounds, and "those, therefore, who go fishing and talking dia-lectics about attorneys and about slaughter-house cases and police regula-tions find themselves entirely wide of the mark."[472]

The Civil Rights Act then was passed by a vote of 38 to 26, with nine recorded as absent.[473] Of the seventeen senators who were in Congress during the vote on the Fourteenth Amendment, all of them had voted for the amendment, and fifteen of them voted for the 1875 act.[474] Of the re-maining two, only Republican William Sprague voted against the bill while Lot M. Morrill was recorded as absent.[475] Even in the cases of these two legislators, it would be difficult to argue that their dispositions in 1875 reflected a long-standing embrace of the court's 1883 doctrine because both men had voted for the first Enforcement Act in 1870 and Morrill had voted for the Ku Klux Klan Act in 1871.[476] Both bills, as has been seen, were inconsistent with the Court's state action doctrine.

The debate over social equality, it finally should be noted, resurfaced in the Forty-Third Congress. Several House Democrats maintained that the bill truly imposed social equality, including Durham,[477] Herndon,[478] Atkins,[479] Southard,[480] John M. Glover,[481] Read,[482] and Ephraim K. Wilson.[483] Republicans Alonzo J. Ransier,[484] Benjamin Butler,[485] Lynch,[486] Joseph H. Rainey,[487] and Charles G. Williams[488] contended otherwise. In the Senate, Republicans Frelinghuysen[489] and Pratt[490] denied that the bill implicated social equality. The question of the Fourteenth Amendment and the bounds of "social rights" shall be explored in fuller detail in the discussion of the Court's more notorious segregation decision of 1896.

d. Conclusion: Reactions to the Court—1883 and Afterward

When the Court issued its decision in the *Civil Rights Cases*, press reactions were generally approving.[491] One such example, the Republican-affiliated *New York Times*, proclaimed,

> Finally after eight years in which the law has been practically a dead letter, the Supreme Court has decided, as it was evident it must decide, that the [Civil Rights] act was unconstitutional. But while the law has, in one sense, been inoperative, in another it has been of great influence, and that mischievous. It has kept alive a prejudice against the negroes and against the Republican Party in the South.[492]

The same paper called Harlan's dissent "a learned, candid, and able paper," but it continued, "The tendency during the war period was toward the construction he favors. Since then a reaction has set in, which, so far, is beneficial."[493] The Court's opinion thus "has satisfied public judgment, and Justice HARLAN's will hardly unsettle it."[494] Approval for the Court occurred despite rather than because of the original understanding.

Although most politicians had long given up on Reconstruction by that time, several original supporters of the Fourteenth Amendment supported Harlan's dissent. During consideration of the *Civil Rights Cases*, Harlan met with Edmunds, with whom he had become friends after the Vermont senator's initial opposition to the Kentuckian's appointment to the Supreme Court, and Edmunds maintained that Congress had fully explored the constitutional questions surrounding the Civil Rights Act. Edmunds' memo to the justice reportedly encouraged his lone dissent.[495] Conkling, who also had opposed Harlan's appointment, wrote the dissenting justice of his "admiration" and even "surprise" toward his opinion, which he predicted "will be widely accepted and adopted as the truth, seen not only, but seen with the foresight of wisdom."[496]

James F. Wilson, who in 1883 was serving as a senator, criticized the Court's decision and asserted his theory of equal protection in terms resembling Republican contentions in the preceding decade:

A failure to enact laws for the equal protection of citizens is a denial of such protection. A neglect to enforce laws enacted to assure such equal protection is a denial of it. Toleration of a custom or practice which asserts inequality in the enjoyment of the common rights of citizenship is a denial of equal protection.[497]

Wilson argued that a "State can not be punished for withholding the equal protection of the laws" and that, under the doctrine of *Prigg*, Congress could directly protect citizens as a substitute for the protection of the state.[498]

In his 1886 memoirs on his years in Congress, James G. Blaine asserted, "By decisions of the Supreme Court, the Fourteenth Amendment has been deprived in part of the power which Congress no doubt intended to impart to it."[499] Under the Court's construction, "little, if any thing, can be done by Congress to correct the evils or avert the injurious consequences arising from" various "outrages" that were

the deeds of individual citizens or of associated masses, acting without authority of law and in defiance of law. Yet when a vitiated public opinion justifies their course, and when indictment and conviction are impossible, the injured citizen loses his rights as conclusively as if the law had denied them, and indeed far more cruelly.

Undoubtedly a large proportion of the members of Congress, while following the lead of those who constructed the Fourteenth Amendment, sincerely believed that it possessed a far greater scope than judicial inquiry and decision have left to it. It is hazarding little to say that if the same political bodies which submitted the Amendment to the people could have measured both the need of its application and the insufficiency of its power, it would have been seriously changed, and would have conferred upon the National Government the unquestioned authority to protect individual citizens in the right of suffrage, so far as that suffrage is used in the choice of officers of the United States. The opportunity was neglected and may never return.[500]

This is a revealing commentary, though its criticism of the amendment seems to be based on a certain view of interpretation that allows text (or at least one potential view of text) to outweigh the meaning imparted by the framers. Henry B. Brown, who would articulate the "separate but equal" doctrine for the Court in 1896, admitted in 1912 on the issue of the *Civil Rights Cases* that "there is still a lingering doubt whether the spirit of the [Reconstruction] amendments was not sacrificed to the letter."[501]

Most Americans paid little attention to the 1883 decision, and protests tended to come from a small minority who remained committed to the goals of Reconstruction long after the nation had largely abandoned them.[502] This is not to say that such protests were not intense. In 1872, Frederick Douglass had condemned the Democratic platform's denial of federal power "to protect the liberties of its citizens in the States" as its "most dangerous feature," and he found the final sections of the Thirteenth, Fourteenth, and Fifteenth Amendments to be their "very essence" without which they "may be evaded and practically rendered null and void."[503] Soon after the *Civil Rights Cases* were handed down, Douglass acknowledged his lack of legal training and inability to speak on constitutional matters, but he felt he could assert that the Court "has utterly ignored and rejected the force and application of object and intention as a rule of interpretation. It has construed the Constitution in defiant disregard of what was the object and intention of the adoption of the Fourteenth Amendment."[504] T. Thomas Fortune, a prominent black journalist, lamented after the *Civil Rights Cases* were decided, "The colored people . . . feel today as they have been baptized in ice water."[505] Robert G. Ingersoll, an attorney and civil rights advocate, asserted that the Court's decision "carries the doctrine of 'State rights' to the Democratic extreme, and renders necessary either another amendment or a new court."[506]

Ingersoll's statement should be qualified by noting that the Court would not quite adopt the most extreme Democratic views of the Fourteenth Amendment as a means of correcting discriminatory state legislation only. In *Yick Wo v. Hopkins* (1886), the Court would unanimously strike down an ordinance that, while racially neutral on its face, was blatantly discriminatory against the Chinese in its administration, and it acknowledged the role of the Equal Protection Clause in controlling the execution of the laws.[507] Still, it is difficult to deny that the Court's opinion in 1883 embraced the views of the opponents of the Fourteenth Amendment and Reconstruction, not those of its framers and other supporters.

Avins is one of the few scholars who does try to deny this, but his analysis ultimately contains conclusions that are unsupported even before questioning his premises.[508] His rejection of the idea that "Radicals deemed Negroes to be the special pets of the law" and his characterization of legislation banning racial discrimination in privately owned businesses as "a denial of equal protection to white persons who could have been rejected on non-racial grounds" sounds more like a rehash of old Democratic beliefs than a true originalist analysis.[509] Avins also places faith in the justices' ability in 1883 to interpret the law in accordance with originalist assumptions without considering the fluctuating historical, political, and institutional contexts in which they were operating.[510]

In addition to the contemporary constructions articulated in this study, several commentators have recognized the understanding of supporters (even taking into account its variations among different Republicans) that the Fourteenth Amendment applies to individuals as well as states and that the state action doctrine contains little pedigree in the legislative debates.[511] The Reconstruction Congresses were interested in congressional power more than federal judicial power[512] and in private action more than state action.[513] Accompanying this priority was the aspiration for congressional power affirmatively to secure equal privileges and immunities to citizens.[514] This point is further supported by the history of the Civil Rights Act of 1866 and Section 2 of the Thirteenth Amendment, which elucidates the pattern of interpretation intended for Section 5 of the Fourteenth Amendment.[515]

Even the notion that the Court adhered to Democratic sentiment is problematic. Before its passage, opponents asserted their fear that the Fourteenth Amendment would centralize the government, yet after its ratification, the same faction in Congress attempted to narrow their interpretation through legal theories that had failed to persuade Congress to defeat the amendment in the first place. As Horace E. Flack put it, "What the one [party] regarded as essential to the Amendment to make it effective, the other regarded as dangerous."[516] Having lost the battle to defeat the amendment, the opponents of Reconstruction employed new interpretations that the Court would incorporate into American constitutional jurisprudence—interpretations that effectively repealed much of Section 5 of the Fourteenth Amendment.

4. *Baldwin v. Franks*

The Court's decision in *Baldwin v. Franks* (1887)[1] carried on the doctrine it had been formulating since Reconstruction. In this case, § 5519, the provision voided in *Harris*, was applied along with §§ 5508 and 5336 to a conspiracy of intimidation and violence against "a class of Chinese aliens" in California, the victims of which were driven from their homes and jobs, having been subject to false imprisonment and sent out of their home county on a steamboat barge.[2] Section 5508 was taken from § 6 of the first Enforcement Act,[3] and § 5336 dealt with seditious conspiracy against the federal government, including the execution of its laws.[4] Included in the case was the issue of rights, privileges, and immunities granted to Chinese aliens by treaties between the United States and China, and while the Court did not doubt the federal government's power to punish those who deprived the Chinese of treaty-secured rights, the question it faced was whether Congress had addressed such a situation.[5]

Regarding § 5519, the Court was presented with the argument that *Baldwin* was distinguishable from *Harris* because it involved a conspiracy to deprive aliens of rights granted by treaty, citing "the well settled rule that a statute may be in part constitutional and in part unconstitutional, and that under some circumstances the part which is constitutional will be enforced, and only that which is unconstitutional rejected."[6] Writing for the Court, Chief Justice Waite rejected this argument on the grounds that the statute was not capable of such separation and cited *Reese*'s holdings for support.[7] The Court could not reach the contrary result, he added, without overruling *Harris* (which it would not do).[8] Waite rejected § 5508 as a basis for punishment by reading its use of the word "citizen" to mean the same as it does in the Fourteenth Amendment without extending it to someone who might be "a person only or an inhabitant."[9] Section 5336 also was deemed insufficient because it involved no attempt to prevent the government from exercising its authority: "The force was exerted in opposition to a class of persons who had the right to look to the government for protection against such wrongs, not in opposition to the government while actually engaged in an attempt to afford that protection."[10]

The Court's holding this time was seven to two. Waite's docket book reveals that Bradley and Harlan initially voted to affirm the convictions with Field and Woods not voting, but Bradley later changed his vote, and only Field decided along with Harlan to dissent.[11] The more senior dissenter's disagreement with the Court was confined to his construction of §§ 5336 and 5508,[12] but Harlan's differences were broader, including an affirmation of the constitutionality of § 5519 with arguments following classic Republican theory on Section 5 of the Fourteenth Amendment.[13]

E. THE TRIUMPH OF SEGREGATION

1. *Louisville v. Mississippi:* Segregation and the Interstate Commerce Clause Revisited

Having invalidated congressional power to enact desegregation during the 1880s, the Supreme Court would face the segregation issue in other contexts during the 1890s, at which time it would have the chance to reveal whether it would recognize alternate channels for desegregation to prevail. The issue returned to the Court, though in the Commerce Clause context, in *Louisville v. Mississippi* (1890),[1] a case involving an indictment of a railroad company for failing to provide separate but equal accommodations on its lines as dictated by a Mississippi law.[2] In a brief decision by Justice Brewer, the Court held that the law did not constitute a regulation of interstate commerce and therefore concluded that it was not beyond state power.[3] The decision was distinguished from *DeCuir* in that the Louisiana Supreme Court had ruled that the law at issue in the 1879 case imposed desegregation on interstate carriers.[4] Here, Brewer explained, the Mississippi Supreme Court had construed the segregation statute to affect only intrastate commerce.[5]

"Without considering other grounds upon which . . . the statute in question might properly be held to be repugnant to the Constitution of the United States," Harlan dissented from the Court's judgment on Commerce Clause grounds.[6] Finding the Court's distinctions unconvincing and discussing the nature of the commerce at issue, Harlan remarked, "I am unable to perceive how" the law in *DeCuir* "is a regulation of interstate commerce, and" this Mississippi law "is not."[7] This time, Bradley joined

Harlan in dissent, leaving one to speculate whether he had omitted to discuss railroad segregation under the Commerce Clause in the *Civil Rights Cases* because he differed on the issue with other justices who joined his majority opinion.[8] If any doubt remained about the ultimate status of segregation under the Reconstruction amendments after *Louisville*, the Court would dispel it six years later.

2. *Plessy v. Ferguson*

a. The Court's Opinion

In 1896, the Court decided the status of segregation under the Fourteenth Amendment in the famous case of *Plessy v. Ferguson*.[1] The petitioner was a man "of seven eighths Caucasian and one eighth African blood" who was arrested in Louisiana for refusing to comply with orders to vacate a railroad car that was designated for whites in accordance with an 1890 Louisiana statute requiring railroad companies to provide "equal but separate accommodations for the white, and colored races" in their coaches.[2]

Writing for the Court, Justice Brown rejected the contention that the Louisiana law conflicted with the Thirteenth Amendment since it "implies merely a legal distinction between the white and colored races" and thus "has no tendency to destroy the legal equality of the two races, or reestablish a state of involuntary servitude."[3] Turning to the Fourteenth Amendment, he both rejected the notion that the amendment abolished racial distinctions and advocated a key characterization of the right that was claimed as a social right:

> The object of the amendment was undoubtedly to enforce the absolute equality of the two races before the law, but in the nature of things it could not have been intended to abolish distinctions based upon color, or to enforce social, as distinguished from political equality, or a commingling of the two races upon terms unsatisfactory to either.[4]

The opinion distinguished "between laws interfering with the political equality of the negro and those requiring the separation of the two races in schools, theatres and railway carriages."[5] Thus, unlike segregation, jury discrimination "implied a legal inferiority in civil society, which lessened the security of the right of the colored race, and was a step toward reducing them to a condition of servility."[6]

The Court cited *Louisville* as "almost directly in point"[7] and asserted that "as applied to the internal commerce of the State," segregation by law does not violate the provisions of Section 1 of the Fourteenth Amendment.[8] The Fourteenth Amendment question thus was reduced to whether the legislation was reasonable, a question the Court answered affirmatively.[9] (In its consideration, the opinion referred to "the established usages, customs and traditions of the people,"[10] but in fact, Southern segregation laws in Louisiana and elsewhere were quite recent.[11]) Brown added that social equality could come about only as "the result of natural affinities," not by legislation, and "[i]f one race be inferior to the other socially, the Constitution of the United States cannot put them upon the same plane."[12] The Court further left "the question of the proportion of colored blood necessary to constitute a colored person" to the states in upholding the statute.[13] Seven justices were in the majority, and Brewer did not participate.[14]

b. Justice Harlan's Dissent

Observing that Louisiana "regulates the use of a public highway by citizens of the United States solely upon the basis of race,"[15] Harlan, again in lone dissent, asserted, "In respect of civil rights, common to all citizens, the Constitution of the United States does not . . . permit any public authority to know the race of those entitled to be protected in the enjoyment of such rights."[16] Without expressly saying so, the dissent had contradicted the majority's characterization of the rights at issue as social rather than civil rights.

Harlan interestingly cited the original understanding to support his argument. The Thirteenth and Fourteenth Amendments, "if enforced according to their true intent and meaning, will protect all the civil rights that pertain to freedom and citizenship."[17] Under the jury discrimination cases, the dissenting justice argued that the Constitution prohibits racial discrimination in civil and political rights, including jury service, and he suggested that under the Court's reasoning, black and white jurors could be separated by a "partition" in the courtroom and during their deliberation.[18]

Harlan added with candor that everyone knew the Louisiana statute was drafted to exclude blacks rather than whites "under the guise of giving equal accommodation for whites and blacks," and he pointed out that the statutory scheme included punishment for failure to abide by it.[19] After commenting on the need for the judiciary to defer to the will of the legislature,[20] Harlan asserted that, despite his belief that the white race would remain dominant,

in the eye of the law, there is in this country no superior, dominant, ruling class of citizens. There is no caste here. Our Constitution is color-blind, and neither knows nor tolerates classes among citizens. In respect of civil rights, all citizens are equal before the law. . . . The law regards man as man, and takes no account of his surroundings or of his color when his civil rights as guaranteed by the supreme law of the land are involved.[21]

Harlan predicted that the Court's opinion would "prove to be quite as pernicious as" the *Dred Scott* decision and encourage the belief that state laws could be used "to defeat the beneficent purposes which the people of the United States had in view when they adopted the recent amendments of the Constitution."[22] He added that the "destinies of the two races, in this country, are indissolubly linked together" and that the segregation statute threatened to instill "race hate" that would undermine both races' interests.[23] Separating citizens by race on a public highway, he maintained, "is a badge of servitude wholly inconsistent with the civil freedom and the equality before the law established by the Constitution."[24] In Harlan's view, the law at issue clearly was premised on the inferiority of black citizens, and the justice closed by condemning the prospect of "sinister legislation" throughout the country that violated the Constitution.[25]

c. The Court's Opinion in View of Contemporary Understandings

Much of the trouble with the Court's opinion from the standpoint of originalism already has been demonstrated by the abundant support the Court had for its decision in *Railroad Co. v. Brown*.[26] Although that particular issue of segregation predated the Reconstruction amendments, it reveals an understanding of equality in the segregation context that usually was not addressed in the debates of the 1860s.

Even besides specific references to segregation in transportation, however, the debates contain numerous references to the assumptions on which segregation rests. Two key propositions on which the Court and Harlan differed were the notions that (1) the right at issue was one of social rather than civil equality, and thus not addressed by the Fourteenth Amendment; and (2) the amendment did not abolish racial distinctions in law (at least omitting the issue of voting rights, which may be seen as exceptional under Section 2).

Looking first at the question of social equality (or the freedom of association) throughout Reconstruction, one finds a familiar division between Democrats and Republicans, though the subject tended to be brought up sporadically before the debates over the civil rights legislation of the 1870s. In 1864, Hendricks equated the absence of separate railroad cars for the races with forcing social equality between them.[27] During the Civil Rights Act debates in 1866, Democratic Representative John L. Dawson equated demands for social equality with efforts to integrate hotels, railroad cars, and churches, among other egalitarian goals.[28] Like Dawson, Doolittle, during debates over the Fifteenth Amendment, considered the imposition of social equality to be the goal of political equality in states containing as many blacks as whites.[29]

Once Summer's civil rights amendment became an issue, opponents of Reconstruction raised the charge of social equality with greater frequency. Thurman described the measure as aiming to secure "the most absolute social equality" under the guise of rights, privileges, and immunities of

citizenship.[30] Similar charges from Eli Saulsbury[31] and Norwood[32] already
have been seen. Garrett Davis both denied that the Fourteenth Amendment
guaranteed desegregated facilities and added that in fact there was a "right
to make the association exclusive as to color" in this context.[33] Thurman
extolled the value of the liberty of association and of the freedom to choose
members of one's social circle.[34] In the House, King denounced Sumner's
"social equality bill,"[35] and Stockton called it "a singular interference undoubtedly with the social rights of the people which was never contemplated in the Constitution."[36] Rice predicted that "this sudden innovation
on our social customs will be severely felt" when public conveyances were
desegregated.[37] He also added that passing the provision of the Sumner bill
abolishing the word "white" in laws "more shamelessly than even the proceeding [sections], parades the scheme of social equality for the blacks and
whites of the South contemplated by this bill."[38]

Figures in the emerging Liberal Republican movement concurred in the
Democratic interpretation. "[B]y discriminating between 'civil' or 'legal
rights' and 'social privileges,' " James G. Blair contended, "we can see that
the object of the bill is to force 'negro social equality' upon the white people
under the most remarkable penalties."[39] The Liberal Republican congressman added that the Republican vote against a House resolution declaring
it unconstitutional to desegregate various public accommodations and
modes of transportation "shows clearly a settled purpose . . . to force negroes into railway and streetcars, hotels, and theaters. . . . Thus . . . by act
of Congress are the white people of this country to be coerced into social
equality with the negroes."[40] Trumbull asserted that what Sumner "calls a
civil rights bill is not a civil rights bill at all," but a measure "proposing
to establish social rights which is unconstitutional in its provisions."[41]

The Forty-Third Congress saw similar comments from Democrats about
the civil rights bill. Alexander Stephens argued that there was "a vast difference between civil rights proper and some of those social rights claimed
by this bill."[42] "You may say these are not social relations provided for in
this bill;" Durham told one of his opponents, "but, sir, if I am compelled
to sit side by side with" the freedman "in the theater, the stage-coach, and
the railroad car, to eat with him at the same table at the hotels, and my
child to be educated at the same schools with his child—if these are not
social relations I do not understand them."[43] Buckner asserted, "It is not
civil rights but social rights that" the bill "seeks to enforce and protect,"
and he found it "inconceivable" that the Equal Protection Clause applied
to the legislation's enumerated rights.[44]

Atkins termed "social equality," the aim he saw behind the bill, as "the
ultima thule of these modern philanthropists and negrophilists."[45] Southard
similarly described the desegregation measure as an attempt "to confer, by
force of law, social privileges—not civil rights as such. It compels to a social

companionship in many of the relations of life that may be against the will and repugnant to the situation, disposition, and tastes of the individual."[46] Glover maintained that the bill infringed on the freedom of association and "should be denominated a bill to regulate the associations, companionship, tastes, and feelings of the people."[47] Vance also found the bill a misnomer on the grounds that it protected only social rights.[48] Read argued that the bill established "beyond doubts . . . what the negro means by civil rights"— "perfect social equality of the races in all the departments of life," which would become "the degradation of the whole country" if it were imposed on Southern whites.[49] Finally, for Ephraim Wilson, "Equal rights do not require identity in time and place of enjoyment; equal privileges do not demand the thrusting of one race upon the other in almost every possible social relation outside of the family circle."[50]

Turning to the Republican proponents of Reconstruction, as seen previously, one finds enough support for the proposition that Congress did not intend to interfere with social rights. The entire difference in the constitutional debate, however, lies in the definitions of social versus civil rights the Republicans employed. It is thus important not to treat social equality and the freedom of association as if all factions shared the Democratic conceptions of these terms.[51]

When Republicans discussed social equality, they tended to do so in contexts conducive to denying that their sought legislation imposed it on society. During Senate debates over the enfranchisement of blacks in Washington, D.C., in 1866, Waitman Willey denied that the "equal enjoyment by the white man and the black man" of the "right of suffrage" could "in anywise change the personal identity of either or affect their social relations."[52] The senator proceeded to observe that the term social rights simply referred to matters beyond the reach of legislation: "Social relations cannot be regulated by law. They are beyond its power. They are not the legitimate subject of legal regulation. Social equality is a matter of taste, of feeling, and of every man's unfettered sense of propriety."[53] In another speech arguing for the ballot for blacks, Senator James W. Patterson, who had been in the House during the vote on the Fourteenth Amendment,[54] maintained that the question was "purely political" and added that the "social status of men is determined by original capacity, and cannot be fixed or safely tampered with by legislation."[55]

During debates over his civil rights amendment, Sumner used a quotation from Frederick Douglass to refute Trumbull's charges of imposing social equality: "We do not aim at any such thing. The colored people desire nothing so intangible. It is unknown to the laws of this country or any other country. I understand what is meant by equality before the law, but social equality I am entirely ignorant of."[56] Indeed, the preeminent black advocate of civil rights for former slaves joined Republicans in distancing the concept of civil rights from that of social equality. Douglass again would deny the social equality characterization in more adamant terms in his later denunciation of the *Civil Rights Cases.*[57]

It will be recalled that President Grant distanced his appeal for civil rights legislation from the notion of social equality in his Second Inaugural Address, stating that "[s]ocial equality is not a subject to be legislated upon."[58] In the new session of Congress, Joseph Rainey, the first black member of the House, prefaced his argument for the civil rights bill by remarking, "Now, gentlemen, let me say the negro is not asking social equality."[59] The opposition's social equality argument became so common that the congressman attacked it as the "bugbear of 'social equality,' " which "the enemies of political and civil equality for the colored man" were using "in place of argument"[60] while Cain called it the opposition's "great bugaboo."[61] The "establishment and regulation" of social equality, in Cain's view, "is not within the province of legislation. No laws enacted by legislators can compel social equality."[62] He even added at one point on behalf of black people, "We have some objections to social equality ourselves, very grave ones."[63] Stowell asserted, "There is no question of social equality in this bill. Gentlemen may choose their personal associates as they please; they may be white or black, or between the two; that is their choice, and no one proposes to interfere with it."[64]

In the Senate, Frelinghuysen asserted that the civil rights bill "does not touch the subject of social equality.... The law which regulates that is found only in the tastes and affinities of the mind; its law is the arbitrary, uncontrolled human will. You cannot enact it."[65] Pratt articulated a similar sentiment in greater detail:

The negro does not seek nor does this bill give him any of your peculiar social rights and privileges. You may still select your own society and invite whom you will to your table. No negro, against your will, may cross your threshold. You may travel in your own private conveyance, occupy your own room at the hotel and have your meals there, and the vision of the colored man will not disturb your serenity. But if you will travel in a public conveyance, you must be content to share your convenience with the Indian, negro, Turk, Italian, Swede, Norwegian, or any other foreigner who avails himself of the same facility, because it is public, and should therefore be open to all. And so, if you choose to set down at a public table in a public inn open to all comers who behave themselves, you must be content to sit beside or opposite to somebody whose skin or language, manners or religion, may shock your sensibilities. No law will force you to talk to him or even look at him, much less make his acquaintance. You may wrap yourself up in your exclusiveness as much as you please, and neither this bill nor any other will compel you to accept or extend any civilities you do not willingly vouchsafe.[66]

The following session of Congress saw the reiteration of earlier Republican arguments in the House. "I repel and repudiate the idea that there is any intention by the provisions of any one of these bills to make social equality," Benjamin Butler asserted. "That is simply an argument to the prejudice."[67] The Massachusetts congressman distinguished the issue "of a common right in a public conveyance" from that of social equality and argued that people under the bill could still associate with whomever they wished.[68] Calling the notion that the bill's passage "can in any manner affect the social status of any one . . . absurd and ridiculous," Lynch pointed out that social distinctions existed between whites who enjoyed the same rights and privileges.[69] "[I]t is not social rights that we desire," he concluded, but "protection in the enjoyment of *public* rights."[70] Rainey[71] and Charles G. Williams[72] described social rights as matters of individual tastes lying beyond the law.

In the end, it is difficult to support the Court's characterization of the rights involved in either *Plessy* or the *Civil Rights Cases* as social rights because such a notion was vehemently denied by supporters of Reconstruction, including several framers of the Fourteenth Amendment. It is clear that, unless one embraces the doctrine of the opponents of civil rights measures during Reconstruction, the Fourteenth Amendment was understood as reaching businesses that were clothed with the public interest and accompanying responsibilities.[73] When they disclaimed the role of social equality in their efforts, Republicans generally were referring simply to matters that they deemed to be beyond the understood reach of the law. Surely, the context of public accommodations and conveyances, long understood to be subject to considerable regulation in the public interest regardless of their private ownership, did not fall into this category.

The "separate but equal" doctrine surfaced in additional contexts during Reconstruction, and it sparked many divisions in Congress. One interesting discussion occurred among several Pennsylvania congressmen a few months before the Fourteenth Amendment was ratified in 1868 when Democrat George W. Woodward cited *West Chester & Philadelphia R.R. v. Miles*, an 1867 Pennsylvania case allowing railroads to segregate blacks.[74] Woodward spoke at length in support of the decision's advocacy of the "separate but equal" doctrine,[75] but several of his colleagues interjected comments. George V. E. Lawrence, a remaining Whig who had voted for the Fourteenth Amendment,[76] contended that nine out of ten people in northwestern Pennsylvania supported the decision and added his own endorsement of it.[77] Woodward said he believed that most Pennsylvania Republicans supported the court, but Pennsylvania Republican Thomas Williams, in seeming disapproval of the decision, retorted that it was truly about one out of every five.[78]

Glenni W. Scofield denied Lawrence's claim as another representative of northwestern Pennsylvania, and he contemptuously remarked of the decision that "no class of citizens indorse" it "except political partisans who concur in the sentiments of that decision because it was their political opinion before."[79] When Lawrence added that Republican papers in his district endorsed the opinion along with "nine out of every ten of the thinking, sensible men of the country," Williams replied that he was mistaken.[80] Blaine also interjected to ask Woodward whether a white person would have been forced out of the railroad car for refusing, as a black woman did in the Pennsylvania case, to comply with the segregated arrangement.[81] Williams, Scofield, and Blaine all had voted for the Fourteenth Amendment.[82]

Besides Lawrence, Lot Morrill provides a rare example of a legislator who voted for the Fourteenth Amendment supporting segregation. His case is a bit more dubious, however, because he had voted for Sumner's earlier cited desegregation amendments in 1864,[83] and his speech tolerating segregation came in 1872. Nonetheless, he took the opportunity during consideration of Sumner's civil rights amendment to suggest that integrating the enumerated facilities could not be characterized as privileges and immunities under the Fourteenth Amendment and that Congress lacked the power it was trying to assert.[84] Morrill did not directly defend the "separate but equal" doctrine, devoting more time to attacking congressional intrusion into inns and places of public amusement (he tolerated desegregating "common carriers" on "national highways"),[85] but it certainly would not follow from his observations that the Fourteenth Amendment bars states from imposing segregation. The other Republican framer who tolerated segregation, whose situation should be familiar enough to the reader at this point not to find it exceptional, was Trumbull. The Illinois senator maintained in 1872 that the Civil Rights Act of 1866 "went to the verge of constitutional authority," and he expressed opposition to congressional efforts to desegregate railroads.[86]

In the Forty-Third Congress, two other Republicans who were not in Congress in 1866 expressed a belief in constitutional tolerance of segregation. Sargent asserted that there was no harm in segregated cars of equal quality on a train that carried all of its occupants at the same speed.[87] Roderick Butler found the "separate but equal" notion acceptable and contended that blacks themselves complained only of not being given accommodations on railroad cars that were as good as those given whites.[88]

Moving beyond sparse and dubious exceptions, there is strong evidence during the Reconstruction debates among Republican framers of the Fourteenth Amendment and their future allies that refutes the *Plessy* Court. This remaining evidence can be placed into two categories: statements that support the proposition that the Fourteenth Amendment abolishes all racial distinctions, thus refuting a fundamental assumption of the *Plessy* Court, and statements expressly supporting desegregation under the Constitution.

Congressional intentions to abolish all racial distinctions in the Thirty-Ninth Congress were manifested before the 1866 Civil Rights Act was debated. During a debate over black suffrage in the nation's capital in January 1866, Farnsworth acknowledged the existence of racial distinctions in the

laws of many states and hoped he would see "these disgraceful distinctions
. . . blotted out immediately in all the States."[89] That same month, Bingham
expressed his desire to have "the American people" approve "the foundation principle" in the proposed new amendment of "the absolute equality
of all citizens of the United States politically and civilly before their own
laws."[90]

When he introduced the Civil Rights Act, the effect of which should be
considered part of Section 1 of the Fourteenth Amendment, Trumbull indicated the measure's intention to secure "practical freedom" to "all persons within the United States," noting that the "laws in the slaveholding
States have made a distinction against persons of African descent on account of their color, whether free or slave."[91] "The purpose of the bill
under consideration," he declared, "is to destroy all these discriminations,
and to carry into effect the [Thirteenth] constitutional amendment."[92] Edgar Cowan, the pro-Johnson Republican, construed the bill as extending
beyond "the abolition of slave codes" and as effecting "the abolition of all
laws in the States which create distinctions between black men and white
ones."[93] Jacob Howard emphasized that the bill went only as far as to
establish "that in respect to all civil rights . . . there is to be hereafter no
distinction between the white race and the black race."[94] Reverdy Johnson
argued that the bill extended beyond race and prevented states from making
distinctions between foreigners and those who were native-born.[95] Condemning "caste exclusion," William Fessenden asked his colleagues, "what
are the objections to putting into the Constitution at once a provision doing
away with all distinctions of this kind?"[96] Garrett Davis pointed out that
"[s]ome of the States make a difference between the civil rights of white
and black people" and asked whether Congress was ready to concede the
principle behind such a "bill declaring that all those differences shall cease,
and that all the people of every State, black and white, shall have the same
civil rights *eo nomine*."[97]

The goal of abolishing racial distinctions also came up during the House
debates over the Civil Rights Act. Thaddeus Stevens called his proposition
for the bill that "[a]ll national and State laws shall be equally applicable
to every citizen, and no discrimination shall be made on account of race
or color" the "genuine proposition" that he loved and hoped the nation
would adopt.[98] Henry Raymond summarized one purpose of the bill as
providing "for that class of persons thus made citizens protection against
anticipated inequality of legislation in the several States."[99] Bingham described the proposal's aim as "[s]imply to strike down by congressional
enactment every State constitution which makes a discrimination on account of race or color in any of the civil rights of the citizen."[100]

Expressing some skepticism toward those attempting to conceptualize
"civil rights" as separate from "political rights," the Ohio congressman, in
his speech denying constitutional power to pass the bill, further defined the

former as including "every right that pertains to the citizen under the Constitution, laws, and Government of this country."[101] The provision of the bill banning "discrimination in civil rights or immunities among citizens of the United States in any State or Territory" based on "race, color, or previous condition of slavery" was eventually stricken out on Bingham's motion in favor of the bill's final form, though James F. Wilson explained that the change did not materially alter the bill; certain rights were specified for the purpose of allaying fears by some that the act would be construed as conferring the right to vote.[102]

William Lawrence's subsequent statement confirmed that the omission was meant to resolve Bingham's reservations, but he added that "this nation must settle the question whether among her own citizens there may be a discrimination in the enjoyment of civil rights."[103] It would not be an unwarranted contention that Wilson was understating the situation when he downplayed the significance of the change in language because other legislators clearly were concerned about it. Nevertheless, even insofar as the provision's deletion made a difference, that would merely suggest that the Civil Rights Act was narrower than the Fourteenth Amendment[104] and in fact fuel the argument that the latter, having employed terms at least as broad as the omitted provision, effected at least as sweeping an abolition of racial distinctions as the 1866 statute before its change. State debates over the ratification of the Fourteenth Amendment, it should be added, included statements supporting the notion that the provision would ban racial distinctions in state law.[105]

General admonitions against racial distinctions resurfaced in the years following the Fourteenth Amendment's passage. While pushing an 1867 amendment to ban discrimination in officeholding and jury eligibility in Washington, D.C., Sumner expressed his desire to "punch that word 'white' out of the statute-book wherever it appears."[106] Noting the jury and officeholding limitations of the amendment, Senator Samuel C. Pomeroy was "willing to go for what I can piece by piece," but he preferred "to bring in one bill to make a clean sweep of the whole legislation on this subject" of racial distinctions.[107] Five months before his death in August 1868, Thaddeus Stevens asserted that whenever someone "undertakes to make a distinction between the black race and our own because of the color of the skin or the formation of the body he forgets his God, and his God will forget him."[108]

The exclusion of voting rights might have muddled the understanding of the Fourteenth Amendment's abolition of racial distinctions somewhat, but not enough to support the Court's conclusions. During debates over the Fifteenth Amendment, when Sumner suggested that Congress make "a guarantee of equal rights universally" by providing that "there shall be no discrimination in any rights on account of race or color," Charles Drake suggested that it would be unnecessary in view of both Section 1 of the

Fourteenth Amendment and the proposal under consideration.[109] Although his party had been defeated in its attempt to ban racial discrimination in voting, John Sherman asserted that the "great body of the party to which I belong have long been in favor of dispensing with and repealing all discriminations on account of color."[110] Joseph Fowler, discontent with the sought amendment, suggested that suffrage should be bestowed even more universally, if in fact "we have arrived at the point of declaring that there are no distinctions whatever so far as citizens are concerned, that we no longer legislate for black men or white men or red men, but legislate for the citizens of the country, for the people alone."[111]

During debates over the Ku Klux Klan Act, Sumner pointed out the bill's "conformity with the Declaration of Independence and with the Constitution of the United States, neither of which knows anything of the word 'white.' "[112] Even Frank Blair's articulation of the Democratic theory that the Fourteenth Amendment addressed only state legislation (which, of course, was involved in *Plessy*) admitted that "[i]t was against discriminating State laws or regulations that both the civil rights bill and the fourteenth amendment were directed."[113]

During the debates over the Sumner civil rights bill during the 1870s, Eli Saulsbury acknowledged the "fanaticism in the land bordering on insanity that affects to regard no distinction between the races," and the Delaware Democrat criticized this phenomenon as the product of "an abnormal condition of mind that excites both pity and contempt."[114] Henry Wilson expressed that he would vote for the proposal precisely because it vindicated what he saw as an understanding that "[w]hatever differences of opinion there may be in regard to" the proposition of white superiority, "one thing is clear, that there should be no [racial] distinction recognized by the laws of the land."[115] Edmunds asserted plainly that race and color were distinctions the states could not make.[116]

Additional informative statements were included in the last month of debate over the 1875 act. "The duty of the law-maker," Lynch asserted, "is to know no race, no color, no religion, no nationality, except to prevent distinctions on any of these grounds, so far as the law is concerned."[117] Republican Representative Stephen W. Kellogg made a similar assertion about "distinctions[s] of color, race, or birthplace" in legislation.[118] In the Senate, Logan asserted the necessity of the bill even in Northern states by pointing out that Connecticut's constitution contained the word "white," which violated the Equal Protection Clause.[119]

Besides legislative support for his views against racial distinctions in the law, the closely analogous propositions in Harlan's dissent that the Constitution forbids class or caste legislation and that it is color-blind also appear in the debates. In 1866, Bingham asserted, "Let the laws which we pass here be of such pure republican character that no person can tell from the reading of them what color is stamped upon the faces of the citizens of the United States. Let us have no class legislation, no class privileges."[120] Ignatius Donnelly found it "as plain to my mind as the sun at noonday, that we must make all the citizens of the country equal before the law; that we must break down all walls of caste; that we must offer equal opportunities to all men."[121] Fessenden agreed with Sumner "that a caste exclusion is entirely contrary to the spirit of our Government, or of any republican form of government."[122] Howard told the Senate in his address introducing the final form of the Fourteenth Amendment in Fessenden's absence that Section 1 "abolishes all class legislation in the States and does away with the injustice of subjecting one caste of persons to a code not applicable to another."[123]

In his earlier cited speech in 1868,[124] James Patterson made a significant observation about the need to adhere to color-blindness despite his conception of the inability to enact social equality:

We cannot level the earth while its internal forces are at work; neither can we bring society to a social equality while the original forces of character are unequally distributed; but social and intellectual differences cannot be made an excuse for any class monopoly of political power. Equality before the law is the groundwork of our civil fabric. Every republic ignores race and class, and assumes sufficient knowledge and self-direction in the people to render them capable of establishing and administering their civil and political institutions.[125]

Similar sentiments followed over the next several years of the Reconstruction Congress. Fowler asserted that "our principle of government recognizes no races."[126] Morton declared that the Fourteenth Amendment "was intended to strike at all class legislation, to provide that laws must be general in their effects."[127] The Indiana senator later made similar statements: "Every discrimination against the negro as a class is denying to them the equal protection of the laws. . . . This amendment was intended to destroy caste, to put all races upon an equality."[128] Rapier identified the phenomenon Congress faced in 1874 as "a desire to establish a system of 'caste,' an anti-republican principle," under which "a drunken white man" was "superior to the most sober and orderly" black man.[129]

The statements against racial distinctions and caste legislation, which undermined the Court's general premises, were supplemented by statements suggesting more specifically that segregation as it confronted the Court in 1896 was inconsistent with the equality under the law that the Reconstruction Congress was incorporating into law. The pre–Thirteenth Amendment context of Washington, D.C., streetcar discrimination has already been reviewed, and that issue clearly linked the desegregation of public conveyances to the absence of racial distinctions.[130] Beyond a warning from Garrett Davis that the Civil Rights Act of 1866 would entail desegregating public accommodations and conveyances, abolishing "discriminations" that were "established by ordinances, regulations, and customs,"[131] more specific suggestions of the Fourteenth Amendment's relationship to segregation in 1866 before congressional passage are generally absent.[132] This is not to suggest, however, that there is warrant to conclude that the original understanding permitted state-sponsored segregation.[133] Not every specific manifestation of an amendment's general principle can be expected to arise in congressional debate before passage. Several newspapers and at least one state legislator did maintain that the Fourteenth Amendment would ban segregation during state ratification debates.[134] The most helpful indication of the original understanding under the circumstances would be statements on segregation by members of Congress after ratification in contexts similar to those that would face the Court.

Thurman criticized the notion of desegregation at length during the Ku Klux Klan Act debates in 1871, but he acknowledged that Sumner's views of segregation in public accommodations, transportation, and schools as entailing "a deprivation of . . . rights, privileges, and immunities" were shared by other senators.[135] Sumner indeed found that the "principle of separation on the ground of hereditary inferiority is the distinctive essence of Caste."[136] He asserted the inconsistency between segregation and the requirement of equality before the law in defense of his civil rights amendment:

[T]his plain requirement is not satisfied, logically or reasonably, by these two concessions [of the right to testify and the right to vote], so that when they are recognized all others are trifles. The court-house and ballot-box are not the only places for the rule. These two are not the only institutions for its operation. The rule is general; how then restrict it to two cases? It is, all are equal before the law—not merely before the law in two cases, but before the law in all cases without limitation or exception. . . .

The new-made citizen is called to travel for business, for health, or for pleasure, but here his trials begin. The doors of the public hotel . . . close against him, and the public conveyances, which the common law declares equally free to all alike, have no such freedom for him. . . .

. . . Separate hotels, separate conveyances, separate theaters, separate schools, separate institutions of learning and science, separate churches, and separate cemeteries—these are the artificial substitutes for Equality; and this is the contrivance by which a transcendent right, involving a transcendent duty, is evaded; for Equality is not only a right but a duty.

How vain it is to argue that there is no denial of Equal Rights when this separation is enforced. The substitute is invariably an inferior article. Does any Senator deny it? Therefore, it is not Equality. At best it is an equivalent only; but no equivalent is equality. Separation implies one thing for a white person and another thing for a colored person; but equality is where all have the same alike. There can be no substitute for equality; nothing but itself. Even if accommodations are the same, as notoriously they are not, there is no Equality. In the process of substitution the vital elixir exhales and escapes.[137]

Edmunds similarly associated segregation with caste and found deseg-regation to be compelled by the Constitution in his explanation of why the Judiciary Committee repeatedly had reported against Sumner's amendment. The Civil Rights Act of 1866 previously had been deemed sufficient, the senator explained, but "history has proved, experienced has proved, that the civil rights bill as it now stands is not adequate to accomplish the end of equality and security which the Constitution commands shall be ob-served."[138] Highlighting the need to adhere to the consequences of the gen-eral principle of equal rights—and suggesting that Trumbull was trying to defeat equal rights[139]—Edmunds lamented,

Everybody is for equal rights in the abstract; but when you come to name what they are, when you come to say that a man independent of his race shall have the same right that another man has to go to a school or into a car, or a right to a trial by jury, or whatever it may be, oh, it is something else.[140]

John Sherman, responding to a question from Trumbull as to what states discriminated in public conveyances, remarked that "the right is denied practically in many of the States."[141] The Ohio senator saw "the right to travel in a public conveyance on the highway" as the equivalent in value to the rights enumerated in the 1866 law. "The right to travel all over this country is just as much a right and privilege and immunity of a citizen as the right to make a contract, or to sue and be sued, to plead and to be impleaded."[142]

In the Forty-Third Congress, Sumner reemphasized the object of his bill as the "complete equality before the law . . . everywhere, in everything reg-ulated by law."[143] William Lawrence cited the example of William Smith, a black man in charge of the House library who was expelled from a train car in the South because of his race, and he expressed his belief that it was the duty of Congress to remedy such violations of the enjoyment of civil rights.[144] The Fourteenth Amendment's object, the congressman asserted,

is to make all men equal before the law. If a State permits inequality in rights to be created or meted out by citizens or corporations enjoying its protection it denies the equal protection of the laws. What the State permits by its sanction, having the power to prohibit, it does in effect itself.[145]

(This proposition went farther than necessary to refute the *Plessy* Court because it addressed state omission to desegregate private corporations un-der its protection.) Robert Elliott argued in terms similar to Lawrence's that the Fourteenth Amendment did not prevent states from denying (with certain exceptions) any rights they themselves conferred, but "[w]hat it does forbid is inequality, . . . discrimination, or" the denial of equal protec-tion.[146] Ransier viewed the legislation as a matter of securing civil equality and the "practical freedom," that the Fourteenth Amendment was intended to secure.[147] Lawrence more forcefully declared that the "fourteenth amendment was designed to secure this equality of rights; and we have no discretion to say that we will not enforce its provisions."[148]

Black people, Stowell asserted, do not seek social equality but "simply ask for equality under the law; that when any institution or privilege is created or regulated by law, it shall be free equally to all, without regard to race or color."[149] Benjamin Butler denied that Congress was attempting to legislate equality insofar as inequalities naturally occur among people. He distinguished the equality for which he was striving in terms of opening up opportunity to all—"not that all men are equal, *but that every man has the right to be the equal of every other man if he can.*"[150] Cain added that the bill was a matter of securing the "rights and immunities" of citizenship.[151]

Morton denied the power of the state to segregate the races under the Equal Protection Clause's prohibition against class legislation.[152] The senator countered Merrimon's charge that his views would entail a ban on sex segregation by pointing out the Fourteenth Amendment's intent "to destroy caste, to put all races upon an equality."[153] "If a State is at liberty to exclude a colored man from the cars on account of his color in traveling," Morton added, "then it has the power to make an odious discrimination because of race, the very thing that the fourteenth amendment intended to stamp out."[154] In full agreement with both the premises and the conclusion of Harlan's dissent, the Indiana senator articulated in greater detail than Edmunds the process of reasoning behind the principle of the Fourteenth Amendment since its framing and its application to the type of situation the Court would face in *Plessy*:

> The Constitution must of necessity employ general terms. All constitutions must. They cannot specify particular cases. The substance and the body of the fourteenth amendment is that it establishes the equality of the races before the law, and in the language of the Supreme Court prevents any State from making any odious discrimination against any class of people. It was not necessary that the Constitution should mention the theater, or should mention the railroad car, or should mention the common school. It lays down the broad and general proposition that men of all races must be placed upon the same level of equality in the enjoyment of civil rights. The States have all the powers left them that they had before; they may make all the conditions of suffrage, make all the conditions in regard to travel, make all the conditions in regard to the courts that they ever could, with one single limitation, that these conditions shall not depend upon the question of race or color; and that is the whole of it. . . .
>
> [A] State may pass a law forbidding a colored man to go into the cars. . . . That law, if carried into the Supreme Court of the United States, would be held to be unconstitutional in the absence of this act. But that is not a thing perhaps which the party injured could do. That is a very imperfect form of remedy, simply to give

the right of appeal from the State courts to the courts of the United States. That was not what was meant by this amendment. The framers of the amendment—and I know something about it—understood that a law passed by a State in contravention of it would be void, and the Supreme Court of the United States would so decide; but they did not intend to leave the victim to that roundabout and costly remedy. They intended to make it a penal offense for any man to violate the rights of another, so that if he did it he should do so at his peril.[155]

Morton added in conclusion that the right "to have the equal enjoyment of every public institution," including "the public conveyance," was "the very highest franchise that belongs to any citizen of the United States as such."[156] The senator's speech remarkably discussed the judicial invalidation of such a law as was at issue in *Plessy* as if it were a foregone conclusion; the real effort behind his argument, it appeared, was offering a justification for congressional legislation. Indeed, one can see how the Democratic theory that the Fourteenth Amendment allowed only judicial invalidation of discriminatory legislation would lead at a minimum to the result Harlan advocated in his dissent. Ultimately, of course, the Court first struck down under the state action doctrine legislation designed to ban discrimination, only to find a way to avoid invalidating a discriminatory statute, the most clear action a state could take, in a decision that apparently did not strike Morton as even feasible.

Later during debate, Edmunds accused Sargent of authorizing states, among other things, "to deny the right to ride in a particular railroad car," and he added, "If there is anything in the fourteenth amendment it is exactly opposite to that."[157] The Vermont senator believed that the amendment proscribed segregation, and he charged his colleague from California with adopting "the democratic idea of the fourteenth amendment . . . that it does not level absolutely and destroy distinctions of race, color, and previous condition of servitude."[158] In the House, first-term Republican Julius C. Burrows described the Civil Rights Act as a measure protecting "rights" that "are conferred both by the common law and the plainest provisions of our Constitution."[159]

Years after his 1896 opinion for the Court, Justice Brown admitted that Justice Harlan had "assumed what is probably the fact, that the [Louisiana] statute had its origin in the purpose, not so much to exclude white persons from railroad cars occupied by blacks, as to exclude colored people from coaches occupied or assigned to white persons."[160] Assessing the sum of the evidence, from the debate during the Civil War over transportation segregation in the nation's capital to general propositions refuting the Court to the more specific articulations against segregation in public conveyances (among other contexts), it must be concluded that *Plessy* was decided with the overwhelming weight of the Reconstruction debates against it. Support for the Court's theory came almost exclusively from those who opposed the Fourteenth Amendment and Reconstruction, which is not to overlook that on this issue, as on the issue of Section 5, Democrats were willing to employ a broader interpretation in order to defeat ratification than they were after the amendment became part of the Constitution.

The exceptions who had voted for the Fourteenth Amendment—Whig George Lawrence and Republicans Lot Morrill and Trumbull—should not be treated as a faction with decisive weight on the question, and the latter two remain a bit dubious in their evolving stands anyway. Some scholars have tried to argue that the Fourteenth Amendment was not intended to address discrimination in areas that were not named in the Civil Rights Act of 1866,[161] but the bulk of Republicans who spoke failed to share this view and were not normally refuted on such grounds. Besides wording the Fourteenth Amendment more broadly, the framers simply did not feel themselves as constrained as the strict terms of the statute, which one must conclude was incorporated into, but not made the outer limit of, the constitutional amendment that soon followed. That segregation was not addressed at the outset proves nothing but that, as with other matters the Court must face, the judiciary should look to the principles that the Constitution articulates and apply them to unanticipated settings rather than abdicating responsibility. The *Plessy* Court's holdings do not become any more feasible under originalism when the issue of segregation is viewed against the principles of the Fourteenth Amendment.

d. School Segregation

Two more cases merit mention as components of the Court's acceptance of segregation in the school context. In *Cumming v. County Board of Education* (1899),[162] the first Supreme Court case about racial discrimination in schools,[163] parents of students in an all-black public high school sued after the local school board closed the school.[164] The plaintiffs specifically objected to a tax levied for the support of primary, intermediate, and high schools insofar as they were paying to support high schools from which their children could derive no benefit, the only remaining high schools in the county being restricted to whites.[165] The board, the suit claimed, could not levy a tax to support high schools without providing equal educational facilities for blacks and whites.[166]

It was Justice Harlan who wrote the opinion for a unanimous Court holding that the board's actions did not violate the Fourteenth Amendment.[167] As the case was pleaded, he wrote, it did not raise the question of the validity of the requirement that blacks and whites be educated in separate schools.[168] Instead, the Court's opinion was based on a difficult standard it set to justify an injunction against the maintenance of an existing public high school for whites only: Federal interference with the management of the schools could be justified only when the case presented "a clear and unmistakable disregard of rights secured by the supreme law of the land," and the board's decision must appear to be "an abuse of its discretion and in hostility to the colored population because of their race."[169]

The Court did not find that this standard had been met. The board had justified closing the high school on the grounds that funds were required for black primary education, and the Court did not find the state court ruling that the board had not acted in bad faith or abused its discretion to be a denial of equal protection.[170] Three and a half years after establishing the "separate but equal" standard, the Court thus deemed itself powerless to enforce the "equal" prong of its rule.[171]

In 1927, the Court dealt squarely with the issue of school segregation in *Gong Lum v. Rice*.[172] In that case, the Court, in a decision by Chief Justice William H. Taft, extended the "separate but equal" doctrine to uphold the exclusion of a citizen of Chinese descent from a school in Mississippi that was reserved for whites.[173] Taft's opinion cited two Supreme Court decisions for support—*Plessy* and *Cumming*—and included little new reasoning, relying primarily on the weight of the 1896 precedent and several state and lower federal court decisions for support.[174] School segregation and the Fourteenth Amendment will be examined in light of the understanding of the Reconstruction Congress following discussion of the Court's more famous school segregation decision in 1954.

F. RETREAT FROM THE FIFTEENTH AMENDMENT

1. *Williams v. Mississippi*

Accompanying the segregation cases was a series of decisions beginning around the turn of the century that brought the Fifteenth Amendment to its own nadir. In *Williams v. Mississippi* (1898),[1] the Court upheld literacy tests and poll taxes designed to disfranchise blacks. The case involved a black murder defendant, Henry Williams, who had been convicted by an all-white jury in Mississippi. Only those who were qualified to vote could serve on juries in the state, and the Mississippi constitution in 1890 had adopted literacy tests and poll tax requirements, dramatically reducing registered black voters to the point that black Mississippians were virtually excluded from jury service.[2] Writing for a unanimous Court, Justice Joseph McKenna distinguished *Yick Wo* by maintaining that *Williams* had not demonstrated that the administration of voting laws in Mississippi was discriminatory.[3]

In his 1901 memoirs, George Boutwell expressed disappointment over the plight of the Fifteenth Amendment, but he also retained hope that it soon would be widely accepted:

It is true that at this time (1901) the operation of the Fifteenth Amendment has been defeated and consequently the governments of States and the Government of the United States have become usurpations, in that they have been in the hands of a minority of men. Nevertheless the influence of the amendment is felt by all, and the time is not distant when it will be accepted by all. Thus our Government will be made to rest upon the wisest and safest foundation yet devised by man: The Equality of Men in the States, and the Equality of States in the Union.[4]

Perhaps Boutwell, who would live until 1905, did not envision the decisions the Supreme Court would hand down two years later, but he would not live to see his aspirations met.

2. *Giles v. Harris*

In *Giles v. Harris*,[1] the first of two key Fifteenth Amendment decisions it handed down in 1903, the Court expressed its impotence to enforce the amendment in a case involving blatant denial of the right to vote on racial grounds. The plaintiff in the case was a black man who was qualified to vote under the Alabama constitution, but he was denied registration as a voter in 1902 on account of his race as "part of a general scheme to disfranchise" blacks.[2] The plaintiff sought the "permanent advantages of registration" as if he had registered before 1903, but the Court, in an opinion by Justice Oliver Wendell Holmes, Jr., asked, "how can we make the court a party to the unlawful scheme by accepting it and adding another voter to its fraudulent lists?"[3] Treating the case as a political question, Holmes maintained that equity could not enforce political rights and that "[i]f the conspiracy and the intent exist," it would not suffice for the Court merely to put "a name on a piece of paper" by adding the plaintiff to the 1902 registration rolls.[4] Rather, "relief from a great political wrong, if done, as alleged, by the people of a State and the State itself, must be given by them or by the legislative and political department of the government of the United States."[5] Justices Harlan, Brown, and Brewer dissented.[6]

It is interesting to compare the Court's use of the "political question" doctrine to defer to Reconstruction laws during the 1860s with its invocation of the same doctrine in a case involving as blatant a violation of the Reconstruction amendments as the Court ever faced, in deference to counter-Reconstruction. An understanding of the broader historical context the Court faced prompts one to ask to what extent *Giles* was itself a political decision. Had the Court reached a different result, its decision might have been enforceable only by measures reminiscent of intervention in the South by federal troops, a prospect the nation had long repudiated by the outset of the twentieth century.

3. *James v. Bowman* and the Fifteenth Amendment State Action Doctrine

a. The Court's Opinion

The next landmark Fifteenth Amendment case, handed down the same year as *Giles*, was *James v. Bowman*,[1] a case involving the constitutionality of § 5507 of the Revised Statutes, which was § 5 of the first Enforcement Act of 1870 in revised form.[2] This provision prohibited any person from preventing, hindering, controlling, or intimidating another from exercising the Fifteenth Amendment right to vote by bribery or various threats, especially from landlords or employers.[3] Based on § 5507, the indictment charged that Henry Bowman had employed bribery to "unlawfully and feloniously" intimidate and prevent certain black citizens from voting in a congressional election in 1898.[4] In an opinion by Justice Brewer, the Court struck down the provision on the grounds that the Fifteenth "amendment relates solely to action 'by the United States or by any State,' and does not contemplate wrongful individual acts."[5]

Brewer compared the amendment to its immediate predecessor, and his opinion cited the *Slaughter-House Cases, Reese, Cruikshank, Harris*, and the *Civil Rights Cases* to support the proposition "that a statute which purports to punish purely individual action cannot be sustained as an appropriate exercise of the power conferred by the Fifteenth Amendment upon Congress to prevent action by the State through some one or more of its official representatives."[6] The Court was further unconvinced by the argument that Congress had the power to punish violations in federal congressional elections, employing the same mode of statutory construction it had employed in *Reese* and *Harris*: on its face § 5507 purported to apply to all elections and thus could not be upheld because Congress could punish bribery only "in respect to elections in which the nation is directly interested, or in which some mandate of the National Constitution is disobeyed."[7] Harlan and Brown dissented without opinion, and McKenna did not take part in the case.[8]

b. Contemporary Understandings of the Fifteenth Amendment and State Action

Much of the originalist refutation of the Court's decision in *James* can be found in the Court's own suggestion that the enforcement clauses of the Fourteenth and Fifteenth Amendments deserve parallel analysis. The overwhelming lack of support for the *Civil Rights Cases* has already been explored, and the state action doctrine finds no stronger basis when one turns to the Fifteenth Amendment context. Among supporters of the amendment, and of Reconstruction more generally, one finds little support for a Fifteenth Amendment state action requirement during the Reconstruction debates.

To find concurrence with the Court's theory, one must turn to those legislators who opposed Reconstruction. William Hamilton, who it will be recalled labeled the Fifteenth Amendment a "wicked amendment,"[9] remarked during debates over the first Enforcement Act in May 1870 that the constitutional provision "is addressed to the State, and to the State solely. . . . The action of the State is the primary consideration or object."[10] Casserly argued at length in favor of a Fifteenth Amendment state action requirement, denying arguments that Section 2 of the amendment permitted Congress to punish individuals and conceding congressional power to act only on "agents of the State."[11] The California senator asserted,

[E]xcept perhaps in the single case of a State officer acting under a State constitution or law, Congress has acquired no right, under the fifteenth amendment, to deal with individuals who interfere with the right of voters of African race. You must leave to the States the correction of all such cases.[12]

During the same debates, Casserly saw the Fourteenth and Fifteenth Amendments as analogous and applied a state action requirement to both.[13] The "primary effect and operation" of the latter amendment was to "operate[] upon the United States and upon the States" and "to make invalid and void any legislation of the United States or of any State that is in conflict with its provisions."[14] Thurman was "wholly at a loss to see how any one can come to a different conclusion than that" of his California colleague and adamantly articulated his own belief that the amendment applied only to the states rather than to an individual or mob.[15] Garrett Davis agreed, pointing out that the "United States" and a "State" could act only "officially" and "politically"—through "some of its organized Departments and officers"—not "by its isolated and straggling citizens."[16] In the House, Democrat Joseph S. Smith contended that "no human ingenuity can torture these few plain, simple words" of the Fifteenth Amendment "so as to make them confer upon Congress any power except to enforce the amendment against the States and persons acting under State or Federal authority."[17]

During debates over the Enforcement Act of February 1871, Charles A. Eldridge charged that there was no basis for the legislation under "the language of this pretended fifteenth amendment," which voided legislation without empowering Congress to punish individuals.[18] Woodward added that the Fifteenth Amendment was "a negative rule to the States, which like the other negatives or inhibitions of the Constitution executes itself, and needs no supplementary legislation."[19] Vickers maintained that "[i]t is only after State action denying or abridging the right to vote that the second clause of the fifteenth amendment can be exercised by Congress," and he found the bill unconstitutional.[20] Thomas Bayard felt similarly and asserted, "The fifteenth amendment . . . has simply the effect of avoiding all provisions of State laws or State constitutions which in any way deny or abridge the right of citizens of the United States to vote on account of their race, color, or previous condition of servitude."[21] Frank Blair[22] and James G. Blair[23] added their own views of the amendment's negative character and inapplicability to individuals, the latter during the April debates. Of all the above cited legislators supporting the Court's doctrine in *James*, Davis, Eldridge, Woodward, and Vickers were in Congress during the vote on the Fifteenth Amendment, and they all voted against the amendment.[24]

On the other side of the debate, Pool denounced Klan violence and the failure to prosecute it at length on April 15, 1870.[25] He tentatively indicated hesitation about whether such terrorism would constitute a violation of the Fifteenth Amendment,[26] but in a lengthy speech he delivered the next month, he repudiated the state action doctrine by explaining that a state omission was sufficient to constitute a violation.[27] Part of his speech defending the first Enforcement Act already has been reviewed in the Fourteenth Amendment context (where he was speaking of the Fifteenth Amendment as well),[28] and to those assertions should be added the following statements from Pool about the Fifteenth Amendment:

It must apply to individuals. . . . [T]he word "deny" is used. There are various ways in which a State may prevent the full operation of this constitutional amendment. It cannot—because the courts would prevent it—by positive legislation, but by acts of omission it may practically deny the right. The legislation of Congress must be to supply acts of omission on the part of the States. If a State shall not enforce its laws by which private individuals shall be prevented by force from contravening the rights of the citizen under the amendment, it is in my judgment the duty of the United States Government to supply that omission, and by its own laws and by its own courts to go into the States for the purpose of giving the amendment vitality there. . . .
[I]ndividuals may prevent the exercise of the right of suffrage. . . . Not only citizens, but organizations of citizens, conspiracies, may be and are . . . in some of the States formed for that purpose. . . . I believe that any bill will be defective which does not make it a highly penal offense for men to conspire together, to organize themselves into bodies, for the express purpose of contravening the right conferred by the fifteenth amendment.[29]

Pool recognized that the "great and most effectual means used to interfere with" black citizens' "exercise of the right secured to them by the fifteenth amendment is by intimidation, by violence," and the Enforcement Act's "purpose . . . is to protect those citizens against intimidation from voting."[30]

In another defense of the bill, John Sherman pointed out that the Fifteenth Amendment's "intention . . . is to secure to every man, without respect to his color, race, or previous condition, the equal right to vote," and he encouraged the punishment of "any man in any community" who would violate this right "by a sure, swift, and severe remedy."[31] The Ohio senator maintained in response to Thurman and Casserly that the bill applied only to the violator who "covers himself under the protection or color of a law or regulation or constitution of a State," but for Sherman this category included preventing "any private person from shielding himself under a State regulation"—"the humblest as well as the highest" citizen.[32]

Other Republican senators indicated their approval of the application of legislation beyond the state. Carl Schurz acknowledged approvingly the bill's application to both states and individuals against Fifteenth Amendment violations.[33] Howard expressed a fear that the courts would narrowly construe the Fifteenth Amendment not to apply to individuals, but he attested that the amendment was not intended to follow the state action doctrine:

I do not think that when Congress passed this amendment and laid it before the States they intended to confine its operation solely to the legislation of Congress by way of prohibition, or to do the same thing in reference to State legislation. They entertained broader views. Their intention and purpose were, beyond a doubt, for I witnessed all the discussion that took place in the Senate, to secure to the colored man by proper legislation the right to go to the polls and quietly and peacefully deposit his ballot there.[34]

Howard proceeded to put himself on record as opposing the construction the Court eventually adopted.[35] A dialogue between Senators William Stewart and George Williams further revealed the intention of preventing mobs from impeding black citizens' right to vote.[36]

Speaking on May 20, 1870, Morton criticized Casserly's interpretation of the Fifteenth Amendment as inconsistent with the intentions of the framers to act directly on individuals, and he declared, "I never heard the construction that has been given to it . . . that it operated only upon States as municipal corporations and upon the United States. . . . I never heard it until to-day."[37] The senator soon afterward submitted § 5 of the Enforcement Act as an amendment, and it passed by a vote of thirty-six to nine.[38] Another amendment offered by Vickers to confine offenses in § 4 to those that occur under color of state authority, characterized by Thurman as a means of showing that Congress was not trying "to punish every ruffian as the embodiment of the State," was rejected by a vote of nine to forty-one.[39]

Morton would take the opportunity to assert in later debates the "hypothesis" of the Enforcement Act that the Fifteenth "amendment conferred upon colored men an absolute right to vote upon the same terms and conditions with white men, and that Congress had the power to protect and enforce this right against individuals or organizations, whether acting in open violence or under color of State law."[40] Congress, he maintained, "intended . . . to make a violation of" the Reconstruction amendments "a personal and criminal offense, and to punish the violator, because that is . . . the only successful enforcement of the amendments that can be had."[41] In the House, Garfield maintained that the Fifteenth Amendment was "not . . . a mere prohibition to the State, a simple negation of power."[42]

Of the eight legislators cited above who expressed understandings contradicting the *James* Court's holdings, all except Schurz were present in Congress during the passage of the Fifteenth Amendment, and seven of these eight remaining members of Congress (all except Pool) had voted for the amendment.[43] Nevertheless, a different understanding of the last amendment ratified in the nineteenth century would prevail in the Court. A 1910 *Harvard Law Review* article entitled "Is the Fifteenth Amendment Void?" made the following observations about the state of Fifteenth Amendment jurisprudence:

Nearly forty years have elapsed since the Fifteenth Amendment was proclaimed by the Secretary of State to be part of the Constitution of the United States. During that time, it has been hated with a deadly hatred by the section of the country it was designed chiefly to affect. It has been despised, flouted, nullified, evaded. Nevertheless, the Supreme Court of the United States, the lawful guardian of the Constitution, has in no single instance held any state or federal statute or the act of any state or federal officer to be in conflict with the Amendment; and no case in that court can be found which would have been decided differently if the Amendment had never existed.

In a number of cases, it is true, the Supreme Court has decided that the Amendment does *not* do this and does *not* do the other; but if the student of constitutional law, not content with such negative information as to what the Amendment does not do, seeks to ascertain affirmatively what, if anything, it has accomplished, he must find his way by the pure light of reason unaided by the binding authority of any actual decision of our highest court.[44]

The amendment indeed appeared to be buried during the first decade of the twentieth century, but the student of constitutional law even then could be enlightened on its meaning apart from unaided intuition by glancing at the debates recorded in the *Congressional Globe*.

4. Grovey v. Townsend

The state action doctrine did not render voting rights so vulnerable that their suppression was always judicially unredressable. In *Nixon v. Herndon* (1927),[1] the Court would find itself capable of relieving a voter from a Texas statute denying the Democratic Party's primary ballot to a black citizen, though it found the statute invalid under the Fourteenth rather than the Fifteenth Amendment.[2]

Nevertheless, the Court was incapable of surmounting a "white primary" scheme in Texas that was more subtle than a racially discriminatory statute, having been based on a state constitutional provision providing for the liberty of political association. In *Grovey v. Townsend* (1935),[3] the Court invoked the state action doctrine to uphold this new scheme. The case involved a suit by a black citizen against a county clerk who refused him a ballot for a Democratic primary on account of his race, in accordance with a resolution offered in a state party convention that excluded blacks from membership and participation in the Democratic Party.[4] In a decision by Justice Owen J. Roberts, the Court reasoned that the exclusion was the result of the decision of party representatives acting in a private capacity and not a result of state action.[5] The Court found no constitutional difficulty with the state constitutional provision guaranteeing the liberty of political associations, and it held that the state Democratic convention did not constitute "a mere instrumentality or agency for expressing the voice or will of the state."[6]

It cannot be said that the Court's retreat from Reconstruction ended at a particular time and that a revival of the Reconstruction amendments immediately ensued. The Court was never monolithic about civil rights, but there did come a point in the twentieth century when civil rights cases based on the amendments tended to be approached with more expansive readings of the Constitution. It remains to explore those twentieth-century cases that revisited Supreme Court decisions retreating from Reconstruction in order to examine the fate of the Court's many distortions (at least from an originalist perspective) of constitutional jurisprudence. Included will be discussion, deferred from the review of *Gong Lum*, on the Reconstruction debates over school segregation, an issue that would stand as the preeminent vehicle for the Supreme Court's repudiation of past civil rights holdings.

4

The Court's Reconsideration of Civil Rights during the Twentieth Century

A. THE WHITE PRIMARY

Less than a decade after it was decided, the Court overturned *Grovey* in *Smith v. Allwright.*[1] That case marked the return of the Texas white primary to the Court, but this time, Justice Stanley F. Reed's majority opinion concluded "that this statutory system for the selection of party nominees for inclusion on the general election ballot makes the party which is required to follow these legislative directions an agency of the State in so far as it determines the participants in a primary election."[2] Because the primaries were "a part of the machinery for choosing officials," they merited the same characterization as the general election and took on "its character as a state agency from the duties imposed upon it by state statutes."[3] The Court thus struck down the white primary, but it was careful not to do so in a way that repudiated the state action requirement, concluding that "[t]his is state action within the meaning of the Fifteenth Amendment."[4] In *Terry v. Adams* (1953),[5] a fragmented Court invalidated a " 'three-step' exclusion process" combining a preprimary election of candidates by a political organization excluding blacks with the Democratic Party primary and general election, which merely ratified the choices of white voters.[6]

B. *BROWN V. BOARD OF EDUCATION* AND SCHOOL SEGREGATION

1. The Court's Opinion

In *Brown v. Board of Education* (1954),[1] the decision most commonly associated with the Supreme Court's role in the "Second Reconstruction,"

Chief Justice Earl Warren began his analysis of the challenged constitutionality of segregated public schools with a note of ambivalence toward history. Evidence surrounding the consideration and ratification of the Fourteenth Amendment, as well as existing practices, the chief justice wrote, were "inconclusive" at best and insufficient "to resolve the problem with which we are faced."[2] Turning to the Court's earliest Fourteenth Amendment cases, Warren cited language in the *Slaughter-House Cases*, quoted also in *Strauder*, construing the amendment "as proscribing all state-imposed discriminations against the Negro race."[3]

The Court's decision ultimately rested, however, on "the effect of segregation itself on public education."[4] To approach this question, Warren reasoned,

we cannot turn the clock back to 1868 when the Amendment was adopted, or even to 1896 when *Plessy* v. *Ferguson* was written. We must consider public education in the light of its full development and its present place in American life throughout the Nation. Only in this way can it be determined if segregation in public schools deprives these plaintiffs of the equal protection of the laws.[5]

He then discussed the importance of education in American society and the psychological damage and other intangible effects resulting from school segregation, including citation to several psychological studies supporting the Court's finding that segregation hindered educational development.[6] "Whatever may have been the extent of psychological knowledge at the time of *Plessy* v. *Ferguson*," the Court rejected any contradictory findings of the 1896 precedent and concluded that "in the field of public education the doctrine of 'separate but equal' has no place. Separate educational facilities are inherently unequal."[7]

Having reached its conclusion in this manner, the Court encouraged the impression with which many constitutional law scholars accepted *Brown*—namely, that its judgment stood against the original understanding of the Fourteenth Amendment.[8] Its very words, as Robert Bork points out, indicate that the high court "thought that it had departed from the original understanding in order to do the socially desirable thing."[9] Combining such an impression with the widespread acceptance of *Brown* as a judgment which any legitimate theory of constitutional interpretation must accept,[10] the Court's defeat of the *Plessy* doctrine might have occurred in a way that ironically encourages the infidelity to originalism in constitutional jurisprudence that allowed the nineteenth-century Court to embark on its retreat from Reconstruction in the first place.

2. School Segregation and the Reconstruction Debates

a. Preliminary Observations about Historical Context

After exploring *Plessy* and its lack of originalist pedigree, one might make a strong argument that extended examination of the Reconstruction

Congress' specific understanding of school segregation is unnecessary. After all, because the Constitution deals with general principles that demand consistent application, it would be difficult to argue that both *Plessy* and *Brown* reached incorrect results. Indeed, the *Gong Lum* Court seems to have recognized this, which explains why the 1927 decision found little need to include new analysis and was justified primarily on the sheer weight of the *Plessy* doctrine. Still, it can only enrich a study of the original understanding of the Reconstruction amendments to discuss specific references to school segregation.

It should be established at the outset, for the sake of keeping the debates in historical context, that school segregation was perhaps the most controversial application of an already controversial principle during Reconstruction. Racially integrated schools were uncommon even in the North, regardless of the dictates of state law, which ranged from mandates for integration to express allowance of voluntary segregation to complete deference to local school officials.[1] Rare exceptions of racially mixed schools in parts of such states as South Carolina and Louisiana, which expressly banned segregated public schools,[2] tended to be short-lived and marred by interracial turmoil.[3] It has been shown already that desegregation statutes often existed on paper without being followed to a great extent in practice, and the congressional debates over the various civil rights proposals of the 1870s, particularly those including schools, were treated like "deadly poison" by both political parties through the Republicans' disastrous election year of 1874.[4]

Several Radicals seem to have manifested a sense that the practical success of their school desegregation efforts was dubious, suggesting that even after their proposal became law, blacks and whites might be able to separate themselves in equal school facilities—as long as they chose to do so without state compulsion.[5] Others feared that integrated schools would infuriate white southerners to the point that they would abolish public schools altogether.[6] Black politicians tended to acquiesce when education officials segregated schools, and most blacks seemed to focus on the new public educational systems as an improvement over a complete denial of schooling.[7] (Frederick Douglass' own *New National Era* called segregated schools "infinitely superior" to no schools at all.[8] There even existed a group of blacks with reservations about mixing schools, some of whom opposed the school segregation measures of the 1870s outright.[9]

The unpopularity of school integration naturally was accompanied by a sense that it would incur considerable political damage on Republicans, which in turn gave legislators—especially Republicans in the border states and the South, who not coincidentally were most responsible for the decline in congressional support for the school integration provision of the civil rights bill in 1874—a difficult balancing test to conduct. Should they risk defeat for the sake of advocating what often appeared a superficial extension of the principle of equality (given indications of its practical failure) that likely would not even be converted into practice?[10]

Given this context, it is immediately apparent that there were sufficient political reasons for legislators to oppose legislation compelling mixed schools apart from any advocacy of the principle of "separate but equal." An elected official could believe that the equality established by the Fourteenth Amendment should lead to desegregation if the principle were carried out consistently, but politics being what it is, there might have been countervailing pressures stronger than one's constitutional interpretation to oppose the result Sumner's bill originally intended. In fact, support for school segregation presented something of a catch-22 situation even from the perspective of those who were most strongly interested in perpetuating Reconstruction: As events ultimately demonstrated, supporting a measure as unpopular as school desegregation by the mid-1870s threatened Republicans with the destruction of the political support on which they relied in the first place to continue and strengthen Reconstruction.[11]

That this unpopularity existed—or that segregation was practiced in so many schools—certainly does not decide the originalist analysis—at least not under the present study's conception of original meaning. The very purpose of adopting constitutional amendments that can be enforced by undemocratic courts occupied by life-tenured judges is the recognition that principles of general application must be applied consistently, regardless of the popular verdict on the consequences of applying a rule in specific contexts. This realization is as relevant in the context of the Fourteenth Amendment as in any other context, for the 1868 amendment made an unusually ambitious claim of bestowing legal equality, a dense and sweeping concept, in a society and legal system permeated in so many areas with a caste system. When specific contexts entail actions mandated by the Constitution that the people would oppose, it is natural to expect politicians to disappoint constitutional expectations, an observation that only affirms the existence of courts in the first place. It is with this in mind that the statements of politicians of the 1860s and 1870s should be examined. Even from this perspective, it will be seen that the record is a remarkable one in favor of the Court's result.

b. Debates Preceding Consideration of the Civil Rights Act of 1875 and Its Precursors

Statements addressing school segregation occurred usually in scattered contexts before the debates over the Sumner proposals of the 1870s brought the issue to the floor on a more consistent basis. Several statements were made on both sides of the debate both before and after the passage of the Fourteenth Amendment. In 1864, Henry Wilson referred to the battle for desegregation undertaken in Massachusetts, recalling "the time when colored children were attempted to be excluded from some of the common schools, where they had as much right by law as your child or mine."[12] Several days after entering the Senate in March 1867, Morton asserted that it was "of the very essence of reconstruction that" the freedmen "shall be educated," which meant for him "a system of common schools established open and free to all, without distinction of race or color."[13] Generally, however, the issue did not arise, and statements before the 1870s debates, with minor exceptions of particular debates over the District of Columbia, address more general propositions about education without getting specific about school segregation.

Several statements in the 1860s assert the general importance of education, a concept that the establishment of public schools affirmed during Reconstruction, without specifically addressing segregation. John Sherman urged early in the first session of the Thirty-Ninth Congress that the freedmen be given "the natural rights of free men," listing "the right to be educated" in this category along with other rights that would be expressly addressed in the Civil Rights Act of 1866.[14] During his attack on the Black Codes, Donnelly criticized the exclusion of blacks from schools that whites were attending and extolled the importance of universal education as an essential companion of universal suffrage, though his statements did not necessarily preclude the possibility of segregation.[15] Republican Representative Josiah B. Grinnell quoted from General O. O. Howard, who headed the Freedmen's Bureau, on the "absolutely essential" attribute of education "to fit [the freedmen] for their new duties and responsibilities."[16] James M. Ashley added comments after ratification on the necessity of "free public schools" as a prerequisite to security "in civil or religious liberty."[17] Such statements, while inconclusive, help counter notions that schools were understood to be constitutionally inferior in importance to other rights such as those named in the 1866 bill.

Other statements suggested the illegality of the exclusion of blacks from public schools without necessarily taking a stand on the possibility of equal facilities that also were separate. During debate over the 1866 Civil Rights Act, Columbus Delano pointed out that the measure would invalidate a law such as that his home state once had, "excluding the black population from any participation in the public schools or in the funds raised for the support of those schools."[18] Michael Kerr argued that a teacher who excluded blacks from a common school, as required by law in Indiana, would be liable to punishment for denying a civil right, despite black citizens' immunity from taxation for the support of schools.[19] The following year, John Sherman urged that "schools ought to be established for the education of all, white and black."[20] Howe affirmed "the right to be educated" and vehemently expressed his unwillingness to readmit into the Union any state with a constitution that "shut up the common schools from the enjoyment of a large portion of their people, white or black."[21] His disposition was different toward a state "constitution which throws open the schoolhouses, which admits the right of poor and rich, of white and black, to receive that education without which no man can be fitted for an American citizen."[22] Howe contributed the only reference to school segregation during debates over the final version of the Fourteenth Amendment, but his statement did not directly address the issue. The Wisconsin senator attacked the inequitable funding of white and black schools in the segregated Florida school system and asked his colleagues whether they "dare hesitate to put in the Constitution . . . a positive inhibition upon exercising this power of local government to sanction such a crime as I have just portrayed."[23]

As far as the Civil Rights Act of 1866 was concerned, however, it is difficult to maintain that the statute addressed school segregation. On one side, Cowan expressed his fear that the act would abolish segregated schools and found that prospect "monstrous."[24] Kerr dissociated integrated schools from the "slavery or involuntary servitude" the Thirteenth Amendment addressed.[25] Rogers suggested that Congress was invading the state's domain by interfering with segregated schools[26]—a charge he also had leveled against Bingham's original proposal of the Fourteenth Amendment.[27]

On the other side, James F. Wilson stated that the "civil rights and immunities" the bill addressed would not include the right to sit on juries or the right to have children "attend the same schools,"[28] the only statement by a supporter of the bill during the debates specifically denying its application to school desegregation.[29] This is the most direct evidence Alexander M. Bickel and Raoul Berger cite to support their theses that the original understanding of the Fourteenth Amendment would have permitted segregation in public schools.[30]

Even conceding that the Civil Rights Act did not address school segregation, there is little warrant to apply the same conclusion to the Fourteenth Amendment. It is clear that the amendment was intended to constitutionalize the act and that legislators often referred to the two measures as having the same effect[31]—indeed they might have been considered almost synonymous for purposes of those debates of the 1860s that did not deal with segregation. Nevertheless, the 1866 law differed materially in that its final form enumerated those rights it protected while the Fourteenth Amendment, like the nondiscrimination provision of the 1866 bill that was omitted over concerns about its breadth,[32] was not similarly contained in its wording.[33] There was in fact no reason for such confines. A statute, unlike a constitutional amendment, must be anchored to a preexisting constitutional provision, and as long as Congress' egalitarian work remained on a statutory level, there were reasons to confine the 1866 bill to terms that would not be too attenuated from the fundamental aspects of freedom covered by the Thirteenth Amendment.

As it turned out, egalitarians such as Bingham who had constitutional scruples over the bill (never cured in the case of the Ohio congressman even after revision) would not be bound by such reservations when it came time to amend the Constitution. It is noteworthy that Bingham, the very congressman who had moved to delete the nondiscrimination provision,[34] would proceed to draft an amendment that was worded in no narrower terms than the provision that he had helped remove from the 1866 statute. Insofar as others in Congress desired to delete the bill's nondiscrimination provision because they did not want rights expanded in any context, constitutional or statutory, the debate over the Civil Rights Act—highlighting that broader terms did make a difference for some—should have served as an additional indication that the broadly worded amendment would not share the confines of its statutory predecessor. Whatever the variations among legislators on the question of the constitutional basis for the 1866 act and the amendment that followed, the Reconstruction debates would not support a view of the latter as confined to the list of rights in the former—perhaps the most common misconception among originalist scholars of the Fourteenth Amendment.

The scattered appearances of the school segregation issue during the 1860s included the context of Washington, D.C., but only indirectly since separate schools for blacks, supported by a special property tax directed toward black property owners, already had been established there by Congress in 1862 soon after emancipation in the nation's capital.[35] In 1864, Congress did away with the tax and required school officials to receive a share of the school funds pro rata without challenging the segregated arrangement.[36] Appropriations similarly were made for the segregated schools in 1866 without debate on segregation itself.[37]

In 1867, Sumner introduced an amendment to compel the former Confederate states to require in their constitutions that their legislatures "establish and sustain a system of public schools open to all, without distinction of race or color."[38] In terms foretelling Justice Harlan's characterization of segregation in the transportation context, Sumner described his motion as a proposition "to require a system of free schools open to all without distinction of caste."[39] The proposition was open to challenge on more than segregationist grounds because congressional power to require the states to establish systems of education in their constitutions was a contentious issue.[40] Frelinghuysen had such an objection to the amendment, but his statement included the significant suggestion that the proposal was unnecessary because the Fourteenth Amendment already abolished racial distinctions:

The proposition is that we shall provide free schools without distinction of race. The reconstruction law already provides that there shall be no discrimination in legislation on account of race or color. The fourteenth amendment has that provision, and that amendment must be a part of the constitution before any one of these States can be introduced. There is, therefore, no necessity for that part of the Senator's amendment.[41]

George Williams asked Sumner specifically whether his amendment would abolish segregated schools, and the Massachusetts senator replied, "If I should have my way, according to the true principle, it would be that the schools, precisely like the ballot box or the rail cars, should be open to all. But the proposition is necessarily general in its character; it does not go into details."[42] It is worthy of note that Sumner both acknowledged the desegregation of railroad cars and suggested that consistency dictated the same results with respect to schools. Still, his response reveals that the issue of school segregation was being addressed—perhaps by design due to political considerations—in terms so general that one wonders how directly the Senate was willing to consider the issue at all. Sumner's amendment was rejected by an even 20–20 vote, with Frelinghuysen included among the "nays."[43] Considering that the Fourteenth Amendment was not yet ratified and that votes against Sumner's proposal did not necessarily infer disapproval of desegregation, the vote indicates the strength of Sumner's position in the Senate[44]—any refusal to consider the consequences of abolishing racial distinctions notwithstanding. Sumner regretted his failure, however, and he did not refrain from expressing his disappointment.[45]

During debates over the Southern states in 1868, school segregation returned on various additional occasions. The discussion surrounding *Miles*, the Pennsylvania segregation decision that George Woodward had quoted on the floor, may be cited in the school segregation context because the opinion upheld this form of segregation among others.[46] Kerr made a vitriolic attack on school integration as a debasement of white children.[47] Beck condemned prospects for integration in Arkansas at length and expressed his disapproval toward the examples of South Carolina and Louisiana.[48]

The Arkansas debate included rare statements of tolerance for segregation by a senator who had voted for the Fourteenth Amendment and by another Republican supporter of Reconstruction. Frelinghuysen, who did not enter Congress until November 1866,[49] responded to a question from John B. Henderson about whether a state could segregate schools as follows:

I cannot answer that question, for I do not think that either the constitutional amendment or the proposition of the Senator's colleague touches that question, as to what school they shall be educated in; but I think that . . . the constitutional amendment, prevents a discrimination in civil or political rights on account of race or color.[50]

Henderson expressed his "desire that the negroes shall have an equal right in the school moneys, but that the State may require them to be educated in different schools from the whites."[51] Henderson's position seems clear enough, but Frelinghuysen's is difficult to accept on its face due to both his earlier expressed views on the subject and (as remains to be seen) his later views staunchly defending school integration.

In 1870, an amendment proposed by Henry Wilson to bind Virginia against various discriminations, including preventing anyone from "participating equally in the school fund or school privileges" on racial grounds, prompted Conkling to express reservations about congressional intervention "so intimately into the social condition."[52] The amendment was defeated,[53] but the outcome could have been motivated by several other expressed reservations, including congressional power to bind a state in the manner that was being attempted.[54] During later House debates over Virginia's readmission, Bingham praised Virginia's constitution for providing "that the schools of the State shall be free and open to all the children of the Commonwealth from the age of five years to the age of twenty-one years, and that none of those children shall be excluded from the benefit of the public schools."[55] The congressman's remark, however, was general enough to leave doubt that it addressed school integration under the Fourteenth Amendment.

The notion that the Fourteenth Amendment was concerned about racial discrimination in schools surfaced more clearly in the debates over the readmission of Mississippi, which followed the Virginia debates in 1870, though as in similar contexts, congressional power to fix conditions under the Guaranty Clause of the Constitution was also a major issue. Howard asserted that "[n]o more humane, benevolent, and . . . necessary provision can be inserted" into the proposed legislation than the condition attached to Mississippi that its constitution "shall never be so amended or changed as to deprive any citizen, or class of citizens of the United States, of the school rights and privileges secured by the constitution of said State."[56] The senator expressed support for a ban on racial discrimination in funding education without addressing segregation, though Trumbull denied that guaranteeing "a republican form of government has anything to do with the establishment of schools in a State."[57] Stewart did not find constitutional power for the school provision under the Guaranty Clause, but he did illustrate how his reservations about the legislation did not change his beliefs about the impact of the Fourteenth Amendment:

I believe that Congress has a good deal of additional power to interfere to protect the people of the South in their civil rights that it did not have previous to our fourteenth amendment. I believe that the first section of the fourteenth amendment, taken in connection with the civil-rights bill and the fifteenth amendment, authorizes the exercise of a good deal of controlling power to keep these people straight; and inasmuch as this question is open, and there is being so much said, that it may not be overlooked I propose to call attention to the fourteenth amendment.

After quoting Section 1 of the amendment, the Nevada senator remarked,

That is one of the conditions-precedent which Congress has matured, and upon which much legislation for the protection of the people of the South may be legitimately predicated as cases arise. The States shall make no discrimination in their laws. I believe if the State of Mississippi should pass a law which would deprive the colored man of the same rights and privileges of schools that the white man has, or make any other discrimination which would deny him the equal protection and benefit of the laws, we have direct constitutional power to interfere; but I do not believe we can say in advance that she shall not change a particular provision of her constitution—in advance, I mean, of any attempt on her part to violate the Constitution of the United States or the principles upon which reconstruction is based.

Stewart found the bill "unnecessary" given Mississippi's "good faith" and added:

We have put in the Constitution of the United States certain powers to enable us to protect the people of the South, to enable us to protect the colored people particularly in their rights. . . . [W]e can go into all the States and secure to all men the equal protection of the laws in their civil rights; we can wipe out all distinctions and discriminations on account of race or color in their political rights.[58]

Willey added that the schools provision "does not seem to accomplish what Senators seem to suppose that it does" because in his view "[t]here is nothing in this system to prevent that discrimination that they shall not have equal benefits with other classes of citizens in that State."[59]

Many of the statements supporting equal school privileges or equal access are too general to be taken as specific statements on segregation. During the Georgia readmission debate, Benjamin Butler pointed out to alleviate objections that "the whole scope and effect of our bill" imposing a restriction on Georgia would be to require "equal rights and privileges in the school fund which will be the product of the taxation of" both races.[60] Other comments of his colleagues might have been similarly limited, but even the more vague language about equal privileges offers support for the notion that public schools were included in the realm of civil rights rather than social rights, which government could not address.

The segregation issue was brought to the floor more directly after Sumner introduced a bill to desegregate schools in Washington, D.C., in 1870.[61] A school reorganization bill that provided for the abolition of racial distinctions in admissions to Washington public schools was reported to the Senate on February 8, 1871, over the objections of James Patterson, the chairman of the Senate District of Columbia Committee.[62] Patterson proposed to strike out the provision abolishing racial distinctions, agreeing with the bill "as to principle" but differing "as to policy" because he predicted that the "amendment will tend to destroy the schools of the city, or to put them back at least ten or fifteen years."[63] Patterson's stand dem-

onstrates the conflict between principle and practicability on the segregation issue. Far from lending support to the notion that Congress'
conception of the principle of equality did not entail integration, his views
illustrate how a legislator might oppose desegregation measures on practical grounds rather than on grounds of principle (the grounds on which
constitutional law is based). Even Patterson added his aspiration that some
day, racial prejudice, which was "transitory, will pass away, and the children of different races and different colors will mix in the schools."[64]

Sumner and Republican John S. Harris of Louisiana expressed their
hopes that the clause would not be removed, the latter senator asserting,
"We have adopted the principle of equality in the Constitution of the
United States, and I think this is a proper place to enact a law in accordance
therewith."[65] Patterson countered with a question as to the success of integration in Harris' home state—adding again, "the principle I do not oppose; it is only the policy"—and the senator from Louisiana replied that
his state had "difficulties to contend with that they have not here in Washington."[66] Sumner compared objections to those of legislators who opposed
the right of blacks to "ride in the horse-cars" and argued,

Now that it is proposed to apply the same principle to the schools, we are again
assured with equal seriousness and gravity that though correct in principle, it is not
practical. Sir, I take issue on that general proposition. I insist that whatever is
correct in principle is practical. Anything else would make this world a failure and
obedience to the laws of God impossible.

The provision which my friend would strike out is simply to carry into education
the same principle which we have carried into the courtroom, into the horse car,
and to the ballot-box; that is all. If there be any argument in favor of the provision
in these other cases, allow me to say that it is stronger in the school-room, inasmuch
as the child is more impressionable than the man. You should not begin life with
a rule that sanctions a prejudice. Therefore do I insist, especially for the sake of
children, for the sake of those tender years most susceptible to human influence,
that we should banish a rule which will make them grow up with a separation
which will be to them a burden—a burden to the white, for every prejudice is a
burden to him who has it, and a burden to the black, who will suffer always under
the degradation. . . .

A great protection to the colored child, and a great assurance of his education,
will be that he is educated on the same benches and by the same teachers with the
white child. You may give him what is sometimes called an equivalent in another
school; but this is not equality. His right is to equality and not to equivality. He
has equality only when he comes into your common school and finds no exclusion
there on account of his skin.[67]

Sumner cited passages from a report from trustees of black schools during
his speech, including a statement that the laws creating segregated schools

in Washington "were enacted as a temporary expedient to meet a condition of things which has now passed away."[68]

Carpenter added a similar statement on the necessity of applying the Constitution's abolition of racial distinctions to the case of schools:

[W]e have said by our Constitution, we have said by our statutes, we have said by our party platforms, we have said through the political press, we have said from every stump in the land, that from this time henceforth forever, where the American flag floats, there shall be no distinction of race or color or on account of previous condition of servitude, but that all men, without regard to these distinctions, shall be equal, undistinguished before the law. Now . . . that principle covers this whole case. We have said that these men, in common with all men, shall vote. We have said that they shall sit in the jury-box and upon the bench; that they may hold office; and we have assumed to destroy all these distinctions. If we insist upon destroying this distinction as to suffrage and holding office, how absurd it is to set up the distinction at the very fountain of life, and to say that in education, which is to shape the course of life, there shall be made the very distinction which we have been amending the Constitution and legislating for ten years to abolish![69]

Carpenter added that "[t]his is no question of social equality" since "here we are providing for the establishment and management of a public institution," where racial discrimination was no more excusable than at the polls.[70]

Patterson argued that his proposal was simply not to address the segregation issue, thus leaving it to the discretion of the school board to determine school arrangements, and he explained that his stand was due only to complaints his committee was getting that many white children would not attend mixed schools.[71] "Even some ten of the most intelligent of the colored people of this District . . . discussed this matter with me," he added, and despite their desire to have both races mix in the schools, "they admitted that in their judgment the colored schools of this District would be injured, and the educational advantages of the colored children would be injured" under an integrated arrangement.[72] School officials from both black and white schools also had visited Patterson and explained that desegregation could not be executed or that it would destroy the white schools.[73] The senator from New Hampshire reiterated his regret, wishing "that these prejudices did not exist and that the children might be thrown together in the schools; but we must take things as we find them."[74] He looked forward to the time when the people would be educated "up to a point where they can exercise these political privileges and rights," and he repeated that he was with Sumner on principle, just not on practice.[75] In his opinion, even most blacks in the nation's capital did not want the desegregation provision.[76] Patterson's candid discussion of the motivations behind his position undermines rather than strengthens the notion, for purposes of constitutional analysis, that those who refused to prevent school segregation were acting out of a deeper belief in the Constitution's tolerance of segregation.

Thurman delivered extended remarks against Sumner's proposal, asking his colleagues not to aggravate objections to the common school system by adding the "terrible difficulty that arises from the distinctions of race."[77] He warned of the mistreatment of black children that would occur in integrated schools and characterized the situation as implicating social equality.[78] He added that he did not object at all to allowing blacks "to ride in the public conveyances of the country"—a noteworthy concession by an opponent of Reconstruction—but he found it "to be a very different question" when the context changed to compulsory integration in schools.[79]

Frederick Sawyer rejected contentions that school desegregation would not work, pointing out that despite the obstacle of prejudice that faced "every other step which has been taken by the Congress . . . toward the establishment of the equal rights of the races," including the integration of public conveyances, such measures had succeeded because people needed such facilities.[80] He feared that striking out the school desegregation clause would be interpreted as "a renunciation on the part of the Senate of their faith in the universal application of the doctrine of the equality of all men before the law."[81] "[T]his prejudice of race," he contended, "is not, perhaps, so deep as it appears."[82] Sawyer refuted Thurman's contention that "social privileges" were involved on the grounds that "[t]he question is whether the privileges of the public schools are privileges which belong to the public. . . . These schools are maintained by . . . common, public funds . . . and those funds should be administered impartially, giving to no class of men any privilege over another class of men."[83] For the South Carolina senator, anything short of keeping the desegregation clause would "revers[e] the action which has been the chief glory of the Republican party" and constitute "a gross sacrifice of principle" because of a prejudice originating in slavery.[84]

Thomas Tipton compared the practice of keeping black regiments during the war with that of school segregation and asked, "is it a crime to be practical?"[85] Separate schools, he thought, would not allow black children to be "overshadowed by the superior advantages of" white children.[86] Republican Hiram R. Revels, the nation's first black senator, asserted that it was the nation's duty to discourage prejudice, and he added that blacks would not act "imprudently" by "hurriedly shov[ing] their children into" schools with whites where there was a strong desire to keep them out.[87] If the Senate adopted Patterson's amendment, however, Revels warned that prejudice would be encouraged, "and, perhaps, after the encouragement thus given, the next step may be to ask Congress to prevent them from riding in the street cars, or something like that."[88] The Mississippi senator also explained how he felt that "mixed schools are very far from bringing about social equality."[89]

Joshua Hill wished to avoid the segregation issue and contended that everyone, including blacks, desired to have their children educated in separate schools.[90] The senator offered an amendment that would have a similar effect to Patterson's, but Henry Wilson reminded his colleagues of the "struggle" in Massachusetts to "destroy caste in our common schools" and hoped that the Senate would "stand upon the principle of equality of rights and privileges" by rejecting the proposal.[91] Wilson acknowledged the possibility of "practical difficulties in carrying out this system of equality; . . . but, sir, it is the mode and manner of educating the people against caste."[92] Sumner's legislation died with no further discussion, and a similar House bill was defeated.[93]

Sumner made a similar effort to desegregate schools in 1872.[94] Stockton argued that his colleague's bill violated "the rights of white people" by compelling mixed schools.[95] Thomas Bayard argued that blacks received a proportionate amount of school funds and suggested that if blacks "cannot get along by themselves," it demonstrated "an absolute inferiority, a confession of some great defects which must exist by the law of nature, and against which these puny efforts of human legislation will prove utterly and absurdly fruitless."[96] The senator also found it unrepublican to impose the scheme on the majority of whites who did not desire it for the sake of a minority.[97] James Harper opposed the proposal and suggested that it involved social equality.[98] Orris Ferry indicated his willingness to see mixed schools if the people wanted them, but he felt that Congress should not attempt to manage the common schools "from the outside."[99] Trumbull did not believe the bill merited the Senate's time, but Edmunds wanted it considered because "it involves a principle that every one . . . says he believes in now."[100] The legislation met with approval on a procedural test, but it was never taken up for a final vote.[101] In the end, the Reconstruction Congress' record with Washington schools, which never included a vote for integration (despite appropriations to preexisting segregated schools), is not informative because it involves at most an omission to address segregation.[102]

The issue of school integration surfaced in the 1872 House debates over a proposed scheme for federal aid to education, but again in an inconclusive way. Democrats opposed such aid out of fear that it would allow the U.S. Commissioner of Education too much power over schools, including power to induce desegregation by withholding funds from noncomplying schools.[103] Democrats expressing apprehensions about mixed schools during these debates included Henry D. McHenry,[104] Kerr,[105] Abram Comingo,[106] John T. Harris,[107] and John Storm,[108] but Republicans Washington Townsend[109] and Austin Blair[110] tried to assure their colleagues that the bill did not address the issue. Rainey asked that if the bill were to impose desegregation, "what harm would result therefrom?"[111] Storm asserted that the bill did "force mixed schools upon the South," because as soon as a state established segregated schools, "the Radicals of the country will denounce it as violating the fourteenth amendment."[112] The House passed an amendment by Democrat Frank Hereford providing that federal funds would not be withheld on grounds of segregated schools,[113] but this demonstrated little more than the debates over schools in Washington, D.C. As was recognized during the debates, there was another bill pending at the time in the Senate that would include school integration[114]—an incentive for the House to decline to address segregation in a funding bill before it would face legislation dealing with the issue directly.

c. Debates over the Civil Rights Act of 1875 and Its Precursors

c.1. The Forty-Second Congress

Given the relative paucity of specific evidence addressing school segregation and the Fourteenth Amendment during preratification debates, the debates over Reconstruction's final civil rights law, which included several framers, offer the most important evidence of the original understanding of the issue.[115] One of the early statements referring to school segregation actually came from Thurman, who argued that the assumption of Sumner's bill—that school segregation violated the rights, privileges, and immunities of citizenship—would allow legislators in a state that segregated schools by law to be sued under the Ku Klux Klan Act.[116]

The school segregation issue was addressed by numerous legislators during consideration of Sumner's rider to the amnesty bill in the second session of the Forty-Second Congress. In his dialogue with Sumner in which he expressed tolerance for other forms of segregation, Hill maintained that there was no "denial of a civil right" in provisions for separate schools that nevertheless provided equal benefits to both races.[117] Others had trouble with Sumner's amendment on the grounds that amnesty bills enjoyed special status under Section 3 of the Fourteenth Amendment and could not have legislation dealing with other matters attached, an argument that did not prevail.[118] Sumner's proposal nevertheless was rejected on December 21, 1871, by a twenty-nine to thirty vote.[119] Significantly, the bill carried among those senators who had voted for the Fourteenth Amendment (whether in the Senate or the House) by a vote of twelve to three, four others being recorded as absent.[120] One senator recorded as "not voting" for the constitutional amendment (James Patterson) voted for the proposal, and Garrett Davis, who voted against the Fourteenth Amendment, also voted against Sumner's rider to the amnesty bill.[121] The Massachusetts senator reintroduced his amendment later that day before the start of Christmas recess.[122]

The Senate resumed its business in January 1872 and debated the amendment with several references to school segregation. After arguing for desegregation in other contexts, Sumner drew an analogy to schools:

The common school . . . is an inn where children rest on the road to knowledge. It is a public conveyance where children are passengers. It is a theater where children resort for enduring recreation. Like the others, it assumes to provide for the public; therefore it must be open to all; nor can there be any exclusion, except on grounds equally applicable to the inn, the public conveyance, and the theater.

But the common school has a higher character. Its object is the education of the young, and it is sustained by taxation to which all contribute. Not only does it hold itself out to the public by its name and its harmony with the other institutions; but it assumes the place of parent to all children within its locality, bound always to a parent's watchful care and tenderness, which can know no distinction of child.[123]

Citing extensive testimony from outside Congress for support, the senator concluded "that the separate school from its very nature must be a failure, and that it never could afford equal education."[124] Sumner called the segregated school "an indignity to the race" that "has for its badge inequality" and contradicts "all that is implied in the recent constitutional amendments."[125]

Among those who expressed opposition to the school desegregation measure in this debate were several Democrats and two Republicans, one of whom had voted for the Fourteenth Amendment. Lot Morrill voiced his opposition on grounds similar to those he held regarding the other desegregation measures, feeling that "taking the direction of the common schools of the States" would be "invading a province . . . which lies outside of the domain of this Government."[126] Orris Ferry, who unlike Morrill was not in Congress when the Fourteenth Amendment was passed, found the matter "immaterial" in his home state of Connecticut, where he claimed both races attended the same schools, but he defended a state's right to control its own school system.[127] Eli Saulsbury attacked the idea of abolishing racial distinctions in schools and charged that the amendment imposed social equality.[128] Garrett Davis included schools in his list of public utilities with which he found a freedom of association.[129] Thurman argued that racially segregated schools did not violate the Fourteenth Amendment any more than separation by sex.[130] The pending proposal forced white and black children "into social intercourse," the senator continued, and would "pull down the poor white child to the level of the black."[131] James Kelly felt school segregation differed from stage-coach discrimination, dreading the assumption of federal jurisdiction "for every little petty misdemeanor of school children" at the exclusion of state courts.[132] Vickers argued that government power to compel integration implied similar power to regulate other aspects of schools, and he predicted that the measure would lead to "intense feeling and opposition, and the destruction of the school system."[133] Saulsbury made the same prediction.[134]

Responding to Thurman's question about the basis of federal power for such an interference in the states as Sumner proposed, Carpenter asserted,

I have no doubt of the power of this Government under the fourteenth amendment, (which applies to common schools and to Legislatures of the States and to the courts of the States, and to every institution in the States and existing under their authority, as much as it does to the citizens of the States,) to say that a colored man shall have his right in the common school.[135]

The senator distinguished between private "voluntary institutions, whether incorporated or not, which we ought not to interfere with, and those great institutions which are supported by law and maintained by general taxation."[136] It "does not take away all power to control" the schools to say that "if you have a school, and support it by taxation on all citizens, then you shall not discriminate between the children of different citizens."[137]

John Sherman viewed the issue as implicating the propositions that attending public schools was "both a right and a privilege" and that "all are entitled to equal privileges in the public schools."[138] Edmunds argued that under the Fourteenth Amendment,

when the law sets up a common school, which is the creature of the law, there cannot be equality of protection and equality of right when the law of the State, if you please, declares that a man of one color of hair or of skin may send his children, and the man of another color of hair may not send his.[139]

As mentioned earlier, the Sumner proposal was narrowly passed on February 9, and of the legislators who had voted for the Fourteenth Amendment, only two (Trumbull and Morrill) voted against it while twelve voted for it, excluding Colfax's tie-breaking vote.[140] Edmunds and James Nye were absent for the February vote, and the show of twelve senators in support included Zachariah Chandler and Aaron Cragin, who had been absent from the December 1871 vote. By this time, therefore, the cumulative endorsement of the original supporters of the amendment was even more impressive than the December vote alone.[141]

As has been seen, the amnesty bill as amended received enough opposition to prevent its passage,[142] and the rest of the Forty-Second Congress included deadlock and ultimately ill-fated attempts to add a significant civil rights provision to the bill.[143] This period nevertheless included significant statements and votes on school segregation. James G. Blair protested the coercion of one race to attend school with another and characterized the issue involved as one of social privilege rather than a civil right.[144] McHenry predicted that in his state "the people will abandon the common-school system rather than submit to this unjust and unconstitutional regulation which is forced upon them by a fanaticism which heeds neither the liberty of the people nor the rights of the States."[145] House opponents of the measure employed a filibustering strategy on April 15, 1872, which eventually led frustrated Republican supporters—who clearly commanded a majority in support of the bill, but not the two-thirds they needed to suspend the rules—to seek an alternative strategy to attain their goals.[146]

In the Senate debates of the following month, Edmunds debated both

Trumbull and Orris Ferry on the validity of the school desegregation measure, arguing in response to the Illinois senator that the right to go to school is a civil rather than a social right and challenging the Connecticut senator to distinguish between integration in schools and in horse-cars.[147] Morton asked Trumbull to characterize the right to attend school, and the Illinois senator replied, "It is not any right at all. It is a matter to be regulated by the localities."[148] He found civil rights to constitute those "rights appertaining to the individual as a free, independent citizen," such as contract and property rights, but Morton responded that

the point . . . is not to be evaded or dodged by saying that the right to go to school is not a civil right. . . . You may call it a civil right or a political right; and if there be a distinction, if a right to participate in these schools is to be governed by color or any other distinction, I say that is a fraud upon those who pay the taxes. . . . [W]here there are public schools supported by common taxation upon everybody, white and black, there there is a civil right that there shall be equal participation in those schools. That is the point.[149]

Soon afterward came the only statement from a supporter of the Sumner amendment throughout the entire debates that might be cited to support a result contrary to *Brown v. Board of Education*.[150] John Sherman expressed approval of the Ohio Supreme Court's decision in *State* ex rel. *Garnes v. McCann*,[151] which upheld segregated schools under the Fourteenth Amendment, but in view of his consistent opposition to "separate but equal" substitutes for Sumner's bill, it is unclear that he understood the decision.[152] It might be that he was relying on newspaper reports because the court's opinion was handed down only the day before.[153] In his discussion of the case, the Ohio senator remarked that there were "certain cases defined by the law" of his state in which "the colored people may have, when they are a certain number, separate schools" with proportional funding, but "[i]n ordinary cases, by the common consent and custom of every one there since the war was over, the whites and the blacks go to the same schools."[154] Despite *Garnes'* actual holding, Sherman could have been referring to voluntary segregation, a prospect he envisioned might temporarily occur in the South by mutual choice, rather than *de jure* segregation.[155] The matter received no further attention, and other statements from both the bill's supporters and opponents indicate overwhelmingly that the civil rights amendment banned school segregation.[156] (Orris Ferry, who endorsed *Garnes* the next day, stated that "it has been the assertion of those who support this bill with regard to the schools that compelling the separation of the races into different buildings was a violation of the fourteenth amendment, notwithstanding that both races, in their separate buildings, enjoyed the same or equal accommodations, facilities, and advantages."[157])

Arthur Boreman expressed his opposition to the school provision "as a question of expediency, not one of constitutional right," and he found no violation of equal rights in laws that had the same application to both races.[158] Frank Blair believed it was "in accordance with good policy to keep" the two races "separate and apart."[159] Orris Ferry felt school integration should not be imposed by Congress on localities and moved to exclude the school provision from the bill.[160] Ferry's amendment was rejected by a vote of twenty-five to twenty-six, with thirteen of the fourteen legislators present who had voted for the Fourteenth Amendment voting no (all except Trumbull).[161]

Blair then proposed a proviso stating, "*Provided, however*, That the people of every city, county, or State shall decide for themselves, at an election to be held for that purpose, the question of mixed or separate schools for the white or black people."[162] James Alcorn stated that the matter of school segregation had been settled in his state and that he would prefer his constituents not to have additional trouble over the issue through the proposal.[163] Blair defended the bill under "the right of local self-government," but Howe felt compelled to vote against it by his desire "to put an end, once and for all, to . . . the spirit of caste."[164] Edmunds added that desegregation was necessary to abolish racial distinctions, just as in other contexts, and that this task could not be relegated to the decisions of communities.[165] Thomas Bayard took issue with Sumner's invocation of caste to support his arguments.[166] Blair's motion was defeated by a vote of twenty-three to thirty, with fourteen of the sixteen legislators present who had voted for the Fourteenth Amendment voting no (Trumbull and William Sprague being the exceptions).[167] The votes on the Ferry and Blair proposals both indicate that a majority of the Senate and an overwhelming majority of those present who had voted for the Fourteenth Amendment found school segregation incompatible with the scheme of equality the amendment had established.[168]

The issue was raised again in several floor statements during the remainder of the session before the passage, in Sumner's absence, of the alternate civil rights amendment without the schools provision. Boreman felt that both races were satisfied with segregated schools and argued that "two separate schools are a better provision for" blacks "than one mixed school where they might be treated unkindly and receive less attention than when they are taught separately."[169] Although he believed the situation might be different after a generation of educating the people against prejudice, Orris Ferry found integration to be against the interests of the races at the time.[170] Thurman again challenged congressional authority to pass the bill and endorsed *Garnes*.[171] Trumbull reiterated his view that school integration was not a civil right but contended that both races should enjoy the benefits of school appropriations.[172]

Several senators argued about the practical destructive effect of school integration. Alcorn praised Mississippi's record with segregation, though he admitted that division among the races made it a "compromise" that "was necessary to perpetuate the cause of education," and he opposed Sumner's amendment chiefly because he thought it would "destroy the school system in the State which I represent."[173] Frank Blair asserted that the proposal would "destroy the public schools throughout a large number of the States" by driving out "hundreds and thousands of white children" from integrated schools.[174] Edward Rice found the school provision "the most ungenerous and infamous clause in the first section of this bill" and predicted an outcome similar to that articulated by Blair.[175]

Edmunds reiterated his belief that school desegregation was consistent with the principle of equal rights applied to other areas and found that "if you can establish separate schools you can establish separate courts."[176] Soon before the vote in Sumner's absence on the amendment striking out schools, Frelinghuysen remarked that "the opinion of the Senate has been expressed over and over again in favor of retaining the provisions in reference to public schools" and that the failure to incorporate them "very much impairs the effect of the bill."[177] The New Jersey senator's reservations did not prevent the success of the compromise amendment or the failure of Sumner's subsequent attempt to add his original amendment.[178]

c.2. The Forty-Third Congress

The Forty-Third Congress' consideration of school segregation in its renewed debates over civil rights legislation, however it would appear from floor statements, would mark one of the most controversial chapters in the Republican Party's history. Grant's Second Inaugural Address had urged the nation to give "the colored man . . . access to the schools,"[179] a statement that was not necessarily clear enough to specify desegregation over equal access more generally. Amid the political turmoil the school integration issue brought in 1874,[180] however, the president did not want the civil rights bill to address schools, and his intention to influence such a result was evidenced by the spreading rumors that he would veto the bill if it compelled mixed schools.[181]

It is unclear that Grant actually would have vetoed the bill, which he had urged in the first place and ultimately signed after it was amended, but to the extent the motives for his stand are apparent, they seem to have been both political and practical. He feared that a measure compelling the integration of schools would result in the abandonment of public education entirely, and after the election, he reportedly remarked that the civil rights legislation did more than all other causes put together to defeat his party because almost all whites found it distasteful.[182] Consistent with his concern over education and equality, however, he appealed to the country a year later for a constitutional amendment "making it the duty of each of the several States to establish and forever maintain free public schools adequate to the education of all the children in the rudimentary branches within their respective limits, irrespective of sex, color, birthplace, or religions."[183]

Former Senator Benjamin F. Wade, the staunch Radical who would have become president had Andrew Johnson been removed from office, remarked that the bill fomented so much opposition from the South, border states, and Midwest that citizens in those areas voted against the Republican Party in the 1874 elections.[184] He agreed with the principle of the measure, but he also found it impracticable, pointing out that "a thing may be right in the abstract, and yet not be expedient, because public sentiment will not tolerate or accept the full application of the principle."[185] Several other politicians agreed on the bill's devastating effect on the Republicans.[186] Among incumbent legislators, however, debates would follow a different track from what one might expect from the external political realities of the time.

In the early House debates, Democrats James Beck,[187] Milton Durham,[188] John Atkins,[189] and Milton Southard[190] attacked the school integration provision as an encroachment on state or local power. Alexander Stephens,[191] Roger Mills,[192] John M. Bright,[193] Hiram P. Bell,[194] John Glover,[195] and Robert Vance[196] charged that the bill violated the freedom of association or imposed social equality. Glover expressly called it his state's "constitutional right" to decide the question of school segregation.[197] Democrats Mills,[198] Durham,[199] James H. Blount,[200] William Herndon,[201] and Atkins[202] also charged that compelling mixed schools would lead to the withdrawal of whites or the shutdown or destruction of the school system.

On the other side, Josiah Thomas Walls, a black Florida Republican, asserted under the Fourteenth Amendment that "the individual rights, privileges, and immunities of the citizens, irrespective of color, to all facilities afforded by corporations, licensed establishments, common carriers, and institutions supported by the public, are sacred, under the law, and that violations of the same will entail punishment safe and certain."[203] William Stowell pointed out that schools were "legal institutions, established and maintained by law," and he categorized them with hotels, railroads, and juries, insisting that "all these legal institutions shall be for the benefit of all alike."[204] Benjamin Butler viewed the argument that the bill would "break up the common-school system of the South" as a "threat" to be disregarded.[205] "All that we ask is equal laws, equal legislation, and equal rights throughout the length and breadth of this land," insisted Richard Cain.[206]

In the Senate, Frelinghuysen delivered a long speech defending the Sumner bill, having assumed a leadership role in promoting the measure after its sponsor's death.[207] "Subjecting to taxation is a guarantee of the right to use," the New Jersey senator asserted, and while "[u]niform discrimination may be made in schools and institutions of learning and benevolence on account of age, sex, morals, preparatory qualifications, health, and the like," the "one idea in the bill" was the "equality of races before the law."[208] The bill's aim was "to destroy . . . the distinctions of race," and he attempted to distinguish *Garnes* by pointing out that the bill would not prevent voluntary segregation in which whites and blacks each would choose to attend different schools.[209] When one turned from such a voluntary arrangement to legal classifications of schools by race, however, the situation became "an enactment of personal degradation" through law.[210] "The objection to such a law on our part is that it would be legislation in violation of the fundamental principles of the nation," Frelinghuysen added.[211] The senator also remarked that "we know that if we establish separate schools for colored people, those schools will be inferior to those for the whites."[212]

Daniel Pratt also pointed out that the bill allowed voluntary segregation and anticipated that in large cities where "the colored people are numerous enough to have separate schools of their own, they would probably prefer their children should be educated by themselves."[213] "[I]n the villages and country" where "separate schools will be impracticable, and the colored children . . . must necessarily be where the great majority of the children are white," Pratt maintained that "here the question must be fairly met whether they shall share or be excluded from the benefits of the public schools."[214] Thurman asserted, "I do not think that any one of the majority of the Judiciary Committee who reported the bill will sustain" the assertion that the bill did not require integrated schools, and he explained by his understanding how schools would not be established under the bill, leaving both races without education.[215] Senator John W. Johnston, a Conservative from Virginia, maintained that his state's separate-but-equal school arrangement was "the only way to make [the schools] successful," and he had an excerpt from a Republican paper read on the floor that included the following argument:

We do not care to discuss any abstract principle involved in this measure. The *practical results* which are *absolutely certain* to follow its adoption alone concern us. We know as well as any future consequence of present action can be known that the attempt to combine the two races in the schools will result *in breaking up the schools altogether*. We recognize this fact as caused by prejudices and antipathies which we have no power to uproot.[216]

This quote articulated very well the practical concerns that faced school integration efforts beyond matters of principle that otherwise might have controlled.

Morton argued that racial segregation in schools was "a gross discrimination" that violated the Equal Protection Clause, and he argued with Augustus Merrimon about the distinction between separation by race and by sex under the Fourteenth Amendment.[217] The North Carolina senator shared many of his colleagues' concerns that public education laws would be repealed if the bill were passed.[218] He defended the "separate but equal" doctrine, but Morton countered him: "the States are left free to establish common schools or not; but if they do establish them at public expense they must extend their benefits equally and in common to the children of all races. . . . That is the great purpose, the spirit, and the body of the fourteenth amendment."[219]

Boutwell argued that to provide

equal facilities . . . in different schools, is to rob your system of public instruction of that quality by which our people, without regard to race or color, shall be assimilated in ideas, personal, political, and public, so that when they arrive at the period of manhood they shall act together upon public questions with ideas formed under the same influences and directed to the same general results.[220]

Stockton attacked the notion that equality entails occupying the same schools and predicted that the bill would "break up the whole common-school system in this country."[221] Howe met such threats by remarking, "Let justice be done though the common schools and the very heavens fall."[222] The Republican senator acknowledged that voluntary segregation was possible under the bill, but he added, "let the individuals and not the superintendent of schools judge of the comparative merits of the schools."[223]

Alcorn went farther in acknowledging the extent to which voluntary segregation would be allowed under the bill, stating that he was "not in favor of mixing" schools and that blacks in Mississippi did not desire integration.[224] When Congress legislated, however, it must keep in mind that "[e]quality before the law demands that legislation should not be colored with the distinctions of class."[225] The Mississippi senator's stand might have seemed internally inconsistent, but his support of the bill did mark a change from his earlier pro-segregation stand, brought on perhaps because his constituents, most of whom were black, had insisted that he change his position.[226] The other Mississippi senator, Republican Henry R. Pease, doubted that schools would close as a result of the bill, foreseeing voluntary segregation as a result, but he felt that segregation by law made a racial distinction—"a distinction the intent of which is to foster a concomitant of slavery."[227] Eli Saulsbury charged his colleagues with pushing a bill that would "not affect their children, while they are avowing their purpose to force the mixed schools whereby the children of the poor white men may be compelled to be educated in associations with the colored children or not educated at all."[228] If pressed "too far," the senator predicted "that the school system of their States" would be "broken up."[229]

The long debates of May 22, 1874, included several amendment proposals, the first of which was an amendment from Senator Sargent providing

That nothing herein contained shall be construed to prohibit any State or school district from providing separate schools for persons of different sex or color, where such separate schools are equal in all respects to others of the same grade established by such authority, and supported by an equal *pro rata* expenditure of school funds.[230]

The Senate rejected the proposal by a vote of twenty-one to twenty-six, and eight of the eleven voting legislators who had voted for the Fourteenth Amendment (six being absent) voted against it.[231] One of the three endorsing the Sargent amendment, William B. Allison, would vote against a subsequent similar proposal from the same senator.[232] Allison and a second of the three approving votes—Stewart—would later vote for the bill without any such amendment.[233]

Boutwell followed with a proposal intended to clarify what he viewed as the bill's intention to desegregate every public school.[234] Stewart, who had voted for the Sargent amendment, stated that he would vote for mixed schools if he thought he "could accomplish that purpose and educate the colored man where he would not otherwise be educated," but because he feared that integrated schools "would not have that precise effect," he thought "it ought to be left optional to have schools mixed or separate as the people themselves desire" without "compel[ling] mixed schools."[235] He did not wish to go farther at that time[236] out of fear that states consequently might choose not to establish free schools at all, but he suggested that the Constitution first should require "every State to have a school system" to empower Congress to make desegregation effective.[237] The Nevada senator objected to the notion that the Boutwell amendment would "not leave it optional even with" blacks "to separate themselves, but must force them into the same school."[238] In a dialogue with Boutwell, Frelinghuysen remarked, "The law as it stands gives them the right to go to a white school," but the Massachusetts senator had his doubts.[239]

The proposal failed by a vote of five to forty-two,[240] but this overwhelming rejection—the votes against including several of the most radical senators who had unequivocally endorsed bans on school segregation—only helps indicates that the vote did not support a result contrary to *Brown v. Board of Education*. Avins erroneously construes the vote to show "that the school clause was not intended to be a school desegregation bill, but was designed to assure Negroes of equal school facilities,"[241] but such a conclusion could only arise from a failure to note the clear interpretation placed on the bill by both supporters and opponents. Whatever Stewart's support of the Sargent amendment may have indicated about the extent of his support of the "separate but equal" concept (or his different understanding of it[242]), the sum of relevant statements reacting to the Bout-well amendment indicates no more than that senators found no need to clarify the bill so that it would preclude voluntary segregation, which was not at issue in *Brown*. Votes on subsequent amendments would help prove as much.

An amendment from John B. Gordon to strike out the school clause entirely failed by a vote of fourteen to thirty, with all eleven of the original Fourteenth Amendment supporters present voting no, including two of the three senators who had voted for the Sargent amendment.[243] An additional amendment from Democrat Thomas C. McCreery to exclude schools that already were established failed with eleven ayes and votes against not counted.[244] Sargent followed not long afterward with a more ambiguous version of his earlier amendment that allowed segregated schools with a proportionate share of funds,[245] prompting an attack from Edmunds:

The whole effect of this proposition is to authorize States on account of color to deny the right to ride in a particular railroad car, or to go to a particular common school. If there is anything in the bill, it is exactly contrary to that. If there is anything in the fourteenth amendment it is exactly opposite to that. The fourteenth amendment does not authorize us to make any trades with States either way on the subject, or regulate the action of States. What the Constitution authorizes us to do is to enforce equality; and it is not half-equality, for there is no such thing as half-equality. . . . To put in these words here or in any part of the bill is merely to say in substance and effect that this bill shall have no force in asserting the equality that the fourteenth amendment to the Constitution asserts, if that asserts any equal-ity at all; and of course the bill goes on the theory that it does.[246]

Sargent denied that the Fourteenth Amendment compelled mixed schools, arguing that the notion "that the fourteenth amendment absolutely levels all distinctions and justifies you in putting heavy penalties to prevent a system of separate schools" would eliminate separation by sex in schools.[247] Edmunds countered that the California senator's conclusion would entail "that the fourteenth amendment does not, as it respects com-mon schools, level a distinction which a State may have a right to make on account of race and color."[248] He pointed out the need for consistency in applying the abolition of racial distinctions in railroads, highways, or steamboats to schools, "for the fourteenth amendment is general and sweeping."[249] It conferred "either an absolute right that the Constitution gives to the citizen, or it is nothing at all and does not touch the case."[250] In an attempt to introduce a practical consideration that supported defeat of Sargent's amendment, Edmunds also cited statistics indicating that black school facilities were being shortchanged.[251] Sargent responded with an analogy of sex segregation in railroad cars and an expression of his desire not to "overthrow" the public education system "into the dust."[252] His amendment was defeated by a vote of sixteen to twenty-eight, with the original Fourteenth Amendment supporters present voting against it by a margin of nine to one (Stewart being the exception).[253] Soon afterward, the Senate passed the Civil Rights Act with the school and jury clauses by a vote of twenty-nine to sixteen, all ten of those who voted for the Fourteenth Amendment casting their votes yes (including Stewart).[254] Among Republicans, the vote was twenty-three to three with Boreman, Carpenter, and John F. Lewis voting no.[255]

In the House, limited discussion of schools occurred in 1874. Roderick Butler expressed his view that the bill would retard education for blacks and was "satisfied that the colored people of my district do not want the school feature of the bill."[256] Chester Darrall of Louisiana cited his state's example to demonstrate that "the granting of the right of attendance in the public schools of the State to colored children does not destroy the usefulness of our schools,"[257] but Democrat John J. Davis warned, "Pass this measure and you strike a fatal blow at the free-school system of the South and in the border States."[258]

The 1874 elections left those who were leading the fight for the civil rights bill demoralized, the legislation—particularly the school provision—having been a major issue in the congressional campaigns.[259] Consideration of the bill in the House in the second session of Congress began on January 27, 1875, and the legislation's opponents initiated a filibuster that frustrated supporters; the ultimate result, however, was the elimination of the House filibuster when a majority was empowered to prevent business from being halted.[260] Under the revised rules, the House Judiciary Committee reported a bill on February 3, 1875, that desegregated inns, public conveyances, and places of public amusement while permitting "separate schools and institutions giving equal educational advantages in all respects for different classes of persons entitled to attend such schools."[261] Lame-duck Republicans maintained their support of the bill, but others who would be up for re-election in 1876 deserted the cause in large numbers.[262]

Three amendments to the bill were proposed by Republicans. John Cessna proposed to restore the Senate bill's language, which would include school desegregation.[263] Alexander White proposed an amendment that would allow segregation in all areas the bill covered.[264] Stephen Kellogg moved to strike out the schools provision without interfering with other desegregation provisions.[265] During debate, John Lynch described school segregation as "contrary to republicanism" and compared it with religious discrimination.[266] Storm argued that "[t]here is no escape from" the "conclusion" that "[i]f it is not a deprivation of equal rights to say that white children shall go into one public-school building and the colored into another building, then it is no deprivation of equal rights when a railroad company makes provision for carrying white passengers in one car and black in another."[267] Ellis Roberts stated that he preferred the House to the Senate bill because he understood the latter as a provision to "insist upon the same schools for the colored children as for the white children."[268]

Julius Burrows pointed out that in the schools clause, "[h]ere for the first time is the daring attempt to be made to enter upon a system of legislation which proposes to make a distinction between American citizens, and separate a people by class legislation which, under the Constitution, are united and equal."[269] He expressed his "warmest adherence to the doctrine of free schools" and asserted that the pending legislation could not be approved "without doing violence to the spirit of your institutions, trampling upon your Constitution, and inaugurating a course of legislation whose legitimate end is the subjugation of the weak of every class and race."[270] Approving segregated schools "would take a step directly backward, and undo in many of the States the work of half a century."[271]

Charles G. Williams predicted that the school segregation issue would plague the country again if it were not settled then, arguing that "temporary strife" was "better . . . than that growing prejudice and growing hate should rend and distract this country ever again."[272] In a similar spirit, William A. Phillips urged his colleagues to "divest" themselves "of prejudice and rise to the dignity of the occasion" by "producing the fruits of this great revolution and this elevation of the colored race."[273] Referring to the bill generally, John P. C. Shanks challenged the "[t]imid men . . . who have been afraid to stand up here and do right," and Garfield expressed his fearlessness: "If ruin comes from this, I welcome ruin."[274] Whatever courage Republicans could muster for other desegregation provisions, the dominant sentiment on mixed schools would not satisfy those Radicals who supported school integration to the end.

However strong the indications were in the previous session that support of the bill would be politically dangerous, this understanding had escalated by 1875, after so many Republican congressional careers had been ended. James B. Sener of Virginia indicated that he had "reasonable ground to apprehend that" passage "may cause the immediate suspension of" the school system "and possibly the permanent destruction of the system to the irretrievable injury of both races."[275] "But," he added, "I oppose this bill for another reason; I was before the people of my district in 1872 and again in 1874."[276] He explained that despite his votes against the civil rights proposals, he was defeated in 1874 because in his district "at the last moment the apprehension was started . . . and circulated through the press, that under the whip and spur of party pressure and party necessity . . . I might yield my honest convictions to the will of the majority."[277] Republican Edwin O. Stanard said that he would support the bill if it "would tend to the elevation of this people without damaging anybody else, . . . but believing that such is not the case, I cannot support it."[278]

Cain argued for the necessity of education for blacks and agreed as a compromise—"for the sake of the welfare of the republican party"—to assent to Kellogg's proposal, as important as he found the school clause (though he did not believe Southern blacks wanted mixed schools).[279] It was better, he asserted, to omit the provision altogether if Congress could not pass it "in its entirety," for "[w]e want no invidious discrimination in the laws of this country."[280] Simeon B. Chittenden spoke because "I do not want to go down with my party quite so deep as the bill will sink it if it becomes the law."[281] He acknowledged the "justice" and

conformity of the bill . . . with the late constitutional amendments. . . . But the bill is nevertheless an offense and menace to the dominant race. Say this is prejudice, or sentiment if you please. I am a practical man, and believe it impolitic unnecessarily to vex white men, North and South, by passing this bill now.[282]

Alexander White, sponsor of the segregation measure, articulated the danger the Republican Party faced and made an important concession about the measure he was proposing for adoption:

This is a question of expediency, not a matter of right. Your committee concede this by providing in their bill for separate schools. Had it been a matter of right or of principle, they could not have provided in their bill for separate schools; but as it was neither, but only a question of expediency, they could do so, and acted wisely and well in so doing.[283]

The Alabama congressman suggested that integration did not comport with the desires of blacks and that it was driving whites out of the Republican Party, citing the example of his state and the diminution of Republican power throughout the South.[284] He concluded,

If the civil-rights bill which is on your table becomes the law, you will drive these [Southern Republicans], whose fidelity to republican principles has been proven by sacrifices and trials to which no northern republican has been subjected, permanently away from you, and you obliterate in a brief time the republican party South.[285]

It is also significant that Kellogg defended his own amendment in the following terms:

As the bill is now drawn, we recognize a distinction in color which we ought not to recognize by any legislation of the Congress of the United States. Sir, in the legislation of this country I recognize no distinction of color, race, or birthplace. All ought to be equal before the law; and the children of all should have an equal right to the best education they can have in the public schools of the country. But this bill proposes to make a distinction by a national law. The proviso to the first section is one that makes a discrimination as to classes of persons attending public schools; and I do not wish to make any such provision in an act of Congress. . . . All are equal before the law, and all should be equal in the enjoyment of their rights. We believe that all men have the same privileges under the law, without distinction of race, color, or anything except as their own character or conduct in life shall make for them. But by the provisions of this bill you ask us to destroy the school system of the Southern States by an enactment which is not asked for by the colored people of the South and which they do not want, for they know it will be used to deprive them of the educational advantages that have been secured to them since their emancipation and since they became entitled to all the rights of citizens under the law of the land.[286]

Coming from the sponsor of the position that would succeed, this statement undermines rather than supports the idea that the "separate but equal" doctrine was consistent with the Fourteenth Amendment command to abolish racial distinctions. Like so many other statements, it reflects a sense of congressional reluctance to address the school issue because expediency precluded it—but without a willingness to have Congress actually place its imprimatur upon government-drawn racial distinctions.

James Monroe remarked that his radical constituents regarded "the bill as it now stands" as "a dangerous precedent" for introducing "formally into the statute law a discrimination between different classes of citizens in regard to their privileges as citizens."[287] He then conveyed the preferences of his black constituents who told him

that they would rather have their people take their chances under the Constitution and its amendments; that they would rather fall back upon the original principles of constitutional law and take refuge under their shadow than to begin with this poor attempt to confer upon them the privileges of education connected with this discrimination.[288]

In other words, Southern blacks "think their chances for good schools will be better under the Constitution with the protection of the courts than under a bill containing such provisions as this."[289] Since the schools clause "will irritate all classes and please nobody" (conservatives interpreting the bill to impose mixed schools in certain cases), the Ohio congressman advocated striking it from the bill altogether.[290]

Republican Barbour Lewis believed "it is right that the colored man should have the same privileges in schools as the white," but "while nothing can be said against it on principle, still you must remember that legislation cannot always control public sentiment and at once mold and fashion and recreate great communities in their ideas, their thoughts, their habits, customs, and modes of life."[291] He predicted that school desegregation would be deemed more acceptable over the progress of future years, but he thought that it was best at that moment to move for the other integration provisions.[292] Charles E. Phelps stated that Sumner could not have left the Republican Party "a legacy so full of the seeds of disintegration and decay as the measure which the majority will this day pass."[293] He spoke of the school system as "young and tender and full of promise, full of hope," but if the schools clause were enacted, "you shut the door of every public school."[294] In a statement epitomizing the precarious position of radicalism at the end of the Forty-Third Congress, Benjamin Butler expressed that despite his preference to "legislate equal privileges to white and black in the schools," he would prefer that all reference to schools be struck out than to break up the Southern school system or disappoint "the colored people, because they say they desire no legislation which shall establish any class distinction."[295]

The Kellogg amendment striking the schools clause passed by a vote of 128 to 48.[296] White's proposal to allow segregated facilities then failed by a vote of 91 to 114.[297] Finally, the Cessna amendment to require school integration by substituting the Senate bill was defeated by a vote of 114 to 148, with about one-third of Republicans joining Democrats against it, before the bill passed without the school provision.[298] Many Republicans who favored school desegregation (a group that included Kellogg), realizing the implausibility of requiring it in their bill, voted for the Kellogg amendment as a better alternative than a bill creating racial distinctions through a "separate but equal" provision.[299] Far from revealing that a third of the Republicans were opposed to mixed schools as an interpretation of the Fourteenth Amendment,[300] the context and content of the debates amply demonstrate how fears based on grave political damage and inexpediency could have determined the outcome.[301] Among lame-duck Republicans who did not face re-election, the vote for the Cessna amendment was seventy-three to ten, while most of those who were re-elected in 1874 voted against it by a forty-one to fifty-three margin.[302] Even amid this situation, of those who had voted for the Fourteenth Amendment in 1866 (one as a senator), the Cessna amendment was supported by a margin of eight to four.[303] Additionally, the two Republicans who were recorded as "not voting" in 1866 voted for the 1875 proposal.[304] Neither the five Democrats who voted against the Fourteenth Amendment nor the additional Democrat who had not voted in 1866 voted for the Cessna amendment.[305]

d. Conclusions

In his excellent *Virginia Law Review* article, "Originalism and the Desegregation Decisions," Michael W. McConnell points out that half or more than half of legislators—though not two-thirds—repeatedly cast votes premised on the unconstitutionality of segregated schools and that motions incorporating the "separate but equal" doctrine were defeated without exception.[306] This trend was even stronger among those who had voted for the Fourteenth Amendment.[307] Viewed as a matter of party division—and the votes for and against the Fourteenth Amendment reflected party almost entirely—school desegregation provisions were supported by at least 70 percent—and more often over 90 percent—of Republicans until the 1874 elections; 64 percent of Republican congressmen supported integration even after that point.[308] The sum of legislative evidence supports the conclusion that the dominant understanding of the Fourteenth Amendment among its supporters did not entail constitutional approval of the "separate but equal" doctrine in schools.[309]

The original understanding of the Fourteenth Amendment runs far beyond legislative evidence specifically regarding school segregation, however. As has been pointed out, amendments necessarily deal with principles, and principles demand consistent application that can address many of the specific issues that are not addressed during initial ratification debates. The school segregation issue was hardly addressed during the ratification period, but the principle that the new regime of equality included the elimination of racial distinctions in law—perhaps with the temporary exception of the ballot under Section 2 of the Fourteenth Amendment—was amply supported. It is interesting to note additionally not only how little support there was for the mode of segregation the Court upheld in *Plessy*, but also how the school segregation debates included several references to desegregation in transportation as if it were consensually viewed as unacceptable under the Fourteenth Amendment. The judge who would have reached a result different from that of *Brown v. Board of Education* would indeed have had a difficult challenge surmounting the overwhelming evidence against the result of *Plessy*. Republicans made numerous statements on the need to apply desegregation consistently, especially in public institutions (which clearly were at issue in *Brown*).

The tolerance for "voluntary segregation" by several Republicans does not change the matter either, for this concept still entailed a ban on *de jure* discrimination, which was involved in *Brown*. In effect, "voluntary segregation" amounts to little more than a recognition that individuals might choose to attend separate schools rather than pursuing courts. By definition, it falls beyond the realm of the type of case a court could hear because judicial intervention in cases such as *Brown* arises from the state's exercise of its coercive powers against an individual's desire to attend a certain school.

It can be a useful exercise to view the Reconstruction debates as a collection of constructions of the Fourteenth Amendment, but the school segregation issue demonstrates as well as any other the need for legal scholars not to analyze members of Congress as if they were merely judges or lawyers and not politicians as well. Once one understands the broader political context that faced legislators, the apparent support for school segregation, to the extent it existed among Reconstruction's supporters, is itself a suspect legitimate indication of constitutional interpretation. Political realities created a situation in which opposition to integration could arise from several factors that for a politician might override the considerations of a life-tenured judge charged with handing down "pure" interpretations of the Constitution. The overwhelming public opposition to and consequent inexpediency of school desegregation is difficult to deny in view of historical evidence. Acknowledgment of the "voluntary segregation" scenario provided an additional incentive to view the integration measures as empty statements of principle that would be accompanied by little substance. For some, there seemed to be no reason under such circumstances to sacrifice political health, which they needed for the successful prosecution of Reconstruction in the first place. Several of those who voted against desegregation actually fueled arguments that the Fourteenth Amendment prohibits segregation in public schools by conceding that they were acting despite considerations of equal privileges or the need to overlook racial distinctions.

In an effort to refute McConnell's findings, Michael J. Klarman attempts to downplay the evidence from the 1870s debates by suggesting that constitutional values had in fact been advancing since 1866,[310] but as McConnell himself recognized, this suggestion is unsupported by evidence.[311] A basic historical understanding of the retreat from Reconstruction indicates that the opposite conclusion would be more appropriate. If there is anything amazing about the behavior of the Reconstruction Congress, it is that its members would come to manifest as much opposition to school segregation as they ultimately did in the political climate in which they were operating.

To be certain, Congress, having to start almost from scratch in defining and protecting the rights of people who recently had been slaves, initially focused its attention on matters other than segregation specifically, not exploring desegregation laws to apply to the states until it was finished passing the Fifteenth Amendment and most accompanying enforcement legislation. That segregated schools were the norm in practice through ratification, a point that has been raised on the other side of this debate,[312] is of limited relevance when one speaks of a constitutional amendment dealing with general principles calling for consistent application. That a specific, popularly approved practice might violate the Constitution's general principles is a classic demonstration of the appropriateness of judicial action, and perhaps no other amendment embraced as dense and demanding a mandate for change as the Fourteenth—given that it was understood to create equality before the law in a context that included pervasive inequalities for a race that had just emerged from slavery into a caste system.

The extent of the amendment's ambitiousness comes not from modern notions, but from the repeatedly broad constructions placed on it by its supporters from the outset. That a particular consequence of an amendment will be unpopular, or otherwise inexpedient, is not a concern of constitutional law or judges who must interpret the nation's blueprint in the same mode in which it was adopted. That the work of the framers of the Fourteenth Amendment was an uphill battle that met with substantial unpopularity was understood, but the framers went about their work regardless. Henry Wilson seemed to acknowledge as much when he asserted in 1869 that

this whole struggle in this country to give equal rights and equal privileges to all citizens of the United States has been an unpopular one; that we have been forced to struggle against passions and prejudices engendered by generations of wrong and oppression; that we have been compelled to struggle against great interests and powerful political organizations. . . . [T]he struggle of the last eight years to give freedom to four and a half millions of men who were held in slavery, to make them citizens of the United States, to clothe them with the right of suffrage, to give them the privilege to be voted for, to make them in all respects equal to the white citizens of the United States, has cost the party with which I act a quarter of a million of votes. There is not to-day a square mile in the United States where the advocacy of the equal rights and privileges of those colored men has not been in the past and is not now unpopular.

But my doctrine is, no matter how unpopular it is, no matter what it costs, no matter whether it brings victory or defeat, it is our duty to hope on and struggle on and work on until we make the humblest citizen of the United States the peer and the equal in rights and privileges of every other citizen of the United States.[313]

Propositions requiring as many steps to be implemented successfully as equality before the law for Black Americans during the 1860s and 1870s can inherently be expected to require several years, as well as several phases; those who dwell on certain manifestations of inequality in 1866 or 1868 seem to miss the point of appreciating the original understanding and tying it to a broader sense of perspective. The Reconstruction debates reflect an ongoing, conscious effort among legislators to implement through several specific legislative steps (preferring not to leave the matter entirely to the courts) the ambitious goal of equality before the law that had been embraced in 1866. During the 1870s, on the issue of segregation in public schools, Congress' efforts reflected the same broad ambition as before, but it collided with public opinion that was retreating from Reconstruction—and which delivered a Republican majority that seemed to be following Henry Wilson's articulated doctrine an electoral punishment that sealed the fate of school desegregation, leaving it to the courts to support an unpopular consequence of a constitutional principle without accompanying legislative enactments. This is what the Reconstruction debates reflect about desegregation, not the narrowly premised conclusions of those who feel that *Brown* reached an incorrect result under the Fourteenth Amendment.

The path the *Brown* Court took to reach its result, however, was different from that of the framers. Rather than employing the more sweeping propositions of equality before the law and the consequent abolition of racial distinctions in government action, it looked to largely empirical studies of social science, ignoring the fact that courts are inherently better suited to employ constitutional principle.[314] Besides not reflecting constitutional principle, Chief Justice Warren's opinion employed assumptions that were both unsupported by the leading study of the issue in the field and potentially subject to change under different circumstances.[315] Social science in the 1870s was not what it was in the 1950s, but even a cursory glance at the grave apprehensions over school integration during Reconstruction suggests that desegregation may have come far from lessening the harm to students that concerned the *Brown* Court. Ironically, *Brown* relied on a methodology that could have worked in different contexts, including Reconstruction, to undermine its result—a result which could have found a more legitimate and enduring basis in the original understanding in the first place.

C. THE REFORMULATION OF CONSTITUTIONAL JURISPRUDENCE ADDRESSING CIVIL RIGHTS LEGISLATION

1. *United States v. Raines* and the Collapse of the *Reese* Doctrine

One distortion of constitutional jurisprudence brought on by the Supreme Court's retreat from Reconstruction was corrected by the invalidation of the *Reese* doctrine in *United States v. Raines* (1960).[1] This case involved the charge that various registrars in a Georgia county had "discriminated on racial grounds against Negroes who desired to register to vote in elections conducted in the State."[2] The defendants had been indicted under § 2004 of the Revised Statutes—§ 1 of the first Enforcement Act of 1870 as amended by § 131 of the Civil Rights Act of 1957—which provided for the attorney general to institute an action to enjoin interference with voting rights.[3] The district court had found the law unconstitutional on the grounds that "the statute on its face was susceptible of application beyond the scope permissible under the Fifteenth Amendment,"[4] but the Supreme Court handed down a different rule of interpretation: "one to whom application of a statute is constitutional will not be heard to attack the statute on the ground that impliedly it might also be taken as applying to other persons or other situations in which its application might be unconstitutional."[5] Fourteen precedents and a concurring opinion were cited to support this proposition.[6]

In his opinion for the Court, Justice William J. Brennan recognized (citing *Reese*) that there might be cases in which applying "a criminal statute would necessitate such a revision of its text as to create a situation in which the statute no longer gave an intelligible warning of the conduct it prohibited," but he found the case at bar "the most typical one for application of the rules" of construction the Court announced.[7] As for *Reese*, Brennan explained that the precedent "may have drawn support from the assumption that if the Court had not passed on the statute's validity *in toto* it would have left standing a criminal statute incapable of giving fair warning of its prohibitions," but the Court refused to follow the 1876 precedent "to the extent *Reese* did depend on an approach inconsistent with what we think the better one and the one established by the weightiest of the subsequent cases."[8]

The Court found the legislation "appropriate," though in terms acknowledging the "conduct charged" as "state action" and thus "subject to the ban of" the Fifteenth Amendment.[9] At the end of the decision, Brennan declined to "compound the error we have found in the District Court's judgment by intimating any views on" the "ultimate scope in which Congress intended this legislation to apply, and concerning its constitutionality under the Fifteenth Amendment in these various applications."[10] The Court had not encountered the opportunity to revisit other lingering questions about the Fifteenth Amendment, but it marked the end of the *Reese* doctrine and aligned federal civil rights legislation with longstanding doctrine on statutory construction in other areas.

Thus the state action requirement for the Fifteenth Amendment remained after *Raines*. Only certain language in *South Carolina v. Katzenbach* (1966), which upheld the Voting Rights Act of 1965, arguably goes farther: "The basic test to be applied in a case involving § 2 of the Fifteenth Amendment is the same as in all cases concerning the express powers of Congress with relation to the reserved powers of the States."[11] The consequences of this holding, however, remain unclear.

2. Sidestepping the Fourteenth Amendment State Action Doctrine: The Uncertain Fate of Section 5

a. *Heart of Atlanta Motel* and *Katzenbach*

When it came time for the Court to assess the constitutionality of civil rights legislation in the 1960s, Section 5 of the Fourteenth Amendment did not enjoy the revival an originalist constitutional lawyer might have expected, considering the results the Court reached. The Civil Rights Act of 1964 was upheld in the landmark case of *Heart of Atlanta Motel, Inc. v. United States* (1964),[1] but under the Interstate Commerce Clause, not Section 5 of the Fourteenth Amendment.[2] The case involved a challenge to Title II's constitutionality through a declaratory judgment action by the owner of an all-white Atlanta motel, three-quarters of whose clientele were interstate travelers.[3]

In his opinion for the Court, Justice Thomas C. Clark explained that the law's legislative history indicated that it was based on Section 5, the Equal Protection Clause, and the Interstate Commerce Clause.[4] In his discussion of the *Civil Rights Cases*, however, he called the 1883 precedent "inapposite, and without precedential value in determining the constitutionality of the present Act."[5] The Civil Rights Act of 1875 was distinguished from its 1964 successor in the following terms:

Unlike Title II of the present legislation, the 1875 Act broadly proscribed discrimination in "inns, public conveyances on land or water, theaters, and other places of public amusement," without limiting the categories of affected businesses to those impinging upon interstate commerce. In contrast, the applicability of Title II is carefully limited to enterprises having a direct and substantial relation to the interstate flow of goods and people, except where state action is involved. Further, the fact that certain kinds of businesses may not in 1875 have been sufficiently involved in interstate commerce to warrant bringing them within the ambit of the commerce power is not necessarily dispositive of the same question today.[6]

Clark noted also that the Court in 1883, acknowledging that the law was not "conceived" under the Commerce Clause, had not faced arguments that the 1875 act could be based on that clause.[7] It was due to this acknowledgment, as well as the Court's express confinement of its holding to cases not involving Congress' plenary power, that Clark was undeterred by the 1883 assertion that "no one will contend that the power to pass [the act] was contained in the Constitution before the adoption of the last three amendments."[8] The Court thus concluded "that the *Civil Rights Cases* have no relevance to the basis of decision here where the Act explicitly relies upon the commerce power, and where the record is filled with testimony of obstructions and restraints resulting from the discriminations found to be existing."[9]

The case produced three concurrences, two of which relied on the Fourteenth Amendment. Justice Black did not rely on the Fourteenth Amendment but added at the end of his concurrence that "nothing in the *Civil Rights Cases* . . . gives the slightest support to the argument that Congress is without power under the Commerce Clause to enact the present legislation" because the Court had expressly declined to consider "the validity of such antidiscrimination legislation if rested on the Commerce Clause."[10]

Justice William O. Douglas expressed his reluctance "to rest solely on the Commerce Clause" because he found the case's result "much more obvious as a protective measure under the Fourteenth Amendment than under the Commerce Clause."[11] By relying on Section 5, Douglas argued that "the Act would apply to all customers in all the enumerated places of public accommodation. And that construction would put an end to all obstructionist strategies and finally close one door on a bitter chapter in American history."[12] The Fourteenth Amendment, he asserted, allowed "every person—whatever his race, creed, or color—to patronize all places of public accommodation without discrimination whether he travels interstate or intrastate."[13] Justice Arthur J. Goldberg delivered the second (and briefest) concurrence relying on the Fourteenth Amendment. "The primary purpose of the Civil Rights Act of 1964," the junior justice emphasized, "is the vindication of human dignity and not mere economics."[14] Citing the views of his concurrence in *Bell v. Maryland*,[15] Goldberg argued that the Civil Rights Act was justifiable under both Section 5 of the Fourteenth Amendment and the Interstate Commerce Clause, both of which granted congressional authority to protect rights covered by Section 1 of the Fourteenth Amendment.[16]

The concurrences also applied to *Heart of Atlanta Motel*'s companion case, *Katzenbach v. McClung*.[17] That case applied its immediate predecessor's ruling to owners of a restaurant that catered to local white customers with only a take-out service for blacks, serving much food that had moved in interstate commerce.[18] The Court found the Civil Rights Act of 1964 "plainly appropriate in the resolution of what the Congress found to be a national commercial problem of the first magnitude."[19]

In *Heart of Atlanta Motel*, the Court seemed unwilling to challenge the *Civil Rights Cases*, and even the two concurrences recognizing Section 5 of the Fourteenth Amendment made no reference to the original understanding of that provision, perhaps because they based their conclusions entirely on other considerations. This study does not intend to reassess the merits of the Court's Commerce Clause jurisprudence, but this does not preclude criticism of the Court's treatment of the *Civil Rights Cases* in 1964. First, Clark's attempt to distinguish the 1883 precedent seems unconvincing. Reading Justice Bradley's opinion on its own terms, it seems difficult to maintain that the justices of that time felt there could be a serious defense of the Civil Rights Act of 1875 on Commerce Clause grounds, regardless of Clark's attempt to downplay such language with other dicta on the plenary power of Congress. The sole exception might have been the railroad prong of the case, which one might argue implicated interstate commerce more than anything involved in the two 1964 cases. It will be recalled that Justice Harlan had cited the Commerce Clause as an alternate ground only in the interstate railroad prong of the 1883 case, and while Bradley might have agreed with him if he had considered this ground, it is difficult to envision any of the justices (including Harlan), let alone a majority, reaching the same conclusion under the Commerce Clause as *Heart of Atlanta Motel*.

A second problem with the Warren Court's analysis, more central to this study, is the peculiar position in which it leaves constitutional jurisprudence: The Court upheld an act passed pursuant to a 177-year-old constitutional provision while leaving intact a decision that struck down a similar law more directly related to the constitutional amendment on which it was based, ratified only seven years earlier. Although one might find the Court's determination that the 1964 act was constitutionally distinguishable from the 1875 act unconvincing, assuming that the Warren Court would have found a way to uphold the earlier law if it ever faced such a case, the Court's 1964 decision on its own terms did leave open the possibility that the 1964 act, but not the 1875 act, could be deemed constitutional. Thus even if much of the result of the *Civil Rights Cases* seemed to be reversed, *Heart of Atlanta Motel's* language indicated that there still was some civil rights legislation that might not be upheld if it was not crafted to conform to the Commerce Clause.

To turn to another difficulty, the later civil rights law derives its recognized constitutional legitimacy only from its connection to commercial matters Congress chose to address, not to federal power over civil rights on the broader grounds of equality under the original meaning of Section 5 of the Fourteenth Amendment, which unquestionably comprises the more primary basis of both pieces of legislation. The question of whether the Court (precedent aside) overstepped the original understanding of the Commerce Clause might be a matter for another study, but if it did, it is of even greater damage to constitutional law that the Court failed to take the opportunity to reverse its mistake in 1883 since it could have prevented yet another distortion—an overexpansion of federal power in one area to compensate for the undue contraction of federal power in another. Without accompanying constitutional amendments imposing equality, the Commerce Clause by itself is a grant of plenary power over a limited area that could be used for purposes of inequality as well as equality because it is value-neutral. The Fourteenth Amendment, on the other hand, was framed precisely with the intention of empowering Congress to legislate equality, which was the primary goal of Congress in 1964 as well as 1875. If the framers were able to witness the Supreme Court's choice of provisions on which to uphold civil rights legislation in 1964, it is not difficult to imagine their befuddlement.

b. Postscript: *Guest* and *Daniel*

The closest the Court ever has come to overruling the *Civil Rights Cases'* holding on the Fourteenth Amendment was *United States v. Guest* (1966),[20] though the Court's opinion dealt with statutory construction and avoided questions of constitutional power.[21] A group of whites involved in violence against blacks had been indicted in part for conspiracy to deprive the victims of their "right to the equal utilization" of state-owned, operated, or managed public facilities, as well as their "right to travel freely" to and from Georgia through the state's highways and other instrumentalities of interstate commerce.[22]

In an opinion by Justice Potter Stewart, the Court upheld the conspiracy indictment under 18 U.S.C. § 241, a surviving part of § 6 of the first Enforcement Act,[23] but without addressing congressional power to punish private conduct under the Fourteenth Amendment because the statute was construed as granting only "remedial[] implementation to any rights secured by" the Equal Protection Clause.[24] The statute also was deemed to enforce constitutional rights beyond those of the Fourteenth Amendment, including the right to interstate travel, which the Court found to be punishable by Congress against private action.[25] Implicit in the Court's discussion is a rejection of the notion (consistent with the *Slaughter-House Cases*) that the Privileges and Immunities Clause might play a role in such an indictment.

When turning to the branch of the indictment under the Equal Protection Clause, Stewart explained that the clause created no new rights and asserted that the "Fourteenth Amendment protects the individual against *state action*, not against wrongs done by *individuals*."[26] This was "the view of the Court from the beginning," Stewart wrote with citations of *Cruikshank, Harris* and the *Civil Rights Cases*, and "[i]t remains the Court's view today."[27] To whatever extent it reaffirmed the state action doctrine, however, the Court added that the state's involvement need not "be either exclusive or direct."[28] The indictment mentioned that a means of executing the conspiracy was by "causing the arrest of Negroes by means of false reports that such Negroes had committed criminal acts," and while "the extent of official involvement" was unclear from the allegations—which might possibly reveal no sufficient cooperative action by state officials in a bill of particulars—the allegations were broad enough to prevent dismissal of the equal protection part of the indictment.[29]

While the Court explicitly addressed only the Equal Protection Clause and not Section 5[30] and in fact reaffirmed the state action doctrine, a separate concurrence by Justice Clark, joined by Justices Black and Abe Fortas, asserted that "the specific language of § 5 empowers the Congress to enact laws punishing all conspiracies—with or without state action—that interfere with Fourteenth Amendment rights."[31] Another concurrence by Justice Brennan, joined by Warren and Douglas, also reached the issue of congressional power under Section 5 of the Fourteenth Amendment, concluding that the section "authorizes Congress to make laws that it concludes are reasonably necessary to protect a right created by and arising under that Amendment; and Congress is thus fully empowered to determine that punishment of private conspiracies interfering with the exercise of such a right is necessary to its full protection."[32] Brennan cited *McCulloch v. Maryland* to support his conception of congressional power under the Fourteenth Amendment and described Section 5 "as a positive grant of legislative power, authorizing Congress to exercise its discretion in fashioning remedies to achieve civil and political equality for all citizens."[33]

Thus, six justices in *Guest* in two separate opinions reached the conclusion that the Fourteenth Amendment applies to purely private conduct. Brennan recognized this and, in an apparent attempt to illustrate a coherent judgment by the Court, contended that "a majority of the Court today rejects" the *Civil Rights Cases'* "interpretation of § 5" as "confined to the adoption of 'appropriate legislation for correcting the effects of . . . prohibited State laws and State acts, and thus to render them effectually null, void, and innocuous.' "[34] Nevertheless, while the *Guest* concurrences placed the durability of the *Civil Rights Cases* in doubt, much confusion remains over the extent of congressional power envisioned by the six justices, and the application of Section 5 to private conduct remains unresolved.[35]

Perhaps an understanding that it had not substantially upset the *Civil Rights Cases* was implicit in the Court's continued reliance on the Commerce Clause for support of the Civil Rights Act of 1964 in *Daniel v. Paul* (1969).[36] That case dealt with the application of Title II to a segregated snack bar in a privately owned recreational facility, "principally engaged in selling food for consumption on the premises," that "serves or offers to serve interstate travelers or" that serves "a substantial portion of" food that "has moved in commerce."[37] Such a facility, the Court held, was a "public accommodation" under Title II because any of these characteristics was sufficient to describe it that way.[38] Justice Brennan's opinion for the Court relied in part on *Katzenbach v. McClung* for support of its Commerce Clause analysis.[39]

Assuming a different posture from his *Heart of Atlanta Motel* concurrence, Justice Black, alone in dissent, argued that the Court had stretched the Commerce Clause power too far—"giv[ing] the Federal Government complete control over every little remote country place of recreation in every nook and cranny of every precinct and county in every one of the 50 States."[40] Black added, however, that he "could and would agree with the Court's holding in this case had Congress in the 1964 Civil Rights Act based its power to bar racial discrimination at places of public accommodations on § 5 of the Fourteenth Amendment," which he observed Congress "did not choose to invoke."[41]

3. Section 2 of the Thirteenth Amendment: The Partial Resuscitation of the Reconstruction Amendments

In 1968 Section 2 of the Thirteenth Amendment underwent a remarkable revival beginning with the case of *Jones v. Alfred H. Mayer Co.*,[1] where the Court faced questions of both the scope and constitutionality of § 1982, a remnant of § 1 of the 1866 Civil Rights Act that grants all citizens equal rights to purchase property.[2] The statute, Justice Stewart wrote for the Court, "bars *all* racial discrimination, private as well as public, in the sale or rental of property," and "thus construed," § 1982 "is a valid exercise of the power of Congress to enforce the Thirteenth Amendment."[3] The merits of the Court's construction of § 1982 shall not be revisited in this study, but its conclusions on Section 2 of the Thirteenth Amendment are noteworthy because they affirmed congressional power to protect civil rights regardless of whether it "reaches beyond state action to regulate the conduct of private individuals."[4] As the Court viewed it, "If Congress cannot say that being a free man means at least" enjoying "the freedom to buy whatever a white man can buy, the right to live wherever a white man can live . . . then the Thirteenth Amendment made a promise the Nation cannot keep."[5]

Although the Court's retreat from Reconstruction did not include the invalidation of the Civil Rights Act of 1866, *Jones* has been viewed as an opinion resurrecting the Thirteenth Amendment from its burial during the previous century.[6] Although the case worked in part from dicta from the *Civil Rights Cases* stating that Congress under the amendment had "power to pass *all laws necessary and proper for abolishing all badges and incidents of slavery in the United States,"*[7] *Jones* seemed effectively to set the stage for invalidating the 1883 precedent's holding on the Thirteenth Amendment.[8]

The Supreme Court largely confirmed its expansion of the Thirteenth Amendment beyond the doctrines of 1883 in *Griffin v. Breckenridge* (1971).[9] In that case, the Court faced § 1985(3), the civil counterpart of the act it had invalidated in *Harris* eighty-eight years earlier and the statutory descendant of § 2 of the Ku Klux Klan Act of 1871.[10] At issue was a damages action charging a conspiracy by a group of whites to assault blacks who were "travelling upon the federal, state and local highways" for the purpose of preventing them "from seeking the equal protection of the laws and from enjoying the equal rights, privileges and immunities of citizens" under both state and federal law.[11]

Griffin found the precedent of *Collins v. Hardyman* (1951),[12] which effectively construed § 1985(3) as addressing "only conspiracies under color of state law," to be problematic, citing "the evolution of decisional law" and its preference "to accord to the words of the statute their apparent meaning" in adherence to judicial interpretations of related laws and legislative history.[13] Justice Stewart pointed out in the Court's opinion "that all indicators—text, companion provisions, and legislative history—point unwaveringly to § 1985(3)'s coverage of private conspiracies."[14] Read in this manner, the Court found that the private conspiracy involved in the case fell within the statute's language and had no doubt of the constitutional power of Congress to enact it.[15] The statute was applied to private parties when there was "some racial, or perhaps otherwise class-based, invidiously discriminatory animus behind the conspirators' action" without deciding "whether a conspiracy motivated by invidiously discriminatory intent other than racial bias" would be covered.[16] While the rule of statutory construction in such cases as *Harris* and *Baldwin* might have urged deciding against the provision's constitutionality, the Court pointed out that it had "long since firmly rejected that rule in such cases as *United States* v. *Raines*," thus rendering it unnecessary to find § 1985(3)'s language to be "constitutional in all its possible applications in order to uphold" it and apply it to the case at bar.[17]

The finding of constitutionality occurred not under Section 5 of the Fourteenth Amendment, which the Court deemed unnecessary to consider,[18] but on two other grounds. First, the Court applied *Jones'* holding that under Section 2 of the Thirteenth Amendment, "Congress has the power . . . rationally to determine what are the badges and the incidents of slavery, and the authority to translate that determination into effective legislation."[19] Second, the Court applied for support the "right of interstate travel," which it claimed precedent had "firmly established . . . is constitutionally protected, does not necessarily rest on the Fourteenth Amendment, and is assertable against private as well as governmental interference."[20]

By declining to face the Fourteenth Amendment in favor of the Thirteenth Amendment and the right of interstate travel, *Griffin*, like those precedents forming its premises, left lingering a major distortion in constitutional jurisprudence. This distortion would remain through future cases the Court would decide concerning § 1985(3) that the nineteenth-century Court had not faced—cases that involved issues other than the civil rights of the formerly enslaved race.[21] The 1883 state action doctrine of the Fourteenth Amendment was allowed to persevere long enough for the Court to revert to the newly revived Thirteenth Amendment, even though it was (if anything) that amendment that, under the original understanding, employed the more disputable basis for upholding § 1985(3).

There is little question that Congress believed it was operating primarily under the Fourteenth Amendment when it passed the Ku Klux Klan Act, which, as has been pointed out, was entitled "An Act to enforce the Provisions of the Fourteenth Amendment to the Constitution of the United States, and for other Purposes."[22] Besides the many statements of legislators during Reconstruction confirming that the Fourteenth Amendment was ratified to dispel any doubts about congressional power to pass civil rights legislation under the Thirteenth Amendment, one could further cite congressional reenactment of the 1866 Civil Rights Act in 1870.[23] Thus, while *Harris* and possibly the *Civil Rights Cases* may be considered overruled on Thirteenth Amendment grounds, they remain (subject to consensual clarification of *Guest*) substantially valid law in their central holdings on the Fourteenth Amendment, which Shellabarger described as including "far more explicit, complete, and careful provisions" than its predecessor.[24] Thus, the resuscitation of the Reconstruction amendments has occurred only partially.

4. Section 5 Returns to the Court

After years of failing to revisit directly its past rulings regarding the amendment that originally was considered the chief basis of civil rights, the

Court in 1997 once again faced Section 5 in *City of Boerne v. Flores*.[1] This case involved the constitutionality of the Religious Freedom Restoration Act of 1993, through which Congress offered broader protections to religious freedom than were available under the Court's earlier interpretation of the Free Exercise Clause of the First Amendment.[2] In an opinion by Justice Anthony M. Kennedy striking down the statute, the Court offered an account of the history of the Fourteenth Amendment that flatly contradicted the framers' understanding of congressional power under Section 5: "The Fourteenth Amendment's history confirms the remedial, rather than substantive, nature of the Enforcement Clause."[3] After the demise of Bingham's first proposal, "the revised Amendment" dictated that "Congress' power was no longer plenary but remedial"[4] and that the "substantive rights" the Fourteenth Amendment "confers . . . against the States . . . are self-executing."[5]

The Court did not stop there. It turned from legislative history to its own precedent and cited none other than *Reese, Harris*, the *Civil Rights Cases*, and *James* to support its assertion that "[a]ny suggestion that Congress has a substantive, non-remedial power under the Fourteenth Amendment is not supported by our case law."[6] Kennedy acknowledged the modifying effect of such cases as *Heart of Atlanta Motel* and *Guest*, but for the *Flores Court*, "their treatment of Congress' § 5 power as corrective or preventive . . . has not been questioned."[7] Thus if there remained any question whether the arguably discredited precedents of the nineteenth and early twentieth century retained any vitality, the Court has given its answer in the affirmative.

5

Conclusion

During its retreat from Reconstruction, the Supreme Court, in case after case, departed from the understanding of the Reconstruction amendments held by those who supported them, adopting in all but a few cases the interpretations of those who opposed both the post–Civil War movement and its resulting innovations to the Constitution. As a result, the intended constitutional innovations did not endure in the face of the nation's broader retreat from Reconstruction. By the time of the depletion of the pro-Reconstruction majority of Congress in 1875, the Court already had begun to narrow the Fourteenth Amendment from its original meaning, and by the presidential abandonment of Reconstruction in 1877, it had gone far-ther on both the Fourteenth and Fifteenth Amendments, besides striking down provisions of enforcement legislation. Subsequent decisions would continue even farther in this direction.

Political science scholars might have expected that the political branches would have reversed the tide of Reconstruction in the face of public op-position before the Court would, but the opposite trend occurred. Whether this speaks more to the dedication of various politicians than to the justices' imposition of their personal views toward Reconstruction is a question that can be debated, but the disappointment of the Court's performance stands regardless. As the only inherently undemocratic branch in the federal gov-ernment, it is the judiciary that one would think best structured to resist a temptation among the people to disregard amendments to the Constitution. Instead, the Supreme Court abdicated such a role on an issue that one could argue demanded the protection of minority rights over majority will more than any other issue in American constitutional history. This chapter is one of the most disappointing in the Court's history, precisely because it could have been the institution's shining moment—its opportunity to stand against the tide of history. Instead, it behaved like a political institution, disavowing the legal framework of Reconstruction even before the political branches did.

As W.E.B. Du Bois saw it, various opponents of Reconstruction

relied upon the court to do what Democratic members of Congress had failed to accomplish—and the court, through a process of reasoning very similar to that of Democratic legislators, deprived the enforcement legislation of nearly all its strength when it rendered its decisions in the cases of United States *vs*. Reese and United States *vs*. Cruikshank.[1]

Given the mood of the 1860s, including the example of Andrew Johnson's fate, it is difficult to imagine that the Court would have met with general acceptance in the first few years after the Civil War had it decided then to hand down the types of decisions it would make in subsequent decades. Indeed, the Court consistently declined to impede the efforts of Radical Republicans through the 1860s, but the situation would change during the next decade. By the time of Chief Justice Waite's death in 1888, even the once radical Shellabarger, a political relic of Reconstruction, would express approval of the departed chief justice's decisions on the Reconstruction amendments—despite what he recognized as their conflict with the framers' intent.[2]

One cannot know the innermost motivations of late–nineteenth-century justices when they decided civil rights cases, but evidence makes it clear that on most of the major issues, they failed to interpret the Constitution in accordance with the original understanding and simultaneously made decisions that met with general public approval. When the twentieth-century Court decided cases that reversed its own earlier retreat from Reconstruction, it often failed to base its conclusions on the central principles of the framers. Civil rights legislation was upheld under the Interstate Commerce Clause—or later, the Thirteenth Amendment—rather than the Fourteenth Amendment, Section 5 of which continues to remain in the limbo of the state action doctrine along with Section 2 of the Fifteenth Amendment. The Court might have relaxed the state action doctrine somewhat, but the requirement of state action still remains.

The Privileges and Immunities Clause also remains substantially interred under the doctrine of the *Slaughter-House Cases*. It seems a fixed assumption of the twentieth-century Court that constitutional rights other than equal protection (such as the right to interstate travel) must rest somewhere other than the Privileges and Immunities Clause—or the rest of the Fourteenth Amendment for that matter. Enforcement legislation once again has become relevant, but not entirely in ways that were intended—and not with an acknowledgment of the extent to which the Fourteenth Amendment comprises its foundation. As for the selective incorporation that has absorbed most of the first eight amendments into the 1868 amendment, even that trend occurred under the Due Process Clause instead of the clause immediately preceding it. Even when the twentieth-century Court has used the best-suited provisions to support its conclusions, as *Brown v. Board of Education* did when it employed the Equal Protection Clause (it might have added the Privileges and Immunities Clause), its rationale did not always comport with the original principles that included more deeply rooted and enduring notions of equality.

The sense one gets from the later decisions is that they were reached by justices who were working from concerns other than the original understanding. *Brown* expressly suggested as much, and even the *Heart of Atlanta Motel* and *Guest* concurrences arguing for the application of Section 5 of the Fourteenth Amendment to private action did not invoke the understanding on which the amendment was adopted for support. Besides the specific distortions the twentieth-century Court continues to manifest in constitutional jurisprudence, the false perception—encouraged at times by the Court's own reasoning—that it has reached its results in civil rights and voting rights cases *despite* the original meaning is additionally damaging in that it encourages constitutional law to depart from the principles incorporated into the Constitution through the people's representatives.

Those who share Justice Thomas' views of the Commerce Clause in *Lopez* might feel doubly troubled that the Court has overexpanded one provision of the Constitution—an equality-neutral provision with serious shortcomings as a potential safeguard of individual rights—while failing to employ the judicially shrunken amendment that *was* appropriately crafted to protect equality. For these critics, the result, besides failing properly to reflect statutory goals, does a worse job of reflecting the basis for the national consensus behind both federal control of commerce and egalitarian goals. The Court's philosophy during its own "Second Reconstruction" might have contained the seeds of some of its own decisions' destruction.

On a broader level, the Court's retreat from Reconstruction contains important lessons for both strict constructionists (some of whom are labeled originalists) and those who advocate the view that the Constitution "evolves" or changes as time progresses. First, the Court's retreat exemplifies the difference between strict constructionism and originalism because judicial innovation of the Reconstruction amendments tended to be narrower and closer to strict textualism than the understanding of the framers. Such a mode of interpretation can be the product of judicial activism as much as constructions that are more liberal than the original understanding. This point has been illustrated in Richard L. Aynes' discussion of the political motivations of the majority in the *Slaughter-House Cases*.[3]

Justice Harlan's dissent in *Plessy*, not widely viewed as an originalist stand, seemed to realize how judges can infuse their policy views to unduly narrow a constitutional provision. Harlan embraced a mode of originalism that properly recognized how the legislature's original understanding of a provision might call for either a strict or a loose construction, but not the infusion of a judge's policy preferences in either direction:

> I do not understand that the courts have anything to do with the policy or expediency of legislation. . . . There is a dangerous tendency in these latter days to enlarge the functions of the courts, by means of judicial interference with the will of the people as expressed by the legislature. Our institutions have the distinguishing characteristic that the three departments of government are coordinate and separate. Each must keep within the limits defined by the Constitution. And the courts best discharge their duty by executing the will of the law-making power, constitutionally expressed, leaving the results of legislation to be dealt with by the people through their representatives. Statutes must always have a reasonable construction. Sometimes they are to be construed strictly; sometimes, liberally, in order to carry out the legislative will. But however construed, the intent of the legislature is to be respected, if the particular statute in question is valid, although the courts, looking at the public interests, may conceive the statute to be both unreasonable and impolitic. If the power exists to enact a statute, that ends the matter so far as the courts are concerned.[4]

In view of the congressional debates, it is difficult to dispute that Harlan correctly characterized the nature of the Reconstruction amendments in his landmark dissents. In 1888, Shellabarger articulated the liberal spirit and context in which the amendments were adopted, as well as his apprehensions toward judges who were truly strict constructionists. The former congressman admitted he had feared Waite's "extreme conservatism" when he became chief justice on the grounds that "neither the *time* nor the *spirit* in which the new Amendments were gendered, nor the text of these Amendments, was characterized by eminent conservatism."[5]

The Court's record also contains an important lesson for jurisprudential liberals who argue that the Constitution changes with time. Implicit in the theory of an evolving Constitution is the notion that the advancement of time necessarily brings with it progress and improvement, but for those who regard the principle of Reconstruction as an ideal, the retreat from Reconstruction marked societal (and correspondingly legal) retrogression rather than progress. To assume that change over time necessarily entails evolution is to disregard the possibility that a society may devolve as well as evolve. It is understandable that one may wish to loosen the reins on judges so that their rulings may incorporate principles progressing from the original meanings imparted by a legislature, but because progress is deemed to mean different things by different societies and individuals, sanctioning judicial departures from originalism can invite dangerous results. The society that followed Reconstruction undoubtedly thought its abandonment

of the post–Civil War movement marked the nation's progress, and subsequent generations of historical interpretation only escalated this sentiment
to the point that the policy of the Reconstruction era was condemned outright. Those who accept the premise of judicial activism have unwittingly
offered endorsement to the Supreme Court's retreat from Reconstruction,
which comported with societal conceptions of progress at the time.

In his criticism of McConnell's defense of desegregation under originalist
constitutional theory, Klarman attacks originalism on two grounds: 1. "under originalism, the constitutional values that happen to be in place at the
time an amendment is ratified extend their sovereignty into the future;"
and 2. "justifying intergenerational binding is especially difficult when the
issue to be resolved implicates attitudes and values that have shifted dramatically over time."[6] For reasons just discussed, Klarman's argument col-
lapses under its own weight, for if the phenomena he identifies as problems
are truly problems—thus demanding that judges avoid them—he has vindicated a principle that adds support to the Court's narrowing of the Reconstruction amendments and corresponding enforcement legislation.

The consequences of originalism are not always easy to accept—it certainly would have agitated post-Reconstruction society—but the alternative
should not be deemed more desirable, regardless of a society's understanding at a particular time. Frederick Douglass was a dissenting voice at the
time the *Civil Rights Cases* were handed down, and he lamented what he
saw as the Court's inconsistency in observing the original intent:

> In the dark days of slavery, this Court, on all occasions, gave the greatest im-
> portance to *intention* as a guide to interpretation. . . . Everything in favor of slavery
> and against the negro was settled by this object and *intention*. . . . Where slavery
> was strong, liberty is now weak.
> O for a Supreme Court of the United States which shall be as true to the claims
> of humanity, as the Supreme Court formerly was to the demands of slavery! When
> that day comes, as come it will, a Civil Rights Bill will not be declared unconsti-
> tutional and void, in utter and flagrant disregard of the objects and *intentions* of
> the National legislature by which it was enacted, and of the rights plainly secured
> by the Constitution.[7]

Douglass' position was far enough out of the American mainstream at that
point that his legal views may have been derided as a relic of sentimental
attachment to an outmoded conception of government. His policy position
having been repudiated by the nation through the termination of Reconstruction in 1877, it is difficult to see how his legal stand could have with-
stood attack without invoking originalism. As history demonstrates,
however, the Supreme Court has not always followed the original understanding of the Constitution. Even when the day came upholding the landmark civil rights law of the twentieth century, it came in a decision based

not on the egalitarian amendment Douglass expected to be revived, but on a constitutional provision dealing with commerce.

The Court during the Civil Rights Movement might have done more for its cause had it learned from its predecessors' mistakes and expressly repudiated the notion that judges may read extraconstitutional views into their opinions that violate the meaning originally imparted to the Constitution's provisions. In that way, it could have better guarded the integrity of the American constitutional system—not to mention the legitimacy of the Court itself—by working to dispel the common criticism that the Constitution effectively can be changed at the will of life-tenured judges. It is true that a strong enough majority of the people can act to amend the Constitution under procedures set by the government's blueprint. Absent such a national consensus, however, it is implicit in the very idea of a Constitution that, whatever else changes, there are certain principles on which the nation can rely without risking their compromise or destruction when the times deem it acceptable to disregard them.

Notes

EPIGRAPH

1. 109 U.S. 3, 26 (1883) (Harlan, J., dissenting).
2. FREDERICK DOUGLASS, THE FREDERICK DOUGLASS PAPERS 113 (John W. Blassingame and John R. McKivigan, eds., 1991).

CHAPTER 1: INTRODUCTION

1. 514 U.S. 549.
2. U.S. CONST. art. I, § 8, cl. 3. *See* 514 U.S. at 567–68.
3. 514 U.S. at 559.
4. *Id.* at 567.
5. 379 U.S. 294 (1964).
6. 395 U.S. 298 (1969).
7. Pub. L. No. 88–352, 78 Stat. 241 (codified as amended at 42 U.S.C. §§ 1971, 2000(a)-2000(h)(6) (1988)).
8. *See* 514 U.S. at 626–27 (Breyer, J., dissenting).
9. *Id.* at 584 (Thomas, J., concurring).
10. *Id.* at 596 (Thomas, J., concurring).
11. *Id.* at 589 (Thomas, J., concurring).
12. *See id.* at 584–85, 599–600 (Thomas, J., concurring) (criticizing "the Court's dramatic departure in the 1930's from a century and a half of precedent" and suggesting that the "substantial effects" test would grant power to Congress over matters that were intended to be left to the states regardless of their effects on interstate commerce).
13. 379 U.S. 241 (1964).
14. Justice Thomas asserted in his *Lopez* concurrence, "Although I might be willing to return to the original understanding, I recognize that many believe that

it is too late in the day to undertake a fundamental reexamination of the past 60 years. Consideration of *stare decisis* and reliance interests may convince us that we cannot wipe the slate clean." 514 U.S. at 601 n.8. This study takes no more decisive position as to whether interpretations of the Interstate Commerce Clause should remain intact on grounds of *stare decisis*.

15. W. E. BURGHARDT DU BOIS, BLACK RECONSTRUCTION IN AMERICA 723 (1935).

16. Monroe v. Pape, 365 U.S. 167, 244 (1961) (Frankfurter, J., dissenting) (quoting Zechariah Chafee, Jr., *Safeguarding Fundamental Human Rights: The Tasks of States and Nation* 27 GEO. WASH. L. REV. 519, 529 (1959)).

17. RECONSTRUCTION AND REDEMPTION IN THE SOUTH 6 (Otto H. Olsen ed., 1980).

18. *See* JOHN HOPE FRANKLIN, RACE AND HISTORY: SELECTED ESSAYS 1938–1988 at 387 (1989); ERIC FONER, RECONSTRUCTION: AMERICA'S UNFINISHED REVOLUTION 1863–1877 at 609 (1988).

19. WILLIAM ARCHIBALD DUNNING, ESSAYS ON THE CIVIL WAR AND RECONSTRUCTION 384–85 (Macmillan & Co. 1897).

20. JOHN W. BURGESS, RECONSTRUCTION AND THE CONSTITUTION 1866–1876 at 133 (1902).

21. *Id.* at 244–45.

22. *See id.* at 246. ("The conduct of the men who now appeared on the scene as the creators of the new South was so tyrannic, corrupt, mean and vulgar as to repel the historian from attempting any detailed account of their doings, and incline him to the vaguest outline.")

23. *See* FRANKLIN, *supra* note 18 at 387; FONER, *supra* note 18 at 609.

24. C. Mildred Thompson, *Carpet-Baggers in the United States Senate, in* STUDIES IN SOUTHERN HISTORY AND POLITICS 175 (1914) [hereinafter DUNNING SCHOOL].

25. *Id.* at 176. Thompson also characterized Republican senators of the Forty-First Congress who (unlike Lyman Trumbull, whom she praised) were strong supporters of Reconstruction as "straight-out party politicians" while Senators George E. Spencer and William P. Kellogg "were unprincipled and corrupt to begin with" in a Senate that could not discipline them. *Id.*

26. *Id.* at 169.

27. J. G. de Roulhac Hamilton, *Southern Legislation in Respect to Freedmen 1865–1866 in* DUNNING SCHOOL, *supra* note 24 at 156.

28. William Watson Davis, *The Federal Enforcement Acts, in* DUNNING SCHOOL, *supra* note 24 at 228.

29. *Id.*

30. James W. Garner, *Southern Politics Since the Civil War, in* DUNNING SCHOOL, *supra* note 24 at 370.

31. *See* FRANKLIN, *supra* note 18 at 387–88.

32. *See id.* at 388; FONER, *supra* note 18 at 609.

33. *See* FRANKLIN, *supra* note 18 at 394.

34. 347 U.S. 483 (1954). The Court itself admitted in its opinion that it regarded evidence of the original understanding of the Fourteenth Amendment as "inconclusive." *Id.* at 489.

35. Adamson v. California, 332 U.S. 46, 64 (1947) (Frankfurter, J., concurring).

36. It should not be assumed that the original meaning is discernible strictly from the ratification debates themselves. While these debates may be of superior probative value, they cover issues of a limited scope, and immediately subsequent Congresses and presidential administrations are traditionally accepted as means of casting reflected light on recent constitutional provisions. *Cf.* Michael W. Mc-Connell, *Originalism and the Desegregation Decisions* 81 VA. L. REV. 947, 1107 (1995) [hereinafter McConnell I] ("The shifts in public opinion between 1866–68 and 1871–75 . . . make any inference based on the latter period uncertain, but they do not push in one direction or the other. In the end, reliance on evidence from this period seems neither more nor less warranted than the accepted practice of relying on evidence from the administrations of the early Presidents in interpreting the Constitution of 1787. If we were to reject this evidence, consistency would demand that we cease looking to the practices of the Washington Administration in interpreting separation of powers or to those of Presidents Jefferson and Madison in interpreting the Religion Clauses."). Concurrence in this statement might be qualified only by a word of caution in tracking the growing disapproval toward Reconstruction during the latter part of this period.

37. The second Justice John M. Harlan pointed out, "Reports of the debates in the state legislatures on the ratification of the Fourteenth Amendment are not generally available." Reynolds v. Sims, 377 U.S. 533, 602 (1964) (Harlan, J., dissenting). *See also* Michael W. McConnell, *The Originalist Justification for* Brown: *A Reply to Professor Klarman* 81 VA. L. REV. 1937, 1944 (1995) [hereinafter McConnell II] ("Although in theory, evidence of the understanding of the state legislatures at the precise time of ratification would be a superior basis for interpretation [to the debates over the Civil Rights Act of 1875], it does not exist.").

38. *Cf.* ROBERT H. BORK, THE TEMPTING OF AMERICA 165 (1990) (citing records of ratifying conventions, contemporary newspaper accounts, constructions of early congresses, interpretations by executive branch officials, early court decisions, and legal treatises among sources to consult for an understanding of particular provisions of the Constitution).

CHAPTER 2: A BRIEF OVERVIEW OF RECONSTRUCTION AND THE NATION'S RETREAT

1. *Cf.* FONER, *supra* note 18, Ch. 1 at xxvii (opening his study of Reconstruction with the Emancipation Proclamation "to indicate that Reconstruction was not merely a specific time period, but the beginning of an extended historical process: the adjustment of American society to the end of slavery").

2. *See id.*

3. The actual date of ratification has been recorded as December 6, *see* 6 CHARLES FAIRMAN, HISTORY OF THE SUPREME COURT OF THE UNITED STATES: RECONSTRUCTION AND REUNION 1864–88 at 1161 (1971) [hereinafter SUPREME COURT HISTORY], December 9, and December 18, *see* Eugene Gressman, *The Unhappy History of Civil Rights Legislation,* 50 MICH. L. REV. 1323, 1324 & n.1 (1952).

4. U.S. CONST. amend. XIII.

5. See FONER, *supra* note 18, Ch. 1 at 183.

6. *See id.*

7. *See id.* at 189.

8. *See id.* at 242–43.

9. *See id.* at 229, 231–32. Believing that "the President's policy endangered the rights of the people and the authority of the nation," Senator Henry Wilson, a Radical, described Reconstruction measures as "a series of legislative measures intended to secure the rights and privileges of the freedmen, protect those who had remained loyal to the Government, preserve order and put [the rebellious] States under the control of men loyal to the country, to liberty and justice." HENRY WILSON, HISTORY OF THE RECONSTRUCTION MEASURES OF THE THIRTY-NINTH AND FORTIETH CONGRESSES iv (Negro Univ. Press 1970) (1868).

10. *See* FONER, *supra* note 18, Ch. 1 at 198–99.

11. *See id.* at 199.

12. *See id.* at 246; John Harrison, *Reconstructing the Privileges and Immunities Clause* 101 YALE L.J. 1385, 1413 (1992); McConnell I, *supra* note 36, Ch. 1 at 958.

13. *See* Act of July 16, 1866, ch. 200, 14 Stat. 173 (1866). *See also* FONER, *supra* note 18, Ch. 1 at 243.

14. Act of Apr. 9, 1866, ch. 31, 14 Stat. 27 (reenacted as Act of May 31, 1870, ch. 114, §§ 16, 18, 16 Stat. 140, 144) (codified as amended in several sections of 42 U.S.C. (1994)). *See also* FONER, *supra* note 18, Ch. 1 at 243.

15. *See* 14 Stat. 27. *See also* FONER, *supra* note 18, Ch. 1 at 243–44.

16. *See* FONER, *supra* note 18, Ch. 1 at 247, 250.

17. *See id.* at 250–51, 248 n.37; THE RECONSTRUCTION AMENDMENTS' DEBATES: THE LEGISLATIVE HISTORY AND CONTEMPORARY DEBATES ON THE 13TH, 14TH, AND 15TH AMENDMENTS 210 (Alfred Avins, ed., 1967) [hereinafter DEBATES] (quoting CONG. GLOBE, 39th Cong., 1st Sess. 1861 (1866)) (repassage of Civil Rights Act).

18. *See* FONER, *supra* note 18, Ch. 1 at 251.

19. *See* CONG. GLOBE, 39th Cong., 1st Sess. 118 (1866) (statements of Rep. Stevens); 6 SUPREME COURT HISTORY, *supra* note 3, Ch. 2 at 1260–61; FONER, *supra* note 18, Ch. 1 at 239.

20. U.S. CONST. amend. XIV, §§ 1, 5.

21. *See* U.S. CONST. amend. XIV, § 2.

22. *See* U.S. CONST. amend. XIV, § 3.

23. *See* U.S. CONST. amend. XIV, § 4.

24. *See* DEBATES, *supra* note 17, Ch. 2 at 211 (quoting CONG. GLOBE, 39th Cong., 1st Sess. 2286 (1866)).

25. *See id.* at 237 (quoting CONG. GLOBE, 39th Cong., 1st Sess. 3042 (1866)).

26. *See id.* at 238 (quoting CONG. GLOBE, 39th Cong., 1st Sess. 3149 (1866)).

27. *See* 6 SUPREME COURT HISTORY, *supra* note 3, Ch. 2 at 133.

28. *See* FONER, *supra* note 18, Ch. 1 at 262.

29. *See id.* at 262–63.

30. *See id.* at 267.

31. *See id.* at 271, 278.

32. *See* Act of Mar. 2, 1867, ch. 153, 14 Stat. 428; Act of Mar. 23, 1867, ch. 6, 15 Stat. 2; Act of July 19, 1867, ch. 30, 15 Stat. 14; Christopher N. May, *Presidential Defiance of 'Unconstitutional' Laws: Reviving the Royal Prerogative*, 21 HASTINGS CONST. L.Q. 865, 906 (1994).

33. *See* DEBATES, *supra* note 17, Ch. 2 at xiii.

34. *See id.*; FONER, *supra* note 18, Ch. 1 at 276.

35. *See id.*

36. Tenure of Office Act of Mar. 2, 1867, ch. 134, 14 Stat. 430 (amended by Act of Apr. 5, 1869, ch. 10, 16 Stat. 6 (repealed 1887)). *See also* FONER, *supra* note 18, Ch. 1 at 333.

37. *See* FONER, *supra* note 18, Ch. 1 at 334.

38. *See id.* at 336.

39. *See id.* at 341.

40. *See id.* at 337.

41. *See* DEBATES, *supra* note 17, Ch. 2 at 335 (quoting CONG. GLOBE, 40th Cong., 3rd Sess. 286 (1869)) (introduction of Fifteenth Amendment in the House of Representatives on January 23).

42. *See* DEBATES, *supra* note 17, Ch. 2 at 410 (quoting CONG. GLOBE, 40th Cong., 3rd Sess. 1564 (1869)).

43. *See* DEBATES, *supra* note 17, Ch. 2 at 417 (quoting CONG. GLOBE, 40th Cong., 3rd Sess. 1641 (1869)).

44. *See* 7 JAMES D. RICHARDSON, A COMPILATION OF THE MESSAGES AND PAPERS OF THE PRESIDENTS 1789–1897, at 8 (Washington, Government Printing Office 1898) ("The question of suffrage is one which is likely to agitate the public so long as a portion of the citizens of the nation are excluded from its privileges in any State. It seems to me very desirable that this question should be settled now, and I entertain the hope and express the desire that it may be by the ratification of the fifteenth article of amendment to the Constitution.")

45. *See* 2 GEORGE S. BOUTWELL, REMINISCENCES OF SIXTY YEARS IN PUBLIC AFFAIRS 48, 229–30 (1902).

46. *See* WILLIAM GILLETTE, RETREAT FROM RECONSTRUCTION 1869–1879, at 86 (1979).

47. *See id.* at 87–88 (discussing temporary restoration of Georgia to military rule following that state's expulsion of black legislators).

48. U.S. CONST. amend. XV.

49. *See* Act of May 31, 1870, ch. 114, 16 Stat. 140 (codified as amended in several sections of 42 U.S.C. (1994)). *See also* 7 SUPREME COURT HISTORY, *supra* note 3, Ch. 2 at 143–49 (discussing the act's legislative history); DEBATES, *supra* note 17, Ch. 2 at 460, 463 (quoting CONG. GLOBE, 41st Cong., 2d Sess. 3809, 3884 (1870)) (recording passage of the act).

50. *See* 16 Stat. 140.

51. *See* FONER, *supra* note 18, Ch. 1 at 454.

52. *See* Act of July 14, 1870, ch. 254, 16 Stat. 254, amended by Act of Feb. 18, 1875, ch. 80, 18 Stat. 316, 318 (repealed 1952).

53. *See* Act of February 28, 1871, ch. 99, 16 Stat. 433, repealed by Act of Feb. 8, 1894, ch. 25, 28 Stat. 36. For other discussions of this act, see 7 SUPREME COURT HISTORY, *supra* note 3, Ch. 2 at 149–51; GILLETTE, *supra* note 46, Ch. 2 at 26.

54. *See* Act of June 22, 1870, ch. 150, 16 Stat. 162; Neal Devins, *Political Will and the Unitary Executive: What Makes an Independent Agency Independent?*, 15 CARDOZO L. REV. 273, 276–77 (1993).

55. Act of Apr. 20, 1871, ch. 22, 17 Stat. 13 (codified as amended at 42 U.S.C. §§ 1983, 1985–1986 (1994)).

56. *See* FONER, *supra* note 18, Ch. 1 at 454.

57. RICHARDSON, *supra* note 44, Ch. 2 at 127.

58. *See* 17 Stat. 13.

59. *See* FONER, *supra* note 18, Ch. 1 at 454.

60. *See* Act of June 10, 1872, ch. 415, 17 Stat. 347, 348; GILLETTE, *supra* note 46, Ch. 2 at 26.

61. Davis, *supra* note 28, Ch. 1 at 228.

62. *See* FONER, *supra* note 18, Ch. 1 at 425–26; GILLETTE, *supra* note 46, Ch. 2 at 27.

63. *See* FONER, *supra* note 18, Ch. 1 at 342, 425–27; GILLETTE, *supra* note 46, Ch. 2 at 28.

64. *See* FONER, *supra* note 18, Ch. 2 at 442.

65. RICHARDSON, *supra* note 44, Ch. 2 at 134–35.

66. *See id.* at 136–38.

67. *See* FONER, *supra* note 18, Ch. 1 at 457–59; Edwin C. Woolley, *Grant's Southern Policy, in* DUNNING SCHOOL, *supra* note 24, Ch. 1 at 184.

68. *See* GILLETTE, *supra* note 46, Ch. 2 at 43, 45, 229.

69. *See id.* at 229.

70. *See id.* at 90–91.

71. *See id.* at 91–92.

72. *See id.* at 110–12.

73. *See id.* at 113.

74. *See id.* at 112, 114–15.

75. *See id.* at 115; Laurent Frantz, *Congressional Power to Enforce the Fourteenth Amendment Against Private Acts*, 73 YALE L.J. 1353, 1365 (1964); FONER, *supra* note 18, Ch. 1 at 437.

76. *See* GILLETTE, *supra* note 46, Ch. 2 at 115. A black Louisiana legislator stated that "on Easter Sunday of 1873, when the sun went down that night, it went down on the corpses of two hundred and eighty negroes." FONER, *supra* note 18, Ch. 1 at 437.

President Grant later called the incident "a butchery of citizens . . . which in bloodthirstiness and barbarity is hardly surpassed by any acts of savage warfare," 7 RICHARDSON, *supra* note 44, Ch. 2 at 307, and he also made the following remarks:

> To hold the people of Louisiana generally responsible for these atrocities would not be just, but it is a lamentable fact that insuperable obstructions were thrown in the way of punishing these murderers; and the so-called conservative papers of the State not only justified the massacre, but denounced as Federal tyranny and despotism the attempt . . . to bring them to justice. Fierce denunciations ring through the country about office holding and election matters in Louisiana, while every one of the Colfax miscreants goes unwhipped of justice, and no way can be found in this boasted land of civilization and Christianity to punish the perpetrators of this bloody and monstrous crime. . . .
>
> To say that the murder of a negro or a white Republican is not considered a crime in Louisiana would probably be unjust to a great part of the people, but it is true that a great number of such murders have been committed and no one has been punished therefor; and manifestly, as to them, the spirit of hatred and violence is stronger than law.

Id. at 308–09.

77. *See* GILLETTE, *supra* note 46, Ch. 2 at 116.

78. *See id.* at 95, 97–98.

79. *See id.* at 101–02; Woolley, *supra* note 67, Ch. 2 at 189–90.

80. *See* DU BOIS, *supra* note 15, Ch. 1 at 552; GILLETTE, *supra* note 46, Ch. 2 at 137.

81. *See* DU BOIS, *supra* note 15, Ch. 1 at 551–52.

82. *See* GILLETTE, *supra* note 46, Ch. 2 at 138–43.

83. *See id.* at 144; Woolley, *supra* note 67, Ch. 2 at 191–92.

84. *See* GILLETTE, *supra* note 46, Ch. 2 at 146–48.

85. *See* FONER, *supra* note 18, Ch. 1 at 497–98, 509.

86. *See* GILLETTE, *supra* note 46, Ch. 2 at 367; FONER, *supra* note 18, Ch. 1 at 528. For examples of this sentiment in 1874, *see* GILLETTE, *supra* note 46, Ch. 2 at 143 (the nation was "sick and tired of the miserable wrangle") (quoting Washington *National Republican* editorial); *id.* at 182 ("Reconstruction, the carpetbaggers, the usurpation of power supported by troops—all this is dead weight, a millstone, that if not speedily disengaged will carry republicanism to the bottom.") (quoting New York *Herald* editorial); *id.* at 184 ("[M]anipulation of the southern states from Washington had been a failure. Perhaps it would have been, even if it had not been so grossly abused; but the abuses have insured its failure, and insured, also, the disgust of the North, and the certainty that, either by this administration or the next, the opposite policy [of noninterference] will be tried.") (quoting Springfield *Republican*). *See also id.* at 192 (citing belief that all efforts to "raise the negro to the station and dignity of the Southern white race, are as silly and futile as the attempt of Xeres to bind the ocean with an iron chain") (quoting Augusta, Georgia, *Chronicle and Sentinel*, 1871); *id* at 184 (acknowledging the existence of an "overwhelming public sentiment *at the North* adverse to the protection of life at the South by the use of the Federal authority") (quoting Chicago *Inter-Ocean*, Jan. 19, 1875); *id.* at 192–93 (observing the general view of Southern Democrats as stigmatizing the black man as "unfit for the suffrage as a child, and . . . disastrous consequences [were] certain to flow from his admission to a share in the work of government. He *was* a child to all practical intents and purposes. . . . [T]o give him the ballot was to put an edged tool in his hands with which to hurt himself and his neighbors. It was at once a folly and a cruelty to thus spoil a good laborer in making [him] an utterly incompetent and preposterous citizen.") (quoting Springfield *Republican*, Sept. 10, 1875).

87. FONER, *supra* note 18, Ch. 1 at 527.

88. *See* GILLETTE, *supra* note 46, Ch. 2 at 197.

89. *See* FONER, *supra* note 18, Ch. 1 at 527.

90. *See id.* at 371–72.

91. *See id.* at 372.

92. *See* GILLETTE, *supra* note 46, Ch. 2 at 188.

93. *See id.* at 197.

94. *See* 7 RICHARDSON, *supra* note 44, Ch. 2 at 221.

95. *See* 2 CONG. REC. 3451, 4176 (1874); GILLETTE, *supra* note 46, Ch. 2 at 197, 205.

96. GILLETTE, *supra* note 46, Ch. 2 at 202.

97. *See id.* at 205.

98. *See id.* at 206.

99. *See id.* at 204, 217–18.

100. *See id.* at 207.

101. *See id.*

102. *See id.* at 217, 258.

103. *See id.* at 246.

104. *See id.* at 246, 261.

105. *See id.* at 247.

106. *See id.* at 247–48.

107. *See* FONER, *supra* note 18, Ch. 1 at 524–25, 527–28.

108. *See* GILLETTE, *supra* note 46, Ch. 2 at 253.

109. *See* Act of March 1, 1875, ch. 114, 18 Stat. 335 (held unconstitutional in part in the *Civil Rights Cases*, 109 U.S. 3 (1883)) (formerly codified in part at 42 U.S.C. § 1984).

110. *See* FRANKLIN, *supra* note 18, Ch. 1 at 116.

111. FONER, *supra* note 18, Ch. 1 at 556.

112. *See id.*; GILLETTE, *supra* note 46, Ch. 2 at 275, 277.

113. *See* GILLETTE, *supra* note 46, Ch. 2 at 201, 217–18, 241–42, 256–58, 274, 278, 292. Amid the storm of opposition, there were only a few who believed the final bill should have gone farther. *See id.* at 274–75.

Rep. William M. Robbins, a Democrat who opposed Reconstruction, remarked during the debates, "If I desired only party advantage, and not the welfare of the people of my country, I would wish you to pass this bill; for no respectable white man in my country is in favor of it; all are bitterly against it, and all will desert you if you pass it." DEBATES, *supra* note 17, Ch. 2 at 671 (quoting 2 CONG. REC. 900 (1874)).

114. 109 U.S. 3. *See infra* Ch. 3.D.2.a.

115. RICHARDSON, *supra* note 44, Ch. 2 at 297.

116. *Id.* at 298–99.

117. *See* GILLETTE, *supra* note 46, Ch. 2 at 151.

118. *See id.* at 118–20.

119. *See id.* at 121.

120. *See id.* at 122.

121. *See id.* at 123–24. Grant defended Sheridan's actions and called it "a deplorable fact that political crimes and murders have been committed in Louisiana which have gone unpunished, and which have been justified or apologized for, which must rest as a reproach upon the State and country long after the present generation has passed away." 7 RICHARDSON, *supra* note 44, Ch. 2 at 312.

122. JAMES A. GARFIELD, THE DIARY OF JAMES A. GARFIELD 6 (Harry James Brown & Frederick D. Williams, eds., 1967–81).

123. *See* GILLETTE, *supra* note 46, Ch. 2 at 131–32.

124. 92 U.S. 214 (1876). *See infra* Ch. 3.B.5.b.

125. 92 U.S. 542 (1876). *See infra* Ch. 3.B.6.a.

126. *See* 92 U.S. at 220–22.

127. *See* 92 U.S. at 559; FONER, *supra* note 18, Ch. 1 at 530–31.

128. *See* C. PETER MAGRATH, MORRISON R. WAITE: THE TRIUMPH OF CHARACTER 134 (1963) (calling the cases "the opening phases of the Compromise of 1877"); Ruth Ann Whiteside, Justice Joseph Bradley and the Reconstruction Amendments 204 (Ph.D. dissertation, 1981) (describing "a series of judicial inter-

pretations that had begun to narrow the reach of the new Amendments" as a "major reason behind the demise of the enforcement program").

129. A. LEON HIGGINBOTHAM, JR., SHADES OF FREEDOM 90 (1996) (citing ROBERT J. KACZOROWSKI, THE POLITICS OF JUDICIAL INTERPRETATION: THE FEDERAL COURTS, DEPARTMENT OF JUSTICE AND CIVIL RIGHTS, 1866–1876, at 175 (1985)); GILLETTE, *supra* note 46, Ch. 2 at 297.

130. *See* GILLETTE, *supra* note 46, Ch. 2 at 304–05, 321, 418.

131. *See* WOOLLEY, *supra* note 67, Ch. 2 at 196–97.

132. *See* GILLETTE, *supra* note 46, Ch. 2 at 162–63.

133. *Cf. id.* at 155–65 (citing various miscommunications between Grant, Gov. Adelbert Ames, and Attorney General Edwards Pierrepont, as well as Ames' failure to provide important information about the urgency of the situation).

134. *See id.* at 318, 315; WILLIAM B. HESSELTINE, ULYSSES S. GRANT: POLITICIAN 410 (1935).

135. *See* FONER, *supra* note 18, Ch. 1 at 575.

136. *See* HESSELTINE, *supra* note 134, Ch. 2 at 421.

137. *See* GILLETTE, *supra* note 46, Ch. 2 at 323–24.

138. *See id.* at 327–33.

139. *See* FONER, *supra* note 18, Ch. 1 at 581.

140. *See id.*

141. *See* GILLETTE, *supra* note 46, Ch. 2 at 333.

142. *See id.* at 344–45; FONER, *supra* note 18, Ch. 1 at 582.

143. *See* GILLETTE, *supra* note 46, Ch. 2 at 355, 434.

144. *See id.* at 362, 375.

145. *See* FONER, *supra* note 18, Ch. 1 at 590.

146. *See id.* at 598, 593.

CHAPTER 3: THE SUPREME COURT'S RETREAT FROM RECONSTRUCTION

A. Prelude to Retreat

1. 71 U.S. (4 Wall.) 475.

2. *See id.* at 501.

3. *See* Georgia v. Stanton, 73 U.S. (6 Wall.) 50, 77 (1868).

4. 74 U.S. (7 Wall.) 506.

5. *See id.* at 515.

6. 74 U.S. (7 Wall.) 700 (1869), *overruled on other grounds*, Morgan v. United States, 113 U.S. 476 (1885).

7. *See id.* at 725–26.

8. *Id.* at 731.

9. 27 F. Cas. 785 (C.C.D. Ky.) (Swayne, Circuit Justice 1866).

10. *See id.* at 791 (citing 17 U.S. (4 Wheat.) 316 (1819)). *McCulloch* will be discussed further in the analysis of the *Civil Rights Cases, infra* Ch. 3.D.2.

11. 27 F. Cas. at 793.

12. *Id.* at 794.

13. *See* In re Turner, 24 F. Cas. 337, 339 (C.C.D. Md.) (Chase, Circuit Justice

1867). Swayne's and Chase's opinions were cited with approval by Senator James Harlan in 1868. *See* DEBATES, *supra* note 17, Ch. 2 at 292 (quoting CONG. GLOBE, 40th Cong., 2d Sess. 1077 (1868)).

B. The Court's Decisions during the 1870s

1. *Blyew v. United States*

1. 80 U.S. (13 Wall.) 581.
2. *See* THE OXFORD COMPANION TO THE SUPREME COURT OF THE UNITED STATES 383 (Kermit L. Hall, ed., 1992) [hereinafter OXFORD].
3. *See* 80 U.S. at 583.
4. *Id.* at 590–91.
5. *Id.* at 593, 595.
6. *See id.* at 592.
7. *See id.* at 593–94.
8. *Id.* at 595 (Bradley, J., dissenting). Bradley added that the act's terms were "broad enough to embrace other persons as well as those of African descent." *Id.* at 596.
9. *See id.* at 596; *supra* note 14, Ch. 2 and accompanying text.
10. *See* 80 U.S. at 596–97 (Bradley, J., dissenting).
11. *Id.* at 599 (Bradley, J., dissenting).
12. *Id.* (Bradley, J., dissenting).
13. *Id.* at 599–600 (Bradley, J., dissenting).
14. *Id.* at 601 (Bradley, J., dissenting).
15. *Id.* (Bradley, J., dissenting).
16. *See supra* note 12, Ch. 2 and accompanying text.
17. *See* Harrison, *supra* note 12, Ch. 2 at 1413.
18. DEBATES, *supra* note 17, Ch. 2 at 98 (quoting CONG. GLOBE, 39th Cong., 1st Sess. 43 (1865)).
19. *Id.* at 108 (quoting CONG. GLOBE, 39th Cong., 1st Sess. 322–23 (1866)). For further support of the notion of the Thirteenth Amendment as including the incidents to slavery, see, e.g., *id.* at 370 (quoting CONG. GLOBE, 40th Cong., 3rd Sess. 153 (1869)) (statement of Sen. Wilson) (stating that "the fetters of slavery were riven" by the Thirteenth Amendment).
20. *Id.* at 480 (quoting CONG. GLOBE, 41st Cong., 3rd Sess. 1253 (1871)).
21. *See* Douglas L. Colbert, *Liberating the Thirteenth Amendment*, 30 HARV. C.R.-C.L. L. REV. 1, 19 (1995).

2. The Privileges and Immunities Clause and the *Slaughter-House Cases*

1. 83 U.S. (16 Wall.) 36 (1873).
2. *See* OXFORD, *supra* note 2, Ch. 3.B.1 at 789.
3. 15 F. Cas. 649 (C.C. La.) (Bradley, Circuit Justice 1870).
4. *See id.*
5. *Id.* at 651.
6. "The Citizens of each State shall be entitled to all Privileges and Immunities of Citizens in the several States."

7. 15 F. Cas. at 652.

8. *Id.*

9. *Id.* at 652–53.

10. *Id.* at 654.

11. 26 F. Cas. 79 (C.C.S.D. Ala. 1871). *See* Whiteside, *supra* note 128, Ch. 2 at 201 (calling *Hall* "in essence Bradley's decision, for he quite literally supplied . . . both the substance and the language of the judgment").

12. *See* Whiteside, *supra* note 128, Ch. 2 at 174–75; Frantz, *supra* note 75, Ch. 2 at 1362.

13. *See* Whiteside, *supra* note 128, Ch. 2 at 138, 181; Richard L. Aynes, *On Misreading John Bingham and the Fourteenth Amendment*, 103 YALE L.J. 57, 97 (1993) [hereinafter *Misreading Bingham*].

14. *See* 26 F. Cas. at 82.

15. *Id.* at 81.

16. *See* 83 U.S. (16 Wall.) 36, 59 (1873).

17. *See* CHARLES FAIRMAN, MR. JUSTICE MILLER AND THE SUPREME COURT 1862–1890, at 124 (1939).

18. *See id.* at 128, 140.

19. 83 U.S. at 71.

20. *Id.* at 73.

21. *Id.* at 81.

22. *See id.* at 73–74.

23. *Id.* at 76 (quoting Corfield v. Coryell, 6 F. Cas. 546, 551–52 (C.C.E.D. Pa.) (Washington, Circuit Justice 1823)).

24. *See* 6 F. Cas. at 551; Richard L. Aynes, *Constricting the Law of Freedom: Justice Miller, the Fourteenth Amendment, and the Slaughter-House Cases*, 70 CHI.-KENT L. REV. 627, 647 (1994) [hereinafter *Constricting the Law of Freedom*].

25. Washington's opinion in its original form stated the following:

[W]hat are the privileges and immunities of citizens in the several states? We feel no hesitation in confining these expressions to those privileges and immunities which are, in their nature, fundamental; which belong, of right, to the citizens of all free governments; and which have, at all times, been enjoyed by the citizens of the several states which compose this Union, from the time of their becoming free, independent, and sovereign. What these fundamental principles are, it would perhaps be more tedious than difficult to enumerate. They may, however, be all comprehended under the following general heads: Protection by the government; the enjoyment of life and liberty, with the right to acquire and possess property of every kind, and to pursue and obtain happiness and safety; subject nevertheless to such restraints as the government may justly prescribe for the general good of the whole.

6 F. Cas. at 551–52.

26. *See* 83 U.S. at 77.

27. *Id.* The Court did provide some examples of federally based privileges and immunities, including the right to come to the seat of government to assert a claim with that government, to transact business with it, seek its protection, share its offices, administer its functions; to have free access to seaports that involve foreign commerce, subtreasuries, land offices, and courts in the states; to demand federal protection of life, liberty, and property on the high seas or within a foreign jurisdiction; to peaceably assemble and petition for redress of grievances and to have

access to the privilege of *habeas corpus*; to use navigable waters of the United States; and to all rights secured by treaties with foreign nations. *See* 83 U.S. at 79–80.

28. *Id.* at 78.

29. *Id.* at 82.

30. *See id.* at 80. The Court also found no unconstitutional deprivation of property under the Due Process Clause. *See id.* at 81.

31. *Id.* at 87 (Field, J., dissenting).

32. *Id.* at 88–89 (Field, J., dissenting).

33. *Id.* at 89 (Field, J., dissenting).

34. *See id.* (Field, J., dissenting).

35. *See id.* at 90–93 (Field, J., dissenting).

36. *See id.* at 93 (Field, J., dissenting).

37. *See id.* at 94 (Field, J., dissenting).

38. *Id.* at 95 (Field, J., dissenting).

39. *Id.* at 96 (Field, J., dissenting).

40. *See id.* at 96–97 (Field, J., dissenting).

41. *See id.* at 97 (Field, J., dissenting). *Cf. supra* notes 23 and 25 and accompanying text.

42. 83 U.S. at 97 (Field, J., dissenting).

43. *See id.* at 98 (Field, J., dissenting).

44. *See id.* at 101 (Field, J., dissenting).

45. *See id.* at 102–09 (Field, J., dissenting).

46. *Id.* at 109–10 (Field, J., dissenting).

47. *Id.* at 112 (Bradley, J., dissenting).

48. *Id.* at 113–14 (Bradley, J., dissenting).

49. *Id.* at 116 (Bradley, J., dissenting).

50. *Id.* (Bradley, J., dissenting).

51. *Id.* at 117 (Bradley, J., dissenting).

52. *See id.* at 118 (Bradley, J., dissenting).

53. *Id.* at 118–19 (Bradley, J., dissenting).

54. *Id.* (Bradley, J., dissenting).

55. *See id.* at 119 (Bradley, J., dissenting).

56. *Id.* at 125 (Swayne, J., dissenting).

57. *Id.* at 129 (Swayne, J., dissenting).

58. *Id.* (Swayne, J., dissenting).

59. *See* 85 U.S. (18 Wall.) 129, 135 (1874) (Bradley, J., concurring).

60. *Id.* at 132–33.

61. *See id.* at 137 (Bradley, J., concurring); *id.* at 138 (Field, J., concurring).

62. *See Constricting the Law of Freedom, supra* note 24, Ch. 3.B.2 at 648–49; 83 U.S. at 91, 96–97 (Field, J., dissenting).

63. DEBATES, supra note 17, Ch. 2 at 136 (quoting CONG. GLOBE, 39th Cong., 1st Sess. 599 (1866)).

64. *See id.* at 148 (quoting CONG. GLOBE, 39th Cong., 1st Sess. app. 105 (1866)) (Freedmen's Bureau bill debates).

65. *See id.* at viii.

66. *See id.* at xi, 237 (quoting CONG. GLOBE, 39th Cong., 1st Sess. 3042 (1866)).

67. *Id.* at 203 (quoting CONG. GLOBE, 39th Cong., 1st Sess. 1782 (1866)).

68. *See id.* at xiii, 259 (quoting CONG. GLOBE, 39th Cong., 2d Sess. 239–40 (1867)).

69. *See id.* at viii, 155 (quoting CONG. GLOBE, 39th Cong., 1st Sess. 1065 (1866)).

70. *See, e.g.,* CHESTER JAMES ANTIEAU, THE ORIGINAL UNDERSTANDING OF THE FOURTEENTH AMENDMENT 23, 25 (1981) (citing the understanding in several states that the amendment would include the protection of Northern whites who traveled South and protection of all races in all sections of the country).

71. *See* DEBATES, *supra* note 17, Ch. 2 at 335 (quoting CONG. GLOBE, 40th Cong., 3rd Sess. 558 (1869)).

72. *See id.* at xx, 428, 449 (quoting CONG. GLOBE, 41st Cong., 2d Sess. 1536, 3658 (1870)).

73. *See id.* at 460 (quoting CONG. GLOBE, 41st Cong., 2d Sess. 3871 (1870)). The language Bingham applied to the equal protection guarantee—"not simply of the State itself, but of the Constitution of the United States as well"—appears in this context to support the proposition that it is not only the states, but also the federal government that cannot deny the equal protection of the laws. This notion is pertinent to the issue that would face the Court in *Bolling v. Sharpe,* 347 U.S. 497 (1954) (holding that the Due Process Clause of the Fifth Amendment restricted the federal government just as the Equal Protection Clause of the Fourteenth Amendment restricts the states), but since the issue lies beyond the Court's retreat from Reconstruction, this study will not explore it in greater detail.

74. DEBATES, *supra* note 17, Ch. 2 at 450 (quoting CONG. GLOBE, 41st Cong., 2d Sess. app. 472 (1870)).

75. *Id.* at 673 (quoting 2 CONG. REC. 3451 (1874)) (Civil Rights Act debates).

76. *See id.* at 688 (quoting 2 CONG. REC. 4148 (1874)) (asserting "upon my soul" that he believes the Fourteenth Amendment condemns "broad discrimination between the rights of white men"). *See also id.* at 716 (quoting 3 CONG. REC. 945 (1875)) (statement of Rep. Lynch) (suggesting religion and nationality as distinctions that lawmakers have a duty to ignore).

77. *See id.* at xxxii, 732 (quoting 3 CONG. REC. 1793 (1875)) (stating that the Civil Rights Act banned only racial discrimination, but the Fourteenth Amendment included the power to address discrimination for other reasons as well).

78. *See id.* at x, 180–82 (quoting CONG. GLOBE, 39th Cong., 1st Sess. 1268–70 (1866)) (statement of Rep. Kerr).

79. *See, e.g., id.* at xii, 248–49 (quoting CONG. GLOBE, 39th Cong., 1st Sess. app. 293–94 (1866)) (statement of Rep. Shellabarger); *id.* at 541 (quoting CONG. GLOBE, 42d Cong., 1st Sess. 500 (1871)) (statement of Sen. Frelinghuysen); *id.* at 560 (quoting CONG. GLOBE, 42d Cong., 1st Sess. 693 (1871)); *id.* at 615 (quoting CONG. GLOBE, 42d Cong., 2d Sess. 844 (1872)) (statement of Sen. Sherman). It should be added that Rep. Samuel Shellabarger, when discussing the clause, cited a list of "fundamental" privileges, derived from national and not state citizenship, that went beyond the Court's interpretation. These privileges "cannot be taken away from any citizen of the United States by the laws of any State." *Id.* at 248 (quoting CONG. GLOBE, 39th Cong., 1st Sess. app. 293 (1866)).

80. *Id.* at 552 (quoting CONG. GLOBE, 42d Cong., 1st Sess. app. 242–43 (1871)).

81. *Id.*

82. *See id.* at 559 (quoting CONG. GLOBE, 42d Cong., 1st Sess. 660 (1871)).

83. *See id.* at xxvii, 627 (quoting CONG. GLOBE, 42d Cong., 2d Sess. app. 42–43 (1872)).

84. *See id.* at 664 (quoting 2 CONG. REC. 420 (1874)).

85. *See id.* at 717 (quoting 3 CONG. REC. 949 (1875)); *id.* at 238 (quoting CONG. GLOBE, 39th Cong., 1st Sess. 3149 (1866)).

86. *See id.* at 679–80 (quoting 2 CONG. REC. 4086–88 (1874)).

87. *See id.* at 736 (quoting 3 CONG. REC. app. 105 (1875)).

88. *See id.* at 618 (quoting CONG. GLOBE, 42d Cong., 2d Sess. app. 26 (1872)).

89. *Id.* at 549–50 (quoting CONG. GLOBE, 42d Cong., 1st Sess. 576–77 (1871)).

90. *See* McConnell I, *supra* note 36, Ch. 1 at 1023; FONER, *supra* note 18, Ch. 1 at 500, 507; RALPH J. ROSKE, HIS OWN COUNSEL: THE LIFE AND TIMES OF LYMAN TRUMBULL 155, 157, 161–70 (1979).

91. DEBATES, *supra* note 17, Ch. 2 at 540 (quoting CONG. GLOBE, 42d Cong., 1st Sess. app. 189 (1871)).

92. *See id.* at 718 (quoting 3 CONG. REC. app. 157 (1875)).

93. *See id.* at 737–38 (quoting 3 CONG. REC. 1862 (1875)).

94. *See id.* at xxxii.

95. *See id.* at 550 (quoting CONG. GLOBE, 42d Cong., 1st Sess. 577 (1871)).

96. *See id.* at 659 (quoting 2 CONG. REC. 384 (1874)).

97. *See id.* at 709 (quoting 2 CONG. REC. 343 (1874)).

98. *Id.* at v, 65–66 (quoting CONG. GLOBE, 38th Cong., 1st Sess. 1202 (1864)).

99. *See id.* at v, 76–77 (quoting CONG. GLOBE, 38th Cong., 1st Sess. 2943, 2984, 2990 (1864)) (statements of Rep. Higby, Rep. Kelley, & Rep. Ingersoll); *id.* at 81–84 (quoting CONG. GLOBE, 38th Cong., 2d Sess. 138, 193, 237 (1865)) (statements of Rep. Ashley, Rep. Kasson, and Rep. Smith).

100. *Id.* at 100 (quoting CONG. GLOBE, 39th Cong., 1st Sess. 158 (1866)).

101. *See id.* at 121 (quoting CONG. GLOBE, 39th Cong., 1st Sess. 474 (1866)).

102. *See id.* at 193 (quoting CONG. GLOBE, 39th Cong., 1st Sess. 1627 (1866)) (statement of Rep. Buckland) ("[I]t is the duty of the Government to provide for its future safety, and insist upon such measures as will secure to every American citizen the natural rights of life, liberty, and property, in all the States."); *id.* at 207 (quoting CONG. GLOBE, 39th Cong., 1st Sess. 1835 (1866)) (statement of Rep. Lawrence) ("Congress may by law secure the citizens of the nation in the enjoyment of their inherent right of life, liberty, and property, and the means essential to that end, by penal enactments to enforce the observance of the provisions of the Constitution, article four, section two, and the equal civil rights which it recognizes or by implication affirms to exist among citizens of the same State.").

103. *See* Gressman, *supra* note 3, Ch. 2 at 1326, 1333.

104. DEBATES, *supra* note 17, Ch. 2 at 122 (quoting CONG. GLOBE, 39th Cong., 1st Sess. 476 (1866)).

105. *Id.* at 236 (quoting CONG. GLOBE, 39th Cong., 1st Sess. 3034–35 (1866)).

106. *See, e.g., id.* at 136 (quoting CONG. GLOBE, 39th Cong., 1st Sess. 599 (1866)) (statement of Sen. Trumbull).

107. 41 U.S. (16 Pet.) 539 (1842).

108. *See* CONG. GLOBE, 39th Cong., 1st Sess. 1292, 1294 (1866). *See also* DEBATES, *supra* note 17, Ch. 2 at 164–65 (quoting CONG. GLOBE, 39th Cong. 1st Sess. 1118–19 (1866)).

109. *See, e.g.*, DEBATES, *supra* note 17, Ch. 2 at 207–08 (quoting CONG. GLOBE, 39th Cong., 1st Sess. 1835–36 (1866)) (statement of Rep. Lawrence) (citing both *Prigg* and *McCulloch v. Maryland* to justify the enforcement of "civil rights constitutionally recognized and affirmed by national authority").

110. *See Constricting the Law of Freedom, supra* note 24, Ch. 3.B.2 at 649–50.

111. *See id.*

112. *See id.* at 156 (quoting CONG. GLOBE, 39th Cong., 1st Sess. 1088 (1866)).

113. *Id.* at 216 (quoting CONG. GLOBE, 39th Cong., 1st Sess. 2538 (1866)).

114. *Id.*

115. *Id.* at 217 (quoting CONG. GLOBE, 39th Cong., 1st Sess. 2542 (1866)).

116. *See id.* The Pennsylvania ratification debates reflected similar understandings of the amendment as including natural rights mentioned in the Declaration of Independence. *See* ANTIEAU, *supra* note 70, Ch. 3 at 29.

117. *See* DEBATES, *supra* note 17, Ch. 2 at 230 (quoting CONG. GLOBE, 39th Cong., 1st Sess. 2961 (1866)).

118. *Id.* at 219 (quoting CONG. GLOBE, 39th Cong., 1st Sess. 2765 (1866)).

119. *Id.*

120. *Id.* at 219–20 (quoting CONG. GLOBE, 39th Cong., 1st Sess. 2765–66 (1866)). *See also id.* at 373 (quoting CONG. GLOBE, 40th Cong., 3rd Sess. 1003 (1869)) (statement of Sen. Howard) (asserting that Section 1 of the Fourteenth Amendment arose out of the inability of the Constitution to secure citizens their rights and privileges under Article IV Section 2).

121. *See id.* at 237 (quoting CONG. GLOBE, 39th Cong., 1st Sess. 3039, 3041 (1866)) (statements of Sen. Hendricks & Sen. Johnson).

122. *See id.* (quoting CONG. GLOBE, 39th Cong., 1st Sess. 3039 (1866)).

123. According to Boutwell, the "euphony and indefiniteness of meaning" of the Privileges and Immunities Clause "were a charm to" Bingham. 2 BOUTWELL, *supra* note 45, Ch. 2 at 42.

124. DEBATES, *supra* note 17, Ch. 2 at 237 (quoting CONG. GLOBE, 39th Cong., 1st Sess. 3148 (1866)).

125. *Id.* at 335 (quoting CONG. GLOBE, 40th Cong., 3rd Sess. 558 (1869)).

126. *See id.* at xxvii, 614 (quoting CONG. GLOBE, 42d Cong., 2d Sess. 843 (1872)); *id.* at 237–38 (quoting CONG. GLOBE, 39th Cong., 1st Sess. 3042, 3149 (1866)) (recording Senate and House votes on the Fourteenth Amendment).

127. *See id.* at 535, 537 (quoting CONG. GLOBE, 42d Cong., 1st Sess. 475, 482 (1871)) (statements of Rep. Dawes & Rep. Wilson).

128. *See id.* at 494, 561 (quoting CONG. GLOBE, 42d Cong., 1st Sess. app. 69, 693 (1871)); *id.* at 237–38 (quoting CONG. GLOBE, 39th Cong., 1st Sess. 3149 (1866)) (recording Senate and House votes on the Fourteenth Amendment).

129. *See id.* at 466 (quoting H.R. REP. NO. 22, 41st Cong., 3rd Sess., pt. 1, at 1 (1871)).

130. *See id.* at 587 (quoting CONG. GLOBE, 42d Cong., 2d Sess. 525 (1872)).

131. *See id.* at 590 (quoting CONG. GLOBE, 42d Cong., 2d Sess. app. 1 (1872)).

132. *See id.* at 541 (quoting CONG. GLOBE, 42d Cong., 1st Sess. 500 (1871)).

133. *Id.*

134. *Id.*

135. *Id.* at 561 (quoting CONG. GLOBE, 42d Cong., 1st Sess. 693 (1871)).

136. *Id.* at 675 (quoting 2 CONG. REC. 3454 (1874)).

137. *Id.* at 679 (quoting 2 CONG. REC. 4087 (1874)).
138. *See id.* at xxx, 686 (quoting 2 CONG. REC. 4116 (1874)).
139. *Id.* at 732 (quoting 3 CONG. REC. 1793 (1875)).
140. *Id.* at 743 (quoting 3 CONG. REC. 1870 (1875)).
141. *See, e.g.,* BORK, *supra* note 38, Ch. 1 at 181 (dismissing the interpretive value of *Corfield* as "a singularly confused opinion in 1823 by a single Justice of the Supreme Court setting out his ideas of what the original privileges and immunities clause . . . meant").
142. For examples of citations of *Corfield* in contexts tending to support the Court's conclusion, *see* DEBATES, *supra* note 17, Ch. 2 at 128 (quoting CONG. GLOBE, 39th Cong., 1st Sess. 505 (1866)) (statement of Sen. Johnson) (citing other parts of the decision to refute its use in support of the 1866 Civil Rights Act); *id.* at 181 (quoting CONG. GLOBE, 39th Cong., 1st Sess. 1269 (1866)) (statement of Rep. Kerr) (stating that Washington's views "were uttered in reference alone to white citizens" and asserting the states' right to exclude blacks "or to limit them in civil or political rights and privileges"); *id.* at 510 (quoting CONG. GLOBE, 42d Cong., 1st Sess. app. 84 (1871)) (statement of Rep. Bingham) (viewing the opinion as an interpretation of the original Privileges and Immunities Clause insuring only that the states would not deny to citizens of other states the general rights of its own citizens); *id.* at 523 (quoting CONG. GLOBE, 42d Cong., 1st Sess. app. 117 (1871)) (statement of Sen. Blair) (criticizing use of the opinion to vest too much power in the central government); *id.* at 540 (quoting CONG. GLOBE, 42d Cong., 1st Sess. app. 188–89 (1871)) (statement of Rep. Willard) (maintaining that a citizen is entitled only to "an equality of privileges and immunities with the citizens of the State in which he may happen to be"); *id.* at 559 (quoting CONG. GLOBE, 42d Cong., 1st Sess. 660 (1871)) (statement of Sen. Vickers) (suggesting that the Ku Klux Klan Act goes beyond protecting privileges and immunities recognized by the opinion); *id.* at 626 (quoting CONG. GLOBE, 42d Cong., 2d Sess. app. 41 (1872)) (statement of Sen. Vickers) (suggesting that the civil rights bill goes beyond protecting privileges and immunities recognized by the opinion); *id.* at 664 (quoting 2 CONG. REC. 420 (1874)) (statement of Rep. Herndon) (citing the opinion before citing the Court's interpretation in the *Slaughter-House Cases*); *id.* at 679–80 (quoting 2 CONG. REC. 4087 (1874)) (statement of Sen. Thurman) (citing the opinion while drawing distinctions between state and national privileges and immunities); *id.* at 718 (quoting 3 CONG. REC. app. 157 (1875)) (statement of Rep. Smith) (same).

For examples of citations of *Corfield* in contexts tending to contradict the Court's conclusion, see *id.* at 122 (quoting CONG. GLOBE, 39th Cong., 1st Sess. 475 (1866)) (statement of Sen. Trumbull) (reading the opinion as a definition of the privileges and immunities of citizens of the United States during the debates over the Civil Rights Act of 1866); *id.* at 163–64 (quoting CONG. GLOBE, 39th Cong., 1st Sess. 1117–18 (1866)) (statement of Rep. Wilson) (citing the case as part of his appeal to supply "the protection which the States deny"); *id.* at 207–08 (quoting CONG. GLOBE, 39th Cong., 1st Sess. 1835–36 (1866)) (statement of Rep. Lawrence) (arguing for "equal fundamental civil rights for all citizens"); *id.* at 219 (quoting CONG. GLOBE, 39th Cong., 1st Sess. 2765 (1866)) (statement of Sen. Howard) (expressing his desire to compel states to respect fundamental guarantees); *id.* at 248 (quoting CONG. GLOBE, 39th Cong., 1st Sess. app. 293 (1866)) (statement of

Rep. Shellabarger) (asserting that no state can take away fundamental rights); *id.* at 466 (quoting H.R. REP. NO. 22, 41st Cong., 3rd Sess., pt. 1, at 2 (1871)) (report of Rep. Bingham for the majority of the House Judiciary Committee) (interpreting original Privileges and Immunities Clause as conferring general citizenship on citizens in each state); *id.* at 468–69 (quoting H.R. REP. NO. 22, 41st Cong., 3rd Sess., pt. 2, at 6–8 (1871)) (report of Rep. Loughridge for the minority of the House Judiciary Committee) (citing the opinion in support of fundamental rights and including the elective franchise among them); *id.* at 494 (quoting CONG. GLOBE, 42d Cong., 1st Sess. app. 69 (1871)) (statement of Rep. Shellabarger) (citing opinion as including "the fundamental rights of citizenship"); *id.* at 502 (quoting CONG. GLOBE, 42d Cong., 1st Sess. 334 (1871)) (statement of Rep. Hoar) (discussing privileges and immunities "fundamental and essential to citizenship"); *id.* at 557 (quoting CONG. GLOBE, 42d Cong., 1st Sess. app. 228 (1871)) (statement of Sen. Boreman) (citing opinion to illustrate fundamental rights that were being violated, thus necessitating the Ku Klux Klan Act); *id.* at 674 (quoting CONG. GLOBE, 43rd Cong., 1st Sess. 3453 (1874)) (statement of Sen. Frelinghuysen) (arguing for legal equality as a privilege of United States citizenship); *id.* at 679 (quoting 2 CONG. REC. 4087 (1874)) (statement of Sen. Morton) (arguing against different treatment of state and national privileges). Besides his dissenting opinion, it should be noted that Justice Bradley, in his earlier letter to Judge Woods, believed *Corfield* described fundamental privileges and immunities that were covered by the Fourteenth Amendment. *See* 7 SUPREME COURT HISTORY, *supra* note 3, Ch. 2 at 190.

It was rare for legislators to dismiss *Corfield*'s importance, but see DEBATES, *supra* note 17, Ch. 2 at 528 (quoting CONG. GLOBE, 42d Cong., 1st Sess. 152 (1871)) (statement of Rep. Garfield) (stating that congressional power is not truly as broad as suggested in the opinion); *id.* at 544 (quoting CONG. GLOBE, 42d Cong., 1st Sess. app. 314 (1871)) (statement of Rep. Burchard) (same).

143. *See* DEBATES, *supra* note 17, Ch. 2 at 657–58 (quoting 2 CONG. REC. 342 (1873)).

144. *See id.* at 659 (quoting 2 CONG. REC. 380 (1874)).

145. *See id.* at 664 (quoting 2 CONG. REC. 420 (1874)).

146. *See id.* at 667 (quoting 2 CONG. REC. 453 (1874)).

147. *See id.* at 668 (quoting 2 CONG. REC. app. 2 (1874)).

148. *See id.* at 676 (quoting 2 CONG. REC. app. 242 (1874)).

149. *See id.* at 679–80 (quoting 2 CONG. REC. 4087–88 (1874)).

150. *See id.* at 708–09 (quoting 2 CONG. REC. app. 342–43 (1874)).

151. *See id.* at 716–17 (quoting 3 CONG. REC. 948–49 (1875)).

152. *See id.* at 718 (quoting 3 CONG. REC. app. 157 (1875)).

153. *See id.* at 737–38 (quoting 3 CONG. REC. 1862 (1875)).

154. *Id.* at 738–39 (quoting 3 CONG. REC. 1863 (1875)).

155. *See id.* at 673, 675 (quoting 2 CONG. REC. 3451, 3454 (1874)).

156. *See id.* at 686 (quoting 2 CONG. REC. 4116 (1874)); *id.* at 731 (quoting 3 CONG. REC. 1792 (1875)).

157. *See id.* at 688 (quoting 2 CONG. REC. 4148 (1874)). After studying the Court's opinion, Howe exclaimed, "The American people would say, as they had said about the Dred Scott decision, that it was not law and could not be law." HOWARD N. MEYER, THE AMENDMENT THAT REFUSED TO DIE 77 (rev. ed., 1978).

158. *Constricting the Law of Freedom, supra* note 24, Ch. 3.B.2 at 681 n.389.

See also DEBATES, *supra* note 17, Ch. 2 at 680 (quoting 2 CONG. REC. 4088 (1874)); *id*. at 743 (quoting 2 CONG. REC. 1870 (1875)).

159. *See id*. at 501 (quoting CONG. GLOBE, 42d Cong., 1st Sess. 334 (1871)).

160. *See id*. at 237 (quoting CONG. GLOBE, 39th Cong., 1st Sess. 3042 (1866)) (recording Senate votes on the Fourteenth Amendment).

161. *See infra* Ch. 3.B.6.b.

162. *See Constricting the Law of Freedom, supra* note 24, Ch. 3.B.2 at 627 & n.4 (asserting that " 'everyone' agrees the Court incorrectly interpreted the Privileges and Immunities Clause").

163. BORK, *supra* note 38, Ch. 1 at 166.

164. 211 U.S. 78, 96.

165. *See* McConnell I, *supra* note 36, Ch. 1 at 1004.

166. 83 U.S. (16 Wall.) 130, 139 (1873).

167. *Id*. at 137.

168. *Id*. at 139.

169. *See id*. at 139–42 (Bradley, J., concurring).

170. *See id*. at 142; 6 SUPREME COURT HISTORY, *supra* note 3, Ch. 2 at 1364, 1474.

3. *Railroad Co. v. Brown*: The Court and Segregation in 1874

1. 84 U.S. (17 Wall.) 445.

2. *See* Act of Mar. 3, 1863, 12 Stat. 805.

3. 84 U.S. at 447–48.

4. *Id*. at 448.

5. *Id*. at 452.

6. *Id*. at 452–53.

7. DEBATES, *supra* note 17, Ch. 2 at 56 (quoting CONG. GLOBE, 38th Cong., 1st Sess. 553 (1864)).

8. *Id*. at 57 (quoting CONG. GLOBE, 38th Cong., 1st Sess. 817 (1864)).

9. *Id*. at 58 (quoting CONG. GLOBE, 38th Cong., 1st Sess. 818 (1864)).

10. *Id*. at 63 (quoting CONG. GLOBE, 38th Cong., 1st Sess. 1158 (1864)).

11. *Id*. at 60 (quoting CONG. GLOBE, 38th Cong., 1st Sess. 839 (1864)).

12. *Id*. For other examples of Democratic senators opposing desegregation, see *id*. at 62 (quoting CONG. GLOBE, 38th Cong., 1st Sess. 1156 (1864)) (statement of Sen. Johnson); *id*. at 63 (quoting CONG. GLOBE, 38th Cong., 1st Sess. 1158 (1864)) (statement of Sen. Saulsbury).

13. *Id*. at 79 (quoting CONG. GLOBE, 38th Cong., 1st Sess. 3133 (1864)).

14. *See id*. at 65 (quoting CONG. GLOBE, 38th Cong., 1st Sess. 1161 (1864)).

15. *Id*. at 80 (quoting CONG. GLOBE, 38th Cong., 1st Sess. 3137 (1864)). Those who voted against the two amendments included Republicans on both occasions, but the "nay" votes are difficult to explain in terms of opposition to desegregation, perhaps because the votes occurred while the war was still raging. That other factors might have been involved is further suggested by the inconsistency in voting. Senator James W. Grimes expressed tolerance for segregated cars "at this time" before the vote on the second amendment, but he and Senator Lafayette S. Foster, both of whom voted against the second amendment, had voted for the first amendment. At the same time, Senator John Sherman, who would later champion the

cause of desegregation, voted against both amendments. *See id.* at 65, 79–80 (quoting CONG. GLOBE, 38th Cong., 1st Sess. 1161, 3133, 3137 (1864)).

16. *Id.* at 281 (quoting S. REP. NO. 131, 40th Cong., 2d Sess. at 2 (1868)).

17. *Id.* at 293 (quoting CONG. GLOBE, 40th Cong., 2d Sess. 1121 (1868)).

18. *Id.* (quoting CONG. GLOBE, 40th Cong., 2d Sess. 1121–22 (1868)).

19. *Id.* at 294 (quoting CONG. GLOBE, 40th Cong., 2d Sess. 1123 (1868)).

20. *Id.* at 295 (quoting CONG. GLOBE, 40th Cong., 2d Sess. 1124 (1868)).

21. *See id.* at 296 (quoting CONG. GLOBE, 40th Cong., 2d Sess. 1125 (1868)).

22. *Id.*

23. *See id.* at 237 (quoting CONG. GLOBE, 39th Cong., 1st Sess. 3042 (1866)) (recording Senate votes on the Fourteenth Amendment).

24. *See* ANTIEAU, *supra* note 70, Ch. 3.B.2 at 28–29, 52, 55.

4. *Minor v. Hapersett* and Suffrage under the Fourteenth Amendment

1. 88 U.S. 162.

2. *Id.* at 171.

3. *See* Samuel Shellabarger, Statement in Memoriam on the Death of Chief Justice Morrison R. Waite, 126 U.S. 596, 600 (1888).

4. *See* 88 U.S. at 171, 178.

5. *See id.* at 174. Section 2 of the Fourteenth Amendment states the following:

Representatives shall be apportioned among the several States according to their respective numbers, counting the whole number of persons in each State, excluding Indians not taxed. But when the right to vote at any election for the choice of electors for President and Vice President of the United States, Representatives in Congress, the Executive and Judicial officers of a State, or the members of the Legislature thereof, is denied to any of the male inhabitants of such State, being twenty-one years of age, and citizens of the United States, or in any way abridged, except for participation in rebellion, or other crime, the basis of representation therein shall be reduced in the proportion which the number of such male citizens shall bear to the whole number of male citizens twenty-one years of age in such State.

6. *See, e.g.,* DEBATES, *supra* note 17, Ch. 2 at 100 (quoting CONG. GLOBE, 39th Cong., 1st Sess. 173 (1866)) (statement of Rep. Wilson) (suffrage "is not a natural right"); *id.* at 105 (quoting CONG. GLOBE, 39th Cong., 1st Sess. 237 (1866)) (statement of Rep. Kasson) (suggesting that suffrage is not a natural right but subject to several restrictions); *id.* at 212 (quoting CONG. GLOBE, 39th Cong., 1st Sess. 2459 (1866)) (statement of Rep. Stevens) (acknowledging the effect of Section 2 as allowing the exclusion of adult male citizens from the right to vote with the penalty of loss of representation); *id.* at 213 (quoting CONG. GLOBE, 39th Cong., 1st Sess. 2462 (1866)) (statement of Rep. Garfield) ("I regret more than I shall be able to tell this House that we have not found the situation of affairs in this country such, and the public virtue such that we might come out on the plain, unanswerable proposition that every adult intelligent citizen of the United States, unconvicted of crime, shall enjoy the right of suffrage."); *id.* (quoting CONG. GLOBE, 39th Cong., 1st Sess. 2469 (1866)) (statement of Rep. Kelley) (expressing dissatisfaction with the Fourteenth Amendment for not proposing "to at once enfranchise every loyal man in the country"); CONG. GLOBE, 39th Cong., 1st Sess. 2498 (1866) (statement

of Rep. Broomall) ("The second proposition is, in short, to limit the representation of the several States as those States themselves shall limit suffrage. . . . And why not? If the negroes of the South are not to be counted as a political element in the government of the South in the States, why should they be counted as a political element in the government of the country in the Union? If they are not to be counted as against the southern people themselves, why should they be counted as against us?"); DEBATES, *supra* note 17, Ch. 2 at 214 (quoting CONG. GLOBE, 39th Cong., 1st Sess. 2505 (1866)) (statement of Rep. McKee) ("[T]his House is not prepared to enfranchise all men; the nation, perhaps, is not prepared for it to-day; the colored race are not prepared for it, probably, and I am sure the rebels are unfit for it; and as Congress has not the moral courage to vote for it, then put in this provision which cuts off the traitor from all political power in the nation, and then we have secured to the loyal men that control which they so richly deserve."); *id.* at 215 (quoting CONG. GLOBE, 39th Cong., 1st Sess. 2506 (1866)) (statement of Rep. Eldridge) ("Why is it that the gentleman from Pennsylvania [Mr. STEVENS] gives up universal suffrage? Why is it that he and other gentlemen give up universal confiscation? Why is it that other gentlemen give up universal butchery of that people? It is a compromise of what they call principle for the purpose of saving their party in the next fall election."); *id.* (quoting CONG. GLOBE, 39th Cong., 1st Sess. 2508 (1866)) (statement of Rep. Boutwell) ("The proposition in the matter of suffrage falls short of what I desire, but so far as it goes it tends to the equalization of the inequality at present existing; and while I demand and shall continue to demand the franchise for all loyal male citizens of this country—and I cannot but admit the possibility that ultimately those eleven States may be restored to representative power without the right of franchise being conferred upon the colored people—I should feel myself doubly humiliated and disgraced, and criminal even, if I hesitated to do what I can for a proposition which equalizes representation."); *id.* at 215 (quoting CONG. GLOBE, 39th Cong., 1st Sess. 2510 (1866)) (statement of Rep. Miller) (asserting that the Fourteenth "amendment will settle the complication in regard to suffrage and representation, leaving each State to regulate that for itself, so that it will be for it to decide whether or not it shall have a representation for all its male citizens not less than twenty-one years of age"); *id.* (quoting CONG. GLOBE, 39th Cong., 1st Sess. 2511 (1866)) (statement of Rep. Eliot) (acknowledging that Section 2 does not preclude the denial of the franchise to a portion of a state's citizens, though approving its tendency to equalize representation); *id.* at 216 (quoting CONG. GLOBE, 39th Cong., 1st Sess. 2530 (1866)) (statement of Rep. Randall) ("Gentlemen here admit that they desire [federal control over suffrage], but that the weak kneed of their party are not equal to the issue. Your purpose is the same, and but for that timidity you would now ingraft negro suffrage upon our Constitution and force it on the entire people of this Union."); *id.* (quoting CONG. GLOBE, 39th Cong., 1st Sess. 2532 (1866)) (statement of Rep. Banks) (stating that the federal government could "extend the elective franchise to the colored population of the insurgent States" but that "public opinion . . . at this precise moment" would "make it impossible," so "[i]t was therefore most wise on the part of the committee on reconstruction to waive this matter in deference to public opinion"); CONG. GLOBE, 39th Cong., 1st Sess. 2535 (1866) (statement of Rep. Eckley) ("If South Carolina persists in withholding the ballot from the colored man, then let her take the alternative we offer, of confining her to the white basis of representation."); DEBATES, *supra* note 17, Ch. 2 at 216 (quoting CONG. GLOBE, 39th Cong., 1st Sess. 2537 (1866)) (statement of Rep. Beaman) ("I did hope to see the rights of the freedmen completely established. I did believe . . . that we should have the manhood and magnanimity to declare that men who have wielded the sword in defense of their country are fit to be intrusted with the ballot. But I am convinced that my expectations, hitherto fondly cherished, are doomed to some disappointment."); *id.* at 217 (quoting CONG. GLOBE, 39th Cong., 1st Sess. 2540 (1866)) (statement of Rep. Farnsworth) ("[A]lthough I should prefer to see incorporated into the Constitution a guarantee of universal suffrage, as we cannot get the required two thirds for that, I cordially support this proposition as the next best."); *id.* (quoting CONG. GLOBE, 39th Cong., 1st Sess. 2542 (1866)) (statement of Rep. Bingham) ("The amendment does not give, as the second section shows, the power to Congress of regulating suffrage in the several States."); *id.* at 220 (quoting CONG. GLOBE, 39th Cong., 1st Sess. 2766 (1866)) (statement of Sen. Howard) (Section 1 of the Fourteenth Amendment does not confer the right to vote since the "right of suffrage is not, in law, one of the privileges or immunities thus secured by the Constitution"); *id.* at 222 (quoting CONG. GLOBE, 39th Cong., 1st Sess. 2769 (1866)) (statement of Sen. Wade) (asserting that "our friends, the colored people of the South, should not be excluded from the right of voting," but because three-fourths of the states would not ratify this proposition, Congress "must accommodate" itself "to the will of majorities"); CONG. GLOBE, 39th Cong., 1st Sess. 2943 (1866) (statement of Sen. Doolittle) ("Your amendment proposes to allow the States to say who shall vote."); DEBATES, *supra* note 17, Ch. 2 at 230 (quoting CONG. GLOBE, 39th Cong., 1st Sess. 2961 (1866)) (statement of Sen. Poland) (calling "the whole system of suffrage of any republican State . . . wholly artificial, founded upon its own ideas of the number and class of persons who will best represent the wishes and interests of the whole people"); CONG. GLOBE, 39th Cong., 1st Sess. 2964 (1866)) (statement of Sen. Stewart) (asserting that the Fourteenth Amendment "declares that all men are entitled to life, liberty, and property, and imposes upon the Government the duty of discharging these solemn obligations, but . . . [i]t refuses the aid of four million people in maintaining the Government of the people. . . . The utter impossibility of a final solution of the difficulties by the means proposed will cause the North to clamor for suffrage"); DEBATES, *supra* note 17, Ch. 2 at 232 (quoting CONG. GLOBE, 39th Cong., 1st Sess. app. 219 (1866)) (statement of Sen. Howe) ("I am sorry to have to put that clause [Section 2] into our Constitution. . . . I wish there was no community and no State in the United States that was not prepared to say with my friend from Nevada [Stewart] that all men may be represented in the Congress of the United States and shall be represented and shall choose their own Representatives. That is the better doctrine; that is the true doctrine. I would much prefer, myself, to unite with the people of the United States in saying that hereafter no man shall be excluded from the right to vote, than to unite with them in saying that hereafter some men may be excluded from the right of representation."); CONG. GLOBE, 39th Cong., 1st Sess. app. 240 (1866) (statement of Sen. Davis) (Section 2's "true meaning was intended to be difficult to be reached, but when understood it is a measure which shrinks from the responsibility of openly forcing negro suffrage upon the late slave States, but attempts by a great penalty to coerce them to accept it."); DEBATES, *supra* note 17, Ch. 2 at 233 (quoting CONG. GLOBE, 39th Cong., 1st Sess. 3027 (1866)) (statement of Sen. Johnson) ("It says that each of the southern States, and, of course, each other State in the Union, has a right to regulate for itself the franchise, and that consequently, as far as the Government of the United States is concerned, if the black man is not permitted the right to the franchise, it will be a wrong (if a wrong) which the Government of the United States will be impotent to redress."); *id.* at 236 (quoting CONG. GLOBE, 39th Cong., 1st Sess. 3035 (1866)) (statement of Sen. Henderson) (admitting that "the country is not yet prepared" to give blacks political power); *id.* at 237 (quoting CONG. GLOBE, 39th Cong., 1st Sess. 3038 (1866)) (statement of Sen. Yates) ("[A]lthough we do not obtain suffrage now, it is not far off, because the grasping desire of the South for office, that old desire to rule and reign over this Government and control its destinies, will at a very early day hasten the enfranchisement of the loyal blacks."); *id.* at 237 (quoting CONG. GLOBE, 39th Cong., 1st Sess. 3039 (1866)) (statement of Sen. Howard) ("[T]he theory of this whole amendment is, to leave the power of regulating the suffrage with the people or Legislatures of the States, and not to assume to regulate it by any clause of the Constitution of the United States."); CONG. GLOBE, 39th Cong., 1st Sess. 3145 (1866) (statement of Rep. Finck) ("While this [second] section admits the right of the States thus to exclude negroes from voting, it says to them, if you do so exclude them they shall also be excluded from all representation; and you shall suffer the penalty by loss of representation."); DEBATES, *supra* note 17, Ch. 2 at 238 (quoting CONG. GLOBE, 39th Cong., 1st Sess. 3169 (1866)) (statement of Rep. Windom) ("The injustice, if any, of the first section [of the Fourteenth Amendment] consists in not including political as well as civil equality among its guarantees."); *id.* at 267 (quoting CONG. GLOBE, 39th Cong., 2d Sess. 237 (1867)) (statement of Rep. Garfield) (asserting that citizens of the United States were never entitled to the privilege of voting in any state under Article IV Section 2); *id.* at 299 (quoting CONG. GLOBE, 40th Cong., 2d Sess. app. 238 (1868)) (statement of Sen. Dixon) ("The proposed amendment proceeded on the ground of exclusive white suffrage. It proposed to leave the question of suffrage where the Constitution left it, with the people of the several States, South as well as North."); *id.* at 319 (quoting CONG. GLOBE, 40th Cong., 2d Sess. 2603 (1868)) (statement of Sen. Morton) ("The right to regulate the question of suffrage belongs to the States under the Constitution. It has been recognized as belonging to the several States ever since the foundation of the Government."); *id.* at 323 (quoting CONG. GLOBE, 40th Cong., 2d Sess. 2665 (1868)) (statement of Sen. Conkling) ("Without going back of the fourteenth amendment of the Constitution, be it ratified now or about to be ratified, it seems to me clear that by the unmistakable force of its language the regulation of suffrage in the States belongs to the States themselves."); *id.* (quoting CONG. GLOBE, 40th Cong., 2d Sess. 2698 (1868)) (statement of Sen. Doolittle) (stating that the Fourteenth Amendment "expressly recognizes in, if it does not confer on, the States the power to disqualify persons from exercising the right of suffrage on account of race or color, or any other reason they choose"); *id.* at 324 (quoting CONG. GLOBE, 40th Cong., 2d Sess. 2741–42 (1868)) (statement of Sen. Morton) (stating that he had taken it for granted that "the States have the right to control suffrage" under the Constitution); *id.* at 338 (quoting CONG. GLOBE, 40th Cong., 3rd Sess. 642–44 (1869)) (statement of Rep. Eldridge) (asserting the longstanding right of the states to regulate suffrage and that "citizenship does not necessarily carry with it the right to vote or hold office"); *id.* at 341 (quoting CONG. GLOBE, 40th Cong.,

3rd Sess. 92 (1869)) (statement of Rep. Miller) (asserting that the Fourteenth Amendment never contemplated infringing the states' right to regulate suffrage); *id.* at 343–44 (quoting CONG. GLOBE, 40th Cong., 3rd Sess. 691–92 (1869)) (statement of Rep. Beck) (asserting under both its legislative history and its text that the Fourteenth Amendment intended to give Congress no power over suffrage in the states); *id.* at 344 (quoting CONG. GLOBE, 40th Cong., 3rd Sess. 699 (1869)) (statement of Rep. Burr) (the Fourteenth Amendment's "intention and effect was to permit every State to do as it might elect on" the subject of suffrage "with the understanding that such States as refused suffrage to the negro would be curtailed in representation to that extent"); *id.* at 350 (quoting CONG. GLOBE, 40th Cong., 3rd Sess. 727 (1869)) (statement of Rep. Shellabarger) (acknowledging that the "power of regulating elections and of passing registration laws" is with the states); *id.* at 359 (quoting CONG. GLOBE, 40th Cong., 3rd Sess. 904 (1869)) (statement of Sen. Vickers) ("There is no natural right to vote."); *id.* at 361 (quoting CONG. GLOBE, 40th Cong., 3rd Sess. app. 152 (1869)) (statement of Sen. Doolittle) (asserting that the Fourteenth Amendment "expressly provides that this very question of suffrage shall be left to the people of the States"); *id.* at 362 (quoting CONG. GLOBE, 40th Cong., 3rd Sess. app. 168 (1869)) (statement of Sen. Bayard) ("I have never been able to accede to the dogma that suffrage is a natural right, or that universal suffrage is essential or even conducive to permanent free government."); *id.* at 365 (quoting CONG. GLOBE, 40th Cong., 3rd Sess. 979–80 (1869)) (statement of Sen. Frelinghuysen) (reading Sections 1 & 2 of the Fourteenth Amendment not to extend congressional power over suffrage); *id.* at 367 (quoting CONG. GLOBE, 40th Cong., 3rd Sess. 985 (1869)) (statement of Sen. Howard) ("Sir, the United States have never granted to any citizen of the United States in the States, nor abridged to him, the right to vote. The Government of the United States has not intermeddled, nor has it the right to intermeddle, with the right of voting."); *id.* at 368 (quoting CONG. GLOBE, 40th Cong., 3rd Sess. 986 (1869)) (statement of Sen. Sumner) ("conceding to every State the power to regulate the suffrage"); *id.* at 372 (quoting CONG. GLOBE, 40th Cong., 3rd Sess. 1002 (1869)) (statement of Sen. Drake) (asserting that "it is impossible that the word 'privileges' as contained in" Section 1 of the Fourteenth Amendment "can embrace the right to vote because a man is a citizen of the United States"); *id.* at 373 (quoting CONG. GLOBE, 40th Cong., 3rd Sess. 1003 (1869)) (statement of Sen. Howard) (asserting that there is no right to vote that can be derived under the Fourteenth Amendment); *id.* (quoting CONG. GLOBE, 40th Cong., 3rd Sess. 1004 (1869)) (statement of Sen. Cragin) (recalling "that it was announced upon this floor by more than one gentleman, and contradicted and denied by no one so far as I recollect, that" the Fourteenth "amendment did not confer the right of voting upon anybody"); *id.* at 374 (quoting CONG. GLOBE, 40th Cong., 3rd Sess. 1004–06 (1869)) (statement of Sen. Yates) (conceding, despite his wishes, that Congress had not intended the Fourteenth Amendment to entitle a man to suffrage by virtue of citizenship); *id.* at 381 (quoting CONG. GLOBE, 40th Cong., 3rd Sess. 1031 (1869)) (statement of Sen. Fessenden) (admitting the states' right to regulate suffrage under the Constitution); *id.* at 450 (quoting CONG. GLOBE, 41st Cong., 2d Sess. app. 472 (1870)) (statement of Sen. Casserly) ("The control of the subject of the suffrage remains in the States full and uncontrolled, as it was before the fifteenth amendment, except" as stated in the latter amendment); *id.* at 464 (quoting S. REP. NO. 187, 41st Cong., 2d Sess. at 1–2 (1870)) (Senate Judiciary

Committee report) (asserting that the Privileges and Immunities Clause does "not include the right of suffrage"); *id.* at 466–67 (quoting H.R. REP. NO. 22, 41st Cong., 3rd Sess., pt. 1, at 2–4 (1871)) (House Judiciary Committee report) (acknowledging state power to regulate suffrage and denying the power to grant voting rights for women); *id.* at 572 (quoting S. REP. NO. 21, 42d Cong., 2d Sess. at 3–4 (1872)) (Senate Judiciary Committee report) (finding an inferential state right to deny a portion of its citizens the right to vote under Section 2 of the Fourteenth Amendment); *id.* at 613–14 (quoting CONG. GLOBE, 42d Cong., 2d Sess. 827–28 (1872)) (statement of Sen. Carpenter) (asserting that Sections 1 & 2 of the Fourteenth Amendment distinguish between "those privileges which pertain to every citizen, and which no State may abridge, and the political right to vote which may be abridged by a State"); *id.* at 684 (quoting 2 CONG. REC. 360 (1874)) (statement of Sen. Morton) ("It was well understood in the adoption of the fourteenth amendment that it was not intended to extend to or cover the right of suffrage.")

Reference also was made during the debates to the 1868 Republican platform that stated that "the question of suffrage in all the loyal States properly belongs to the people of those States." *See id.* at 341 (quoting CONG. GLOBE, 40th Cong., 3rd Sess. 92 (1869)) (statement of Rep. Miller); *id.* at 343 (quoting CONG. GLOBE, 40th Cong., 1st Sess. 691 (1869)) (statement of Rep. Beck); *id.* at 364 (quoting CONG. GLOBE, 40th Cong., 3rd Sess. 939 (1869)) (statement of Sen. Corbett); *id.* at 370 (quoting CONG. GLOBE, 40th Cong., 3rd Sess. app. 154 (1869)) (statement of Sen. Wilson) (stating that the 1868 Republican platform declared "that under the Constitution it belonged to the people of each of the loyal States to regulate suffrage therein").

7. *See* DEBATES, *supra* note 17, Ch. 2 at xv, 304–05 (quoting CONG. GLOBE, 40th Cong., 2d Sess. 1966–67 (1868)) (statement of Rep. Stevens) (suggesting that the privileges secured by Section 1 of the Fourteenth Amendment extended to voting); *id.* at 316 (quoting CONG. GLOBE, 40th Cong., 2d Sess. 2462–63 (1868)) (statement of Rep. Bingham) (suggesting the possibility of congressional power to protect political as well as civil privileges); *id.* at 336 (quoting CONG. GLOBE, 40th Cong., 3rd Sess. 559 (1869)) (statement of Rep. Boutwell) (explaining Section 2 as a means of imposing "a political penalty for doing that which in the first section it is declared the State has no right to do"); *id.* at 345 (quoting CONG. GLOBE, 40th Cong., 3rd Sess. app. 94 (1869)) (statement of Rep. Corley) ("A citizen of the United States is the political equal of every other citizen, and cannot be constitutionally denied the right to the ballot in any State except for rebellion or crime."); *id.* at 366 (quoting CONG. GLOBE, 40th Cong., 3rd Sess. 982 (1869)) (statement of Sen. Ross) (asserting that "the right of suffrage is one of nature's ordination, and therefore universal, not to be restricted except for incompetency or the commission of crime"); *id.* at 370–73 (quoting CONG. GLOBE, 40th Cong., 3rd Sess. 1000–03 (1869)) (statements of Sen. Edmunds) (asserting his belief that the Fourteenth Amendment covers political privileges and immunities); *id.* at 375 (quoting CONG. GLOBE, 40th Cong., 3rd Sess. 1008 (1869)) (statement of Sen. Corbett) (indicating that the Fourteenth Amendment is already sufficient to confer voting rights on blacks); *id.* at 468–71 (quoting H.R. REP. NO. 22, 41st Cong., 3rd Sess., pt. 2, at 4–10, 12–17 (1871)) (House Judiciary Committee minority report) (asserting that the right of suffrage is a fundamental right inherent in citizenship under Section 1); *id.* at 541 (quoting CONG. GLOBE, 42d Cong., 1st Sess. 501 (1871)) (statement of

Sen. Frelinghuysen) ("I believe that the ballot is one of the privileges of the citizen.").

During the debates over the Civil Rights Act of 1866, Congressman Rogers contended that the bill "would prevent a State from refusing negro suffrage under the broad acceptation of the term 'civil rights or immunities.' " *Id.* at 166 (quoting CONG. GLOBE, 39th Cong., 1st Sess. 1122 (1866)). He also remarked that "[t]he right to vote is a privilege" in a speech suggesting the ambiguity and breadth of the Privileges and Immunities Clause. *Id.* at 216 (quoting CONG. GLOBE, 39th Cong., 1st Sess. 2538 (1866)). Rogers had delivered a vitriolic white supremacist attack on the principle of blacks voting in the previous debate over black suffrage in the District of Columbia, *see* CONG. GLOBE, 39th Cong., 1st Sess. 198 (1866), and the second Justice Harlan perceptively argued for the innocuity of his comments by pointing out that given the strength of his convictions, Rogers approached the Fourteenth Amendment with calmness inconsistent with any belief that it enfranchised the freedmen. Harlan concluded that Rogers "did not seriously interpret the Amendment" as conferring black suffrage. Oregon v. Mitchell, 400 U.S. 112, 183 (1970) (Harlan, J., concurring in part and dissenting in part).

For examples of suggestions during state ratification debates that the Fourteenth Amendment could extend federal power over suffrage, see ANTIEAU, *supra* note 70, Ch. 3.B.2 at 28–29 (statement of Gov. Morton) ("As a question of natural right, it is hard to say that suffrage is not a natural right, when upon its exercise may depend the possession and enjoyment of all other acknowledged natural rights."); *id.* at 55 ("If, when other remedies have failed, it be the clear and deliberate judgment of Congress that loyal Republican State governments cannot be maintained except by conferring the elective franchise upon the Negro race in those States, Congress may confer it."); *id.* at 49–50 (statement of Sen. Landon) ("The amendments now under consideration guarantee to all persons born upon American soil the privileges of citizenship and the immunities of impartial suffrage.") *id.* at 50 (statement of Sen. Wallace) ("I oppose these amendments because they force the States to yield their right to regulate suffrage."); *id.* (statement of Sen. Burnett) (suggesting that the amendment possibly could be construed as authorizing Congress to confer black suffrage); *id.* (statement of Rep. Chalfant) (fearing that suffrage would be construed as a privilege and immunity and that the Fourteenth Amendment would lead to universal suffrage).

8. *See* Frank Scaturro, To What Extent Does the Original Meaning of the Fourteenth Amendment Sanction the Warren Court's Assertion of Federal Power over Suffrage? 28–29, 33–34 (1996) (on file with author). *Cf. also supra* notes 5 & 6, Ch. 3.B.4.

9. *See id.* at 38.

5. The Fifteenth Amendment and *United States v. Reese*

1. 25 F. Cas. 1324 (C.C.D. Del.) (Strong, Circuit Justice 1873).
2. *Id.* at 1325.
3. *Id.*
4. *See* U.S. CONST. art. IV, § 2, cl. 3.
5. 25 F. Cas. at 1326.
6. *Id.*
7. *Id.*

8. *See id.* at 1327–28.

9. *Id.* at 1328.

10. *Cf.* Frantz, *supra* note 75, Ch. 2 at 1364–65 ("Seven years after the four-teenth amendment was proposed, five years after its ratification, the notion that congressional enforcement power under the fourteenth and fifteenth amendments cannot reach 'private acts' was so far from Justice Strong's mind that, even in dealing with the case of a state official charged with making racially discriminatory use of his official powers, the Justice did not even bother to stress the 'state action' aspects of the case before him.").

11. 92 U.S. 214 (1876).

12. *See* Oxford, *supra* note 2, Ch. 3.B.1 at 714.

13. *See* 92 U.S. at 215–16.

14. *Id.* at 217.

15. *Id.* at 218.

16. *See id.*

17. *See id.* at 219–20.

18. *Id.* at 220.

19. *Id.*

20. *Id.*

21. *Id.* at 221.

22. *See id.* at 222–38 (Clifford, J., dissenting).

23. *Id.* at 241 (Hunt, J., dissenting).

24. *Id.* (Hunt, J., dissenting).

25. *Id.* (Hunt, J., dissenting).

26. *Id.* at 238–39, 241–42 (Hunt, J., dissenting).

27. *Id.* at 242 (Hunt, J., dissenting).

28. *Id.* (Hunt, J., dissenting).

29. *Id.* (Hunt, J., dissenting).

30. *See id.* at 243 (Hunt, J., dissenting).

31. *Id.* (Hunt, J., dissenting).

32. *Id.* at 244 (Hunt, J., dissenting) (quoting United States v. Hartwell, 73 U.S. (6 Wall.) 385, 395–96 (1868)).

33. *Id.* at 245 (Hunt, J., dissenting).

34. *See id.* (Hunt, J., dissenting).

35. *Id.* at 246–47 (Hunt, J., dissenting).

36. *Id.* at 247–48 (Hunt, J., dissenting).

37. *Id.* at 248–49 (Hunt, J., dissenting).

38. *Id.* at 251–52 (Hunt, J., dissenting).

39. *Id.* at 252–54 (Hunt, J., dissenting).

40. *Id.* at 253–54 (Hunt, J., dissenting).

41. *See id.* at 254–56 (Hunt, J., dissenting).

42. *Id.* at 256 (Hunt, J., dissenting).

43. *See* Debates, *supra* note 17, Ch. 2 at 347 (quoting Cong. Globe, 40th Cong., 3rd Sess. app. 98 (1869)) (statement of Sen. Morton); *id.* at 354 (quoting Cong. Globe, 40th Cong., 3rd Sess. 862 (1869)) (statement of Sen. Warner); *id.* at 355 (quoting Cong. Globe, 40th Cong., 3rd Sess. 863 (1869)) (statement of Sen. Morton); *id.* at 361 (quoting Cong. Globe, 40th Cong., 3rd Sess. 912 (1869)) (statement of Sen. Willey); *id.* at 363 (quoting Cong. Globe, 40th Cong., 3rd Sess.

938 (1869)) (statement of Sen. Williams); *id.* at 364 (quoting CONG. GLOBE, 40th Cong., 3rd Sess. 979 (1869)) (statement of Sen. Frelinghuysen); *id.* at 398 (quoting CONG. GLOBE, 40th Cong., 3rd Sess. 1304 (1869)) (statement of Sen. Trumbull); *id.* at 399 (quoting CONG. GLOBE, 40th Cong., 3rd Sess. 1305 (1869)) (statement of Sen. Edmunds); *id.* at 411 (quoting CONG. GLOBE, 40th Cong., 3rd Sess. 1625 (1869)) (statement of Sen. Howard); *id.* at 417 (quoting CONG. GLOBE, 40th Cong., 3rd Sess. app. 294 (1869)) (statement of Rep. Higby); *id.* at 422 (quoting CONG. GLOBE, 41st Cong., 2d Sess. 600 (1870)) (statement of Sen. Howard); *id.* at 425 (quoting CONG. GLOBE, 41st Cong., 2d Sess. 1363 (1870)) (statement of Sen. Trumbull); *id.* at 442 (quoting CONG. GLOBE, 41st Cong., 2d Sess. 3571 (1870)) (statement of Sen. Morton); *id.* at 450 (quoting CONG. GLOBE, 41st Cong., 2d Sess. app. 472 (1870)) (statement of Sen. Casserly) ("[T]he intent of the fifteenth amendment was single; to protect one race of people in the country, and only one, that known as 'the colored race.' To that class of citizens, therefore, its effects are confined."); *id.* at 460 (quoting CONG. GLOBE, 41st Cong., 2d Sess. 3872–73 (1870)) (statement of Rep. Kerr) (asserting that the Fifteenth Amendment "does not confer the right to vote" but "only forbids the denial by the States or by Congress of the right to vote on account of race, color, or previous condition of servitude"); *id.* at 482 (quoting CONG. GLOBE, 41st Cong., 3rd Sess. app. 161 (1871)) (statement of Sen. Bayard).

44. *See, e.g., id.* at 351 (quoting CONG. GLOBE, 40th Cong., 3rd Sess. 863 (1869)) (statement of Rep. Jenckes); *id.* at 356 (quoting CONG. GLOBE, 40th Cong., 3rd Sess. 863 (1869)) (statement of Sen. Morton); *id.* at 391 (quoting CONG. GLOBE, 40th Cong., 3rd Sess. 1226 (1869)) (statement of Rep. Lawrence).
In this section, comments on the Fifteenth Amendment shall include comments on an earlier proposal that expressly included the right to hold office because the two versions contain no difference that is relevant for present purposes.

45. *Id.* at 339 (quoting CONG. GLOBE, 40th Cong., 3rd Sess. 668 (1869)) (statement of Sen. Stewart). *Cf.* 7 RICHARDSON, *supra* note 44, Ch. 2 at 306 (message of President Grant) (asserting that the Fifteenth Amendment secured "the political equality of colored citizens").

46. DEBATES, *supra* note 17, Ch. 2 at 404 (quoting CONG. GLOBE, 40th Cong., 3rd Sess. 1315 (1869)).

47. *See id.* at 238 (quoting CONG. GLOBE, 39th Cong., 1st Sess. 3149 (1866)) (recording House votes on the Fourteenth Amendment); *id.* at 410 (quoting CONG. GLOBE, 40th Cong., 3rd Sess. 1564 (1869)) (recording House votes on the Fifteenth Amendment). Dixon was recorded as "not voting" for both amendments.

48. *Id.* at 380 (quoting CONG. GLOBE, 40th Cong., 3rd Sess. 1030 (1869)).

49. *Id.* at 350 (quoting CONG. GLOBE, 40th Cong., 3rd Sess. 727 (1869)).

50. RICHARDSON, *supra* note 44, Ch. 2 at 55–56.

51. DEBATES, *supra* note 17, Ch. 2 at 399 (quoting CONG. GLOBE, 40th Cong., 3rd Sess. 1304 (1869)). Howard also feared that the negative terms of the amendment might be construed to infer an affirmative grant of power to Congress to regulate suffrage in all other aspects, including imposition of religious tests, but Edmunds refuted this apprehension. *See id.* (quoting CONG. GLOBE, 40th Cong., 3rd Sess. 1304–05 (1869)).

52. RICHARDSON, *supra* note 44, Ch. 2 at 306.

53. *See* DEBATES, *supra* note 17, Ch. 2 at 437 (quoting CONG. GLOBE, 41st Cong., 2d Sess. 3480 (1870)).

54. *Id.* at 437–38 (quoting CONG. GLOBE, 41st Cong., 2d Sess. 3485 (1870)).

55. *Id.* at 440 (quoting CONG. GLOBE, 41st Cong., 2d Sess. 3561 (1870)).

56. *Id.*

57. *Id.* (quoting CONG. GLOBE, 41st Cong., 2d Sess. 3562 (1870)).

58. *See id.*

59. *Id.* at 441 (quoting CONG. GLOBE, 41st Cong., 2d Sess. 3568 (1870)).

60. *Id.*

61. *Id.* at 442 (quoting CONG. GLOBE, 41st Cong., 2d Sess. 3568–69 (1870)).

62. *Id.* (quoting CONG. GLOBE, 41st Cong., 2d Sess. 3569 (1870)).

63. *Id.*

64. *Id.*

65. *Id.* (quoting CONG. GLOBE, 41st Cong., 2d Sess. 3571 (1870)).

66. *Id.* at 443 (quoting CONG. GLOBE, 41st Cong., 2d Sess. 3571 (1870)).

67. *Id.* at 443–44 (quoting CONG. GLOBE, 41st Cong., 2d Sess. app. 353–54 (1870)).

68. *See id.* at 445 (quoting CONG. GLOBE, 41st Cong., 2d Sess. app. 357–59 (1870)) (contending that the provisions applied beyond color or race and subverted registration laws).

69. *See* FONER, *supra* note 18, Ch. 1 at 507. Schurz saw "Negro supremacy," as he viewed Reconstruction, as "the horror, the nightmare, of the Southern people." JOHN G. SPROAT, "THE BEST MEN": LIBERAL REFORMERS IN THE GILDED AGE 11 (1968).

70. *See* DEBATES, *supra* note 17, Ch. 2 at 446 (quoting CONG. GLOBE, 41st Cong., 2d Sess. 3608 (1870)).

71. *See id.* at 448 (quoting CONG. GLOBE, 41st Cong., 2d Sess. 3613 (1870)).

72. *Id.* (quoting CONG. GLOBE, 41st Cong., 2d Sess. 3655 (1870)).

73. *Id.* at 453 (quoting CONG. GLOBE, 41st Cong., 2d Sess. 3663 (1870)).

74. *Id.* at 417 (quoting CONG. GLOBE, 40th Cong., 3rd Sess. 1641 (1869)) (recording Senate votes on the Fifteenth Amendment).

75. *Id.* (quoting CONG. GLOBE, 41st Cong., 2d Sess. app. 421–22 (1870)).

76. *Id.* at 455 (quoting CONG. GLOBE, 41st Cong., 2d Sess. app. 421 (1870)).

77. *Id.* (quoting CONG. GLOBE, 41st Cong., 2d Sess. 3670 (1870)).

78. *See id.* at 458 (quoting CONG. GLOBE, 41st Cong., 2d Sess. 3690 (1870)).

79. *See id.* at 460 (quoting CONG. GLOBE, 41st Cong., 2d Sess. 3872–73 (1870)).

80. *See id.* at 461 (quoting CONG. GLOBE, 41st Cong., 2d Sess. 3875 (1870)) (asserting that the bill places "in the hands of Congress all matters growing out of State elections in any form whatever").

81. *See id.* (quoting CONG. GLOBE, 41st Cong., 2d Sess. 3876 (1870)) (finding the bill's control over suffrage and penal provisions "as dangerous as unconstitutional").

82. *See id.* at 462 (quoting CONG. GLOBE, 41st Cong., 2d Sess. 3882 (1870)) (defending the notion of Congress using its own instrumentalities and federal courts to enforce the Constitution rather than trusting state authority).

83. *See id.* at 463 (quoting CONG. GLOBE, 41st Cong., 2d Sess. app. 392–93 (1870)) (asserting the necessity of "appropriate legislation" from Congress and expressing distrust of the states).

84. *See id.* at 458, 463 (quoting CONG. GLOBE, 41st Cong., 2d Sess. 3690, 3884 (1870)). The Senate vote occurred after the rejection of an amendment by Senator Vickers proposing to add the words "on account of race, color, or previous condition of servitude" to § 3. *Id.* at 457 (quoting CONG. GLOBE, 41st Cong., 2d Sess. 3687 (1870)).

85. *See id.* at 483 (quoting CONG. GLOBE, 41st Cong., 3rd Sess. app. 158 (1871)).

86. *See id.* at 481 (quoting CONG. GLOBE, 41st Cong., 3rd Sess. 1283 (1871)) (referring to the Enforcement Act as a bill to "make good" the Fifteenth Amendment by securing the "equal right to the ballot among citizens of the United States having equal qualifications, without regard to race, color, or previous condition of servitude").

87. *See id.* at 524 (quoting CONG. GLOBE, 42d Cong., 1st Sess. app. 251 (1871)) (the Enforcement Act "proceeded upon the hypothesis that the amendment conferred upon colored men and absolute right to vote upon the same terms and conditions with white men").

88. *See id.* at 526 (quoting CONG. GLOBE, 42d Cong., 1st Sess. app. 150 (1871)) (asserting that the Enforcement Act was passed pursuant to congressional power under the Fifteenth Amendment and the power to regulate elections and suffrage involving federal officials); *id.* at 530 (quoting CONG. GLOBE, 42d Cong., 1st Sess. app. 154 (1871)) ("[W]ith the fifteenth amendment superadded, Congress is armed with more than a mere negative power, and had the right to pass the enforcement law of May last.").

89. *See, e.g.,* GILLETTE, *supra* note 46, Ch. 2 at 34 ("The enforcement acts were, in fact, vulnerable to judicial scrutiny. Often the hastily planned and framed statutes were so worded that effective administration could not be provided and the legal limits were uncertain."); *id.* at 365 (criticizing "the flimsiness of all the statutory words" and "the inadequacies of the laws themselves"); 7 SUPREME COURT HISTORY, *supra* note 3, Ch. 2 at 276 ("An inquiry into why the experience with the enforcement legislation was disappointing should begin with the performance of Congress and federal prosecutors."). For an example of a similar sentiment on the Fourteenth Amendment, see Gressman, *supra* note 3, Ch. 2 at 1340 ("[T]he framers had assumed too much and incorporated too little when they drafted the [Fourteenth] amendment. They failed to anticipate the judicial process of interpretation with its ever-present possibility of strict constructionism.").

90. *See* Robert L. Stern, *Separability and Separability Clauses in the Supreme Court,* 51 HARV. L. REV. 76, 82 (1937); Frantz, *supra* note 75, Ch. 2 at 1360.

91. United States v. Salerno, 481 U.S. 739, 745 (1987). The joint opinion of Justices Sandra Day O'Connor, Anthony M. Kennedy, and David Souter in Planned Parenthood v. Casey, 505 U.S. 833, 895 (1992), however, held that a law imposing a spousal notification requirement as a prerequisite to abortion was facially unconstitutional as a substantial obstacle "in a large fraction of the cases in which" it "is relevant." A majority of the Court has never specified whether it intends this modification of the *Salerno* standard.

Justice John P. Stevens, who had dissented from *Salerno,* later dismissed its "no set of circumstances" statement as "rigid and unwise dictum" that "was unsupported by citation or precedent." Janklow v. Planned Parenthood, 517 U.S. 1174, 1175 (1996) (memorandum of Stevens, J., respecting denial of certiorari). However, he did quote the following proposition as the "long established principle of our jurisprudence" recognized in *Salerno:* " '[T]he fact that [a legislative] Act might operate unconstitutionally under some conceivable set of circumstances is insufficient to render it wholly invalid.' " *Id.* (quoting 481 U.S. at 745). It can be argued that even this understanding of *Salerno* calls into question the Court's holding in *Reese.*

92. *See* Frantz, *supra* note 75, Ch. 2 at 1360.

6. *United States v. Cruikshank*

1. 92 U.S. 542 (1876). *Reese* and *Cruikshank* were both handed down on March 27, 1876. *See* Frantz, *supra* note 75, Ch. 2 at 1360.

2. Act of May 31, 1870, ch. 114, § 6, 16 Stat. 140, 141 (codified as amended in several sections of 42 U.S.C. (1994)). *See also* DEBATES, *supra* note 17, Ch. 2 at 458 (quoting CONG. GLOBE, 41st Cong., 2d Sess. 3689 (1870)).

3. 92 U.S. at 548.

4. *Id.* at 549.

5. *See id.* at 549–50.

6. *Id.* at 550–51.

7. *Id.* at 551.

8. U.S. CONST. amend. I.

9. 92 U.S. at 552.

10. *Id.* at 552–53.

11. *Id.* at 553.

12. *Id.* at 553–54.

13. *Id.* at 554.

14. *Id.*

15. *Id.*

16. *Id.* at 554–55.

17. *Id.* at 555.

18. *Id.* at 555–56.

19. *Id.* at 556.

20. *Id.*

21. *Id.*

22. *Id.*

23. *Id.* at 556–57.

24. *Id.* at 557.

25. *Id.*

26. *Id.* at 557–59.

27. *See Id.* at 559–69 (Clifford, J., dissenting).

Justice Bradley, who decided *Cruikshank* on the circuit level with the same result as the Court, *see* United States v. Cruikshank, 25 F. Cas. 707 (C.C.D. La.) (Bradley, Circuit Justice 1874), articulated some different holdings in his opinion even though he would join Waite's opinion. In his decision, Bradley spoke of both the Thirteenth and Fifteenth Amendments in terms that acknowledged congressional power to legislate against racial discrimination by private parties, including recognition of the constitutionality of the Civil Rights Act of 1866. *See id.* at 711–13. When he turned to the Privileges and Immunities Clause, he spoke of "those inherited privileges which belong to every citizen, as his birthright, or from that body of natural rights which are recognized and regarded as sacred in all free governments," *id.* at 714, in terms that were consistent with the application of the Bill of Rights to the states, which he had endorsed in his *Slaughter-House* dissent. *See* Michael G. Collins, *Justice Bradley's Civil Rights Odyssey Revisited*, 70 Tul. L. Rev. 1979, 1993–94 (1996). The enforcement of the amendment, however, depended on whether "the privilege or immunity in question" was "simply prohibitory of governmental action," in which case "there will be nothing to enforce until such action is undertaken." 25 F. Cas. at 714. Bradley placed the right to peaceably assemble, to bear arms, and to due process in this category, precluding affirmative power on the part of Congress to punish disturbances simply by individuals. *See id.* at 714–15.

Months after the Supreme Court's *Cruikshank* opinion, Bradley reached the following conclusion about the effect of the decision:

The effect of the decision in the Grant Parish Case was to declare that offences committed by private individuals against colored persons were to be left for punishment to the State laws, unless committed against some valid law of the United States, or committed for the purpose of injuring the colored persons on account of their race and color. Now these decisions leave the way clear for Congress to pass laws to enforce rights and privileges granted by the Constitution, and to prevent persons from being oppressed on account of their race and color.

I need not advert to the old Constitution. The recent amendments have the effect to give universal liberty and entire equality before the laws to persons of every race, color and condition.

7 Supreme Court History, *supra* note 3, Ch. 2 at 288.

28. *See* 7 Supreme Court History, *supra* note 3, Ch. 2 at 281, 287.

29. 92 U.S. at 544.

30. Charles Fairman makes precisely this suggestion, along with others on how the *Cruikshank* counts could have been worded to have been upheld, *see* 7 Supreme Court History, *supra* note 3, Ch. 2 at 287, but the present study's divergent conclusions on the correctness of the *Slaughter-House Cases* and the incorporation doctrine suggest that *Cruikshank* departed from the original understanding as it was.

31. 92 U.S. at 554.

32. 14 Stat. 27. *See* 7 Supreme Court History, *supra* note 3, Ch. 2 at 276 (finding "[n]o serious fault" with the Civil Rights Act and mentioning its acceptance in three circuit opinions by Supreme Court justices).

33. 92 U.S. at 545.

34. *See generally supra* Ch. 3.B.2.d.

35. *See* Debates, *supra* note 17, Ch. 2 at 493–94 (quoting Cong. Globe, 42d Cong., 1st Sess. app. 68–69 (1871)) (statement of Rep. Shellabarger). Shellabarger said that § 6 of the 1870 Enforcement Act "rests upon exactly the same legal ground" as § 2 of the Ku Klux Klan Act, "and is in its constitutional aspects identical with it, the only difference being that the section of this bill defines the offense with greater exactness." *Id.* at 494 (quoting Cong. Globe, 42d Cong., 1st Sess. app. 69 (1871)).

36. 92 U.S. at 553–54.

37. 16 Stat. 141.

38. 4 Cong. Rec. 5585 (1876).

39. *See Misreading Bingham, supra* note 13, Ch. 3.B.2 at 62.

40. Samuel Shellabarger, Statement in Memoriam on the Death of Chief Justice Morrison R. Waite, 126 U.S. 596, 600 (1888).

41. SUPREME COURT HISTORY, *supra* note 3, Ch. 2 at 190.

42. *See supra* note 27.

43. 92 U.S. 90 (1876).

44. *Id.* at 92.

45. 110 U.S. 516.

46. *See id.* at 558 (Harlan, J., dissenting).

47. *See id.* at 538.

48. 144 U.S. 323.

49. *See id.* at 361–64 (Field, J., dissenting); *id.* at 370–71 (Harlan, J., dissenting).

50. 176 U.S. 581.

51. *See id.* at 602.

52. *See id.* at 602–04.

53. *See id.* at 592–93, 597–98.

54. *Id.* at 601–02.

55. *Id.* at 612 (Harlan, J., dissenting).

56. 166 U.S. 226, 240.

57. 268 U.S. 652, 665 (1925).

58. 302 U.S. 319, *overruled*, Benton v. Maryland, 395 U.S. 784 (1969).

59. *See id.* at 324–25.

60. *See id.* at 323.

61. 332 U.S. 46 (1947).

62. *See id.* at 59 (Frankfurter, J., concurring).

63. *See id.* at 68 (Black, J., dissenting).

64. *Id.* at 62, 64–65 (Frankfurter, J., concurring).

65. *Id.* at 90 (Black, J., dissenting). *See also id.* at 92–123 (Black, J., dissenting) (appendix).

66. *See* Stephen J. Wermiel, *Rights in the Modern Era: Applying the Bill of Rights to the States*, 1 WM. & MARY BILL RTS. J. 121, 128 (1992).

67. *See* Mapp v. Ohio, 367 U.S. 643 (1961).

68. *See* Robinson v. California, 370 U.S. 660 (1962).

69. *See* Malloy v. Hogan, 378 U.S. 1 (1964).

70. *See* Gideon v. Wainwright, 372 U.S. 335 (1963).

71. *See* Pointer v. Texas, 380 U.S. 400 (1965).

72. *See* Klopfer v. North Carolina, 386 U.S. 213 (1967).

73. *See* Washington v. Texas, 388 U.S. 14 (1967).

74. *See* Duncan v. Louisiana, 380 U.S. 145 (1968).

75. *See* Wermiel, *supra* note 66, Ch. 3.B.6 at 129.

76. DEBATES, *supra* note 17, Ch. 2 at viii, 157–58 (quoting CONG. GLOBE, 39th Cong., 1st Sess. 1088–90 (1866)).

77. *See id.* at 158–59 (quoting CONG. GLOBE, 39th Cong., 1st Sess. 1093–94 (1866)).

78. 32 U.S. (7 Pet.) 243 (1833).

79. *See* DEBATES, *supra* note 17, Ch. 2 at 157–58 (quoting CONG. GLOBE, 39th Cong., 1st Sess. 1089–90 (1866) (citing 32 U.S. at 247)).

80. *See* MICHAEL KENT CURTIS, NO STATE SHALL ABRIDGE: THE FOURTEENTH

AMENDMENT AND THE BILL OF RIGHTS 216 (1986); DEBATES, *supra* note 17, Ch. 2 at 189 (quoting CONG. GLOBE, 39th Cong., 1st Sess. 1294 (1866)).

81. *See* DEBATES, *supra* note 17, Ch. 2 at 187 (quoting CONG. GLOBE, 39th Cong., 1st Sess. 1292 (1866)).

82. *Id.* at 186–87 (quoting CONG. GLOBE, 39th Cong., 1st Sess. 1291–92 (1866)).

83. *See* Charles Fairman, *Does the Fourteenth Amendment Incorporate the Bill of Rights?*, 2 STAN. L.R. 5, 29, 31 (1949) [hereinafter *Incorporation*].

84. *See* DEBATES, *supra* note 17, Ch. 2 at 154 (quoting CONG. GLOBE, 39th Cong., 1st Sess. 1064 (1866)); CURTIS, *supra* note 80, Ch. 3.B.6 at 69–70, 100.

85. *See* DEBATES, *supra* note 17, Ch. 2 at 154 (quoting CONG. GLOBE, 39th Cong., 1st Sess. 1064 (1866)).

86. *Id.* at 155 (quoting CONG. GLOBE, 39th Cong., 1st Sess. 1065 (1866)).

87. *Id.* at 154 (quoting CONG. GLOBE, 39th Cong., 1st Sess. 1064 (1866)).

88. *See* Adamson v. California, 332 U.S. 46, 98 (Black, J., dissenting) (appendix).

89. DEBATES, *supra* note 17, Ch. 2 at 154 (quoting CONG. GLOBE, 39th Cong., 1st Sess. 1064 (1866)). *See also* CURTIS, *supra* note 80, Ch. 3.B.6 at 100–01.

90. *See* DEBATES, *supra* note 17, Ch. 2 at 188 (quoting CONG. GLOBE, 39th Cong., 1st Sess. 1293 (1866)).

91. *Id.* at 193 (quoting CONG. GLOBE, 39th Cong., 1st Sess. 1629 (1866)).

92. *See id.* at xi, 217 (quoting CONG. GLOBE, 39th Cong., 1st Sess. 2542 (1866)).

93. *Id.* at 219 (quoting CONG. GLOBE, 39th Cong., 1st Sess. 2765 (1866)).

94. HORACE EDGAR FLACK, THE ADOPTION OF THE FOURTEENTH AMENDMENT 87 (1908).

Statements in the Pennsylvania and Wisconsin ratifying debates reflected an understanding that freedom of speech and of the press would be secured to the states. See ANTIEAU, *supra* note 70, Ch. 3.B.2 at 32. Four members of the Massachusetts Committee on Federal Relations opposed ratification on the grounds that Section 1 was "needless" since privileges and immunities already were protected by the First, Second, Fifth, Sixth, and Seventh Amendments. *See id.* at 40.

95. *See* DEBATES, *supra* note 17, Ch. 2 at 408 (quoting CONG. GLOBE, 40th Cong., 3rd Sess. 1427 (1869)).

96. *See id.* at 420 (quoting CONG. GLOBE, 41th Cong., 2d Sess. 515 (1870)).

97. *See id.* at 479–80 (quoting CONG. GLOBE, 41st Cong., 3rd Sess. 1245 (1871)).

98. *See id.* at 541 (quoting CONG. GLOBE, 42d Cong., 1st Sess. 499 (1871)).

99. *Id.* at 466 (quoting H.R. REP. NO. 22, 41st Cong., 3rd Sess., pt. 1, at 1 (1871)).

100. *Id.* at 472 (quoting H.R. REP. NO. 37, 41st Cong., 3rd Sess. 7 (1871)).

101. *Id.* at xxiii, 503 (quoting CONG. GLOBE, 42d Cong., 1st Sess. app. 310 (1871)).

102. *Id.* at 510 (quoting CONG. GLOBE, 42d Cong., 1st Sess. app. 84 (1871)).

103. *Id.*

104. *See id.* at 238 (quoting CONG. GLOBE, 39th Cong., 1st Sess. 3149 (1866)) (recording House votes on the Fourteenth Amendment).

105. *See id.* at 535 (quoting CONG. GLOBE, 42d Cong., 1st Sess. 475–76 (1871)).

106. *Id.* at 615 (quoting CONG. GLOBE, 42d Cong., 2d Sess. 844 (1872)).

107. *Id.*

108. *Id.*

109. *Id.*

110. *See id.* at 615–16, 621 (quoting CONG. GLOBE, 42d Cong., 2d Sess. 844–45, 847 (1872)).

111. *Id.* at 344 (quoting CONG. GLOBE, 40th Cong., 3rd Sess. 692 (1869)).

112. *See* 2 CONG. REC. 312, 342, 412, 427 (1874); FONER, *supra* note 18, Ch. 1 at 533.

113. DEBATES, *supra* note 17, Ch. 2 at 548 (quoting CONG. GLOBE, 42d Cong., 1st Sess. 572 (1871)).

114. *See id.* at 676 (quoting 2 CONG. REC. app. 242 (1874)).

115. Fairman, *Incorporation, supra* note 83, Ch. 3.B.6 at 139.

116. *Cf.* Alfred Avins, *Incorporation of the Bill of Rights: The Crosskey-Fairman Debates Revisited,* 6 HARV. J. ON LEGIS. 1, 9 (1968) [hereinafter *Incorporation*] ("At best, Fairman's evidence is of a negative sort. In essence, it concludes that because a large number of lawyers did not know of incorporation, this proves that it did not occur.")

117. *See id.*

118. *See id.* at 4.

119. *See Misreading Bingham, supra* note 13, Ch. 3.B.2 at 70–71.

120. *Id.* at 67, 74.

121. *See* CURTIS, *supra* note 80, Ch. 3.B.6 at 219; RAOUL BERGER, THE FOURTEENTH AMENDMENT AND THE BILL OF RIGHTS 145 (1989).

122. *See* CURTIS, *supra* note 80, Ch. 3.B.6 at 219. *See also* FONER, *supra* note 18, Ch. 1 at 258 ("[I]t is abundantly clear that Republicans wished to give constitutional sanction to states' obligation to respect such key provisions as freedom of speech, the right to bear arms, trial by impartial jury, and protection against cruel and unusual punishment and unreasonable search and seizure").

123. *See id.;* Fairman, *Incorporation, supra* note 83, Ch. 3.B.6 at 76–77.

124. *See* CURTIS, *supra* note 80, Ch. 3.B.6 at 218.

125. *See id.*

126. *See id.*

127. Duncan v. Louisiana 391 U.S. 145, 165 (1968) (Black, J., concurring).

128. *See* OXFORD, *supra* note 2, Ch. 3.B.1 at 426.

129. *See* Avins, *Incorporation, supra* note 116, Ch. 3.B.6 at 26; FLACK, *supra* note 94, Ch. 3.B.6 at 94. This is not necessarily to reject the notion that, if the Due Process Clause were the only issue, selective incorporation under an "ordered liberty" doctrine would be misguided.

7. *Hall v. Decuir*: Segregation and the Interstate Commerce Clause

1. 95 U.S. 485.

2. *Id.* at 487.

3. *Id.*

4. *Id.* at 490.

5. *See* MAGRATH, *supra* note 128, Ch. 2 at 140; ROBERT FRIDLINGTON, THE RECONSTRUCTION COURT 1864–1888, at 204 (1987).

6. 95 U.S. at 500–01 (Clifford, J., concurring in the judgment).
7. *Id.* at 503 (Clifford, J., concurring in the judgment).
8. *See* MAGRATH, *supra* note 128, Ch. 2 at 141.

C. The Jury Discrimination Cases: Exception to the Retreat

1. The Court and Jury Discrimination, 1880–1883

1. *See* Frantz, *supra* note 75, Ch. 2, at 1373.
2. 100 U.S. 303.
3. *See id.* at 304.
4. *Id.* at 307.
5. *Id.*
6. *Id.* at 310.
7. *Id.* at 309.
8. *Id.* at 310.
9. *Id.*
10. *See id.* at 304.
11. *Id.* at 312.
12. 100 U.S. 313 (1880).
13. *See id.* at 315.
14. *See id.* at 315, 320–21.
15. *See id.* at 315.
16. *See id.*
17. *Id.* at 318.
18. *See id.* at 318–19.
19. *Id.* at 319–20.
20. *See id.* at 319, 321–22.
21. *Id.* at 321–22.
22. *Id.* at 323.
23. 100 U.S. 339 (1880).
24. *See id.* at 340, 344.
25. *Id.* at 344–45.
26. *Id.* at 345.
27. *See id.* at 346.
28. *See id.* at 348.
29. *See id.* at 349 (Field, J., dissenting).
30. 103 U.S. 370, 385–86.
31. *Id.* at 387–88.
32. *Id.* at 389–93.
33. *See id.* at 392–97.
34. *Id.* at 397.
35. *See id.* at 398 (Waite, C. J., dissenting); *id.* at 398–99, 407–08 (Field, J., dissenting).
36. 107 U.S. 110, 118.
37. *See id.* at 122.
38. *See id.* at 121–22.

39. *See id.* at 115–16.

40. *See id.* at 123 (dissents of Field, J., & Waite, C. J.).

2. Contemporary Legislative Views on Jury Discrimination and the Constitution

1. *Id.* at xix, 418 (quoting CONG. GLOBE, 41st Cong., 2d Sess. 403 (1870)).

2. *See id.* at 419 (quoting CONG. GLOBE, 41st Cong., 2d Sess. 463 (1870)).

3. *Id.* at 420 (quoting CONG. GLOBE, 41st Cong., 2d Sess. 495 (1870)). Bingham had reservations about congressional power to subject any state to any disability or restriction as a condition of representation "which by the text of the Constitution may not legitimately by Congress be enforced upon every State." *Id.* at 423 (quoting CONG. GLOBE, 41st Cong., 2d Sess. 716 (1870)).

4. *Id.* at 609 (quoting CONG. GLOBE, 42d Cong., 2d Sess. 820 (1872)).

5. *See id.* at 621 (quoting CONG. GLOBE, 42d Cong., 2d Sess. 847 (1872)) (to say that a man "shall not sit upon a jury because he is a colored man, that becomes class legislation at once, and that class of people are not entitled and do not receive the equal protection of benefit of the laws"); *id.* at 626 (quoting CONG. GLOBE, 42d Cong., 2d Sess. 898 (1872)) ("Any law which prevents colored men from sitting on a jury is class legislation, and directly in violation of the spirit, and I think the letter of the fourteenth amendment, which says that every person in every State shall be entitled to the equal protection of the laws; that is, the equal benefit of the laws."); *id.* at 683 (quoting 2 CONG. REC. app. 359 (1874)) (asserting that the Equal Protection Clause "denies the power to exclude negroes from courts of justice because they are negroes"); *id.* at 732 (quoting 3 CONG. REC. 1793 (1875)) ("Does a State that gives the exclusive right to sit upon juries to white men, give the equal protection of the laws of that State to colored men? I say no."); *id.* at 739 (quoting 3 CONG. REC. 1863 (1875)) ("[T]o give the exclusive right to white men to sit upon juries and to adjudicate upon the rights of colored men is denying to colored men the equal protection of the laws, because it is placing the adjudication of their rights exclusively in the hands of another race, filled with a prejudice and passion in many States that would prevent them from doing justice.").

6. *See id.* at 609 (quoting CONG. GLOBE, 42d Cong., 2d Sess. 820 (1872)).

7. *See id.* at 610, 615 (quoting CONG. GLOBE, 42d Cong., 2d Sess. 822–23, 845 (1872)).

8. *See id.* at 615–16 (quoting CONG. GLOBE, 42d Cong., 2d Sess. 844–45 (1872)).

9. *Id.* at 618, 628 (quoting CONG. GLOBE, 42d Cong., 2d Sess. app. 26, 900 (1872)). *See also id.* at 742 (quoting 3 CONG. REC. 1866 (1875)) (statement of Sen. Edmunds) (asserting that the Constitution protects the privilege or duty of citizens to serve on juries).

10. *See id.* at 673, 675 (quoting 2 CONG. REC. 3451, 3454–55 (1874)); *See also id.* at 622 (quoting CONG. GLOBE, 42d Cong., 2d Sess. 848 (1872)) (statement of Sen. Frelinghuysen) ("[I]t is the right of a large class that their whole class shall not be excluded from the jurybox.").

11. *See id.* at 731–32 (quoting 3 CONG. REC. 1792–93 (1875)).

12. *See id.* at 237–38 (quoting CONG. GLOBE, 39th Cong., 1st Sess. 3042, 3149 (1866)) (recording Senate and House votes on the Fourteenth Amendment).

13. *See* ANTIEAU, *supra* note 70, Ch. 3.B.2 at 48 (citing Florida and Texas committees).

14. *See* DEBATES, *supra* note 17, Ch. 2 at 420 (quoting CONG. GLOBE, 41st Cong., 2d Sess. app. 58 (1870)).

15. *See id.* at 618 (quoting CONG. GLOBE, 42d Cong., 2d Sess. app. 26 (1872)); *id.* at xxxii, 731–32, 734 (quoting 3 CONG. REC. 1791–93, 1795 (1875)).

16. *See id.* at xxvii, 629–30 (quoting CONG. GLOBE, 42d Cong., 2d Sess. 912–13 (1872)).

17. *See id.* at 635 (quoting CONG. GLOBE, 42d Cong., 2d Sess. app. 219 (1872)).

18. *Id.* at 739 (quoting 2 CONG. REC. 1864 (1875)).

19. *See id.* at xxxii, 734–35 (quoting 3 CONG. REC. 1796–97 (1875)).

20. *Id.* at 737 (quoting 3 CONG. REC. app. 105 (1875)).

21. *See id.* at xxvi, 601 (quoting CONG. GLOBE, 42d Cong., 2d Sess. 760 (1872)); *id.* at 738 (quoting 3 CONG. REC. 1863 (1875)).

22. *Id.* at 601, 609–10 (quoting CONG. GLOBE, 42d Cong., 2d Sess. 760, 820–22 (1872)).

23. *See id.* at 609, 613 (quoting CONG. GLOBE, 42d Cong., 2d Sess. 821, 827 (1872)).

24. *See id.* at 738 (quoting 3 CONG. REC. 1862–63 (1875)).

25. *See id.* at 648 (quoting CONG. GLOBE, 42d Cong., 2d Sess. 3263 (1872)).

D. The Fourteenth Amendment State Action Doctrine: *United States v. Harris,* the *Civil Rights Cases,* and *Baldwin v. Franks*

1. *United States v. Harris*

1. 106 U.S. 629 (1883).
2. *See id.* at 629–31.
3. *See* 17 Stat. 13 (1871); 106 U.S. at 629; 7 SUPREME COURT HISTORY, *supra* note 3, Ch. 2 at 485.
4. 106 U.S. at 632.
5. *See* 106 U.S. at 637.
6. *See* 92 U.S. at 555; *supra* note 16, Ch. 3.B.6 and accompanying text.
7. 106 U.S. at 639.
8. *Id.* at 640.
9. *Id.* at 641–42.
10. *Id.* at 643.
11. *Id.*
12. *See id.* at 644.

2. The *Civil Rights Cases*

1. Whiteside, *supra* note 128, Ch. 2 at 179.
2. *Id.*
3. *Id.* at 179–80.
4. 7 SUPREME COURT HISTORY, *supra* note 3, Ch. 2 at 192.
5. 109 U.S. 3.
6. *See id.* at 4–5.
7. *Id.* at 10.
8. *Id.* at 11.

9. *Id.*
10. *Id.*
11. *Id.* at 13.
12. *Id.* at 13–14.
13. *Id.* at 15.
14. *Id.* at 18–19.
15. *Id.* at 20–21.
16. *Id.* at 22.
17. *Id.* Compare this holding with the following excerpt from an essay by Bradley on the meaning of equality:

Does it mean social eq[u]ality? Such a state would make all the classes . . . of society commingle their intercourse; would introduce the cobbler into the most elegant drawing room to take a cup of tea with the gayest belle of the town, or else, perhaps, to debate with grave Senators on the affairs of State. Could this have been meant? Certainly not. This is the least possible of all meanings that could be attached to the term. Men *will* choose their own company in whatever state of society you may choose to place them. This is the last vestige of liberty with which they are willing to part.

WILLIAM DRAPER LEWIS, MISCELLANEOUS WRITINGS OF THE LATE HON. JOSEPH P. BRADLEY 91–92 (1901).
18. 109 U.S. at 24. "Mere discriminations on account of race or color were not regarded as badges of slavery," Bradley later added. *Id.* at 25.
19. *Id.* at 25–26.
20. Swayne wrote Harlan concerning his dissent that "in my judgment, it is one of the great—indeed one of the greatest—opinions of the Court—does you infinite honor—is all that could be desired—and will make a profound and lasting impression upon the Country." Alan F. Westin, *John Marshall Harlan and the Constitutional Rights of Negroes: The Transformation of a Southerner*, 66 YALE L.J. 637, 681–82 (1957). Strong called the dissent "a *very* able opinion," LOREN P. BETH, JOHN MARSHALL HARLAN: THE LAST WHIG JUSTICE 231 (1992), and told Harlan, "At first I was inclined to agree with the Court but since reading your opinion, I am in great doubt. It may be that you are right. The opinion of the Court, as you said, is too narrow—sticks to the letter, while you aim to bring out the Spirit of the Constitution." Westin, *supra*, at 681.
21. 109 U.S. at 26 (Harlan, J., dissenting); *supra* note 1, Epigraph.
22. *See* 109 U.S. at 28–29 (Harlan, J., dissenting) (citing 41 U.S. (16 Pet.) 539, 615, 623 (1843)).
23. *Id.* at 35 (Harlan, J., dissenting). *See also supra* note 9, Ch. 3.C.1 and accompanying text for the reference to *Prigg* in *Strauder*.
24. 109 U.S. at 35–37 (Harlan, J., dissenting).
25. *Id.* at 38–39 (Harlan, J., dissenting). *Cf.* Chicago, Burlington, and Quincy R.R. v. Iowa, 94 U.S. 155, 161 (1877) ("Railroad companies are . . . engaged in a public employment affecting the public interest, and . . . subject to legislative control as to their rates of fare and freight, unless protected by their charters.").
26. 109 U.S. at 39 (Harlan, J., dissenting).
27. *Id.* at 40 (Harlan, J., dissenting).
28. *Id.* at 40–41 (Harlan, J., dissenting).
29. *Id.* at 41 (Harlan, J., dissenting).

30. 94 U.S. 113.
31. *Id.* at 126.
32. *See* 109 U.S. at 42 (Harlan, J., dissenting).
33. *Id.* at 42–43 (Harlan, J., dissenting).
34. *Id.* at 43 (Harlan, J., dissenting).
35. *Id.* at 43–44 (Harlan, J., dissenting).
36. *See id.* at 44 (Harlan, J., dissenting).
37. *Id.* at 45–46, 52 (Harlan, J., dissenting).
38. *Id.* at 46 (Harlan, J., dissenting).
39. *Id.* at 47–48 (Harlan, J., dissenting).
40. *Id.* at 48 (Harlan, J., dissenting).
41. *Id.* at 49–50 (Harlan, J., dissenting).
42. *Id.* at 50 (Harlan, J., dissenting).
43. *Id.* at 51 (Harlan, J., dissenting) (quoting McCulloch v. Maryland, 17 U.S. (4 Wheat.) 316, 421 (1819)).
44. *Id.* at 52, 54 (Harlan, J., dissenting).
45. *Id.* at 53 (Harlan, J., dissenting).
46. *Id.* at 54 (Harlan, J., dissenting).
47. *See id.* (Harlan, J., dissenting).
48. *Id.* at 55–56 (Harlan, J., dissenting).
49. *See id.* at 56 (Harlan, J., dissenting).
50. *See id.* (Harlan, J., dissenting).
51. *Id.* at 57 (Harlan, J., dissenting).
52. *Id.* at 57–58 (Harlan, J., dissenting).
53. *Id.* at 59 (Harlan, J., dissenting).
54. *See id.* at 60 (Harlan, J., dissenting).
55. *Id.* at 61–62 (Harlan, J., dissenting).
56. *Id.* at 62 (Harlan, J., dissenting).

3. The State Action Doctrine and Section 5 of the Fourteenth Amendment: The Constitutional Basis for § 2 of the Ku Klux Klan Act of 1871 and §§ 1 and 2 of the Civil Rights Act of 1875

1. *See* DEBATES, *supra* note 17, Ch. 2 at 108 (quoting CONG. GLOBE, 39th Cong., 1st Sess. 319 (1866)).
2. *See id.* at 112, 123 (quoting CONG. GLOBE, 39th Cong., 1st Sess. 363, 477 (1866)).
3. *See id.* at 140 (quoting CONG. GLOBE, 39th Cong., 1st Sess. 628 (1866)).
4. *See id.* at 165, 167 (quoting CONG. GLOBE, 39th Cong., 1st Sess. 1120–21, 1123 (1866)).
5. *See id.* at 170 (quoting CONG. GLOBE, 39th Cong., 1st Sess. 1156 (1866)).
6. *See id.* at 69 (quoting CONG. GLOBE, 38th Cong., 1st Sess. 1490 (1864)).
7. *See id.* at 126 (quoting CONG. GLOBE, 39th Cong., 1st Sess. 499 (1866)).
8. *See id.* at x, 189 (quoting CONG. GLOBE, 39th Cong., 1st Sess. 1294 (1866)).
9. *See id.* at 187 (quoting CONG. GLOBE, 39th Cong., 1st Sess. 1292 (1866)); *supra* note 81, Ch. 3.B.6.

10. *See* DEBATES, *supra* note 17, Ch. 2 at 177–79 (quoting CONG. GLOBE, 39th Cong., 1st Sess. app. 156–59 (1866)).

11. *See id.* at 190–91 (quoting CONG. GLOBE, 39th Cong., 1st Sess. 1295–96 (1866)).

12. *See id.* at 191, 210 (quoting CONG. GLOBE, 39th Cong., 1st Sess. 1367, 1861 (1866)).

13. *Id.* at 77 (quoting CONG. GLOBE, 38th Cong., 1st Sess. 2990 (1864)).

14. *See id.* at 97 (quoting CONG. GLOBE, 39th Cong., 1st Sess. 41–42 (1865)).

15. *Id.* at 98–99 (quoting CONG. GLOBE, 39th Cong., 1st Sess. 111 (1865)).

16. *Id.* at 108 (quoting CONG. GLOBE, 39th Cong., 1st Sess. 322 (1866)). *See also id.* at 121 (quoting CONG. GLOBE, 39th Cong., 1st Sess. 474 (1866)) (statement of Sen. Trumbull) ("[A]ny statute which is not equal to all, and which deprives any citizen of civil rights which are secured to other citizens, is an unjust encroachment upon his liberty; and is, in fact, a badge of servitude which, by the Constitution, is prohibited.").

17. *Id.* at 122 (quoting CONG. GLOBE, 39th Cong., 1st Sess. 475 (1866)).

18. *Id.* at 114 (quoting CONG. GLOBE, 39th Cong., 1st Sess. 406 (1866)).

19. *See id.* at 168 (quoting CONG. GLOBE, 39th Cong., 1st Sess. 1124 (1866)).

20. *See id.* at 169 (quoting CONG. GLOBE, 39th Cong., 1st Sess. 1152 (1866)).

21. *See id.* at 173 (quoting CONG. GLOBE, 39th Cong., 1st Sess. 1255 (1866)).

22. *See id.* at 203 (quoting CONG. GLOBE, 39th Cong., 1st Sess. 1785 (1866)).

23. *See* CONG. GLOBE, 39th Cong., 1st Sess. 3037 (1866).

24. *See* DEBATES, *supra* note 17, Ch. 2 at 173 (quoting CONG. GLOBE, 39th Cong., 1st Sess. 1255 (1866)); *id.* at 203 (quoting CONG. GLOBE, 39th Cong., 1st Sess. 1785 (1866)).

25. *Id.* at 168 (quoting CONG. GLOBE, 39th Cong., 1st Sess. 1124 (1866)).

26. *Id.* at 236 (quoting CONG. GLOBE, 39th Cong., 1st Sess. 3035 (1866)).

27. *Id.*

28. *See supra* text accompanying notes 11–13, Ch. 3.A; *supra* note 27, Ch. 3.B.6.

29. *See* DEBATES, *supra* note 17, Ch. 2 at 123 (quoting CONG. GLOBE, 39th Cong., 1st Sess. 476 (1866)).

30. *Id.* at 177 (quoting CONG. GLOBE, 39th Cong., 1st Sess. app. 156 (1866)).

31. *See id.* at 213 (quoting CONG. GLOBE, 39th Cong., 1st Sess. 2461 (1866)).

32. *Id.* at 228 (quoting CONG. GLOBE, 39th Cong., 1st Sess. 2896 (1866)).

33. *Id.* at 214 (quoting CONG. GLOBE, 39th Cong., 1st Sess. 2502 (1866)). *See also id.* at 215 (quoting CONG. GLOBE, 39th Cong., 1st Sess. 2512 (1866)) (stating that the bill "contained a provision by which the Government of the United States undertook to secure to [the freedman] and to all other citizens the enjoyment of certain rights, and to provide for their violation certain remedies within State jurisdiction, where it seemed to me Congress under the existing Constitution had not the right so to act").

34. *Id.* at 215 (quoting CONG. GLOBE, 39th Cong., 1st Sess. 2511 (1866)).

35. *See, e.g., id.* at 212 (quoting CONG. GLOBE, 39th Cong., 1st Sess. 2459 (1866)) (statement of Rep. Stevens) (pointing out, in reference to the Civil Rights Act, that "a law is repealable by a majority"); *id.* at 213 (quoting CONG. GLOBE, 39th Cong., 1st Sess. 2462 (1866)) (statement of Rep. Garfield) ("[E]very gentleman knows [the Civil Rights Act] will cease to be a part of the law whenever the sad

moment arrives when [the Democratic] party comes into power. It is precisely for that reason that we propose to lift that great and good law above the reach of political strife, beyond the reach of the plots and machinations of any party, and fix it in the serene sky, in the eternal firmament of the Constitution, where no storm of passion can shake it and no cloud can obscure it. For this reason, and not because I believe the civil rights bill unconstitutional, I am glad to see that first section here."); FLACK, *supra* note 94, Ch. 3.B.6 at 95.

36. *See* DEBATES, *supra* note 17, Ch. 2 at 458 (quoting CONG. GLOBE, 41st Cong., 2d Sess. 3689 (1870)).

37. During the Ku Klux Klan Act debates, Shellabarger asserted that if it was constitutional for "Congress to define and punish as a crime against the United States any act of deprivation of the rights of the newly made American citizenship" under the Thirteenth Amendment, "surely, . . . the far more explicit, complete, and careful provisions of the fourteenth much more did it by declaring all our people United States citizens." *Id.* at 493 (quoting CONG. GLOBE, 42d Cong., 1st Sess. app. 68 (1871)). During the debates over the Civil Rights Act of 1875, Lawrence reviewed the Fourteenth Amendment's adoption and asserted that the amendment was intended "to remove all doubt" about the constitutionality of the 1866 act "and to give Congress power to secure equal civil rights to all." *Id.* at 663 (quoting 2 CONG. REC. 413 (1874)).

38. 17 Stat. 13 (1871).

39. *See* DEBATES, *supra* note 17, Ch. 2 at xi, 212 (quoting CONG. GLOBE, 39th Cong., 1st Sess. 2459 (1866)) (statement of Rep. Stevens) (conceding that it "is partly true" that the Fourteenth Amendment "secures the same things" as the Civil Rights Act, but the latter "is repealable by a majority"); *id.* at 213 (quoting CONG. GLOBE, 39th Cong., 1st Sess. 2467 (1866)) (statement of Rep. Boyer) (Section 1 of the Fourteenth Amendment "embodies the principles of the civil rights bill"); *id.* at 214 (quoting CONG. GLOBE, 39th Cong., 1st Sess. 2498 (1866)) (statement of Rep. Broomall) ("[A]ll who will vote for the pending measure . . . voted for this proposition in another shape, in the civil rights bill."); ANTIEAU, *supra* note 70, Ch. 3.B.2 at 4; FLACK, *supra* note 94, Ch. 3.B.6 at 94; Gressman, *supra* note 3, Ch. 2 at 1329.

40. DEBATES, *supra* note 17, Ch. 2 at 96 (quoting CONG. GLOBE, 39th Cong., 1st Sess. 40 (1865)): *See also id.* at 201 (quoting CONG. GLOBE, 39th Cong., 1st Sess. 1777 (1866)) (statement of Sen. Johnson) (charging that the bill "invades the jurisdiction of the States over their criminal code").

41. *Id.* at 123 (quoting CONG. GLOBE, 39th Cong., 1st Sess. 478 (1866)).

42. *Id.* at 140 (quoting CONG. GLOBE, 39th Cong., 1st Sess. 623 (1866)). *See also id.* at 182 (quoting CONG. GLOBE, 39th Cong., 1st Sess. 1270 (1866)) (statement of Rep. Kerr) (asserting that the bill denied the "right of the State to regulate its own internal and domestic affairs, to select its own local policy, and make and administer its own laws for the protection and welfare of its own citizens").

43. *Id.* at 165–66 (quoting CONG. GLOBE, 39th Cong., 1st Sess. 1120–21 (1866)).

44. *Id.* at 191, 205 (quoting CONG. GLOBE, 39th Cong., 1st Sess. 1414, app. 183 (1866)).

45. *Id.* at 121 (quoting CONG. GLOBE, 39th Cong., 1st Sess. 474 (1866)).

46. *Id.* at 628–29 (quoting CONG. GLOBE, 42d Cong., 2d Sess. 901 (1872)).

47. *Id*. at 138 (quoting CONG. GLOBE, 39th Cong., 1st Sess. 603 (1866)).

48. *Id*. at 140 (quoting CONG. GLOBE, 39th Cong., 1st Sess. 632 (1866)).

49. *Id*.

50. *Id*. at 163 (quoting CONG. GLOBE, 39th Cong., 1st Sess. 1117 (1866)). Wilson's conception of rights excluded the right to vote, sit on juries, or attend the same schools. *See also id*. at 214 (quoting CONG. GLOBE, 39th Cong., 1st Sess. 2505 (1866)) (articulating a similar definition of the bill as "a declaration that all persons without distinction of race or color should enjoy in all of the States and Territories civil rights and immunities").

51. *Id*. at 243 (quoting CONG. GLOBE, 39th Cong., 1st Sess. 3215 (1866)).

52. *See id*. at viii, 150 (quoting CONG. GLOBE, 39th Cong., 1st Sess. app. 133 (1866)).

53. *See id*. at 210 (quoting CONG. GLOBE, 39th Cong., 1st Sess. 2080–81 (1866)).

54. *Id*. at 156 (quoting CONG. GLOBE, 39th Cong., 1st Sess. 1066 (1866)).

55. *Id*. at 160 (quoting CONG. GLOBE, 39th Cong., 1st Sess. 1094 (1866)).

56. *Id*. at 214 (quoting CONG. GLOBE, 39th Cong., 1st Sess. 2502 (1866)).

57. *Id*. at 220 (quoting CONG. GLOBE, 39th Cong., 1st Sess. 2766 (1866)).

58. *Id*. at 231 (quoting CONG. GLOBE, 39th Cong., 1st Sess. app. 219 (1866)).

59. *Id*. at 238 (quoting CONG. GLOBE, 39th Cong., 1st Sess. app. 227 (1866)). During a debate over suffrage in the nation's capital not long afterward, Willey asserted,

We owe to the freedman the guarantee of every civil right of man. He must be fully protected in the enjoyment of "life, liberty, and the pursuit of happiness." He must have the same rights in these respects that you or I have; and the securities and guarantees surrounding them must be as ample for him as they are for you or for me. To this extent he must be made equal before the law.

Id. at 246 (quoting CONG. GLOBE, 39th Cong., 1st Sess. 3436 (1866)).

60. *See* ANTIEAU, *supra* note 70, Ch. 3.B.2 at 14–17, 18–19, 23, 38; FLACK, *supra* note 94, Ch. 3.B.6 at 172–73.

61. *See* DEBATES, *supra* note 17, Ch. 2 at 137 (quoting CONG. GLOBE, 39th Cong., 1st Sess. 600 (1866)) (statement of Sen. Trumbull) ("The bill draws to the Federal Government no power whatever if the States will perform their constitutional obligations."); *id*. at 198 (quoting CONG. GLOBE, 39th Cong., 1st Sess. 1758 (1866)) (statement of Sen. Trumbull) ("If an offense is committed against a colored person simply because he is colored, in a State where the law affords him the same protection as if he were white, this act neither has nor was intended to have anything to do with his case, because he has adequate remedies in the State courts; but if he is discriminated against under color of State laws because he is colored, then it becomes necessary to interfere of his protection."); *id*. at 204 (quoting CONG. GLOBE, 39th Cong., 1st Sess. 1785 (1866)) (statement of Sen. Stewart) (stating that the bill would not operate in any state without a law or custom authorizing the proscribed activity and that it would operate only on those who act under color of a law).

62. *Id*. at 179–80 (quoting CONG. GLOBE, 39th Cong., 1st Sess. app. 158–59 (1866)).

63. *See id.* at 238 (quoting CONG. GLOBE, 39th Cong., 1st Sess. 3149 (1866)) (recording House votes on the Fourteenth Amendment).

64. *Supra* note 67, Ch. 3.B.5.

65. DEBATES, *supra* note 17, Ch. 2 at 444 (quoting CONG. GLOBE, 41st Cong., 2nd Sess. app. 355 (1870)).

66. *Id.* at 451 (quoting CONG. GLOBE, 41st Cong., 2d Sess. app. 473 (1870)).

67. *See id.*

68. *See id.*

69. *See id.* at xxiii, 506–08 (quoting CONG. GLOBE, 42d Cong., 1st Sess. app. 115–17 (1871)).

70. *See infra* Ch. 3.D.3.b.1.

71. *See* DEBATES, *supra* note 17, Ch. 2 at xxiii, 506–07 (quoting CONG. GLOBE, 42d Cong., 1st Sess. app. 115–16 (1871)).

72. *See id.*

73. *Id.* at 506 (quoting CONG. GLOBE, 42d Cong., 1st Sess. app. 115 (1871) (quoting CONG. GLOBE, 39th Cong., 1st Sess. 1034 (1866))).

74. *See id.* at 506–07, 570 (quoting CONG. GLOBE, 42d Cong., 1st Sess. app. 115–16, 808, 831 (1871)). Poland, who was a representative in 1871, expressed general agreement with Farnsworth's propositions, but he differed with him enough to vote for the bill. The basis of his own support for the bill remains to be discussed.

75. *See id.* at xxv, 553 (quoting CONG. GLOBE, 42d Cong., 1st Sess. app. 231 (1871)).

76. *See id.*

77. *See id.* at xxv, 535 (quoting CONG. GLOBE, 42d Cong., 1st Sess. app. 160 (1871)).

78. *Id.* at 535 (quoting CONG. GLOBE, 42d Cong., 1st Sess. app. 259 (1871)).

79. *Id.* at 520 (quoting CONG. GLOBE, 42d Cong., 1st Sess. 396 (1871)).

80. *Id.* at 533 (quoting CONG. GLOBE, 42d Cong., 1st Sess. app. 305 (1871)).

81. *Id.* at 548 (quoting CONG. GLOBE, 42d Cong., 1st Sess. 572 (1871)).

82. *See id.* at 558 (quoting CONG. GLOBE, 42d Cong., 1st Sess. 648 (1871)).

83. *Id.* at 518 (quoting CONG. GLOBE, 42d Cong., 1st Sess. app. 208 (1871)).

84. *See id.* at 237–38 (quoting CONG. GLOBE, 39th Cong., 1st Sess. 3042, 3149 (1866)) (recording Senate and House votes on the Fourteenth Amendment).

85. *See* Frantz, *supra* note 75, Ch. 2 at 1356–57.

86. DEBATES, *supra* note 17, Ch. 2 at 138 (quoting CONG. GLOBE, 39th Cong., 1st Sess. 603 (1866)).

87. *Id.* at 206 (quoting CONG. GLOBE, 39th Cong., 1st Sess. 1833 (1866)).

88. *Id.* at 150 (quoting CONG. GLOBE, 39th Cong., 1st Sess. 1034 (1866)).

89. *Id.* at 420 (quoting CONG. GLOBE, 41st Cong., 2d Sess. 466 (1870)).

90. *See supra* note 12, Ch. 3.D.2 and accompanying text. *See also* text accompanying *supra* note 49, Ch. 3.B.5 (assertion by Bingham during Fifteenth Amendment debates that "[w]henever Congress has the power under the Constitution to enforce the limitations of that instrument, even upon States, the exercise of the power will be as uniform as the exercise of any affirmative power can possibly be").

91. *See* DEBATES, *supra* note 17, Ch. 2 at 442 (quoting CONG. GLOBE, 41st Cong., 2d Sess. 3570 (1870)) (statement of Sen. Sherman); *id.* at 458 (quoting

252 Notes

Cong. Globe, 41st Cong., 2d Sess. 3690, 3702 (1870)) (statements of Sen. Stewart & Sen. Thurman).

92. *See* 7 Supreme Court History, *supra* note 3, Ch. 2 at 278.

93. *See* Debates, *supra* note 17, Ch. 2 at xx.

94. *Id*. at 447–48 (quoting Cong. Globe, 41st Cong., 2d Sess. 3611, 3613 (1870)).

95. *Id*. at 447 (quoting Cong. Globe, 41st Cong., 2d Sess. 3611 (1870)).

96. *See id*. at 551–52 (quoting Cong. Globe, 42d Cong., 1st Sess. 604, 607–08 (1871)).

97. *See id*. at xxiii, 508–09, 511 (quoting Cong. Globe, 42d Cong., 1st Sess. app. 81–83, 85 (1871)).

98. *Id*. at 509 (quoting Cong. Globe, 42d Cong., 1st Sess. app. 82 (1871)).

99. *Id*. (quoting Cong. Globe, 42d Cong., 1st Sess. app. 83 (1871)).

100. *Id*. at 510–11 (quoting Cong. Globe, 42d Cong., 1st Sess. app. 84–85 (1871)).

101. *Id*. at 511 (quoting Cong. Globe, 42d Cong., 1st Sess. app. 85 (1871)).

102. *See id*.

103. *Id*. at 513 (quoting Cong. Globe, 42d Cong., 1st Sess. app. 80 (1871)) (statement of Rep. Perry).

104. *Id*. at 552 (quoting Cong. Globe, 42d Cong., 1st Sess. 608 (1871)) (statement of Sen. Pool).

105. *Id*. at 563 (quoting Cong. Globe, 42d Cong., 1st Sess. 697 (1871)).

106. *Id*. at 562 (quoting Cong. Globe, 42d Cong., 1st Sess. 696 (1871)).

107. 17 Stat. 13, 14 (1871). *See also* Debates, *supra* note 17, Ch. 2 at 495, 536 (quoting Cong. Globe, 42d Cong., 1st Sess. app. 70–71, 477 (1871)).

108. *See* Debates, *supra* note 17, Ch. 2 at xxii.

109. *Id*. at 496 (quoting Cong. Globe, 42d Cong., 1st Sess. app. 71 (1871)).

110. *Id*. at 513 (quoting Cong. Globe, 42d Cong., 1st Sess. app. 80 (1871)).

111. *Id*.

112. *Id*. (quoting Cong. Globe, 42d Cong., 1st Sess. 368 (1871)).

113. *Id*. at 530 (quoting Cong. Globe, 42d Cong., 1st Sess. app. 154 (1871)).

114. *Id*. at 522 (quoting Cong. Globe, 42d Cong., 1st Sess. 428 (1871)).

115. *Id*. at 530 (quoting Cong. Globe, 42d Cong., 1st Sess. 437 (1871)).

116. *Id*. at 532 (quoting Cong. Globe, 42d Cong., 1st Sess. 448 (1871)).

117. *Id*. at 534 (quoting Cong. Globe, 42d Cong., 1st Sess. 459 (1871)).

118. *Id*. (quoting Cong. Globe, 42d Cong., 1st Sess. 459–60 (1871)).

119. *Id*. at 538 (quoting Cong. Globe, 42d Cong., 1st Sess. 482 (1871)).

120. *Id*. at 541 (quoting Cong. Globe, 42d Cong., 1st Sess. 501 (1871)).

121. *Id*. at 542 (quoting Cong. Globe, 42d Cong., 1st Sess. 506 (1871)).

122. *Id*. at 543 (quoting Cong. Globe, 42d Cong., 1st Sess. 506 (1871)).

123. *Id*. at 561 (quoting Cong. Globe, 42d Cong., 1st Sess. 695 (1871)).

124. *Id*. at 563 (quoting Cong. Globe, 42d Cong., 1st Sess. 697 (1871)).

125. Richardson, *supra* note 44, Ch. 2 at 299. *See also supra* note 116 and accompanying text, Ch. 2.

126. Debates, *supra* note 17, Ch. 2 at 220 (quoting Cong. Globe, 39th Cong., 1st Sess. 2766 (1866)).

127. *Id*.

128. *Id*. at 221–22 (quoting Cong. Globe, 39th Cong., 1st Sess. 2768 (1866)).

129. *See* FLACK, *supra* note 94, Ch. 3.B.6 at 138.

130. DEBATES, *supra* note 17, Ch. 2 at 230 (quoting CONG. GLOBE, 39th Cong., 1st Sess. 2961 (1866)).

131. CONG. GLOBE, 39th Cong., 1st Sess. 2940 (1866). Making a similar criticism during House debates over Bingham's original proposal, Rogers stated that the proposed amendment would "enable and empower Congress to pass laws compelling the abrogation of all the statutes of the States which makes a distinction, for instance, between a crime committed by a white man and a crime committed by a black man, or allow white people privileges, immunities, or property not allowed to a black man." DEBATES, *supra* note 17, Ch. 2 at 151 (CONG. GLOBE, 39th Cong., 1st Sess. app. 134 (1866)).

132. *See, e.g.,* ANTIEAU, *supra* note 70, Ch. 3.B.2 at 64 (statements of Pennsylvania Sen. Landon, Rep. Mann, & Rep. Deise); *id.* at 65 (report of Arkansas Senate Committee on Federal Relations and statement of Gov. Cox of Ohio).

133. *See id.* at 40–41 (statement of Pennsylvania Rep. Kurtz); *id.* at 41 (statement of Pennsylvania Sen. Burnett and reports of the Texas House Committee on Federal Relations, Texas Senate Committee on Federal Relations, & North Carolina Joint Select Committee on Federal Relations); *id.* at 42 (report of Arkansas House Committee on Federal Relations); *id.* at 64 (statement of Pennsylvania Rep. Jones); *id.* at 65 (statements of Pennsylvania Sen. Wallace, Pennsylvania Rep. Kurtz, & Gov. Orr of South Carolina and report of Arkansas House Committee on Federal Relations); FLACK, *supra* note 94, Ch. 3.B.6 at 192 (statement of Gov. Jenkins of Georgia); *id.* at 198 (report of North Carolina Joint Select Committee on Federal Relations).

134. *See* ANTIEAU, *supra* note 70, Ch. 3.B.2 at 63–64 (report of North Carolina Joint Select Committee on Federal Relations); *id.* at 65 (minority report of Tennessee Senate & statement of Gov. Humphreys of Mississippi); *id.* at 68 (statements of Gov. Humphreys of Mississippi & Gov. Swann of Maryland, reports of the Arkansas Senate Committee on Federal Relations & Florida House Committee on Federal Relations, and statement of Pennsylvania Rep. Jones); FLACK, *supra* note 94, Ch. 3 at 180 (statement of Pennsylvania Sen. Wallace); *id.* at 185–86 (statement of Pennsylvania Rep. Jones); *id.* at 196 (statement of Gov. Worth of North Carolina); *id.* at 200 (report of North Carolina Joint Select Committee on Federal Relations); *id.* at 206 (report of Maryland Joint Committee on Federal Relations).

135. FLACK, *supra* note 94, Ch. 3.B.6 at 206.

136. *See id.* at 152–53, 156–57 (citing the Washington *National Intelligencer*, Raleigh *Sentinel*, Nashville *Union & American*, *Florida Union*, & *Louisville Journal*).

137. DEBATES, *supra* note 17, Ch. 2 at 372 (quoting CONG. GLOBE, 40th Cong., 3rd Sess. 1002 (1869)).

138. *Id.* at 447–48 (quoting CONG. GLOBE, 41st Cong., 2d Sess. 3611, 3613 (1870)).

139. *Id.* at 495 (quoting CONG. GLOBE, 42d Cong., 1st Sess. app. 70 (1871)).

140. *Id.* at 550 (quoting CONG. GLOBE, 42d Cong., 1st Sess. 577 (1871)).

141. *Id.* at 501 (quoting CONG. GLOBE, 42d Cong., 1st Sess. 322 (1871)).

142. *Id.* at 524 (quoting CONG. GLOBE, 42d Cong., 1st Sess. app. 251 (1871)).

143. *Id.* at 536 (quoting CONG. GLOBE, 42d Cong., 1st Sess. 476 (1871)).

144. *Id.* at 537 (quoting CONG. GLOBE, 42d Cong., 1st Sess. 481 (1871)).

145. *See id.* (quoting CONG. GLOBE, 42d Cong., 1st Sess. 481–82 (1871)).

146. *Id.* (quoting CONG. GLOBE, 42d Cong., 1st Sess. 482 (1871)).

147. *Id.* at 538 (quoting CONG. GLOBE, 42d Cong., 1st Sess. 483 (1871)).

148. *Id.*

149. *See id.* at xxiv, 541–42 (quoting CONG. GLOBE, 42d Cong., 1st Sess. 500–02 (1871)).

150. *See id.* at xxiv, 542 (quoting CONG. GLOBE, 42d Cong., 1st Sess. 505–06 (1871)). Pratt emphasized that Section 1 applied to "all persons who are made citizens . . . whether Caucasian, African, or Asiatic in origin. There is no torturing of language by which we can strike out the word 'all' in this article." *Id.* at 542 (quoting CONG. GLOBE, 42d Cong., 1st Sess. 506 (1871)).

151. *Id.* at 542 (quoting CONG. GLOBE, 42d Cong., 1st Sess. 501–02 (1871)).

152. *Id.* at 557–58 (quoting CONG. GLOBE, 42d Cong., 1st Sess. app. 228–29 (1871)).

153. *Id.* at 543 (quoting CONG. GLOBE, 42d Cong., 1st Sess. app. 182 (1871)).

154. *See id.* at 178 (quoting CONG. GLOBE, 39th Cong., 1st Sess. app. 157 (1866)).

155. *See id.* at 208 (quoting CONG. GLOBE, 39th Cong., 1st Sess. 1836 (1866)).

156. *See id.* at 597 (quoting CONG. GLOBE, 42d Cong., 2d Sess. 728 (1872)).

157. *See id.* at 663 (quoting 2 CONG. REC. 414 (1874)).

158. *See id.* at 723 (quoting 3 CONG. REC. 980 (1875)).

159. *See id.* at ix, 164, 190 (quoting CONG. GLOBE, 39th Cong., 1st Sess. 1118, 1295 (1866)) (arguing for the constitutionality of the Civil Rights Act of 1866).

160. *See id.* at 495 (quoting CONG. GLOBE, 42d Cong., 1st Sess. app. 70 (1871)) (arguing for the constitutionality of the Ku Klux Klan Act). Shellabarger also invoked the rules of construction of Chief Justice Marshall and Justice Joseph Story from other sources to support his argument. *See id.* at 493 (quoting CONG. GLOBE, 42d Cong., 1st Sess. app. 68 (1871)).

161. *See id.* at 516 (quoting CONG. GLOBE, 42d Cong., 1st Sess. 375 (1871)) (arguing for the constitutionality of the Ku Klux Klan Act).

162. *See id.* at 558 (quoting CONG. GLOBE, 42d Cong., 1st Sess. app. 229 (1871)) (same).

163. *See id.* at 663 (quoting 2 CONG. REC. 414 (1874)) (arguing for the constitutionality of the Civil Rights Act of 1875).

164. *Id.* at 150 (quoting CONG. GLOBE, 39th Cong., 1st Sess. 1034 (1866)).

165. *Id.* at 135 (quoting CONG. GLOBE, 39th Cong., 1st Sess. 586 (1866)).

166. *Id.* at 158 (quoting CONG. GLOBE, 39th Cong., 1st Sess. 1090 (1866)).

167. *Id.* at 160 (quoting CONG. GLOBE, 39th Cong., 1st Sess. 1094 (1866)).

168. *Id.* at 189 (quoting CONG. GLOBE, 39th Cong., 1st Sess. 1294 (1866)).

169. *Id.* at 151 (quoting CONG. GLOBE, 39th Cong., 1st Sess. app. 134 (1866)).

170. *See id.* at 238 (quoting CONG. GLOBE, 39th Cong., 1st Sess. 3149 (1866)) (recording House votes on the Fourteenth Amendment).

171. *Id.* at 153 (quoting CONG. GLOBE, 39th Cong., 1st Sess. 1063 (1866)).

172. *Id.* at 154 (quoting CONG. GLOBE, 39th Cong., 1st Sess. 1064 (1866)). *See also id.* at 155 (quoting CONG. GLOBE, 39th Cong., 1st Sess. 1065 (1866)) (fearing that the vague language will allow Congress "to legislate upon all matters pertaining to the life, liberty, and property of all the inhabitants of the several States").

173. *Id.* at 156 (quoting CONG. GLOBE, 39th Cong., 1st Sess. 1087 (1866)).

174. *Id.*

175. *See id.* at 160 (quoting CONG. GLOBE, 39th Cong., 1st Sess. 1094–95 (1866)).

176. *Id.* (quoting CONG. GLOBE, 39th Cong., 1st Sess. 1095 (1866)).

177. *Id.*

178. *Id.*

179. *See id.*

180. *Id.* at ix, 161 (quoting CONG. GLOBE, 39th Cong., 1st Sess. 1082 (1866)).

181. *Id.*

182. *Id.*

183. *Id.* at ix.

184. *Id.* at 509 (quoting CONG. GLOBE, 42d Cong., 1st Sess. app. 82 (1871)). *Cf.* FONER, *supra* note 18, Ch. 1 at 258 ("The final version [of the Fourteenth Amendment] . . . was far stronger than Bingham's earlier proposal . . . for this would become a dead letter if Democrats regained control of the House or Senate.").

185. DEBATES, *supra* note 17, Ch. 2 at 510 (quoting CONG. GLOBE, 42d Cong., 1st Sess. app. 84 (1871) (quoting Barron v. Baltimore, 32 U.S. (7 Pet.) 243, 250 (1833)).

186. *See id.*

187. *Id.* at 179 (quoting CONG. GLOBE, 39th Cong., 1st Sess. app. 158 (1866)).

188. *Id.* at 233 (quoting CONG. GLOBE, 39th Cong., 1st Sess. app. 240 (1866)).

189. *Id.* at 236 (quoting CONG. GLOBE, 39th Cong., 1st Sess. 3036 (1866)).

190. *Id.* at 238 (quoting CONG. GLOBE, 39th Cong., 1st Sess. app. 227 (1866)).

191. *Id.* at 248 (quoting CONG. GLOBE, 39th Cong., 1st Sess. app. 256 (1866)).

192. *See* ANTIEAU, *supra* note 70, Ch. 3.B.2 at 20, 64.

193. *See id.* at 62–63.

194. *Id.* at 62.

195. *Id.* at 63.

196. *Id.* at 64.

197. DEBATES, *supra* note 17, Ch. 2 at 341 (quoting CONG. GLOBE, 40th Cong., 3rd Sess. app. 92 (1869)).

198. *Id.* at 420 (quoting CONG. GLOBE, 41st Cong., 2d Sess. 515 (1870)).

199. *Id.* at 451 (quoting CONG. GLOBE, 41st Cong., 2d Sess. app. 473 (1870)).

200. *Id.* at 472 (quoting H.R. REP. NO. 37, 41st Cong., 3rd Sess. 4 (1871)).

201. JAMES A. GARFIELD, THE WORKS OF JAMES ABRAM GARFIELD 397 (Burke A. Hinsdale, ed., Books for Libraries Press 1970) (1882).

202. 7 RICHARDSON, *supra* note 44, Ch. 2 at 127.

203. *Id.*

204. These events were discussed in Jett v. Dallas Independent School Dist., 491 U.S. 701, 722 (1989) (plurality).

205. *See, e.g.,* DEBATES, *supra* note 17, Ch. 2 at 485–89, 499–500 (quoting CONG. GLOBE, 42d Cong., 1st Sess. 155–60, 166, 320–21 (1871)).

206. *Id.* at 489 (quoting CONG. GLOBE, 42d Cong., 1st Sess. 173 (1871)).

207. *Id.* at 484 (quoting CONG. GLOBE, 42d Cong., 1st Sess. 130 (1871)).

208. *Id.* at 491 (quoting CONG. GLOBE, 42d Cong., 1st Sess. 197 (1871)).

209. *Id.* at 492 (quoting CONG. GLOBE, 42d Cong., 1st Sess. 210 (1871)).

210. *Id.* (quoting CONG. GLOBE, 42d Cong., 1st Sess. 222 (1871)).

211. *Id.* (quoting CONG. GLOBE, 42d Cong., 1st Sess. 236 (1871)).

212. *See id.* at xxii.

213. *Id.* at 493–94 (quoting CONG. GLOBE, 42d Cong., 1st Sess. app. 68–69 (1871)).

214. *Id.* at 493 (quoting CONG. GLOBE, 42d Cong., 1st Sess. app. 68 (1871)).

215. *See id.*

216. *Id.* at 494 (quoting CONG. GLOBE, 42d Cong., 1st Sess. app. 69 (1871)).

217. *Id.*

218. *See id.* at 494–95 (quoting CONG. GLOBE, 42d Cong., 1st Sess. app. 69–70 (1871)); *supra note* 139 and accompanying text.

219. DEBATES, *supra* note 17, Ch. 2 at xxii, 496–97 (quoting CONG. GLOBE, 42d Cong., 1st Sess. app. 47–48 (1871)).

220. *Id.* at 497–98 (quoting CONG. GLOBE, 42d Cong., 1st Sess. app. 47–48 (1871)).

221. *Id.* at 498 (quoting CONG. GLOBE, 42d Cong., 1st Sess. app. 48–49 (1871)).

222. *Id.* (quoting CONG. GLOBE, 42d Cong., 1st Sess. app. 50 (1871)).

223. *See id.* at 499–500 (quoting CONG. GLOBE, 42d Cong., 1st Sess. 320–21 (1871)).

224. *Id.* at 501 (quoting CONG. GLOBE, 42d Cong., 1st Sess. 322 (1871)).

225. *Id.*

226. *See id.* (quoting CONG. GLOBE, 42d Cong., 1st Sess. 332–33 (1871)).

227. *Id.* (quoting CONG. GLOBE, 42d Cong., 1st Sess. 334 (1871)).

228. *See id.* at 501–02 (quoting CONG. GLOBE, 42d Cong., 1st Sess. 334 (1871)).

229. *See id.* at 503 (quoting CONG. GLOBE, 42d Cong., 1st Sess. app. 73 (1871)).

230. *See id.* (quoting CONG. GLOBE, 42d Cong., 1st Sess. app. 310 (1871)); *supra* note 101, Ch. 3.B.6 and accompanying text.

231. DEBATES, *supra* note 17, Ch. 2 at 503 (quoting CONG. GLOBE, 42d Cong., 1st Sess. app. 310 (1871)).

232. *Id.* at 532 (quoting CONG. GLOBE, 42d Cong., 1st Sess. 448 (1871)).

233. *See id.* at 512 (quoting CONG. GLOBE, 42d Cong., 1st Sess. app. 78 (1871)).

234. *See id.* at xxiii, 514 (quoting CONG. GLOBE, 42d Cong., 1st Sess. 370 (1871)).

235. *See id.* at xxiii, 516 (quoting CONG. GLOBE, 42d Cong., 1st Sess. 374–75 (1871)).

236. *Id.* at 518 (quoting CONG. GLOBE, 42d Cong., 1st Sess. 393 (1871)).

237. *Id.* at 524–25 (quoting CONG. GLOBE, 42d Cong., 1st Sess. app. 251 (1871)).

238. *Id.* at 525 (quoting CONG. GLOBE, 42d Cong., 1st Sess. app. 252 (1871)).

239. *See id.* at 502 (quoting CONG. GLOBE, 42d Cong., 1st Sess. 337 (1871)).

240. *See id.* at 514–15 (quoting CONG. GLOBE, 42d Cong., 1st Sess. 373, app. 139 (1871)).

241. *See id.* at 515 (quoting CONG. GLOBE, 42d Cong., 1st Sess. app. 87 (1871)).

242. *See id.* at 520 (quoting CONG. GLOBE, 42d Cong., 1st Sess. 396 (1871)).

243. *Id.* at 515 (quoting CONG. GLOBE, 42d Cong., 1st Sess. app. 87 (1871)).

244. *See id.* at xxiv, 522 (quoting CONG. GLOBE, 42d Cong., 1st Sess. 429–31 (1871)).

245. *Id.* at 533 (quoting CONG. GLOBE, 42d Cong., 1st Sess. app. 304 (1871)).

246. SAMUEL S. COX, THREE DECADES OF FEDERAL LEGISLATION 257 (Books for

Libraries Press 1970) (1885). Cox asserted the following about the Fourteenth Amendment:

> This amendment introduced into the organic law a principle so abhorrent to liberty and justice, that from time immemorial it had been regarded by the American people and their ancestors as one of the vilest which could be resorted to, under the worst forms of tyranny. . . . It is a warning to succeeding generations of the excesses of partisan lust. It is the highest glory that any party can claim, that it opposed with all its might, this amendment that is so obnoxious to every other feature of our government.

Id.

247. DEBATES, *supra* note 17, Ch. 2 at 534 (quoting CONG. GLOBE, 42d Cong., 1st Sess. 455 (1871)).

248. *See id.* at 518–19 (quoting CONG. GLOBE, 42d Cong., 1st Sess. app. 208–09 (1871)).

249. *See id.* at 523 (quoting CONG. GLOBE, 42d Cong., 1st Sess. app. 117–18 (1871)).

250. *See supra* note 69, Ch. 3.D.3 and accompanying text.

251. *See* DEBATES, *supra* note 17, Ch. 2 at xxiii, 504–05 (quoting CONG. GLOBE, 42d Cong., 1st Sess. app. 113–14 (1871)).

252. *See id.* at 570 (quoting CONG. GLOBE, 42d Cong., 1st Sess. 808 (1871)).

253. *See id.* at 516 (quoting CONG. GLOBE, 42d Cong., 1st Sess. app. 112 (1871)).

254. *Id.* at 517 (quoting CONG. GLOBE, 42d Cong., 1st Sess. 382 (1871)).

255. *Id.*

256. *See id.* (quoting CONG. GLOBE, 42d Cong., 1st Sess. 383 (1871)).

257. *See* GILLETTE, *supra* note 46, Ch. 2 at 52 ("I have never suffered more perplexity of mind, on any matter of legislation, than on that we are now attempting, concerning the Ku Klux. We are working on the very verge of the Constitution, and many of our members are breaking over the lines, and, it seems to me, exposing us, to the double danger, of having our work overthrown by the Supreme Court and of giving the Democrats new material for injuring us, on the stump.") (letter from Garfield to Burke A. Hinsdale).

258. *See* DEBATES, *supra* note 17, Ch. 2 at 526 (quoting CONG. GLOBE, 42d Cong., 1st Sess. app. 149 (1871)).

259. *Id.* at 526–27 (quoting CONG. GLOBE, 42d Cong., 1st Sess. app. 150–51 (1871)).

260. *See id.* at 527 (quoting CONG. GLOBE, 42d Cong., 1st Sess. app. 209 (1871)).

261. *See id.* (quoting CONG. GLOBE, 42d Cong., 1st Sess. app. 151 (1871)). Such statements could have referred to a variety of issues other than life and property, including the right to vote, generally a matter of greater attention from that time through the Fifteenth Amendment's passage.

262. *Id.* at 528 (quoting CONG. GLOBE, 42d Cong., 1st Sess. app. 152 (1871)).

263. *Id.*

264. *See also id.* at 528–29 (quoting CONG. GLOBE, 42d Cong., 1st Sess. app. 152–53 (1871)).

265. *Id.* at 529 (quoting CONG. GLOBE, 42d Cong., 1st Sess. app. 153 (1871)).

266. *Id.*

267. *Id.*

268. *Id.*

269. *See id.*

270. *See id.* at 529–30 (quoting CONG. GLOBE, 42d Cong., 1st Sess. app. 153–54 (1871)).

271. *Id.* at 530 (quoting CONG. GLOBE, 42d Cong., 1st Sess. app. 154 (1871)).

272. *See id.* at 570 (quoting CONG. GLOBE, 42d Cong., 1st Sess. 808 (1871)).

273. *See id.* at xxiv, 536 (quoting CONG. GLOBE, 42d Cong., 1st Sess. 477 (1871)).

274. *Id.* at 536 (quoting CONG. GLOBE, 42d Cong., 1st Sess. 478 (1871)).

275. *See id.* at 237–38 (quoting CONG. GLOBE, 39th Cong., 1st Sess. 3149 (1866)) (recording House votes on the Fourteenth Amendment); *id.* at xxiv, 538 (quoting CONG. GLOBE, 42d Cong., 1st Sess. 485 (1871)).

276. *Id.* at 538–39 (quoting CONG. GLOBE, 42d Cong., 1st Sess. 485 (1871)).

277. *Id.* at 538 (quoting CONG. GLOBE, 42d Cong., 1st Sess. 485 (1871)).

278. *See id.*

279. *Id.* at 539 (quoting CONG. GLOBE, 42d Cong., 1st Sess. 486 (1871)).

280. *Id.* at xxiv, 539–40 (quoting CONG. GLOBE, 42d Cong., 1st Sess. app. 187–88 (1871)).

281. *Id.* at 540 (quoting CONG. GLOBE, 42d Cong., 1st Sess. app. 189 (1871)).

282. *See id.* at xxiv, 544–46 (quoting CONG. GLOBE, 42d Cong., 1st Sess. app. 313–15 (1871)).

283. *See id.* at 545 (quoting CONG. GLOBE, 42d Cong., 1st Sess. app. 314 (1871)).

284. *Id.*

285. *Id.* (quoting CONG. GLOBE, 42d Cong., 1st Sess. app. 315 (1871)).

286. *Id.*

287. *Id.* at 546 (quoting CONG. GLOBE, 42d Cong., 1st Sess. app. 315 (1871)).

288. *Id.*

289. *See id.* (quoting CONG. GLOBE, 42d Cong., 1st Sess. 514 (1871)).

290. *See id.*

291. *See id.* at xxiv, 547 (quoting CONG. GLOBE, 42d Cong., 1st Sess. 522 (1871)). Note that Farnsworth would not vote for the Ku Klux Klan Act in its final form, which included additional revision beyond the scope of this study. *See id.* at 570 (quoting CONG. GLOBE, 42d Cong., 1st Sess. 808 (1871)).

292. *Id.* at xxiv, 547 (quoting CONG. GLOBE, 42d Cong., 1st Sess. 567 (1871)). *See also id.* at 562 (quoting CONG. GLOBE, 42d Cong., 1st Sess. 696 (1871)) ("If you wish to employ the powers of the Constitution to preserve the lives and liberties of white people against attacks by white people, against rapine and murder and assassination and conspiracy, . . . contrived in order to deprive them of the liberty of having a political opinion, contrived for the purpose of driving them from a city or town where they have endeavored to carry on a peaceable and lawful business or to cultivate the soil, then the whole strength of the Democratic party and all its allies is arrayed against the constitutionality and propriety of such an act.").

293. *See id.* at 548 (quoting CONG. GLOBE, 42d Cong., 1st Sess. 568 (1871)).

294. *See id.* at 562–63 (quoting CONG. GLOBE, 42d Cong., 1st Sess. 696–97 (1871)).

295. *Id.* at 551 (quoting CONG. GLOBE, 42d Cong., 1st Sess. 578–79 (1871)).

296. *Id.* at xxiv, 551 (quoting CONG. GLOBE, 42d Cong., 1st Sess. 578–80 (1871)).

297. *See id.* at 563, 570 (quoting CONG. GLOBE, 42d Cong., 1st Sess. 709, 831 (1871)).

298. *See id.* at 551 (quoting CONG. GLOBE, 42d Cong., 1st Sess. 580 (1871)).

299. *See id.* at 552 (quoting CONG. GLOBE, 42d Cong., 1st Sess. app. 243 (1871)).

300. *See id.* at xxv, 554–56 (quoting CONG. GLOBE, 42d Cong., 1st Sess. app. 217–19 (1871)). Thurman later stated he would not vote for the bill because Section 2 applied to state and not merely federal laws. *See id.* at 570 (quoting CONG. GLOBE, 42d Cong., 1st Sess. 822 (1871)).

301. *See id.* at xxv, 555–56 (quoting CONG. GLOBE, 42d Cong., 1st Sess. app. 218–19 (1871)).

302. *Id.* at 559–60 (quoting CONG. GLOBE, 42d Cong., 1st Sess. 661–62 (1871)).

303. *See id.* at xxv, 563 (quoting CONG. GLOBE, 42d Cong., 1st Sess. 709 (1871)). In the vote on the final version of the bill, Trumbull and Schurz were recorded as absent rather than voting no. *See id.* at 570 (quoting CONG. GLOBE, 42d Cong., 1st Sess. 831 (1871)).

304. *See* Frantz, *supra* note 75, Ch. 2 at 1358 (describing the minority "consisting almost exclusively of Democrats" who maintained " 'that congressional power was limited to the elimination of unequal laws and the correction of official or state action alone' " (quoting ROBERT J. HARRIS, THE QUEST FOR EQUALITY 45 (1960))).

305. These three other legislators were Rep. John Lynch, Rep. Oakes Ames, and Senator William Sprague. Senator Lot M. Morrill was recorded as absent during the first vote on the bill but voted for it when it was approved by the Senate. *See* DEBATES, *supra* note 17, Ch. 2 at 547, 563, 570 (quoting CONG. GLOBE, 42d Cong., 1st Sess. 522, 709, 808, 831 (1871)).

306. *See id.* at 460, 463 (quoting CONG. GLOBE, 41st Cong., 2d Sess. 3809, 3884 (1871)).

307. *See* Alfred Avins, *The Ku Klux Klan Act of 1871: Some Reflected Light on State Action and the Fourteenth Amendment*, 11 ST. LOUIS U. L.J. 331, 380 (1967).

308. *See id.* at 377–81.

309. *Supra* note 241, Ch. 3.B.6 and accompanying text.

310. *See supra* notes 12–13, 37, Ch. 3.B.6 and accompanying text.

311. *See supra* note 59, Ch. 3.B.6 and accompanying text.

312. Rep. William S. Holman asserted at one point during the House debates,

No attempt has been made by the friends of this bill to draw a line of demarkation between the powers of the Federal Government and those of the States in regard to legislation affecting life, liberty, and property. It is manifest the gentlemen recognize no such limit. I have heard no attempt to define the limit between Federal and State jurisdiction.

DEBATES, *supra* note 17, Ch. 2 at 535 (quoting CONG. GLOBE, 42d Cong., 1st Sess. app. 260 (1871)).

313. *See id.* at xxv–xxvi, 577 (quoting CONG. GLOBE, 42d Cong., 2d Sess. 244 (1871)).

314. *Id.* at 575 (quoting CONG. GLOBE, 42d Cong., 2d Sess. 242 (1871)).

315. *See id.* at 579 (quoting CONG. GLOBE, 42d Cong., 2d Sess. 279–80 (1871)).

316. *Id.* (quoting CONG. GLOBE, 42d Cong., 2d Sess. 280 (1872)).

317. *Id.* (quoting CONG. GLOBE, 42d Cong., 2d Sess. 382 (1872)).

318. *See id.* at 580 (quoting CONG. GLOBE, 42d Cong., 2d Sess. 383 (1872)).

319. *See id.* at xxvi, 580 (quoting CONG. GLOBE, 42d Cong., 2d Sess. 383 (1872)).

320. *Id.* at 586 (quoting CONG. GLOBE, 42d Cong., 2d Sess. 492 (1872)).

321. *Id.*

322. *Id.* at 582 (quoting CONG. GLOBE, 42d Cong., 2d Sess. 386 (1872)).

323. *See id.* at 626–27 (quoting CONG. GLOBE, 42d Cong., 2d Sess. app. 41–44 (1872)).

324. *See id.* at xxvi, 586–87 (quoting CONG. GLOBE, 42d Cong., 2d Sess. 494, 496 (1872)).

325. *See id.* at 620–21 (quoting CONG. GLOBE, 42d Cong., 2d Sess. app. 28–29 (1872)).

326. *Id.* at 587 (quoting CONG. GLOBE, 42d Cong., 2d Sess. 524–25 (1872)).

327. *Id.* at 588 (quoting CONG. GLOBE, 42d Cong., 2d Sess. 525 (1872)).

328. *Id.*

329. *See id.* at 588–89 (quoting CONG. GLOBE, 42d Cong., 2d Sess. 526–27 (1872)).

330. *Id.* at 589 (quoting CONG. GLOBE, 42d Cong., 2d Sess. 527 (1872)).

331. *See id.* at xxvi, 603 (quoting CONG. GLOBE, 42d Cong., 2d Sess. 764 (1872)).

332. *Id.* at 586 (quoting CONG. GLOBE, 42d Cong., 2d Sess. 436 (1872)).

333. *See id.* at xxvi, 585–86, 589 (quoting CONG. GLOBE, 42d Cong., 2d Sess. 435–36, 530–31 (1872)).

334. *See id.* at xxvi, 590 (quoting CONG. GLOBE, 42d Cong., 2d Sess. app. 1 (1872)); *id.* at 69 (quoting CONG. GLOBE, 38th Cong., 1st Sess. 1490 (1864)) (recording Senate votes on the Thirteenth Amendment); *id.* at 237–38 (quoting CONG. GLOBE, 39th Cong., 1st Sess. 3042 (1866)) (recording Senate votes on the Fourteenth Amendment).

335. *See id.* at xxvi, 590–91 (quoting CONG. GLOBE, 42d Cong., 2d Sess. 435–36, app. 2–3 (1872)).

336. *Id.* at 591 (quoting CONG. GLOBE, 42d Cong., 2d Sess. app. 3 (1872)).

337. *Id.*

338. *Id.*

339. *See id.* at xxvi, 591–92 (quoting CONG. GLOBE, 42d Cong., 2d Sess. app. 3–4 (1872)).

340. *Id.* at 593 (quoting CONG. GLOBE, 42d Cong., 2d Sess. app. 5 (1872)).

341. *Id.* at 597 (quoting CONG. GLOBE, 42d Cong., 2d Sess. 728 (1872)). *See also id.* at 622 (quoting CONG. GLOBE, 42d Cong., 2d Sess. 872 (1872)) ("Congress has plenary power to bring all the legislation of this country in harmony with the national Constitution, especially since the recent amendments. . . . Therefore in abolishing slavery Congress must, would it complete its work, abolish all the offshoots of slavery, all that grows out of slavery.").

342. *See id.* at xxvi, 599 (quoting CONG. GLOBE, 42d Cong., 2d Sess. 730 (1872)).

343. *Id.* at xxvi, 600 (quoting CONG. GLOBE, 42d Cong., 2d Sess. 731 (1872)).

344. *Id.* (quoting CONG. GLOBE, 42d Cong., 2d Sess. 759 (1872)).

345. *See id.* at 601 (quoting CONG. GLOBE, 42d Cong., 2d Sess. 760 (1872)).

346. *Id.* (quoting CONG. GLOBE, 42d Cong., 2d Sess. 761 (1872)).

347. *See id.* at xxvi, 602 (quoting CONG. GLOBE, 42d Cong., 2d Sess. 762 (1872)).

348. *See id.* at xxvii, 614–16 (quoting CONG. GLOBE, 42d Cong., 2d Sess. 843–45 (1872)). Sherman included in his discussion access to public inns and the right to travel on public highways. The Fourteenth Amendment, he felt, "was passed for the express purpose of correcting" the failure of the original Privileges and Immunities Clause to provide congressional power to enforce the privileges and immunities of citizenship. *Id.* at 615 (quoting CONG. GLOBE, 42d Cong., 2d Sess. 844 (1872)).

349. *See id.* at xxvii, 624 (quoting CONG. GLOBE, 42d Cong., 2d Sess. 893 (1872)).

350. *Id.* at 624 (quoting CONG. GLOBE, 42d Cong., 2d Sess. 893 (1872)).

351. *See id.* at xxvii, 624–25 (quoting CONG. GLOBE, 42d Cong., 2d Sess. 893–94 (1872)).

352. *Id.* at 625 (quoting CONG. GLOBE, 42d Cong., 2d Sess. 895 (1872)).

353. *Id.* at 630 (quoting CONG. GLOBE, 42d Cong., 2d Sess. 913–14 (1872)).

354. *See id.* (quoting CONG. GLOBE, 42d Cong., 2d Sess. 919 (1872)); *id.* at 238 (quoting CONG. GLOBE, 39th Cong., 1st Sess. 3149 (1866)).

355. *See id.* at 630 (quoting CONG. GLOBE, 42d Cong., 2d Sess. 919 (1872)); *id.* at 237–38 (quoting CONG. GLOBE, 39th Cong., 1st Sess. 3042, 3149 (1866)) (recording Senate and House votes on the Fourteenth Amendment).

356. *See id.* at xxvii, 631 (quoting CONG. GLOBE, 42d Cong., 2d Sess. 928–29 (1872)); McConnell I, *supra* note 36, Ch. 1 at 1055.

357. DEBATES, *supra* note 17, Ch. 2 at xxvi, 575 (quoting CONG. GLOBE, 42d Cong., 2d Sess. 242 (1871)). *See also id.* at 579 (quoting CONG. GLOBE, 42d Cong., 2d Sess. 381 (1872)).

358. *Id.* at 579 (quoting CONG. GLOBE, 42d Cong., 2d Sess. 382 (1872)).

359. *Id.*

360. *Id.* at xxvi, 593 (quoting CONG. GLOBE, 42d Cong., 2d Sess. app. 9 (1872)).

361. *Id.* at 608 (quoting CONG. GLOBE, 42d Cong., 2d Sess. 819 (1872)).

362. *Id.* at 621 (quoting CONG. GLOBE, 42d Cong., 2d Sess. app. 29 (1872)).

363. *Id.* at 608 (quoting CONG. GLOBE, 42d Cong., 2d Sess. 819–20 (1872)).

364. *See id.* at xxviii, 631 (quoting CONG. GLOBE, 42d Cong., 2d Sess. 1116 (1872)).

365. *See id.* at 632 (quoting CONG. GLOBE, 42d Cong., 2d Sess. app. 142 (1872)).

366. *See* CONG. GLOBE, 42d Cong., 2d Sess. 372 (1872).

367. *See* DEBATES, *supra* note 17, Ch. 2 at xxviii, 635 (quoting CONG. GLOBE, 42d Cong., 2d Sess. 219 (1872)).

368. *See id.* at 635 (quoting CONG. GLOBE, 42d Cong., 2d Sess. app. 383 (1872)).

369. *See id.* at 631–32 (quoting CONG. GLOBE, 42d Cong., 2d Sess. app. 142, 144 (1872)).

370. *See id.* at 634 (quoting CONG. GLOBE, 42d Cong., 2d Sess. app. 217 (1872)).

371. *See id.* at xxviii, 641–42 (quoting CONG. GLOBE, 42d Cong., 2d Sess. 3189–91 (1872)).

372. *See id.* at xxviii, 642–43 (quoting CONG. GLOBE, 42d Cong., 2d Sess. 3191–92 (1872)).

373. *See id.* at 644 (quoting CONG. GLOBE, 42d Cong., 2d Sess. 3195 (1872)).

374. *Id.* at 649 (quoting CONG. GLOBE, 42d Cong., 2d Sess. 3264 (1872)).

375. *See id.* at 647 (quoting CONG. GLOBE, 42d Cong., 2d Sess. 3261 (1872)).

376. *See id.* at 648 (quoting CONG. GLOBE, 42d Cong., 2d Sess. 3261 (1872)).

377. *See id.* at xxviii, 649 (quoting CONG. GLOBE, 42d Cong., 2d Sess. 3264–65 (1872)); McConnell I, *supra* note 36, Ch. 1 at 1055, 1057.

378. *See* DEBATES, *supra* note 17, Ch. 2 at xxviii, 650–51 (quoting CONG. GLOBE, 42d Cong., 2d Sess. 3266–67 (1872)).

379. *See id.* at xxviii, 651–52 (quoting CONG. GLOBE, 42d Cong., 2d Sess. 3267–68, 3270 (1872)); McConnell I, *supra* note 36, Ch. 1 at 1057.

380. *See* McConnell I, *supra* note 36, Ch. 1 at 1058.

381. *See* DEBATES, *supra* note 17, Ch. 2 at xxviii.

382. *See id.* at xxviii, 652 (quoting CONG. GLOBE, 42d Cong., 2d Sess. 3261 (1872)).

383. *Id.* at 655 (quoting CONG. GLOBE, 42d Cong., 2d Sess. 3733 (1872)).

384. *See id.* (quoting CONG. GLOBE, 42d Cong., 2d Sess. 3735 (1872)).

385. *See id.* at xxviii, 654–55 (quoting CONG. GLOBE, 42d Cong., 2d Sess. 3730, 3735–38 (1872)); McConnell I, *supra* note 36, Ch. 1 at 1059–60.

386. *See* McConnell I, *supra* note 36, Ch. 1 at 1060 (citing CONG. GLOBE, 42d Cong., 2d Sess. 3932, 4322 (1872)).

387. 7 RICHARDSON, *supra* note 44, Ch. 2 at 221.

388. *Id.* at 255.

389. *See* DEBATES, *supra* note 17, Ch. 2 at xxix; McConnell I, *supra* note 36, Ch. 1 at 1063.

390. *See* McConnell I, *supra* note 36, Ch. 1 at 1063.

391. *See* DEBATES, *supra* note 17, Ch. 2 at 657 (quoting 2 CONG. REC. 340 (1873)).

392. *Id.* (quoting 2 CONG. REC. 341 (1873)).

393. *See id.* at xxix, 661 (quoting 2 CONG. REC. 408–09 (1874)).

394. *See id.* at xxix, 662 (quoting 2 CONG. REC. 412 (1874)).

395. *See id.* at xxix, 663 (quoting 2 CONG. REC. 414 (1874)).

396. *Id.* at xxix, 662 (quoting 2 CONG. REC. 412 (1874)).

397. *Id.* at 663 (quoting 2 CONG. REC. 413 (1874)).

398. *Id.* at 665 (quoting 2 CONG. REC. 427 (1874)).

399. *Id.* at 670 (quoting 2 CONG. REC. 566 (1874)).

400. *See id.* at 657 (quoting 2 CONG. REC. 342 (1873)).

401. *See id.* at xxix, 660 (quoting 2 CONG. REC. 384–85 (1874)).

402. *See id.* (quoting 2 CONG. REC. 405 (1874)).

403. *See id.* at 663 (quoting 2 CONG. REC. 415 (1874)).

404. *See id.* at 671 (quoting 2 CONG. REC. 741 (1874)).

405. *See id.* at 667 (quoting 2 CONG. REC. 454 (1874)) ("The fourteenth amendment only makes an inhibition on the States; but this bill empowers Congress to disregard the State and invade the domain of the people, and operate by its pen-

alties, through Federal courts upon individuals directly, although the State may have observed strictly the inhibition.").

406. *See id.* at 664 (quoting 2 CONG. REC. 421 (1874)).

407. *See id.* at 666 (quoting 2 CONG. REC. 429 (1874)).

408. *See id.* at 668 (quoting 2 CONG. REC. app. 2 (1874)).

409. *Id.* at 666 (quoting 2 CONG. REC. 428 (1874)).

410. *See id.* at 667 (quoting 2 CONG. REC. 453–54 (1874)).

411. *See id.* at 671 (quoting 2 CONG. REC. 945 (1874)).

412. *See id.* at xxix.

413. *Id.* at 673 (quoting 2 CONG. REC. 3452 (1874)).

414. *Id.* at 674 (quoting 2 CONG. REC. 3453 (1874)).

415. *Id.*

416. *See id.* (quoting 2 CONG. REC. 3453–54 (1874)).

417. *Id.* (quoting 2 CONG. REC. 3454 (1874) (citing Slaughter-House Cases, 83 U.S. (16 Wall.) 36, 81 (1873))).

418. *See id.* at 675 (quoting 2 CONG. REC. 3454 (1874)).

419. *See id.* at xxx, 677 (quoting 2 CONG. REC. 4081–82 (1874)).

420. *Id.* (quoting 2 CONG. REC. app. 244 (1874)).

421. *See id.* at 677–78 (quoting 2 CONG. REC. 4083–84 (1874)).

422. *See id.* at 678 (quoting 2 CONG. REC. 4084–85 (1874)).

423. *Id.* at xxx, 683 (quoting 2 CONG. REC. app. 358 (1874)).

424. *Id.*

425. *See id.* at 684 (quoting 2 CONG. REC. app. 360 (1874)).

426. *Id.* at 685 (quoting 2 CONG. REC. app. 360–61 (1874)).

427. *See id.* at 687 (quoting 2 CONG. REC. 4144 (1874)).

428. *Id.* at 688 (quoting 2 CONG. REC. 4147–48 (1874)). *See also id.* at 237 (quoting CONG. GLOBE, 39th Cong., 1st Sess. 3042 (1866)) (recording Senate votes on the Fourteenth Amendment).

429. *Id.* (quoting 2 CONG. REC. 4150 (1874)).

430. *See id.* at xxx, 689–90 (quoting 2 CONG. REC. app. 304–05 (1874)).

431. *Id.* at 690 (quoting 2 CONG. REC. 306 (1874)).

432. *See id.* at xxx.

433. *Id.* at 692 (quoting 2 CONG. REC. 4156 (1874)).

434. *See id.* at xxx, 695–96 (quoting 2 CONG. REC. app. 313, 315 (1874)).

435. *See id.* at 697, 701 (quoting 2 CONG. REC. app. 361–62, 367 (1874)).

436. *See id.* at 706 (quoting 2 CONG. REC. 4172–73 (1874)).

437. *See id.* at xxx, 707 (quoting 2 CONG. REC. 4174–75 (1874)).

438. *See id.* at 708 (quoting 2 CONG. REC. 4176 (1874)).

439. *See id.* at 708–09 (quoting 2 CONG. REC. app. 342–43 (1874)).

440. *See id.* at 710 (quoting 2 CONG. REC. 4592–93 (1874)).

441. *Id.* at xxxi, 711 (quoting 2 CONG. REC. 4782–85 (1874)).

442. *See id.* at xxxi, 712 (quoting 2 CONG. REC. app. 478 (1874)).

443. *See id.* at xxxi.

444. *See id.* at 715 (quoting 3 CONG. REC. 944 (1875)).

445. *Id.* at 716–17 (quoting 3 CONG. REC. 947–49 (1875)).

446. *See id.* at 717 (quoting 3 CONG. REC. app. 119 (1875)).

447. *See id.* at 717–18 (quoting 3 CONG. REC. app. 119, 157 (1875)).

448. *Id.* at 720 (quoting 3 CONG. REC. 952 (1875)).

449. *See id.* at 238 (quoting CONG. GLOBE, 39th Cong., 1st Sess. 3149 (1866)) (recording House votes on the Fourteenth Amendment).

450. *Id.* at 722 (quoting 3 CONG. REC. 979 (1875)).

451. *Id.* at 723 (quoting 3 CONG. REC. 980 (1875)).

452. *See id.*

453. *Id.*

454. *See id.* at 731 (quoting 3 CONG. REC. 1011 (1875)).

455. In this category were Hezekiah S. Bundy, Henry Dawes, Garfield, Hale, Samuel Hooper, John A. Kasson, Kelley, Lawrence, Leonard Myers, Charles O'Neill, Godlove S. Orth, Philetus Sawyer, Glenni W. Scofield, and Poland, who had been a senator in 1866. Kasson and Lawrence were recorded as "not voting" in 1866. *See id.* at 237–38 (quoting CONG. GLOBE, 39th Cong., 1st Sess. 3042, 3149 (1866)); *id.* at 731 (quoting 3 CONG. REC. 1011 (1875)).

456. *See id.* at 237 (quoting CONG. GLOBE, 39th Cong., 1st Sess. 3042 (1866)); *id.* at 731 (quoting 3 CONG. REC. 1011 (1875)).

457. Charles A. Eldridge (whose name was recorded in the 43rd Congress as "Eldredge"), William Finck, William Niblack, and Samuel J. Randall all voted against both measures, and Samuel S. Marshall, who had voted against the Fourteenth Amendment, was recorded as "not voting" for the 1875 act. *See id.* at 238 (quoting CONG. GLOBE, 39th Cong., 1st Sess. 3149 (1866)); *id.* at 731 (quoting 3 CONG. REC. 1011 (1875)).

458. *See id.* at 731 (quoting 3 CONG. REC. 1792 (1875)).

459. *See id.* at 732 (quoting 3 CONG. REC. 1793 (1875)).

460. *See id.* at xxxii, 732–34 (quoting 3 CONG. REC. 1793–95 (1875)).

461. *Id.* at 733 (quoting 3 CONG. REC. 1794 (1875)).

462. *See id.* at 731–32, 734 (quoting 3 CONG. REC. 1792–93, 1795 (1875)).

463. *Id.* at 736 (quoting 3 CONG. REC. app. 103–04 (1875)).

464. *Id.* (quoting 3 CONG. REC. app. 105 (1875)).

465. *See supra* notes 153–54, Ch. 3.B.2 and accompanying text; McConnell I, *supra* note 36, Ch. 1 at 1004–05.

466. *See* DEBATES, *supra* note 17, Ch. 2 at xxxii, 737–38 (quoting 3 CONG. REC. 1862–63 (1875)).

467. *Id.* at 737 (quoting 3 CONG. REC. 1861 (1875)).

468. *See id.* at 740 (quoting 3 CONG. REC. 1865 (1875)).

469. *Id.* at 741 (quoting 3 CONG. REC. app. 113 (1875)).

470. *Id.* at 743 (quoting 3 CONG. REC. 1870 (1875)).

471. *Id.*

472. *Id.*

473. *See id.*

474. These fifteen senators (some of whom served in the House nine years earlier) were Henry B. Anthony, William B. Allison, Boutwell, Zachariah Chandler, Conkling, Aaron H. Cragin, Edmunds, Thomas W. Ferry, Howe, Justin S. Morrill, Alexander Ramsey, Sherman, Stewart, William B. Washburn, and William Windom. *See id.* at 237–38 (quoting CONG. GLOBE, 39th Cong., 1st Sess. 3042, 3149 (1866)); *id.* at 743 (quoting 3 CONG. REC. 1870 (1875)).

475. *See id.* at 743 (quoting 3 CONG. REC. 1870 (1875)).

476. *See id.* at 460 (quoting CONG. GLOBE, 41st Cong., 2d Sess. 3809 (1870)); *id.* at 570 (quoting CONG. GLOBE, 42d Cong., 1st Sess. 831 (1871)).

477. *See id.* at 660 (quoting 2 Cong. Rec. 405–06 (1874)).

478. *See id.* at 664 (quoting 2 Cong. Rec. 422 (1874)).

479. *See id.* at 667 (quoting 2 Cong. Rec. 454 (1874)).

480. *See id.* at 668 (quoting 2 Cong. Rec. app. 3 (1874)).

481. *See id.* at 669 (quoting 2 Cong. Rec. app. 4 (1874)).

482. *See id.* at 709 (quoting 2 Cong. Rec. app. 343 (1874)).

483. *See id.* at 710 (quoting 2 Cong. Rec. app. 419 (1874)).

484. *See id.* at 711 (quoting 2 Cong. Rec. 4784 (1874)).

485. *See id.* at 714, 730 (quoting 3 Cong. Rec. 940, 1006 (1875)).

486. *See id.* at 715 (quoting 3 Cong. Rec. 944 (1875)).

487. *See id.* at 722 (quoting 3 Cong. Rec. 960 (1875)).

488. *See id.* at 730 (quoting 3 Cong. Rec. 1003 (1875)).

489. *See id.* at 673 (quoting 2 Cong. Rec. 3451 (1874)).

490. *See id.* at 677 (quoting 2 Cong. Rec. 4082 (1874)).

491. *See* 7 Supreme Court History, *supra* note 3, Ch. 2 at 569–82; Whiteside, *supra* note 128, Ch. 2 at 283.

492. 7 Supreme Court History, *supra* note 3, Ch. 2 at 571 (quoting N.Y. Times, Oct. 18, 1883, at 4).

493. Westin, *supra* note 20, Ch. 3.D.2 at 682 (quoting N.Y. Times, Nov. 19, 1883, at 41).

494. *Id.*

495. *See* Beth, *supra* note 20, Ch. 3.D.2 at 228.

496. *Id.* at 231.

497. 15 Cong. Rec. 135 (1883).

498. *Id.*

499. James G. Blaine, Twenty Years of Congress: From Lincoln to Garfield 419 (Norwich, Henry Bill Publishing Co. 1886).

500. *Id.* at 419–20.

501. Charles A. Lofgren, The Plessy Case: A Legal-Historical Interpretation 251 n.21 (1987).

502. *See* Whiteside, *supra* note 128, Ch. 2 at 283.

503. 4 Douglass, *supra* note 2, Epigraph at 340–41.

504. 5 Douglass, *supra* note 2, Epigraph at 118. *See also id.* at 121 ("What does it matter to a colored citizen that a State may not insult and outrage him, if a citizen of a State may? The effect upon him is the same, and it was just this effect that the framers of the Fourteenth Amendment plainly intended by that article to prevent.").

505. John Hope Franklin, *Race and the Constitution in the Nineteenth Century,* *in* African Americans and the Living Constitution 30 (John Hope Franklin and Genna Rae McNeil, eds., 1995).

506. 7 Supreme Court History, *supra* note 3, Ch. 2 at 570.

507. *See* 118 U.S. 356, 374.

508. Avins seems to equate originalism with advocacy of the most conservative supporters of a constitutional amendment, but even if this premise were conceded, he does not provide sufficient evidence to prove his conclusions. *See* Alfred Avins, *The Civil Rights Act of 1875: Some Reflected Light on the Fourteenth Amendment and Public Accommodations*, 66 Colum. L. Rev. 873, 876 (1966) [hereinafter Avins, *Civil Rights Act of 1875*]. The author criticizes Harlan's opinion and calls

his application of the *Prigg* doctrine an error even though the case itself emerged several times during the debates. *Cf.* Alfred Avins, *What Is a Place of "Public" Accommodation?* 52 MARQ. L. REV. 1, 11 (1968) [hereinafter Avins, *Public Accommodation*]; *supra* notes 160–63, and accompanying text.

509. Avins, *Civil Rights Act of 1875, supra* note 508, Ch. 3 at 914.

510. *See id.* at 876.

511. *See, e.g.*, FLACK, *supra* note 94, Ch. 3.B.6 at 277 ("[N]early all the evidence goes to sustain the position of Congress as far as the question of power and authority is concerned. . . . [A]ccording to the purpose and intention of the Amendment as disclosed in the debates in Congress and in the several state Legislatures and in other ways, Congress had the constitutional power to enact direct legislation to secure the rights of citizens against violation by individuals as well as by States."); HARRIS, *supra* note 304, Ch. 3.D.3 at 53 ("[D]espite differences of opinion concerning the scope of congressional power under the amendment, a majority of the members of the Thirty-ninth, Forty-second, and Forty-third Congresses, some of whom were members of all three and of the Committee of Fifteen on Reconstruction, believed that the equal protection clause did more than condemn official or state action. They believed that it vested Congress at the very least with a primary power to set aside unequal state laws and a secondary power to afford protection to all persons in their enjoyment of constitutional rights when the states failed in their primary responsibility to do so either by neglecting to enact laws or by refusal or impotence to enforce them."); Frantz, *supra* note 75, Ch. 2 at 1353–54 ("[T]he consensus is almost as general" as the understanding of the effect of Supreme Court decisions of the 1870s and 1880s "that, whatever the original understanding may have been as to the new legislative powers being conferred on the Congress, it certainly did not correspond to this state-action-only formula.") (footnotes omitted); *id.* at 1381–82 ("The theory that congressional power to enforce the fourteenth amendment can deal only with 'state action' will not stand up. It is obviously at odds with the original understanding. Even if we are not certain precisely what the original understanding was, we know that it could not have been this.").

512. *See* Frantz, *supra* note 75, Ch. 2 at 1356.

513. *See id.* at 1355; Gressman, *supra* note 3, Ch. 2 at 1326, 1329–30.

514. *See* FLACK, *supra* note 94, Ch. 3.B.6 at 97, 271–72.

515. *Cf. id.* at 137 ("Whatever claim was made in regard to the second section of that Amendment applies with equal force to the fifth section of the Fourteenth Amendment.").

516. *Id.* at 139.

4. *Baldwin v. Franks*

1. 120 U.S. 678.

2. *Id.* at 680–82.

3. *See* 14 Stat. 27 (1870); 120 U.S. at 684.

4. *See* 120 U.S. at 684; 7 SUPREME COURT HISTORY, *supra* note 3, Ch. 2, at 495.

5. *See* 120 U.S. at 682–83.

6. *Id.* at 685.

7. *See id.* at 685–86.

8. *See id.* at 689–90.

9. *Id.* at 691–92. For a criticism of the Court's reading of this statute, see 7 SUPREME COURT HISTORY, *supra* note 3, Ch. 2 at 496–97.

10. 120 U.S. at 693.

11. *See* 7 SUPREME COURT HISTORY, *supra* note 3, Ch. 2 at 494.

12. *See* 120 U.S. at 701–07 (Field, J., dissenting).

13. *See id.* at 694–701 (Harlan, J., dissenting).

E. The Triumph of Segregation

1. *Louisville v. Mississippi*: Segregation and the Interstate Commerce Clause Revisited

1. 133 U.S. 587 (1890).

2. *See id.* at 588.

3. *See id.* at 589, 592.

4. *See id.* at 589.

5. *See id.* at 592.

6. *Id.* at 594–95 (Harlan, J., dissenting).

7. *Id.* at 594 (Harlan, J., dissenting).

8. *See id.* at 595; BETH, *supra* note 20, Ch. 3.D.2 at 232.

2. *Plessy v. Ferguson*

1. 163 U.S. 537 (1896).

2. *Id.* at 538, 540.

3. *Id.* at 542–43.

4. *Id.* at 544.

5. *Id.* at 545.

6. *Id.*

7. *Id.* at 547.

8. *Id.* at 548.

9. *See id.* at 260.

10. *Id.* at 550.

11. *See* McConnell I, *supra* note 36, Ch. 1 at 983–84.

12. 163 U.S. at 551–52.

13. *Id.* at 552.

14. *See id.* at 564.

15. *Id.* at 553 (Harlan, J., dissenting).

16. *Id.* at 554 (Harlan, J., dissenting).

17. *Id.* at 555 (Harlan, J., dissenting).

18. *See id.* at 556, 562–63 (Harlan, J., dissenting).

19. *Id.* at 557 (Harlan, J., dissenting).

20. *See id.* at 558–59 (Harlan, J., dissenting); *infra* note 4, Ch. 5 and accompanying text.

21. 163 U.S. at 559 (Harlan, J., dissenting).

22. *Id.* at 559–60 (Harlan, J., dissenting).

23. *Id.* at 560 (Harlan, J., dissenting).

24. *Id.* at 562 (Harlan, J., dissenting).

25. *Id.* at 560, 563 (Harlan, J., dissenting).

26. *See supra* Ch. 3.B.3.

27. *See* DEBATES, *supra* note 17, Ch. 2 at 60 (quoting CONG. GLOBE, 38th Cong., 1st Sess. 839 (1864)).

28. *See id.* at 133 (quoting CONG. GLOBE, 39th Cong., 1st Sess. 541 (1866)).

29. *See id.* at 378 (quoting CONG. GLOBE, 40th Cong., 3rd Sess. 1011 (1869)).

30. *Id.* at 553–54 (quoting CONG. GLOBE, 42d Cong., 1st Sess. app. 216–17 (1871)). *See also supra* note 362, Ch. 3.D.3.

31. *See supra* note 360, Ch. 3.D.3.

32. *See supra* note 361, Ch. 3.D.3.

33. DEBATES, *supra* note 17, Ch. 2 at 603 (quoting CONG. GLOBE, 42d Cong., 2d Sess. 764 (1872)).

34. *See id.* at 619 (quoting CONG. GLOBE, 42d Cong., 2d Sess. app. 27 (1872)).

35. *Id.* at 635 (quoting CONG. GLOBE, 42d Cong., 2d Sess. app. 383 (1872)).

36. *Id.* at 648 (quoting CONG. GLOBE, 42d Cong., 2d Sess. 3261 (1872)).

37. *Id.* at 656 (quoting CONG. GLOBE, 42d Cong., 2d Sess. app. 597 (1872)).

38. *Id.* (quoting CONG. GLOBE, 42d Cong., 2d Sess. app. 599 (1872)).

39. *Id.* at 632 (quoting CONG. GLOBE, 42d Cong., 2d Sess. app. 142 (1872)).

40. *Id.*

41. *Id.* at 648, 652 (quoting CONG. GLOBE, 42d Cong., 2d Sess. 3264, 3270 (1872)).

42. *Id.* at 659 (quoting 2 CONG. REC. 379 (1874)).

43. *Id.* at 660 (quoting 2 CONG. REC. 406 (1874)).

44. *Id.* at 666 (quoting 2 CONG. REC. 428 (1874)).

45. *Id.* at 667 (quoting 2 CONG. REC. 454 (1874)).

46. *Id.* at 668 (quoting 2 CONG. REC. app. 3 (1874)).

47. *Id.* at 669 (quoting 2 CONG. REC. app. 4 (1874)).

48. *See id.* (quoting 2 CONG. REC. 555 (1874)).

49. *Id.* at 709 (quoting 2 CONG. REC. app. 343 (1874)).

50. *Id.* at 710 (quoting 2 CONG. REC. app. 419 (1874)).

51. Alfred Avins concludes from the debates that the Fourteenth Amendment, under the original understanding, actually "guarantees, against state legislation or other state action, the right of private individuals and groups or clubs of any kind to refuse admission into their society to any person whom they find undesirable for any reason which seems sufficient to them." Alfred Avins, *Social Equality and the Fourteenth Amendment: The Original Understanding*, 4 HOUS. L. REV. 640, 656 (1967). In his view, a law against discrimination by a private club, "far from being an enforcement of the fourteenth amendment as originally understood, is a violation of this amendment as originally intended by its framers, for it constitutes the taking of liberty without due process of law." *Id.* Besides taking the Democratic theory of interpretation an analytical step beyond the opponents of Reconstruction, who did not cite the Due Process Clause for their views on the liberty of association, Avins' view finds little support from the framers of the Fourteenth Amendment and other supporters of Reconstruction.

52. DEBATES, *supra* note 17, Ch. 2 at 247 (quoting CONG. GLOBE, 39th Cong., 1st Sess. 3437 (1866)).

53. *Id.* Willey later called the charge of imposing social equality "the silliest of all pretensions, the silliest of all objections. Social equality is not a matter to be adjusted by law. It is a matter of taste; it is a matter of choice; it cannot be enforced by any legislation; it always regulates itself." *Id.* at 330 (quoting CONG. GLOBE, 40th Cong., 2d Sess. app. 337 (1868)).

54. Patterson was recorded as "not voting" when the final vote was taken on the amendment. *See id.* at 238 (quoting CONG. GLOBE, 39th Cong., 1st Sess. 3149 (1866)).

55. *Id.* at 296 (quoting CONG. GLOBE, 40th Cong., 2d Sess. 1409 (1868)).

56. *Id.* at 652 (quoting CONG. GLOBE, 42d Cong., 2d Sess. 3270 (1872)).

57. In his 1883 speech, Douglass had the following to say about the charge that the Civil Rights Act of 1875 was a "social rights bill":

Another illustration of this tendency to put opponents in a false position, is seen in the persistent effort to stigmatize the "Civil Rights Bill" as a "Social Rights Bill." Now, nowhere under the whole heavens, outside of the United States, could any such perversion of truth have any chance of success. . . . Social equality and civil equality rest upon an entirely different basis, and well enough the American people know it; yet to inflame a popular prejudice, respectable papers . . . persist in describing the Civil Rights Bill as a Social Rights Bill.

When a colored man is in the same room or in the same carriage with white people, as a servant, there is no talk of social equality, but if he is there as a man and a gentleman, he is an offence. . . . To say that because a man rides in the same car with another, he is therefore socially equal, is one of the wildest absurdities. . . .

. . . Equality, social equality, is a matter between individuals. . . . Social equality does not necessarily follow from civil equality, and yet for the purpose of a hell black and damning prejudice, our papers still insist that the Civil Rights Bill is a Bill to establish social equality.

5 DOUGLASS, *supra* note 2, Epigraph at 122–23 (footnote omitted). *See also* 4 DOUGLASS, *supra* note 2, Epigraph at 405 (questioning criticisms of the bill as a bill for social equality soon before its passage in 1875).

58. *Supra note* 387, Ch. 3.D.3 and accompanying text.

59. DEBATES, *supra* note 17, Ch. 2 at 658 (quoting 2 CONG. REC. 344 (1873)).

60. *Id.* at 659 (quoting 2 CONG. REC. 382 (1874)).

61. 3 CONG. REC. 957 (1875).

62. DEBATES, *supra* note 17, Ch. 2 at 670 (quoting 2 CONG. REC. 565 (1874)).

63. *Id.* at 671 (quoting 2 CONG. REC. 902 (1874)).

64. *Id.* at 665 (quoting 2 CONG. REC. 427 (1874)).

65. *Id.* at 673 (quoting 2 CONG. REC. 3451 (1874)).

66. *Id.* at 677 (quoting 2 CONG. REC. 4082 (1874)).

67. *Id.* at 714 (quoting 3 CONG. REC. 940 (1875)).

68. *Id. See also id.* at 730 (quoting 3 CONG. REC. 1006 (1875)).

69. *Id.* at 715 (quoting 3 CONG. REC. 944 (1875)).

70. *Id.*

71. *See id.* at 722 (quoting 3 CONG. REC. 960 (1875)).

72. *See id.* at 730 (quoting 3 CONG. REC. 1003 (1875)).

73. *See* McConnell I, *supra* note 36, Ch. 1 at 1028–29. On this issue, Avins again misses the point by extolling "[f]reedom of choice" in largely the same way that Democratic opponents of the Civil Rights Act of 1875 had. *See* Avins, *Public Accommodation, supra* note 508, Ch. 3.D.3 at 73.

74. *See* DEBATES, *supra* note 17, Ch. 2 at xv, 303–04 (quoting CONG. GLOBE, 40th Cong., 2d Sess. 1964 (1868) (citing 55 (5 P.F. Smith) Pa. St. 209 (1867))).

75. *See id.* at 301 (quoting CONG. GLOBE, 40th Cong., 2d Sess. 1959 (1868)).

76. *See id.* at 762, 238 (quoting CONG. GLOBE, 39th Cong., 1st Sess. 3149 (1866)).

77. *See id.* at 304 (quoting CONG. GLOBE, 40th Cong., 2d Sess. 1965 (1868)).

78. *See id.*

79. *Id.*

80. *Id.*

81. *See id.* at 301 (quoting CONG. GLOBE, 40th Cong., 2d Sess. 1959 (1868)).

82. *See id.* at 238 (quoting CONG. GLOBE, 39th Cong., 1st Sess. 3149 (1866)).

83. *See id.* at 65, 80 (quoting CONG. GLOBE, 38th Cong., 1st Sess. 1161, 3137 (1864)).

84. *See supra* notes 338–40, Ch. 3.D.3 and accompanying text; DEBATES, *supra* note 17, Ch. 2 at 592 (quoting CONG. GLOBE, 42d Cong., 2d Sess. app. 4 (1872)).

85. DEBATES, *supra* note 17, Ch. 2 at 592 (quoting CONG. GLOBE, 42d Cong., 2d Sess. app. 4 (1872)); *supra* note 339, Ch. 3.D.3 and accompanying text.

86. DEBATES, *supra* note 17, Ch. 2 at xxvii, 629 (quoting CONG. GLOBE, 42d Cong., 2d Sess. 901 (1872)).

87. *See id.* at 707 (2 CONG. REC. 4174 (1874)).

88. *See id.* at 710 (2 CONG. REC. 4593 (1874)).

89. *Id.* at 103 (quoting CONG. GLOBE, 39th Cong., 1st Sess. 205 (1866)).

90. *Id.* at 119 (quoting CONG. GLOBE, 39th Cong., 1st Sess. 431 (1866)).

91. *Id.* at 121 (quoting CONG. GLOBE, 39th Cong., 1st Sess. 474 (1866)). *See also id.* at 136 (quoting CONG. GLOBE, 39th Cong., 1st Sess. 599 (1866)).

92. *Id.* at 121 (quoting CONG. GLOBE, 39th Cong., 1st Sess. 474 (1866)).

93. *Id.* at 138 (quoting CONG. GLOBE, 39th Cong., 1st Sess. 603 (1866)). *See also id.* at 127 (quoting CONG. GLOBE, 39th Cong., 1st Sess. 500 (1866)) (asserting that "all State laws making discriminations are swept away" under the bill).

94. *Id.* at 127 (quoting CONG. GLOBE, 39th Cong., 1st Sess. 504 (1866)).

95. *See id.* at 128 (quoting CONG. GLOBE, 39th Cong., 1st Sess. 505 (1866)).

96. *Id.* at 143 (quoting CONG. GLOBE, 39th Cong., 1st Sess. 704 (1866)).

97. *Id.* at 192 (quoting CONG. GLOBE, 39th Cong., 1st Sess. 1415 (1866)).

98. *Id.* at 133 (quoting CONG. GLOBE, 39th Cong., 1st Sess. 537 (1866)).

99. *Id.* at 176 (quoting CONG. GLOBE, 39th Cong., 1st Sess. 1266 (1866)).

100. *Id.* at 186 (quoting CONG. GLOBE, 39th Cong., 1st Sess. 1291 (1866)). *See also id.* at 188 (quoting CONG. GLOBE, 39th Cong., 1st Sess. 1293 (1866)) (contending that the bill proposes "[t]o reform the whole civil and criminal code of every State government by declaring that there shall be no discrimination between citizens on account of race or color in civil rights or in the penalties prescribed by their laws").

101. *Id.* at 186 (quoting CONG. GLOBE, 39th Cong., 1st Sess. 1291 (1866)).

102. *Id.* at 191 (quoting CONG. GLOBE, 39th Cong., 1st Sess. 1296, 1366–67 (1866)).

103. *Id.* at 209 (quoting CONG. GLOBE, 39th Cong., 1st Sess. 1837 (1866)).

104. *See infra* notes 31–33, Ch. 4.B.2 and accompanying text.

105. *See e.g.*, ANTIEAU, *supra* note 70, Ch. 3.B.2. at 15 (statement of Indiana

Rep. Ross) (asserting that the Fourteenth Amendment "will repeal all our State laws making distinctions because of race or color"); *id*. at 19 (statement of Pennsylvania Rep. Jenks) ("By the first section [the Fourteenth Amendment] is intended to destroy every distinction founded upon a difference in the caste, nationality, race or color of persons who have been or may be born in and subject to the jurisdiction of the United States, which has found its way into the laws of the Federal or State Governments which regulate the civil relations or rights of the people.").

106. DEBATES, *supra* note 17, Ch. 2 at 277 (quoting CONG. GLOBE, 40th Cong., 1st Sess. 728 (1867)).

107. *Id*. at 284 (quoting CONG. GLOBE, 40th Cong., 2d Sess. 39 (1867)).

108. *Id*. at 304 (quoting CONG. GLOBE, 40th Cong., 2d Sess. 1966 (1868)).

109. *Id*. at 375 (quoting CONG. GLOBE, 40th Cong., 3rd Sess. 1008 (1869)).

110. *Id*. at 387 (quoting CONG. GLOBE, 40th Cong., 3rd Sess. 1039 (1869)).

111. *Id*. at 398 (quoting CONG. GLOBE, 40th Cong., 3rd Sess. 1303 (1869)).

112. *Id*. at 484 (quoting CONG. GLOBE, 42d Cong., 1st Sess. 21 (1871)).

113. *Id*. at 523 (quoting CONG. GLOBE, 42d Cong., 1st Sess. app. 117 (1871)).

114. *Id*. at 594 (quoting CONG. GLOBE, 42d Cong., 2d Sess. app. 10 (1872)).

115. *Id*. at 608 (quoting CONG. GLOBE, 42d Cong., 2d Sess. 819 (1872)).

116. *See id*. at 647 (quoting CONG. GLOBE, 42d Cong., 2d Sess. 3260 (1872)).

117. *Id*. at 716 (quoting 3 CONG. REC. 945 (1875)).

118. *Id*. at 725 (quoting 3 CONG. REC. 997 (1875)).

119. *See id*. at 740 (quoting 3 CONG. REC. 1865 (1875)).

120. *Id*. at 100 (quoting CONG. GLOBE, 39th Cong., 1st Sess. 174 (1866)).

121. *Id*. at 135 (quoting CONG. GLOBE, 39th Cong., 1st Sess. 589 (1866)).

122. *Id*. at 143 (quoting CONG. GLOBE, 39th Cong., 1st Sess. 704 (1866)).

123. *Id*. at 220 (quoting CONG. GLOBE, 39th Cong., 1st Sess. 2766 (1866)).

124. *See supra* note 55.

125. DEBATES, *supra* note 17, Ch. 2 at 296 (quoting CONG. GLOBE, 40th Cong., 2d Sess. 1409 (1868)).

126. *Id*. at 366 (quoting CONG. GLOBE, 40th Cong., 3rd Sess. app. 197 (1869)).

127. *Id*. at 621 (quoting CONG. GLOBE, 42d Cong., 2d Sess. 847 (1872)).

128. *Id*. at 683 (2 CONG. REC. app. 359 (1874)).

129. *Id*. at 711 (2 CONG. REC. app. 4785 (1874)).

130. *See id*. at 57, 63 (quoting CONG. GLOBE, 38th Cong., 1st Sess. 817, 1158 (1864)) (statements of Sen. Sumner).

131. *Id*. at 204 (quoting CONG. GLOBE, 39th Cong., 1st Sess. app. 183 (1866)).

132. *See* McConnell I, *supra* note 36, Ch. 1 at 984.

133. Although he would arrive at an originalist justification for desegregation, Bork maintained without citing evidence that "[t]he inescapable fact is that those who ratified the amendment did not think it outlawed segregated education or segregation in any aspect of life." BORK, *supra* note 38, Ch. 1 at 75–76.

134. *See* ANTIEAU, *supra* note 70, Ch. 3.B.2 at 59; FLACK, *supra* note 94, Ch. 3.B.6 at 158. During the Pennsylvania ratification debates, state Senator George Connell cited an 1866 Mississippi law barring blacks from riding in first-class passenger cars and said the Fourteenth Amendment's adoption would change that situation. *See* ANTIEAU, *supra* note 70, Ch. 3.B.2 at 59.

135. DEBATES, *supra* note 17, Ch. 2 at 554 (quoting CONG. GLOBE, 42d Cong., 1st Sess. app. 217 (1871)).

136. *Id.* at 580 (quoting CONG. GLOBE, 42d Cong., 2d Sess. 383 (1872)).

137. *Id.* at 579–80 (quoting CONG. GLOBE, 42d Cong., 2d Sess. 381–83 (1872)). *See also id.* at 611 (quoting CONG. GLOBE, 42d Cong., 2d Sess. 823 (1872)) ("All that I ask is that, in harmony with the Declaration of Independence, there be complete equality before the law everywhere, in the inn, on the highway, in the common school, in the church.").

138. *Id.* at 600 (quoting CONG. GLOBE, 42d Cong., 2d Sess. 731 (1872)). *See also supra* note 470, Ch. 3.D.3 (statement by Edmunds asserting the right under the Constitution to protect citizens "against caste prejudice").

139. *See* DEBATES, *supra* note 17, Ch. 2 at 649 (quoting CONG. GLOBE, 42d Cong., 2d Sess. 3264 (1872)). Sumner made a similar charge. *See id.* at 648 (quoting CONG. GLOBE, 42d Cong., 2d Sess. 3264 (1872)).

140. *Id.* at 649 (quoting CONG. GLOBE, 42d Cong., 2d Sess. 3264 (1872)).

141. *Id.* at 643 (quoting CONG. GLOBE, 42d Cong., 2d Sess. 3192 (1872)).

142. *Id.*

143. *Id.* at 657 (quoting 2 CONG. REC. 11 (1873)).

144. *See id.* (quoting 2 CONG. REC. 341 (1873)).

145. *Id.* at 662 (quoting 2 CONG. REC. 412 (1874)).

146. *Id.* at 661 (quoting 2 CONG. REC. 409 (1874)).

147. *Id.* at 659 (quoting 2 CONG. REC. 382–83 (1874)).

148. *Id.* at 663 (quoting 2 CONG. REC. 414 (1874)).

149. *Id.* at 665 (quoting 2 CONG. REC. 427 (1874)).

150. *Id.* at 667 (quoting 2 CONG. REC. 455–56 (1874)).

151. *Id.* at 670 (quoting 2 CONG. REC. 565 (1874)).

152. *Id.* at 683 (quoting 2 CONG. REC. app. 359 (1874)).

153. *Id.*

154. *Id.* at 684 (quoting 2 CONG. REC. app. 360 (1874)).

155. *Id.* at 685 (quoting 2 CONG. REC. app. 360 (1874)).

156. *Id.* (quoting 2 CONG. REC. app. 361 (1874)).

157. *Id.* at 705 (quoting 2 CONG. REC. 4171 (1874)).

158. *Id.* at xxxi, 705–06 (quoting 2 CONG. REC. 4171–72 (1874)). *See supra* notes 436–37, Ch. 3.D.3 and accompanying text for examples of Sargent's tolerance of segregation.

159. *Id.* at 727 (quoting 3 CONG. REC. 999 (1875)).

160. LOFGREN, *supra* note 501, Ch. 3.D.3 at 251 n.21.

161. *See* Bickel, *The Original Understanding and the Segregation Decision*, 69 HARV. L. REV. 1, 58 (1956).

Avins concluded both that race was not subject to greater scrutiny than other forms of discrimination and that laws "singling out racial and religious discrimination for special condemnation, except in respect to voting, cannot justify themselves on the letter of the fourteenth amendment." Alfred Avins, *Fourteenth Amendment Limitations on Banning Racial Discrimination: The Original Understanding*, 8 ARIZ. L. REV. 236 (1967). This conclusion is virtually unsupported in the debates, and it seems to rely on a particular application of text rather than any true original understanding.

162. 175 U.S. 528.

163. *See* OXFORD, *supra* note 2, Ch. 3.B.1 at 210.

164. *See* 175 U.S. at 529–30.
165. *See id.* at 529–31.
166. *See id.* at 529–30.
167. *See id.* at 543.
168. *See id.*
169. *Id.* at 545.
170. *See id.* at 544–45.
171. *See* OXFORD, *supra* note 2, Ch. 3.B.1 at 210.
172. 275 U.S. 78 (1927).
173. *See id.* at 80, 87.
174. *See id.* at 85–87.

F. Retreat from the Fifteenth Amendment

1. *Williams v. Mississippi*

1. 170 U.S. 213.
2. *See id.* at 221–22.
3. *See id.* at 222–25.
4. 2 BOUTWELL, *supra* note 45, Ch. 2 at 48.

2. *Giles v. Harris*

1. 189 U.S. 475 (1903).
2. *Id.* at 482.
3. *Id.* at 484, 486.
4. *Id.* at 487–88.
5. *Id.* at 488.
6. *See id.* at 488–504 (dissents of Brewer, J., & Harlan, J.).

3. *James v. Bowman* and the Fifteenth Amendment State Action Doctrine

1. 190 U.S. 127 (1903).
2. *See id.* at 128; 16 Stat. 140, 141.
3. *See id.*
4. 190 U.S. at 127.
5. *Id.* at 136.
6. *Id.* at 136–40, 142.
7. *Id.* at 139–40, 142.
8. *See id.* at 142.
9. *See supra* note 67, Ch. 3.B.5 and accompanying text.
10. DEBATES, *supra* note 17, Ch. 2 at 444 (quoting CONG. GLOBE, 41st Cong., 2d Sess. app. 355 (1870)).
11. *Id.* at 450–51 (quoting CONG. GLOBE, 41st Cong., 2d Sess. app. 472–73 (1870)).
12. *Id.* at 451 (quoting CONG. GLOBE, 41st Cong., 2d Sess. app. 473 (1870)).
13. *See id.; supra* note 68, Ch. 3.D.3 and accompanying text.
14. DEBATES, *supra* note 17, Ch. 2 at 455 (quoting CONG. GLOBE, 41st Cong., 2d Sess. 3671 (1870)).

15. *Id.* at 452–53 (quoting CONG. GLOBE, 41st Cong., 2d Sess. 3661–63 (1870)).

16. *Id.* at 454 (quoting CONG. GLOBE, 41st Cong., 2d Sess. 3666 (1870)).

17. *Id.* at 463 (quoting CONG. GLOBE, 41st Cong., 2d Sess. app. 416 (1870)).

18. *Id.* at 480 (quoting CONG. GLOBE, 41st Cong., 3rd Sess. 1272 (1871)).

19. *Id.* (quoting CONG. GLOBE, 41st Cong., 3rd Sess. app. 124 (1871)).

20. *Id.* at 482 (quoting CONG. GLOBE, 41st Cong., 3rd Sess. 1635, 1637 (1871)).

21. *Id.* (quoting CONG. GLOBE, 41st Cong., 3rd Sess. app. 166 (1871)).

22. *See id.* (quoting CONG. GLOBE, 41st Cong., 3rd Sess. app. 157 (1871)).

23. *See id.* at 518 (quoting CONG. GLOBE, 42d Cong., 1st Sess. app. 208 (1871)).

24. *See id.* at 410, 417 (quoting CONG. GLOBE, 40th Cong., 3rd Sess. 1564, 1641 (1869)) (recording House and Senate votes on the Fifteenth Amendment).

25. *See id.* at 436 (quoting CONG. GLOBE, 41st Cong., 2d Sess. 2718–19, 2722 (1870)).

26. *See id.* (quoting CONG. GLOBE, 41st Cong., 2d Sess. 2722 (1870)).

27. *See id.* at 447 (quoting CONG. GLOBE, 41st Cong., 2d Sess. 3611 (1870)).

28. *See supra* notes 94–95 & 138, Ch. 3.D.3 and accompanying text.

29. DEBATES, *supra* note 17, Ch. 2 at 447 (quoting CONG. GLOBE, 41st Cong., 2d Sess. 3611 (1870)). *See also id.* at 453 (quoting CONG. GLOBE, 41st Cong., 2d Sess. 3662 (1870)) (restating his views to refute Sen. Thurman).

30. *Id.* at 440 (quoting CONG. GLOBE, 41st Cong., 2d Sess. 3564 (1870)).

31. *Id.* at 442 (quoting CONG. GLOBE, 41st Cong., 2d Sess. 3570 (1870)).

32. *Id.* at 454 (quoting CONG. GLOBE, 41st Cong., 2d Sess. 3663 (1870)).

33. *See id.* at 446 (quoting CONG. GLOBE, 41st Cong., 2d Sess. 3608 (1870)).

34. *Id.* at 448 (quoting CONG. GLOBE, 41st Cong., 2d Sess. 3655 (1870)).

35. *See also supra* note 72, Ch. 3.B.5 and accompanying text.

36. *See* DEBATES, *supra* note 17, Ch. 2 at 449 (quoting CONG. GLOBE, 41st Cong., 2d Sess. 3656, 3658 (1870)).

37. *Id.* at 455 (quoting CONG. GLOBE, 41st Cong., 2d Sess. 3671 (1870)).

38. *See id.* at 456 (quoting CONG. GLOBE, 41st Cong., 2d Sess. 3678 (1870)).

39. *Id.* (quoting CONG. GLOBE, 41st Cong., 2d Sess. 3684 (1870)).

40. *Id.* at 524 (quoting CONG. GLOBE, 42d Cong., 1st Sess. app. 251 (1871)).

41. *Id.* at 685 (quoting 2 CONG. REC. app. 360 (1874)).

42. *Id.* at 530 (quoting CONG. GLOBE, 42d Cong., 1st Sess. app. 154 (1871)).

43. *See id.* at 410, 417 (quoting CONG. GLOBE, 40th Cong., 3rd Sess. 1564, 1641 (1869)) (recording House and Senate votes on the Fifteenth Amendment).

44. Arthur W. Machen, Jr., *Is the Fifteenth Amendment Void?*, 23 HARV. L. REV. 169 (1910).

4. *Grovey v. Townsend*

1. 273 U.S. 536.

2. *See id.* at 540–41.

3. 295 U.S. 45.

4. *See id.* at 46–47.

5. *See id.* at 48.

6. *Id.* at 53–54.

CHAPTER 4: THE COURT'S RECONSIDERATION OF CIVIL RIGHTS DURING THE TWENTIETH CENTURY

A. The White Primary

1. 321 U.S. 649 (1944).
2. *Id.* at 663.
3. *Id.* at 663–64.
4. *Id.* at 664.
5. 345 U.S. 461.
6. *See id.* at 463–66, 472–74, 476 (opinions of Black, J., and Frankfurter, J.).

B. *Brown v. Board of Education* and School Segregation

1. The Court's Opinion

1. 347 U.S. 483.
2. *Id.* at 489.
3. *Id.* at 490 & n.5 (citing 83 U.S. (16 Wall.) 36, 67–72 (1873); 100 U.S. 303, 307–08 (1880)).
4. *Id.* at 492.
5. *Id.* at 492–93.
6. *See id.* at 493–94 & n.11.
7. *Id.* at 494–95.
8. *See* BORK, *supra* note 38, Ch. 1 at 76–77.
9. *Id.*
10. *See id.* at 77.

2. School Segregation and the Reconstruction Debates

1. *See* FONER, *supra* note 18, Ch. 1 at 366; GILLETTE, *supra* note 46, Ch. 2 at 194.
2. *See* McConnell I, *supra* note 36, Ch. 1 at 964.
3. *See* GILLETTE, *supra* note 46, Ch. 2 at 194–95.
4. *See supra* notes 88–102, Ch. 2 and accompanying text.
5. *See* GILLETTE, *supra* note 46, Ch. 2 at 204.
6. *See id.* at 200–01.
7. *See* FONER, *supra* note 18, Ch. 1 at 367.
8. *See id.*
9. *See* GILLETTE, *supra* note 46, Ch. 2 at 201.
10. *Cf. id.* at 206, 209, 220–21, 224, 226 (expressing several opinions as to the grave political damage that would be incurred by school integration and characterizing the 1874 civil rights bill as "empty idealism" from the perspective of Republicans in the South and border states who risked defeat at the polls). "By 1875, it was the Republicans' fear of voters' reprisals which in large part persuaded them to kill that section of the pending civil rights bill mandating mixed schools." *Id.* at 374.
11. *See id.* at 371.

12. DEBATES, *supra* note 17, Ch. 2 at 79 (quoting CONG. GLOBE, 38th Cong., 1st Sess. 3133 (1864)).

13. *Id.* at 269 (quoting CONG. GLOBE, 40th Cong., 1st Sess. 69 (1867)).

14. *Id.* at 97 (quoting CONG. GLOBE, 39th Cong., 1st Sess. 42 (1865)).

15. *See id.* at 135–36 (quoting CONG. GLOBE, 39th Cong., 1st Sess. 589–90 (1866)).

16. *Id.* at 142 (quoting CONG. GLOBE, 39th Cong., 1st Sess. 651 (1866)).

17. *Id.* at 287 (quoting CONG. GLOBE, 40th Cong., 2d Sess. 118 (1868)).

18. *Id.* at 179 (quoting CONG. GLOBE, 39th Cong., 1st Sess. app. 158 (1866)).

19. *Id.* at 183 (quoting CONG. GLOBE, 39th Cong., 1st Sess. 1271 (1866)).

20. *Id.* at 269 (quoting CONG. GLOBE, 40th Cong., 1st Sess. 52 (1867)).

21. *Id.* at 270 (quoting CONG. GLOBE, 40th Cong., 1st Sess. 71 (1867)).

22. *Id.*

23. *Id.* at 231–32 (quoting CONG. GLOBE, 39th Cong., 1st Sess. app. 219 (1866)). *See also id.* at xx, 434 (quoting CONG. GLOBE, 41st Cong., 2d Sess. 2611 (1870)) (similar attack on segregated schools in Florida).

24. *Id.* at 127 (quoting CONG. GLOBE, 39th Cong., 1st Sess. 500 (1866)).

25. *Id.* at 180 (quoting CONG. GLOBE, 39th Cong., 1st Sess. 1268 (1866)).

26. *See id.* at 166 (quoting CONG. GLOBE, 39th Cong., 1st Sess. 1121 (1866)).

27. *See id.* at 151 (quoting CONG. GLOBE, 39th Cong., 1st Sess. app. 134 (1866)).

28. *Id.* at 163 (quoting CONG. GLOBE, 39th Cong., 1st Sess. 1117 (1866)).

29. *See* McConnell I, *supra* note 36, Ch. 1 at 960.

30. *See id.*; Bickel, *supra* note 161, Ch. 3.E.2 at 56; RAOUL BERGER, GOVERNMENT BY JUDICIARY 119 (1977).

31. *See* McConnell I, *supra* note 36, Ch. 1 at 960.

32. *See supra* note 102, Ch. 3.E.2.

33. *See* McConnell I, *supra* note 36, Ch. 1 at 961.

34. *See* DEBATES, *supra* note 17, Ch. 2 at 191 (quoting CONG. GLOBE, 39th Cong., 1st Sess. 1296 (1866).

35. *See* McConnell I, *supra* note 36, Ch. 1 at 977.

36. *See id.* at 977–78.

37. *See id.* at 978; DEBATES, *supra* note 17, Ch. 2 at 143–44 (quoting CONG. GLOBE, 39th Cong., 1st Sess. 708–09, 727 (1866)).

38. DEBATES, *supra* note 17, Ch. 2 at 270 (quoting CONG. GLOBE, 40th Cong., 1st Sess. 165 (1867)).

39. *Id.* (quoting CONG. GLOBE, 40th Cong., 1st Sess. 166 (1867)).

40. Sumner himself acknowledged this objection. *See id.* (quoting CONG. GLOBE, 40th Cong., 1st Sess. 166 (1867)).

41. *Id.* at 271 (quoting CONG. GLOBE, 40th Cong., 1st Sess. 167 (1867)).

42. *Id.* at 272 (quoting CONG. GLOBE, 40th Cong., 1st Sess. 169 (1867)).

43. *See id.* (quoting CONG. GLOBE, 40th Cong., 1st Sess. 170 (1867)).

44. *Cf.* McConnell I, *supra* note 36, Ch. 1 at 964 (discussing the "show of strength for Sumner's position").

45. *See id.* at 276 (quoting CONG. GLOBE, 40th Cong., 1st Sess. 625 (1867)).

46. *See id.* at 304 (quoting CONG. GLOBE, 40th Cong., 2d Sess. 1964–65 (1868)); *supra* notes 74–82, Ch. 3.E.2 and accompanying text.

47. *See* DEBATES, *supra* note 17, Ch. 2 at 310 (quoting CONG. GLOBE, 40th Cong., 2d Sess. 2197 (1868)).

48. *See id.* at 312–14 (quoting CONG. GLOBE, 40th Cong., 2d Sess. 2395, 2447–48 (1868)).

49. *See id.* at 758.

50. *Id.* at 325 (quoting CONG. GLOBE, 40th Cong., 2d Sess. 2748 (1868)).

51. *Id.*

52. *Id.* at 419 (quoting CONG. GLOBE, 41st Cong., 2d Sess. 463 (1870)).

53. *Id.* (quoting CONG. GLOBE, 41st Cong., 2d Sess. 464 (1870)).

54. *See, e.g., id.* at 420 (quoting CONG. GLOBE, 41st Cong., 2d Sess. 464 (1870)) (statement of Sen. Williams) (expressing doubt about congressional power to bind a state to the extent Congress was attempting to bind Virginia); *id.* (quoting CONG. GLOBE, 41st Cong., 2d Sess. 466 (1870)) (statement of Sen. Conkling) (expressing reservations about congressional restrictions on officeholding); *id.* (statement of Sen. Stewart) (asserting that the Fourteenth Amendment better provides for civil rights and that any of the rights in the Virginia amendment could be protected in all the states under the Constitution).

55. *Id.* at 424 (quoting CONG. GLOBE, 41st Cong., 2d Sess. 716–17 (1870)).

56. *Id.* (quoting CONG. GLOBE, 41st Cong., 2d Sess. 1253 (1870)).

57. *Id.* at 424–25 (quoting CONG. GLOBE, 41st Cong., 2d Sess. 1253, 1365 (1870)).

58. *Id.* at 425 (quoting CONG. GLOBE, 41st Cong., 2d Sess. 1329 (1870)).

59. *Id.* (quoting CONG. GLOBE, 41st Cong., 2d Sess. 1331 (1870)).

60. *Id.* at 432 (quoting CONG. GLOBE, 41st Cong., 2d Sess. 1704 (1870)).

61. *See* CONG. GLOBE, 41st Cong., 2d Sess. 323 (1870).

62. *See* CONG. GLOBE, 41st Cong., 3rd Sess. 1054 (1871).

63. DEBATES, *supra* note 17, Ch. 2 at 473 (quoting CONG. GLOBE, 41st Cong., 3rd Sess. 1054 (1871)).

64. *Id.*

65. *Id.* (quoting CONG. GLOBE, 41st Cong., 3rd Sess. 1055 (1871)).

66. *Id.*

67. *Id.*

68. *Id.*

69. *Id.* at 474 (quoting CONG. GLOBE, 41st Cong., 3rd Sess. 1056 (1871)).

70. *Id.*

71. *See id.* at 474–75 (quoting CONG. GLOBE, 41st Cong., 3rd Sess. 1056–57 (1871)).

72. *Id.* at 475 (quoting CONG. GLOBE, 41st Cong., 3rd Sess. 1057 (1871)).

73. *See id.*

74. *Id.*

75. *Id.*

76. *Id.* at 477 (quoting CONG. GLOBE, 41st Cong., 3rd Sess. 1059 (1871)).

77. *Id.* at 475 (quoting CONG. GLOBE, 41st Cong., 3rd Sess. 1057 (1871)).

78. *See id.*

79. *Id.* at 475–76 (quoting CONG. GLOBE, 41st Cong., 3rd Sess. 1057–58 (1871)). Thurman said he "can understand how a common carrier is bound to carry any man who comes decently and is a respectable man and tenders his fare

for his conveyance," but he "never could understand" the desegregation of privately owned places of amusement. *Id.*

80. *Id.* at 476 (quoting CONG. GLOBE, 41st Cong., 3rd Sess. 1058 (1871)).

81. *Id.*

82. *Id.*

83. *Id.* at 477 (quoting CONG. GLOBE, 41st Cong., 3rd Sess. 1059 (1871)).

84. *Id.*

85. *Id.*

86. *Id.*

87. *Id.*

88. *Id.*

89. *See id.* at 478 (quoting CONG. GLOBE, 41st Cong., 3rd Sess. 1060 (1871)).

90. *See id.* at 478–79 (quoting CONG. GLOBE, 41st Cong., 3rd Sess. 1060–61 (1871)).

91. *Id.*

92. *Id.* at 479 (quoting CONG. GLOBE, 41st Cong., 3rd Sess. 1061 (1871)).

93. *See* McConnell I, *supra* note 36, Ch. 1 at 978–79; CONG. GLOBE, 41st Cong., 3rd Sess. 1366–67 (1871).

94. *See* DEBATES, *supra* note 17, Ch. 2 at 636 (quoting CONG. GLOBE, 42d Cong., 2d Sess. 2539 (1872)).

95. *See id.* at xxviii, 636 (quoting CONG. GLOBE, 42d Cong., 2d Sess. 2539 (1872)).

96. *Id.* at 637 (quoting CONG. GLOBE, 42d Cong., 2d Sess. app. 353 (1872)).

97. *See id.* at xxviii, 638 (quoting CONG. GLOBE, 42d Cong., 2d Sess. app. 354–55 (1872)).

98. *See id.* at 639–40 (quoting CONG. GLOBE, 42d Cong., 2d Sess. app. 370–71 (1872)).

99. *Id.* at 640 (quoting CONG. GLOBE, 42d Cong., 2d Sess. 3124 (1872)).

100. *Id.* (quoting CONG. GLOBE, 42d Cong., 2d Sess. 3123 (1872)).

101. *See* McConnell I, *supra* note 36, Ch. 1 at 979; CONG. GLOBE, 42d Cong., 2d Sess. 3124 (1872).

102. *See* McConnell I, *supra* note 36, Ch. 1 at 980.

103. *See* DEBATES, *supra* note 17, Ch. 2 at xxvi.

104. *See id.* at 604 (quoting CONG. GLOBE, 42d Cong., 2d Sess. 788–89 (1872)).

105. *See id.* at 605 (quoting CONG. GLOBE, 42d Cong., 2d Sess. 791 (1872)).

106. *See id.* at 606 (quoting CONG. GLOBE, 42d Cong., 2d Sess. app. 18 (1872)).

107. *See id.* at 606–07 (quoting CONG. GLOBE, 42d Cong., 2d Sess. 855–56 (1872)).

108. *See id.* at 607 (quoting CONG. GLOBE, 42d Cong., 2d Sess. 856 (1872)).

109. *See id.* at 605 (quoting CONG. GLOBE, 42d Cong., 2d Sess. 794 (1872)).

110. *See id.* at 606 (quoting CONG. GLOBE, 42d Cong., 2d Sess. 854 (1872)).

111. *Id.* (quoting CONG. GLOBE, 42d Cong., 2d Sess. app. 15 (1872)).

112. *Id.* at 607 (quoting CONG. GLOBE, 42d Cong., 2d Sess. 856 (1872)).

113. *See id.* (quoting CONG. GLOBE, 42d Cong., 2d Sess. 882 (1872)).

114. *See id.* (quoting CONG. GLOBE, 42d Cong., 2d Sess. 856 (1872)) (statement of Rep. Storm). Avins contends that the debates support the notion that school segregation was not considered a Fourteenth Amendment violation, *see id.* at xxvi, but his conclusion is unsupported. He fails to assess this and other events during

the Reconstruction Congress in their broader political contexts, seemingly treating an individual debate as if it existed in a vacuum, and he falls short of treating politicians like politicians. It should be realized additionally that Avins works from assumptions that "protection of the law" was not broad enough to encompass education, see Alfred Avins, *The Equal "Protection" of the Laws: The Original Understanding*, 12 N.Y.L.F. 385, 426 (1966), and "[t]o the extent that the four-teenth amendment has anything to do with school segregation, it merely guarantees individual freedom of choice, consistent with the choice of all other individuals," not the "right to force himself on others," Alfred Avins, *De Facto and De Jure School Segregation: Some Reflected Light on the Fourteenth Amendment from the Civil Rights Act of 1875*, 38 MISS. L.J. 179, 247 (1967). Such views may be con-sistent with those of Democrats who opposed the Reconstruction amendments, but they do not reflect the original understanding of the Fourteenth Amendment held by supporters.

115. *Cf.* McConnell II, *supra* note 37, Ch. 1 at 1944 ("In a nutshell, I consider the debates the best evidence of meaning in this context because they occur very shortly after ratification and provide the only significant body of evidence of the legal interpretation of the Amendment by those who participated in the process. Although in theory, evidence of the understanding of the state legislatures at the precise time of ratification would be a superior basis for interpretation, it does not exist. The debates over the 1875 Act are the best we have.").

116. *See* DEBATES, *supra* note 17, Ch. 2 at 553–54 (quoting CONG. GLOBE, 42d Cong., 1st Sess. app. 216–17 (1871)).

117. *Id.* at 575 (quoting CONG. GLOBE, 42d Cong., 2d Sess. 241 (1871)).

118. *See* McConnell I, *supra* note 36, Ch. 1 at 1053–54.

119. *See* DEBATES, *supra* note 17, Ch. 2 at 578 (quoting CONG. GLOBE, 42d Cong., 2d Sess. 274 (1871)).

120. Among those who had voted for the Fourteenth Amendment, Henry B. Anthony, Conkling, Edmunds, Thomas W. Ferry, Justin S. Morrill, James W. Nye, Pomeroy, Alexander Ramsey, Sherman, Sumner, Henry Wilson, and William Win-dom all voted for the Sumner amendment, and Lot Morrill, Stewart, and Trumbull voted against it. Zachariah Chandler, Aaron H. Cragin, Howe, and William Sprague were recorded absent. *See id.* at 237–38 (quoting CONG. GLOBE, 39th Cong., 1st Sess. 3042, 3149 (1866)) (recording Senate and House votes on the Fourteenth Amendment); *id.* at 578 (quoting CONG. GLOBE, 42d Cong., 2d Sess. 274 (1871)).

121. *See id.*

122. *See* McConnell I, *supra* note 36, Ch. 1 at 1054.

123. DEBATES, *supra* note 17, Ch. 2 at 580–81 (quoting CONG. GLOBE, 42d Cong., 2d Sess. 383–84 (1872)). *See also id.* at 611 (quoting CONG. GLOBE, 42d Cong., 2d Sess. 823 (1872)) ("All that I ask is that, in harmony with the Declaration of Independence, there be complete equality before the law everywhere, in the inn, on the highway, in the common school, in the church.").

124. *Id.* at 583 (quoting CONG. GLOBE, 42d Cong., 2d Sess. 432 (1872)).

125. *Id.* at 584 (quoting CONG. GLOBE, 42d Cong., 2d Sess. 433–34 (1872)).

126. *Id.* at 592 (quoting CONG. GLOBE, 42d Cong., 2d Sess. app. 4 (1872)).

127. *Id.* at xxvii, 623 (quoting CONG. GLOBE, 42d Cong., 2d Sess. 892 (1872)).

128. *See id.* at 593–94 (quoting CONG. GLOBE, 42d Cong., 2d Sess. app. 9–10 (1872)).

129. *See id.* at 603 (quoting CONG. GLOBE, 42d Cong., 2d Sess. 764 (1872)).

130. *See id.* at 618–19 (quoting CONG. GLOBE, 42d Cong., 2d Sess. app. 26–27 (1872)).

131. *Id.* at 619 (quoting CONG. GLOBE, 42d Cong., 2d Sess. app. 27 (1872)).

132. *Id.* at 625 (quoting CONG. GLOBE, 42d Cong., 2d Sess. 894–95 (1872)).

133. *See id.* at xxvii, at 627 (quoting CONG. GLOBE, 42d Cong., 2d Sess. app. 42 (1872)).

134. *See id.* at 595 (quoting CONG. GLOBE, 42d Cong., 2d Sess. app. 11 (1872)).

135. *Id.* at 603 (quoting CONG. GLOBE, 42d Cong., 2d Sess. 763 (1872)).

136. *Id.*

137. *Id.*

138. *Id.* at 615 (quoting CONG. GLOBE, 42d Cong., 2d Sess. 844 (1872)).

139. *Id.* at 618 (quoting CONG. GLOBE, 42d Cong., 2d Sess. app. 26 (1872)).

140. *See id.* at 630 (quoting CONG. GLOBE, 42d Cong., 2d Sess. 919 (1872)); *id.* at 237–38 (quoting CONG. GLOBE, 39th Cong., 1st Sess. 3042, 3149 (1866)) (recording Senate and House votes on the Fourteenth Amendment); *supra* note 355, Ch. 3.D.3 and accompanying text.

141. *See id.*

142. *See supra* note 356, Ch. 3.D.3 and accompanying text.

143. *See supra* notes 378–86, Ch. 3.D.3 and accompanying text.

144. *See* DEBATES, *supra* note 17, Ch. 2 at 632–33 (quoting CONG. GLOBE, 42d Cong., 2d Sess. app. 142–44 (1872)). During later debates, Andrew King, a colleague of Blair's who was also from Missouri, also characterized school integration as a social right. *See id.* at 635 (quoting CONG. GLOBE, 42d Cong., 2d Sess. app. 383 (1872)).

145. *Id.* at 634 (quoting CONG. GLOBE, 42d Cong., 2d Sess. app. 218 (1872)).

146. *See* McConnell I, *supra* note 36, Ch. 1 at 1063.

147. *See* DEBATES, *supra* note 17, Ch. 2 at 641 (quoting CONG. GLOBE, 42d Cong., 2d Sess. 3189–90 (1872)).

148. *Id.* at 642 (quoting CONG. GLOBE, 42d Cong., 2d Sess. 3190 (1872)).

149. *Id.*

150. *See* McConnell I, *supra* note 36, Ch. 1 at 989.

151. 21 Ohio St. 198 (1872).

152. *See* DEBATES, *supra* note 17, Ch. 2 at 643 (quoting CONG. GLOBE, 42d Cong., 2d Sess. 3193 (1872)); McConnell I, *supra* note 36, Ch. 1 at 989–90.

153. *See* McConnell I, *supra* note 36, Ch. 1 at 990.

154. DEBATES, *supra* note 17, Ch. 2 at 643 (quoting CONG. GLOBE, 42d Cong., 2d Sess. 3193 (1872)).

155. *See id.;* McConnell I, *supra* note 36, Ch. 1 at 990.

156. *See* McConnell I, *supra* note 36, Ch. 1 at 990.

157. DEBATES, *supra* note 17, Ch. 2 at 645 (quoting CONG. GLOBE, 42d Cong., 2d Sess. 3257 (1872)).

158. *Id.* at 644 (quoting CONG. GLOBE, 42d Cong., 2d Sess. 3195 (1872)).

159. *Id.* (quoting CONG. GLOBE, 42d Cong., 2d Sess. 3251 (1872)).

160. *See id.* at 645 (quoting CONG. GLOBE, 42d Cong., 2d Sess. 3256 (1872)).

161. *See id.* at 646 (quoting CONG. GLOBE, 42d Cong., 2d Sess. 3258 (1872)).

162. *Id.*

163. *See id.*

164. *Id.* (quoting CONG. GLOBE, 42d Cong., 2d Sess. 3259 (1872)).

165. *See id.* at 647 (quoting CONG. GLOBE, 42d Cong., 2d Sess. 3260 (1872)).

166. *See id.* (quoting CONG. GLOBE, 42d Cong., 2d Sess. 3261 (1872)).

167. *See id.* at 648 (quoting CONG. GLOBE, 42d Cong., 2d Sess. 3262 (1872)).

168. *See* McConnell I, *supra* note 36, Ch. 1 at 1056.

169. DEBATES, *supra* note 17, Ch. 2 at 652–53 (quoting CONG. GLOBE, 42d Cong., 2d Sess. 3422 (1872)).

170. *Id.* at 653 (quoting CONG. GLOBE, 42d Cong., 2d Sess. 3422 (1872)).

171. *See id.* (quoting CONG. GLOBE, 42d Cong., 2d Sess. 3423 (1872)).

172. *Id.* at 654 (quoting CONG. GLOBE, 42d Cong., 2d Sess. 3426 (1872)).

173. *Id.* at 648, 654 (quoting CONG. GLOBE, 42d Cong., 2d Sess. 3262, 3425 (1872)).

174. *Id.* at 654 (quoting CONG. GLOBE, 42d Cong., 2d Sess. 3425 (1872)).

175. *Id.* at 656 (quoting CONG. GLOBE, 42d Cong., 2d Sess. app. 597 (1872)).

176. *Id.* at 649, 654 (quoting CONG. GLOBE, 42d Cong., 2d Sess. 3264, 3427 (1872)).

177. *Id.* at 655 (quoting CONG. GLOBE, 42d Cong., 2d Sess. 3735 (1872)).

178. *See supra* note 385, Ch. 3.D.3 and accompanying text; DEBATES, *supra* note 17, Ch. 2 at 655 (quoting CONG. GLOBE, 42d Cong., 2d Sess. 3737 (1872)). Sawyer subsequently commented, "It is not all I desire, but it was perfectly evident to me from the expression in the Senate at that time that it was all we could get at this session of Congress." *Id.* at 656 (quoting CONG. GLOBE, 42d Cong., 2d Sess. 3739 (1872)).

179. *Supra* note 387, Ch. 3.D.3 and accompanying text. Historian William Gillette erroneously infers that Grant's Second Inaugural's disclaimer on legislating social equality undermined the strength of his recommendation to Congress, *see* GILLETTE, *supra* note 46, Ch. 2 at 208, but the author seems to presume the universality of the Democratic definition of social equality. It has been shown that the most radical Republicans disclaimed the impact of their proposals on social equality, but they used the term only to refer to matters that government generally did not address. That Grant's invocation of the term "social equality" followed the Radical definitions and rhetoric is apparent by his stand in his Inaugural and by his ultimate signing of the bill.

180. *See generally supra* Ch. 4.B.2.a.

181. *See* GILLETTE, *supra* note 46, Ch. 2 at 208.

182. *See* BROOKS D. SIMPSON, THE RECONSTRUCTION PRESIDENTS 169 (1998); GILLETTE, *supra* note 46, Ch. 2 at 256.

183. RICHARDSON, *supra* note 44, Ch. 2 at 334. Grant's views, though considerably ambiguous, might be compared to those of Senator Stewart, who doubted the expediency of school integration while states were allowed to shut down the schools altogether, but who added that he would be more open to school integration after the ratification of a constitutional amendment compelling the establishment of schools. *See infra* notes 235–37, Ch. 4.B.2 and accompanying text.

184. *See* GILLETTE, *supra* note 46, Ch. 2 at 256.

185. *Id.*

186. *See, e.g., id.* at 256–57.

187. *See* DEBATES, *supra* note 17, Ch. 2 at 658 (quoting 2 CONG. REC. 343 (1873)).

188. *See id.* at 660 (quoting 2 CONG. REC. 405 (1874)).

189. *See id.* at 667 (quoting 2 CONG. REC. 453 (1874)).

190. *See id.* at 668 (quoting 2 CONG. REC. app. 2 (1874)).

191. *See id.* at 659 (quoting 2 CONG. REC. 381 (1874)).

192. *See id.* at 660 (quoting 2 CONG. REC. 385 (1874)).

193. *See id.* at 663 (quoting 2 CONG. REC. 415 (1874)).

194. *See id.* at 668 (quoting 2 CONG. REC. app. 3 (1874)).

195. *See id.* at 669 (quoting 2 CONG. REC. app. 4 (1874)).

196. *See id.* (quoting 2 CONG. REC. 555 (1874)).

197. *Id.* (quoting 2 CONG. REC. app. 5 (1874)).

198. *See id.* at 660 (quoting 2 CONG. REC. 385 (1874)).

199. *See id.* at 661 (quoting 2 CONG. REC. 406 (1874)).

200. *See id.* (quoting 2 CONG. REC. 411 (1874)).

201. *See id.* at 664 (quoting 2 CONG. REC. 421 (1874)).

202. *See id.* at 667 (quoting 2 CONG. REC. 453 (1874)).

203. *Id.* at 664 (quoting 2 CONG. REC. 416 (1874)).

204. *Id.* at 665 (quoting 2 CONG. REC. 427 (1874)).

205. *Id.* at 667 (quoting 2 CONG. REC. 456 (1874)).

206. *Id.* at 670 (quoting 2 CONG. REC. 566 (1874)).

207. *See* McConnell I, *supra* note 36, Ch. 1 at 1069.

208. DEBATES, *supra* note 17, Ch. 2 at 673 (quoting 2 CONG. REC. 3452 (1874)).

209. *Id.* at xxix, 673 (quoting 2 CONG. REC. 3452 (1874)).

210. *Id.* at xxix, 674 (quoting 2 CONG. REC. 3452 (1874)).

211. *Id.* at 674 (quoting 2 CONG. REC. 3452 (1874)).

212. *Id.*

213. *Id.* at 677 (quoting 2 CONG. REC. 4082 (1874)).

214. *Id.*

215. *Id.* at 680–81 (quoting 2 CONG. REC. 4088–89 (1874)).

216. *Id.* at 682 (quoting 2 CONG. REC. 4115 (1874)).

217. *Id.* at 683 (quoting 2 CONG. REC. app. 359 (1874)).

218. *See id.* at 696 (quoting 2 CONG. REC. app. 318 (1874)).

219. *Id.* at 684 (quoting 2 CONG. REC. app. 359 (1874)). *See also id.* at 685 (quoting 2 CONG. REC. app. 361 (1874)) (calling "the equal enjoyment of every public institution, whether it be the court, . . . the school, or . . . the public conveyance, or . . . any other public institution, for pleasure, business, or enjoyment, created or regulated by law," the "very highest franchise that belongs to any citizen of the United States as such").

As governor of Indiana, Morton had stated in 1867 that blacks probably would be able to attend public schools after the Fourteenth Amendment was ratified. He argued for the establishment of schools for blacks in order to preserve the peace, but in view of his repeated stands in Congress, any accommodation of segregation he had made in the statehouse should be deemed an arrangement based on practical considerations rather than an interpretation of the Fourteenth Amendment. *See* ANTIEAU, *supra* note 70, Ch. 3.B.2 at 58.

220. DEBATES, *supra* note 17, Ch. 2 at 685 (quoting 2 CONG. REC. 4116 (1874)).

221. *Id.* at 687 (quoting 2 CONG. REC. 4144–45 (1874)).

222. *Id.* at 688 (quoting 2 Cong. Rec. 4151 (1874)).
223. *Id.* at 689 (quoting 2 Cong. Rec. 4151 (1874)).
224. *Id.* (quoting 2 Cong. Rec. app. 305 (1874)).
225. *Id.*
226. *See id.* at xxx.
227. *Id.* at 691 (quoting 2 Cong. Rec. 4154 (1874)).
228. *Id.* at 693 (quoting 2 Cong. Rec. 4158 (1874)).
229. *Id.* at 694 (quoting 2 Cong. Rec. 4161 (1874)).
230. *Id.* at 702 (quoting 2 Cong. Rec. 4167 (1874)).
231. *See id.* at 237–38 (quoting Cong. Globe, 39th Cong., 1st Sess. 3042, 3149 (1866)) (recording Senate and House votes on the Fourteenth Amendment); *id.* at 702 (quoting 2 Cong. Rec. 4167 (1874)).
Members of the Senate in the Forty-Third Congress included the following legislators who had voted for the Fourteenth Amendment in 1866: William B. Allison, Henry B. Anthony, Boutwell, Chandler, Conkling, Cragin, Edmunds, Thomas W. Ferry, Howe, Justin S. Morrill, Lot Morrill, Alexander Ramsey, John Sherman, Sprague, Stewart, William B. Washburn, and William Windom. Allison, Boutwell, and Washburn had not sat in the Senate during the previous session of Congress. *See* Avins, *Civil Rights Act of 1875, supra* note 508, Ch. 3.D.3 at 875 n.6. Allison, Lot Morrill, and Stewart voted for the amendment, and six others were absent from the vote: Anthony, Sherman, Chandler, Cragin, Sprague, and Ferry: *See id.* at 702 (quoting 2 Cong. Rec. 4167 (1874)). Of the absent senators, all but Sprague previously supported school desegregation.
232. *See infra* note 253, Ch. 4.B.2 and accompanying text.
233. *See infra* note 254, Ch. 4.B.2 and accompanying text.
234. Boutwell's proposal actually was to strike out the words, "And also of common schools and public institutions of learning or benevolence, supported in whole or in part by general taxation," and to replace it with "And also of every common school and public institution of learning or benevolence endowed by the United States or founded by any State; or that may hereafter be endowed by any State, or supported in whole or in part by public taxation." Debates, *supra* note 17, Ch. 2 at 702, 704 (quoting 2 Cong. Rec. 4167, 4169 (1874)).
235. *Id.* at 702–03 (quoting 2 Cong. Rec. 4167 (1874)).
236. "At all events," Stewart concluded, "before a measure of this kind is passed we might wait one year." *Id.* at 703 (quoting 2 Cong. Rec. 4167 (1874)).
237. *Id.*
238. *Id.* at 704 (quoting 2 Cong. Rec. 4168 (1874)).
239. *Id.* at 703 (quoting 2 Cong. Rec. 4168 (1874)).
240. *See id.* at 704 (quoting 2 Cong. Rec. 4169 (1874)).
241. *Id.* at xxxi.
242. Looking at his vote for the Sargent amendment, his statements emphasizing his openness to voluntary segregation, and his later support for the bill, it might be that Stewart's understanding of the Fourteenth Amendment endorsed some hybrid of *de jure* segregation and a "freedom of choice" concept. That is, he might have supported state designation of schools for separate races, but without the state preventing students from choosing to go to a school designated for another race. If this were the case, it is questionable that such a stand would contradict the result in *Brown*. However, it is at least as plausible, especially given the practical consid-

erations expressed behind his hesitation to support the Boutwell amendment—including his openness to voting for such a provision at a later time—that his stand on the amendment was flatly against *de jure* segregation and that votes to the contrary were based on considerations other than constitutional principle.

243. Allison and Stewart were the senators in the latter category. *See* DEBATES, *supra* note 17, Ch. 2 at 237–38 (quoting CONG. GLOBE, 39th Cong., 1st Sess. 3042, 3149 (1866)) (recording Senate and House votes on the Fourteenth Amendment); *id.* at 705 (quoting 2 CONG. REC. 4170 (1874)).

244. *See id.* at 705 (quoting 2 CONG. REC. 4171 (1874)).

245. *See id.* at xxxi, 705 (quoting 2 CONG. REC. 4171 (1874)).

246. *Id.* at 705 (quoting 2 CONG. REC. 4171 (1874)).

247. *Id.* at 705–06 (quoting 2 CONG. REC. 4171–72 (1874)).

248. *Id.* at 706 (quoting 2 CONG. REC. 4172 (1874)).

249. *Id.*

250. *Id.*

251. *Id.* at xxxi, 706–07 (quoting 2 CONG. REC. 4173 (1874)).

252. *Id.* at 707 (quoting 2 CONG. REC. 4175 (1874)).

253. Allison, who had voted for the previous Sargent amendment, voted against this one. *See id.* at 237–38 (quoting CONG. GLOBE, 39th Cong., 1st Sess. 3042, 3149 (1866)) (recording Senate and House votes on the Fourteenth Amendment); *id.* at 708 (quoting 2 CONG. REC. 4175 (1874)).

254. These ten senators were Allison, Boutwell, Conkling, Edmunds, Howe, Justin Morrill, Ramsey, Stewart, Washburn, and Windom. Senators Anthony, Chandler, Cragin, Thomas Ferry, Lot Morrill, Sherman, and Sprague were recorded absent. *See id.* at 237–38 (quoting CONG. GLOBE, 39th Cong., 1st Sess. 3042, 3149 (1866)) (recording Senate and House votes on the Fourteenth Amendment); *id.* at 708 (quoting 2 CONG. REC. 4176 (1874)).

255. *See* McConnell I, *supra* note 36, Ch. 1 at 1078. Given his demonstrated discomfort with the jury provision and his support of the school provision, it would be unwarranted to conclude that it was the school issue that caused Carpenter to withhold his support.

256. DEBATES, *supra* note 17, Ch. 2 at 710 (quoting 2 CONG. REC. 4592 (1874)).

257. *Id.* at 712 (quoting 2 CONG. REC. app. 478 (1874)).

258. *Id.* at 713 (quoting 2 CONG. REC. app. 481 (1874)).

259. *See id.* at xxxi; McConnell I, *supra* note 36, Ch. 1 at 1080.

260. *See* McConnell I, *supra* note 36, Ch. 1 at 1081.

261. DEBATES, *supra* note 17, Ch. 2 at 714 (quoting 3 CONG. REC. 939 (1875)).

262. *See* McConnell I, *supra* note 36, Ch. 1 at 1080.

263. *See id.* at 1081; 3 CONG. REC. 938 (1875).

264. *See* DEBATES, *supra* note 17, Ch. 2 at 714 (quoting 3 CONG. REC. 939 (1875)).

265. *See id.*

266. *Id.* at 716 (quoting 3 CONG. REC. 945 (1875)).

267. *Id.* at 717 (quoting 3 CONG. REC. 951 (1875)).

268. *Id.* at 723 (quoting 3 CONG. REC. 981 (1875)).

269. *Id.* at 727 (quoting 3 CONG. REC. 999 (1875)).

270. *Id.*

271. *Id.* at 728 (quoting 3 CONG. REC. 1000 (1875)).

272. *Id.* at 729 (quoting 3 CONG. REC. 1002 (1875)).

273. *Id.* at 730 (quoting 3 CONG. REC. 1003 (1875)).

274. *Id.* (quoting 3 CONG. REC. 1003, 1005 (1875)).

275. *Id.* at 722 (quoting 3 CONG. REC. 978 (1875)).

276. *Id.*

277. *Id.*

278. *Id.* at 724 (quoting 3 CONG. REC. 981 (1875)).

279. *Id.*

280. *Id.*

281. *Id.* (quoting 3 CONG. REC. 982 (1875)).

282. *Id.*

283. *Id.* at 725 (quoting 3 CONG. REC. app. 15 (1875)).

284. *See id.* at xxxii, 725 (quoting 3 CONG. REC. app. 15, 17 (1875)).

285. *Id.* at 725 (quoting 3 CONG. REC. app. 20 (1875)).

286. *Id.* at 725–26 (quoting 3 CONG. REC. 997 (1875)).

287. *Id.* at 726 (quoting 3 CONG. REC. 997 (1875)).

288. *Id.*

289. *Id.* (quoting 3 CONG. REC. 998 (1875)).

290. *See id.* (quoting 3 CONG. REC. 997–98 (1875)).

291. *Id.* (quoting 3 CONG. REC. 998 (1875)).

292. *See id.*

293. *Id.* at 728 (quoting 3 CONG. REC. 1001 (1875)).

294. *Id.* at 729 (quoting 3 CONG. REC. 1002 (1875)).

295. *Id.* at 730 (quoting 3 CONG. REC. 1005–06 (1875)).

296. *See id.* (quoting 3 CONG. REC. 1010 (1875)).

297. *See id.*

298. *See id.* at xxxii, 731 (quoting 3 CONG. REC. 1011 (1875)).

299. *See* McConnell I, *supra* note 36, Ch. 1 at 1083–84.

300. Avins concludes that "a third of the Republicans were opposed to compelling desegregation." DEBATES, *supra* note 17, Ch. 2 at xxxii.

301. *Cf.* McConnell I, *supra* note 36, Ch. 1 at 1083 ("Fear of political fallout seems to be the reason for the decline in Republican support, as compared to the previous year.").

302. *See id.*

303. Henry Dawes, Garfield, Samuel Hooper, William Kelley, Leonard Myers, Charles O'Neill, Godlove S. Orth, and Philetus Sawyer all voted for the Cessna amendment. Hezekiah S. Bundy, Robert Hale, Glenni W. Scofield, and Luke Poland, who had been a senator in 1866, voted against the proposal. *See id.* at 237–38 (quoting CONG. GLOBE, 39th Cong., 1st Sess. 3042, 3149 (1866)); *id.* at 731 (quoting 3 CONG. REC. 1011 (1875)).

304. John A. Kasson and William Lawrence fell into this category. *See id.* at 238 (quoting CONG. GLOBE, 39th Cong., 1st Sess. 3149 (1866)); *Id.* at 731 (quoting 3 CONG. REC. 1011 (1875)).

305. Charles A. Eldridge (whose name was recorded in the Forty-Third Congress as "Eldredge"), William Finck, William Niblack, and Samuel J. Randall all voted against both the Fourteenth Amendment and the Cessna amendment. Samuel S. Marshall, who had voted against the Fourteenth Amendment, was recorded as "not voting" for Cessna's proposal. James W. Nesmith, who was recorded as absent for

the Senate vote in 1866, voted against the Cessna amendment. *See id.* at 237–38 (quoting CONG. GLOBE, 39th Cong., 1st Sess. 3042, 3149 (1866)); *id.* at 731 (quoting 3 CONG. REC. 1011 (1875)).

306. *See* McConnell I, *supra* note 36, Ch. 1 at 986, 1093, 1098.

307. *See id.* at 1094, 1096.

308. *See id.* at 1096–98.

309. *See id.* at 1098–99.

310. *See* Michael J. Klarman, *Brown, Originalism, and Constitutional Theory: A Response to Professor McConnell* 81 VA. L. REV. 1881, 1903–11 (1995).

311. *See* McConnell II, *supra* note 37, Ch. 1 at 1945 ("Although at one point he says there is 'abundant evidence' that this is the case, he does not present any, and a few pages later he concedes that 'it is possible that McConnell is right,' acknowledging that 'Northern support for federal civil rights legislation' was 'waning' and that it was 'fairly common by the mid-1870s to find former defenders of black suffrage confessing the possibility that the Fifteenth Amendment had been a mistake.' ") (footnotes omitted).

312. *See, e.g.*, Klarman, *supra* note 310, Ch. 4.B.2 at 1884–93.

313. DEBATES, *supra* note 17, Ch. 2 at 340 (quoting CONG. GLOBE, 40th Cong., 3rd Sess. 672 (1869)).

314. *See* McConnell I, *supra* note 36, Ch. 1 at 1137, 1139; BORK, *supra* note 38, Ch. 1 at 76. Bork reached the conclusion that segregation violated the Fourteenth Amendment on grounds of inequality even supposing that the framers deemed segregation and equality to be compatible since, as the "text itself demonstrates . . . the equality under law was the primary goal." *Id.* at 81–82.

315. *See* McConnell I, *supra* note 36, Ch. 1 at 1137–38.

C. The Reformulation of Constitutional Jurisprudence Addressing Civil Rights Legislation

1. *United States v. Raines* and the Collapse of the *Reese Doctrine*

1. 362 U.S. 17.

2. *Id.* at 19.

3. *See id.* at 19 & n.1; 16 Stat. 140 (1870); 71 Stat. 637 (1957) (codified as amended by 42 U.S.C. § 1971).

4. 362 U.S. at 20.

5. *Id.* at 21.

6. *See id.*

7. *Id.* at 22–24.

8. *Id.* at 24.

9. *Id.* at 25.

10. *Id.* at 28.

11. 383 U.S. 301, 326.

2. Sidestepping the Fourteenth Amendment State Action Doctrine: The Uncertain Fate of Section 5

1. 379 U.S. 241.

2. *See id.* at 261.

3. *See id.* at 242–43.

4. *See id.* at 249.

5. *Id.* at 250.

6. *Id.* at 250–51.

7. *Id.* at 251–52.

8. *Id.* at 251. *See also supra* note 7, Ch. 3.D.2 and accompanying text.

9. 379 U.S. at 252.

10. *Id.* at 278 (Black, J., concurring).

11. *Id.* at 279 (Douglas, J., concurring).

12. *Id.* at 280 (Douglas, J., concurring).

13. *Id.* at 286 (Douglas, J., concurring).

14. *Id.* at 291 (Goldberg, J., concurring).

15. 378 U.S. 226 (1964).

16. *See* 379 U.S. at 293 (Goldberg, J., concurring).

17. 379 U.S. 294 (1964).

18. *See id.* at 296.

19. *Id.* at 305.

20. 383 U.S. 745.

21. *See id.* at 749.

22. *Id.* at 747 n.1.

23. *See* Gressman, *supra* note 41, Ch. 3 at 1345.

24. 383 U.S. at 754–55.

25. *See id.* at 757–60.

26. *Id.* at 755 (quoting *United States v. Williams*, 341 U.S. 70, 92 (1951) (Douglas, J., dissenting)).

27. *Id.*

28. *Id.*

29. *Id.* at 756–57.

30. *See id.* at 755.

31. *Id.* at 762 (Clark, J., concurring).

32. *Id.* at 782 (Brennan, J., concurring).

33. *Id.* at 783–84 (Brennan, J., concurring).

34. *Id.* at 782–83 (Brennan, J., concurring).

35. *See* Note, *Membership Has Its Privileges and Immunities: Congressional Power to Define and Enforce the Rights of National Citizenship.* 102 HARV. L. REV. 1925, 1928 (1989); Samuel Estreicher, *Federal Power to Regulate Private Discrimination: The Revival of the Enforcement Clauses of the Reconstruction Era Amendments*, 74 COLUM. L. REV. 449, 513 (1974) [hereinafter Estreicher].

36. 395 U.S. 298.

37. *Id.* at 301, 304.

38. *Id.* at 304.

39. *See id.* at 305.

40. *Id.* at 315 (Black, J., dissenting).

41. *Id.* at 309 (Black, J., dissenting).

3. Section 2 of the Thirteenth Amendment: The Partial Resuscitation of the Reconstruction Amendments

1. 392 U.S. 409 (1968).

2. *See id.* at 422; Act of Apr. 9, 1866, ch. 31, 14 Stat. 27.

3. 392 U.S. at 412.

4. *Id.* at 439.

5. *Id.* at 443.

6. *See* Colbert, *supra* note 21, Ch. 3.B.1 at 2.

7. 392 U.S. at 439 (quoting 109 U.S. 3, 20 (1883)) (emphasis added by Court).

8. *See* Estreicher, *supra* note 35, Ch. 4.C.2 at 467.

9. 403 U.S. 88.

10. *See id.* at 97, 99.

11. *Id.* at 89–92.

12. 341 U.S. 651.

13. 403 U.S. at 92, 96.

14. *Id.* at 101.

15. *See id.* at 96, 104.

16. *Id.* at 102 & n.9.

17. *Id.* at 104.

18. *See id.* at 107.

19. *Id.* at 105 (quoting 392 U.S. at 440).

20. *Id.*

21. *See, e.g.,* Novotny v. Great Am. Federal Sav. & L. Ass'n, 442 U.S. 366 (1979) (holding that § 1985(3) may not be used to redress violations of Title VII of the Civil Rights Act of 1964); United Brotherhood of Carpenters and Joiners of Am. v. Scott, 463 U.S. 825 (1983) (holding that § 1985(3) does not reach conspiracies motivated by bias toward others due to their economic views, status, or activities); Bray v. Alexandria Women's Health Clinic, 506 U.S. 263 (1993) (holding that § 1985(3) does not cover conspiracies to obstruct women's access to abortion clinics).

The dissent in *Scott* recognized that "Congress did not intend any requirement of state involvement in either a civil or criminal action under § 2" of the Ku Klux Klan Act. 463 U.S. at 847 (Blackmun, J., dissenting). A review of that case observed that "[t]he dissenters' position requires a reinterpretation of the fourteenth amendment which . . . would generate a wealth of unwanted litigation for the Court." Taunya Lovell Banks, *Rethinking* Novotny *in Light of* United Brotherhood of Carpenters & Joiners v. Scott: *The Scope and Constitutionally Permissible Periphery of Section 1985(3)*, 27 How. L.J. 1497, 1510 (1984) (footnotes omitted).

22. A federal Court of Appeals made this point in Novotny v. Great Am. Federal Sav. & L. Ass'n, 584 F.2d 1235, 1253 (3rd Cir. 1978), *vacated*, 442 U.S. 366 (1979).

23. *See* Act of May 31, 1870, ch. 114, § 18, 16 Stat. 140, 144; DEBATES, *supra* note 17, Ch. 2 at 458 (quoting CONG. GLOBE, 41st Cong., 2d Sess. 3689 (1870)).

24. *Supra* note 37, Ch. 3.D.3.

4. Section 5 Returns to the Court

1. ____U.S.____, 117 S. Ct. 2157 (1997).

2. 117 S. Ct. at 2160–62. In *Employment Div. v. Smith*, 494 U.S. 872 (1990), the Court upheld a state law of general applicability criminalizing the use of peyote under the Free Exercise Clause, declining to employ a balancing test that required laws substantially burdening religious practices to be justified by a compelling state interest. The Religious Freedom Restoration Act purported to restore the applica-

tion of this balancing test in challenges of laws substantially burdening the exercise of religion. *See* 117 S.Ct. at 2160–62.

    3. 117 S.Ct. at 2164.

    4. *Id.* at 2165.

    5. *Id.* at 2166.

    6. *Id.* at 2166–67.

    7. *Id.* at 2166.

CHAPTER 5: CONCLUSION

    1. DU BOIS, *supra* note 15, Ch. 1 at 690–91.

    2. Samuel Shellabarger, Statement in Memoriam on the Death of Chief Justice Morrison R. Waite, 126 U.S. 596, 600–01 (1888). Shellabarger concluded about Waite, "I am inclined to think the judgment of history will be that he has been, in the main, steadily right regarding these Amendments; especially in view of the restraining effect of the later decisions." *Id.* at 601.

    3. *See Constricting the Law of Freedom, supra* note 24, Ch. 3.B.2 at 655–78. The author might overstate his case as to how the backgrounds and supposed motivations of the justices explain the disposition of every member of the 1873 Court, but his essential suggestion is well taken.

    4. 163 U.S. 537, 558–59 (Harlan, J., dissenting).

    5. 126 U.S. at 600.

    6. Klarman, *supra* note 310, Ch. 4.B.2 at 1916.

    7. DOUGLASS, *supra* note 2, Epigraph at 119–20.

Table of Cases

Index

About the Author

FRANK J. SCATURRO is currently an associate at Cadwalader, Wicker-sham, and Taft in New York. With a lifelong interest in history, he founded the Grant Monument Association in 1994 to draw public attention to the disrepair of Grant's Tomb in New York City. He is the author of *President Grant Reconsidered*, and he has written articles in the fields of Supreme Court jurisprudence and American history, as well as civil procedure.

ISBN 0-313-31105-6

9 780313 311055

90000>

EAN

HARDCOVER BAR CODE